WHAT a WONDERFUL WORLD!

STORY & ART BY
Inio Asano

volume **one**

VIZ Signature Edition

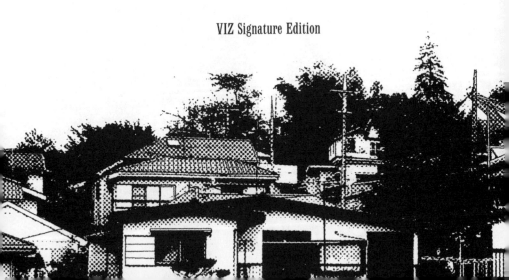

TRACK LIST

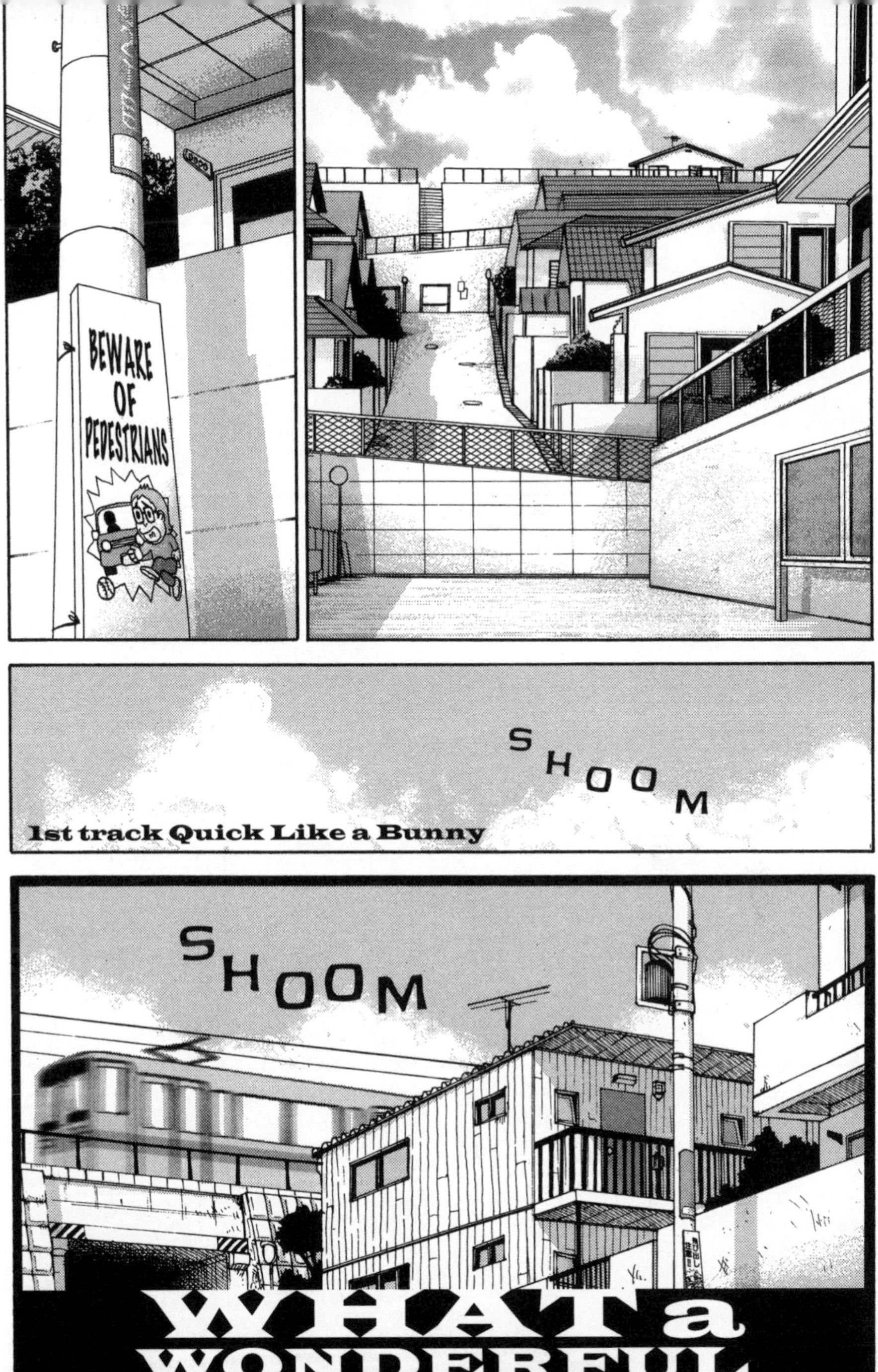
BEWARE OF PEDESTRIANS
SHOOM
1st track Quick Like a Bunny
SHOOM
WHAT a WONDERFUL WORLD!

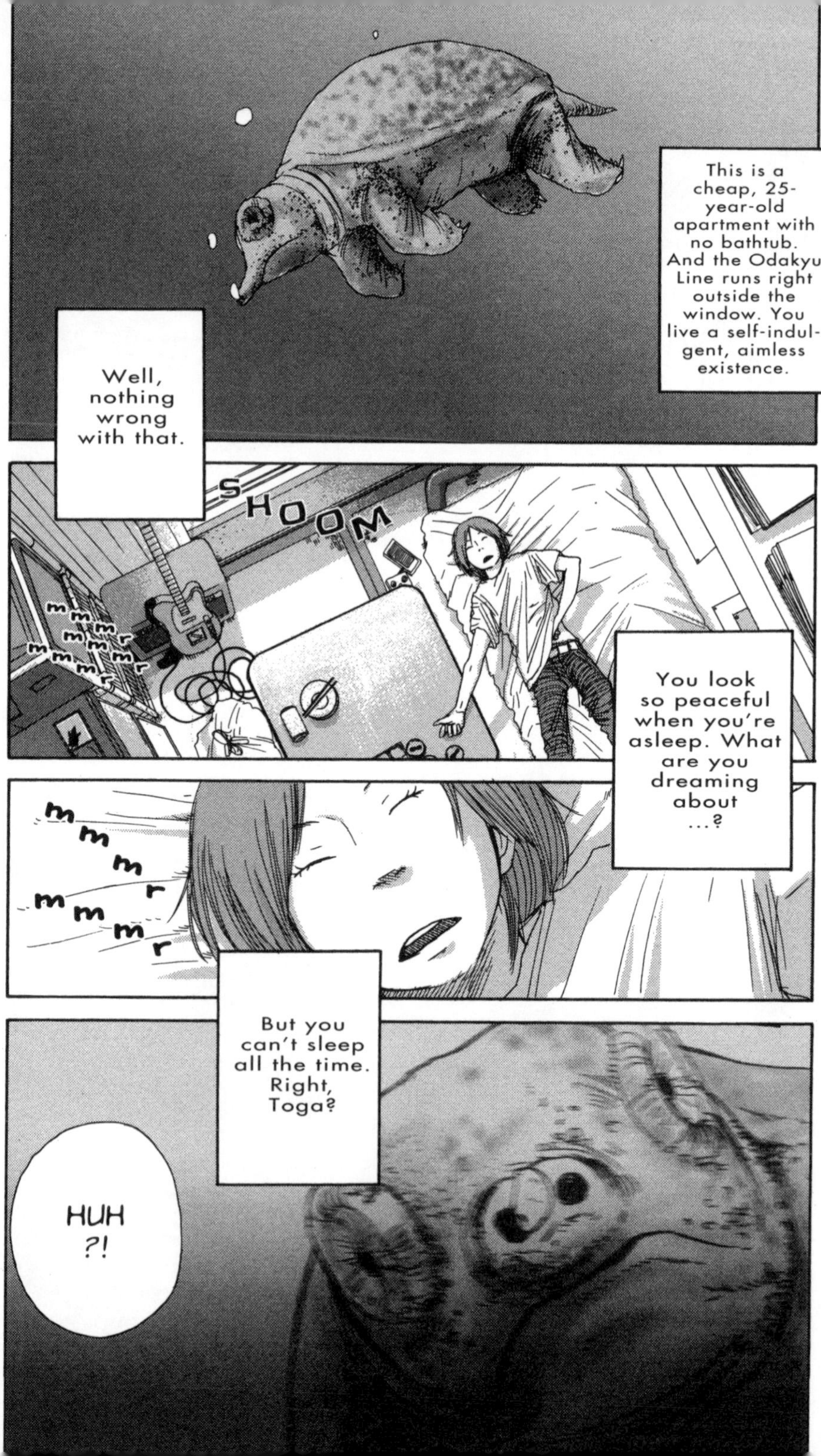
This is a cheap, 25-year-old apartment with no bathtub. And the Odakyu Line runs right outside the window. You live a self-indulgent, aimless existence.
Well, nothing wrong with that.
SHOOM
mmmr
mmmr
mmmr
You look so peaceful when you're asleep. What are you dreaming about ...?
mmmr
mmmr
But you can't sleep all the time. Right, Toga?
HUH ?!

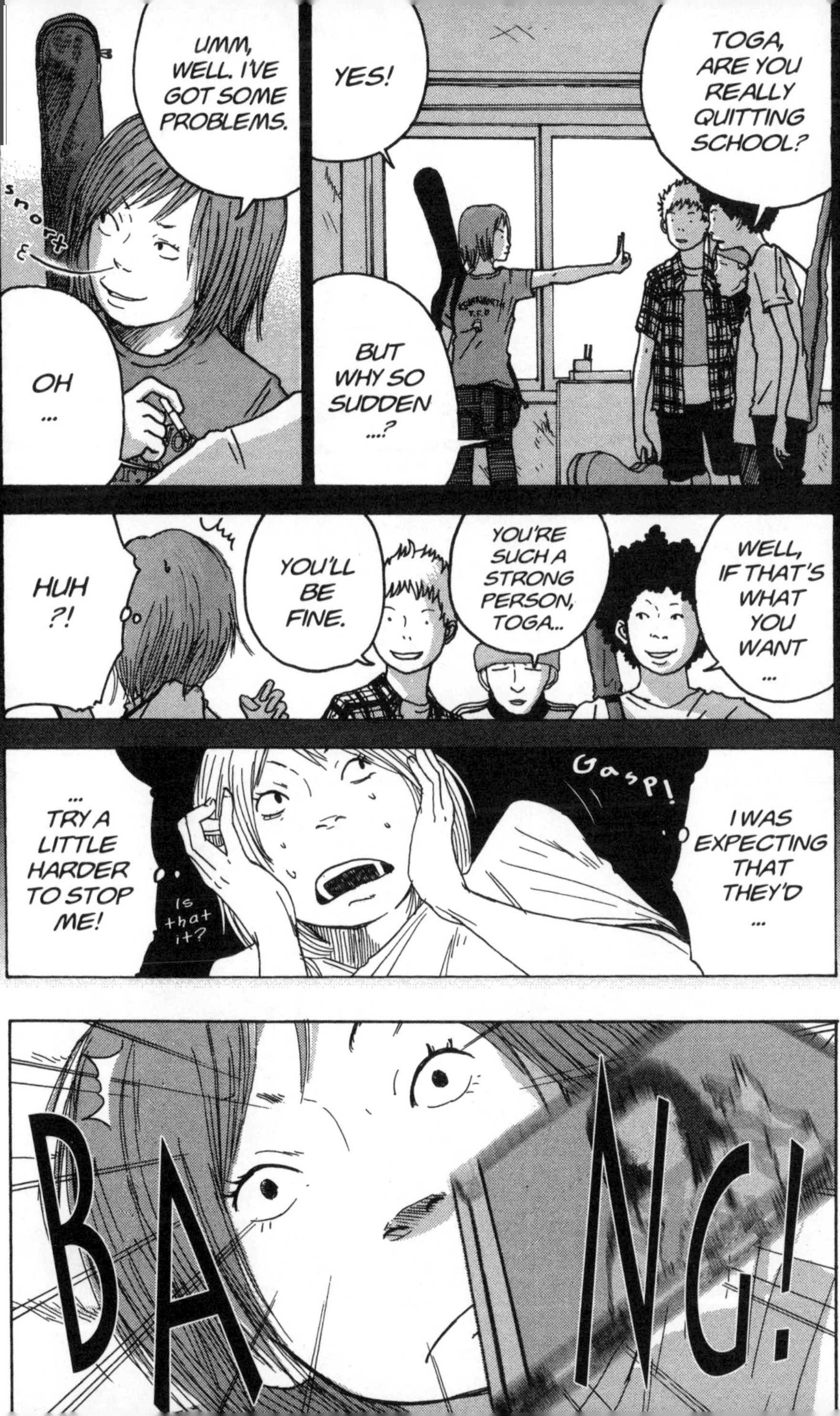
TOGA, ARE YOU REALLY QUITTING SCHOOL?
YES!
BUT WHY SO SUDDEN ...?
UMM, WELL. I'VE GOT SOME PROBLEMS.
snort
OH ...
WELL, IF THAT'S WHAT YOU WANT ...
YOU'RE SUCH A STRONG PERSON, TOGA...
YOU'LL BE FINE.
HUH ?!
Gasp!
I WAS EXPECTING THAT THEY'D ...
is that it?
... TRY A LITTLE HARDER TO STOP ME!
BANG!

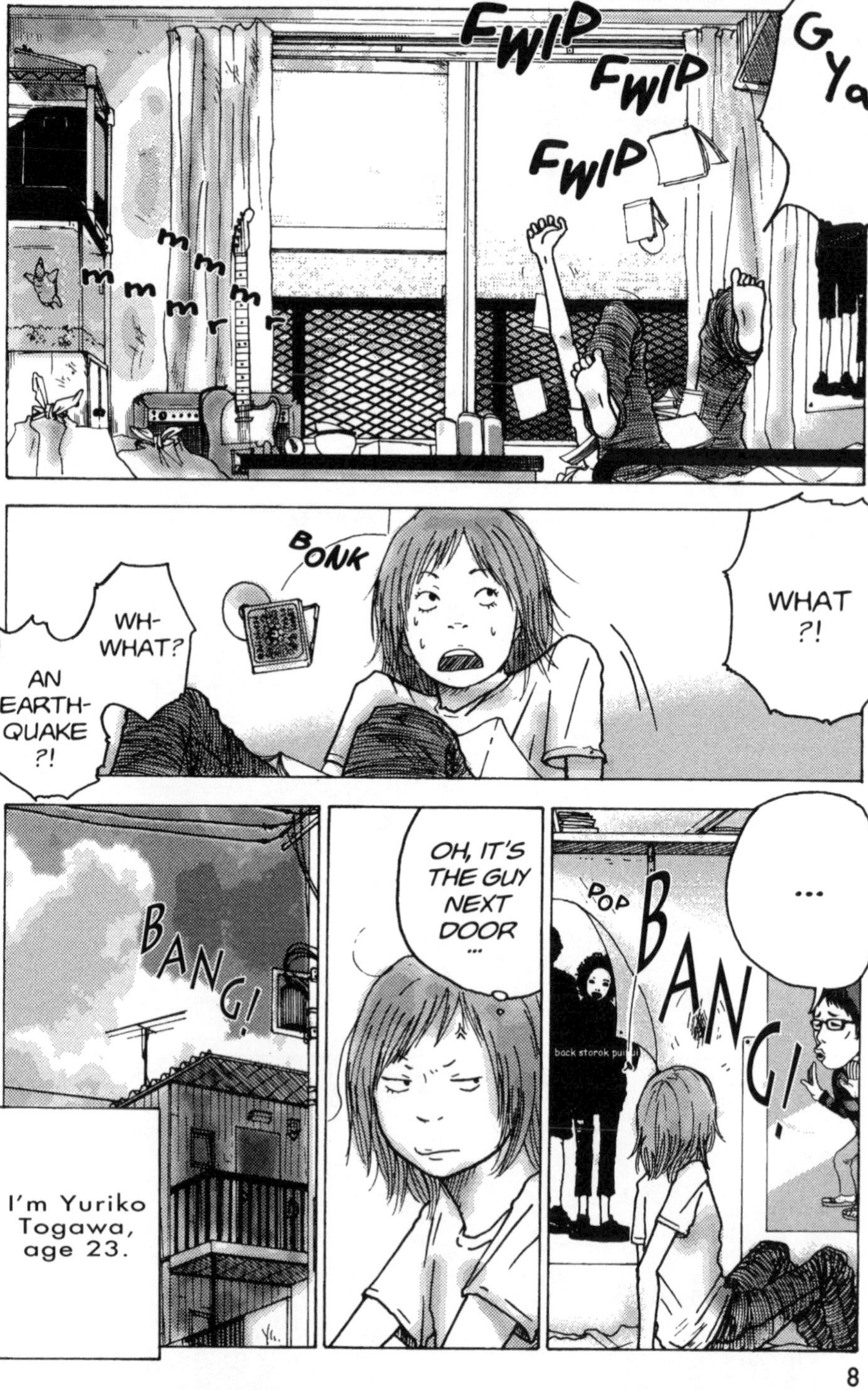
Gyah!
FWIP
FWIP
FWIP
mmmmmmmr
WHAT ?!
BONK
WH- WHAT?
AN EARTH-QUAKE ?!
...
BANG!
POP
OH, IT'S THE GUY NEXT DOOR ...
BANG!
I'm Yuriko Togawa, age 23.

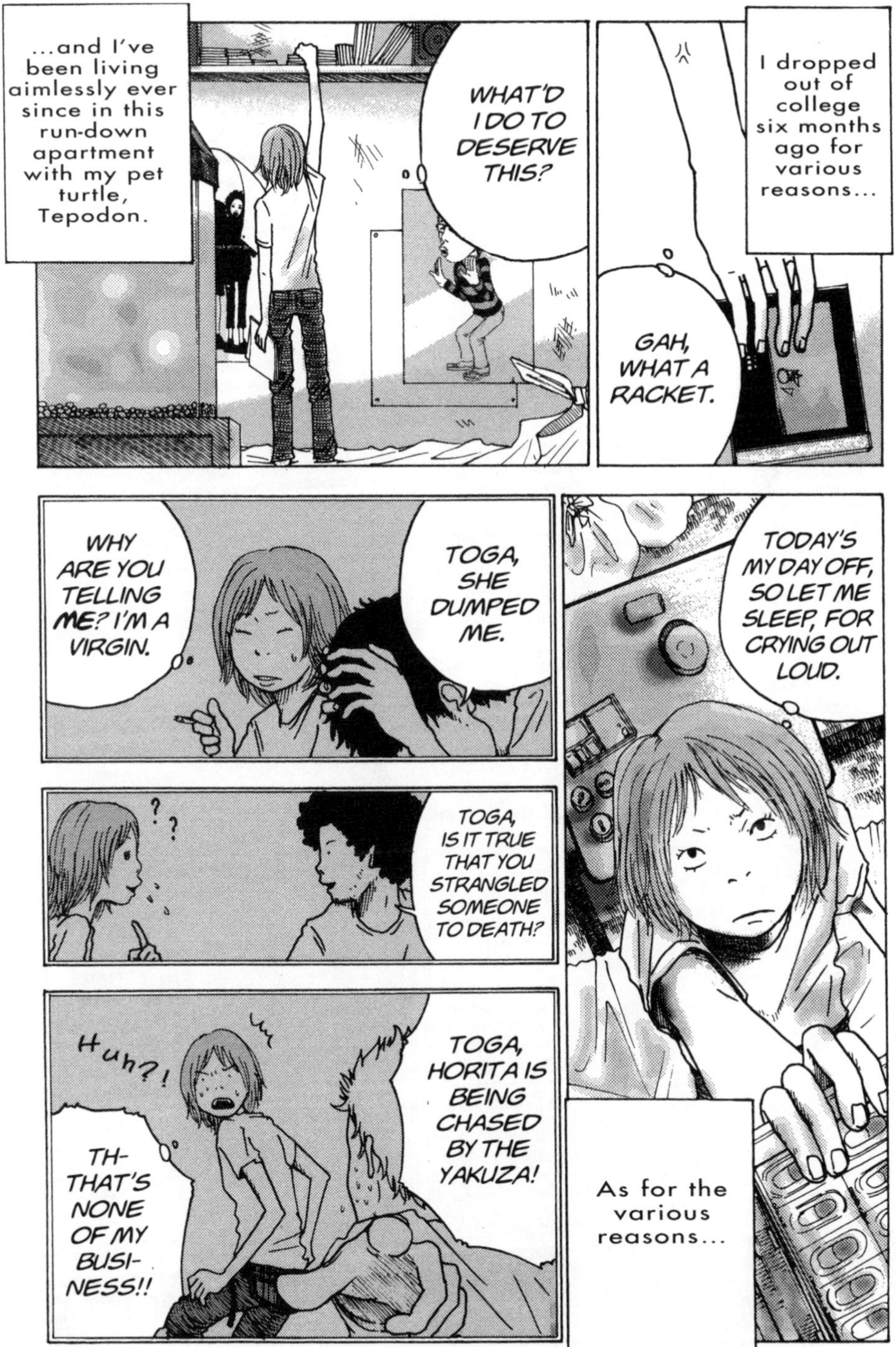
I dropped out of college six months ago for various reasons...
GAH, WHAT A RACKET.
WHAT'D I DO TO DESERVE THIS?
...and I've been living aimlessly ever since in this run-down apartment with my pet turtle, Tepodon.
TODAY'S MY DAY OFF, SO LET ME SLEEP, FOR CRYING OUT LOUD.
As for the various reasons...
TOGA, SHE DUMPED ME.
WHY ARE YOU TELLING ME? I'M A VIRGIN.
TOGA, IS IT TRUE THAT YOU STRANGLED SOMEONE TO DEATH?
TOGA, HORITA IS BEING CHASED BY THE YAKUZA!
Huh?!
TH- THAT'S NONE OF MY BUSINESS!!

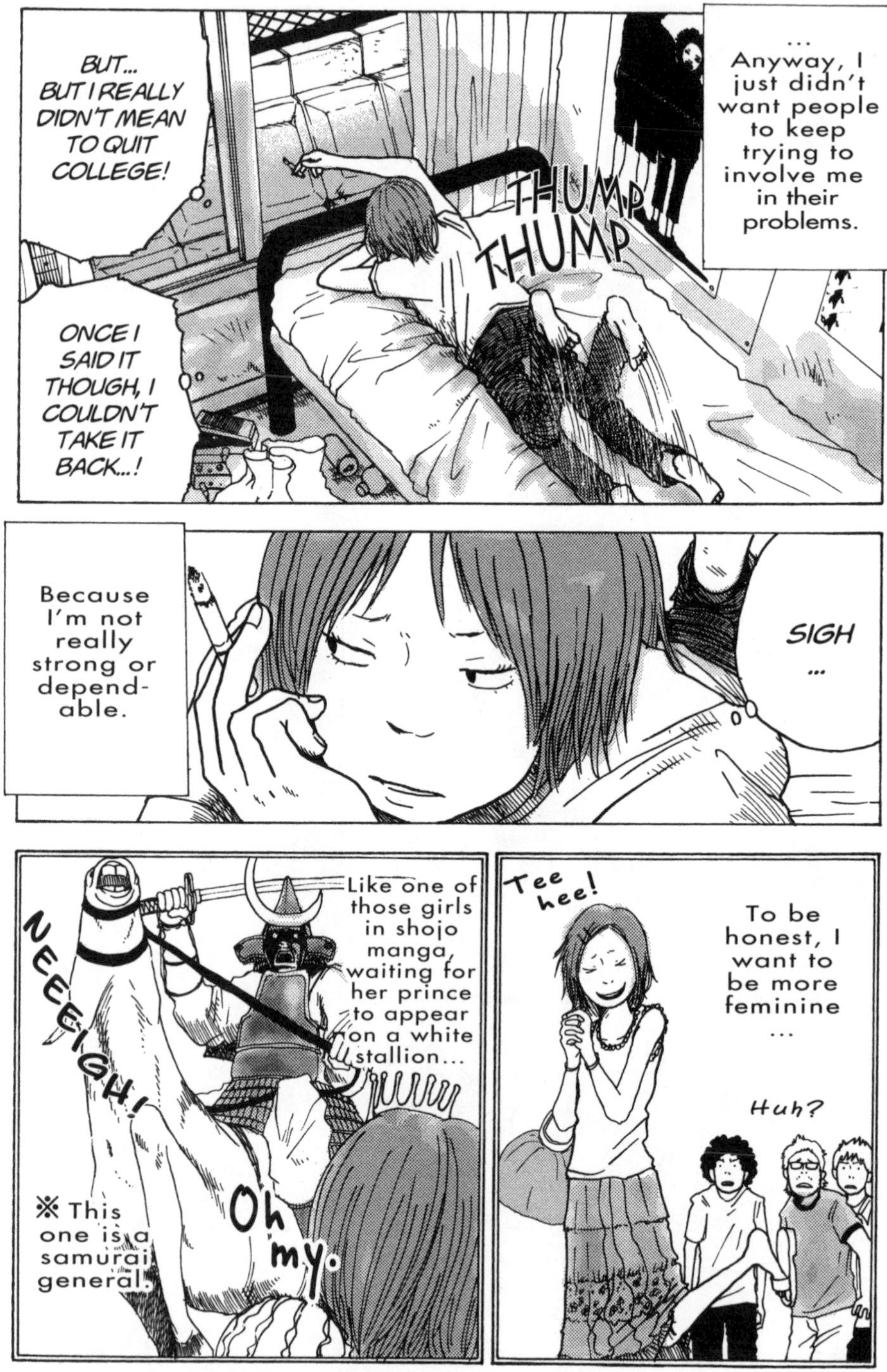
...Anyway, I just didn't want people to keep trying to involve me in their problems.
THUMP THUMP
BUT... BUT I REALLY DIDN'T MEAN TO QUIT COLLEGE!
ONCE I SAID IT THOUGH, I COULDN'T TAKE IT BACK...!
SIGH...
Because I'm not really strong or depend-able.
Tee hee!
To be honest, I want to be more feminine...
Huh?
Like one of those girls in shojo manga, waiting for her prince to appear on a white stallion...
NEEEIGH!
Oh my.
※ This one is a samurai general.

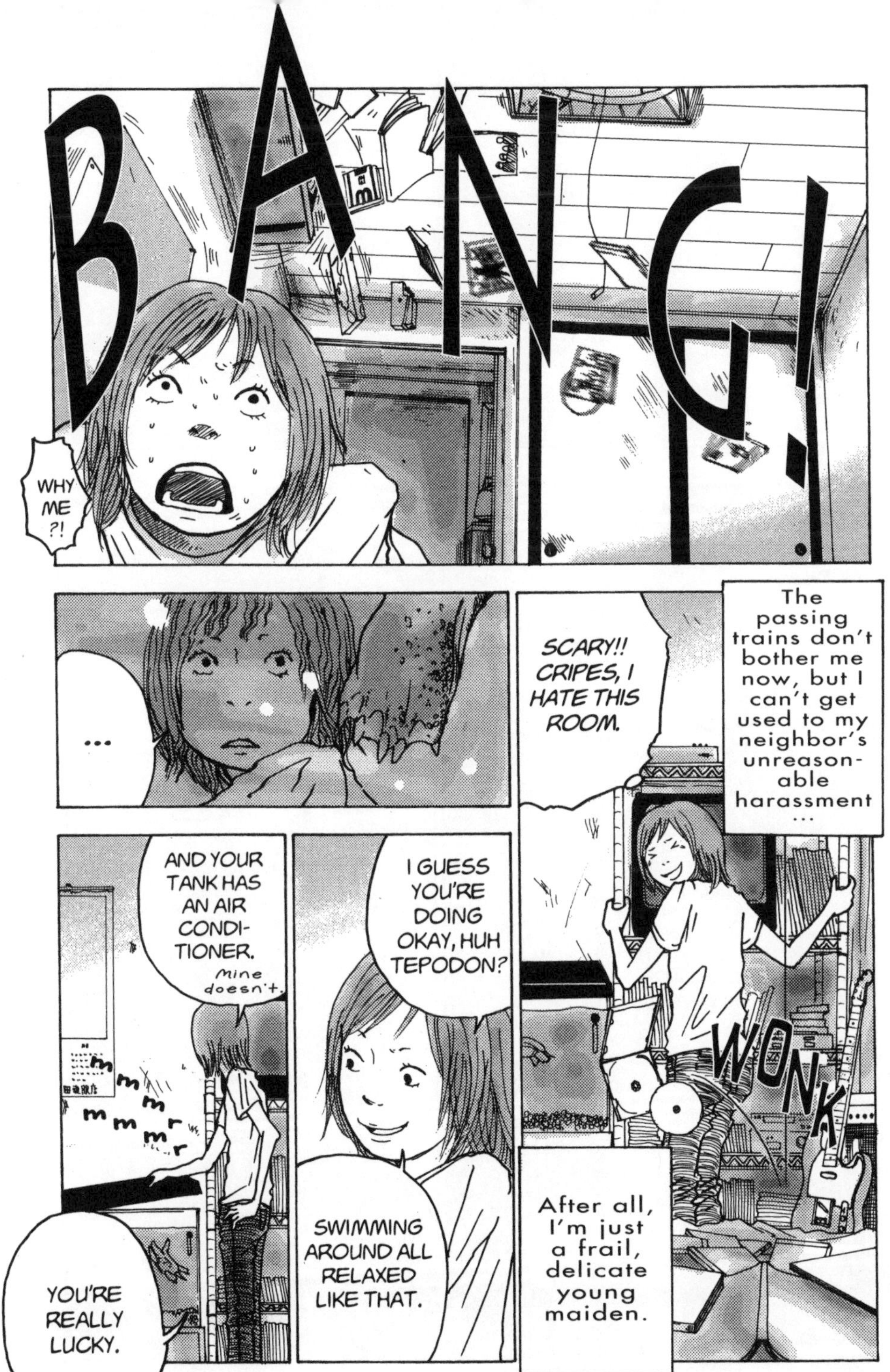
BANG!
WHY ME ?!
The passing trains don't bother me now, but I can't get used to my neighbor's unreasonable harassment ...
SCARY!! CRIPES, I HATE THIS ROOM.
WONK
After all, I'm just a frail, delicate young maiden.
...
I GUESS YOU'RE DOING OKAY, HUH TEPODON?
SWIMMING AROUND ALL RELAXED LIKE THAT.
AND YOUR TANK HAS AN AIR CONDITIONER.
Mine doesn't.
mmmr mmmr
YOU'RE REALLY LUCKY.

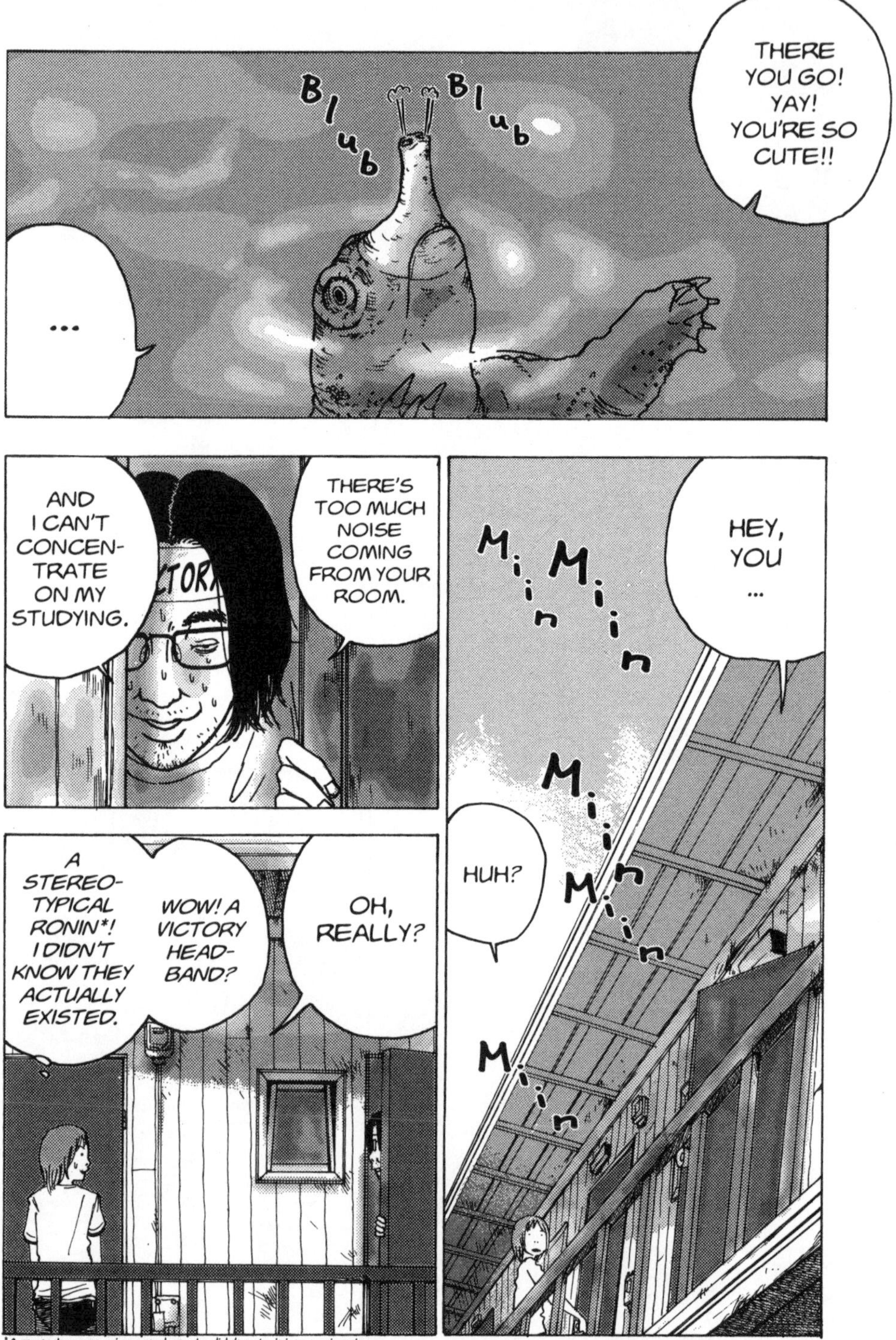
THERE YOU GO! YAY! YOU'RE SO CUTE!!
Blub Blub
...
HEY, YOU ...
Miin Miin
Miin Miin
Miin
HUH?
THERE'S TOO MUCH NOISE COMING FROM YOUR ROOM.
AND I CAN'T CONCEN-TRATE ON MY STUDYING.
OH, REALLY?
WOW! A VICTORY HEAD-BAND?
A STEREO-TYPICAL RONIN*! I DIDN'T KNOW THEY ACTUALLY EXISTED.

*A masterless samurai or a student who didn't make it into a university.

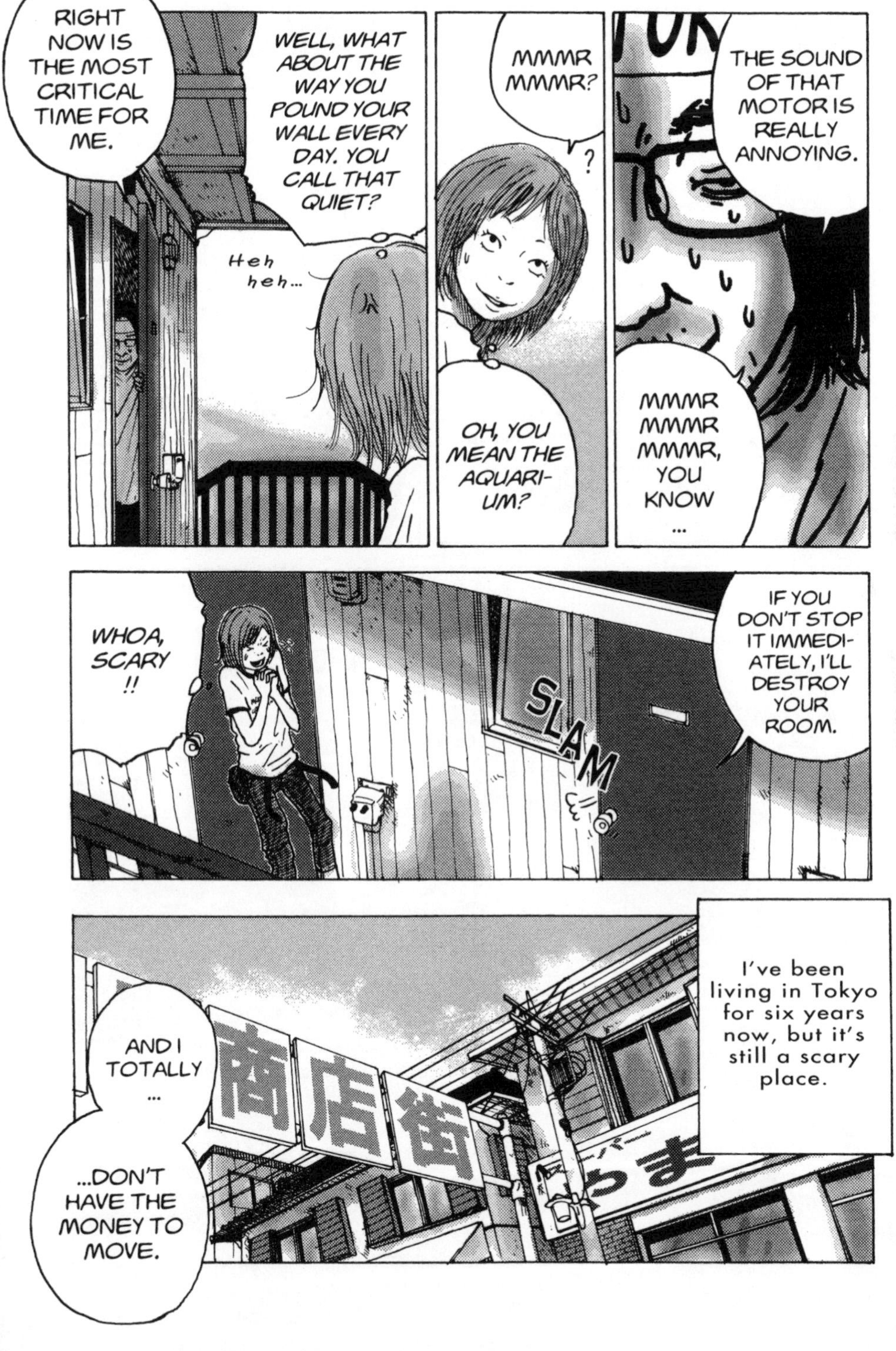
THE SOUND OF THAT MOTOR IS REALLY ANNOYING.
MMMR MMMR MMMR, YOU KNOW ...
MMMR MMMR?
?
OH, YOU MEAN THE AQUARI-UM?
RIGHT NOW IS THE MOST CRITICAL TIME FOR ME.
WELL, WHAT ABOUT THE WAY YOU POUND YOUR WALL EVERY DAY. YOU CALL THAT QUIET?
Heh heh...
IF YOU DON'T STOP IT IMMEDI-ATELY, I'LL DESTROY YOUR ROOM.
SLAM
WHOA, SCARY !!
I've been living in Tokyo for six years now, but it's still a scary place.
商店街
AND I TOTALLY ...
...DON'T HAVE THE MONEY TO MOVE.

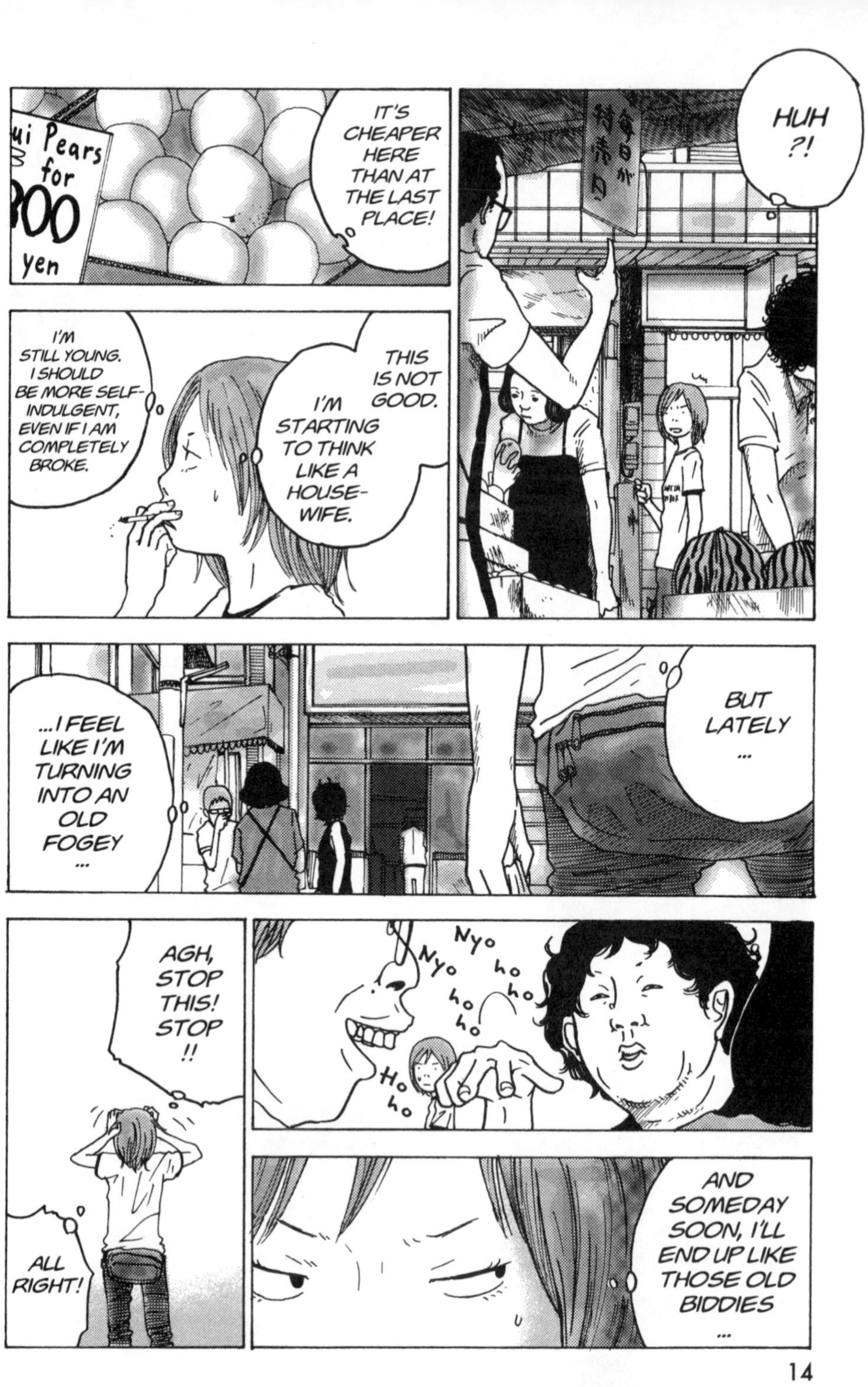
HUH ?!
IT'S CHEAPER HERE THAN AT THE LAST PLACE!
THIS IS NOT GOOD.
I'M STARTING TO THINK LIKE A HOUSE-WIFE.
I'M STILL YOUNG. I SHOULD BE MORE SELF-INDULGENT, EVEN IF I AM COMPLETELY BROKE.
BUT LATELY ...
...I FEEL LIKE I'M TURNING INTO AN OLD FOGEY ...
Nyo ho ho
Nyo ho ho
Ho ho
AND SOMEDAY SOON, I'LL END UP LIKE THOSE OLD BIDDIES ...
AGH, STOP THIS! STOP !!
ALL RIGHT!

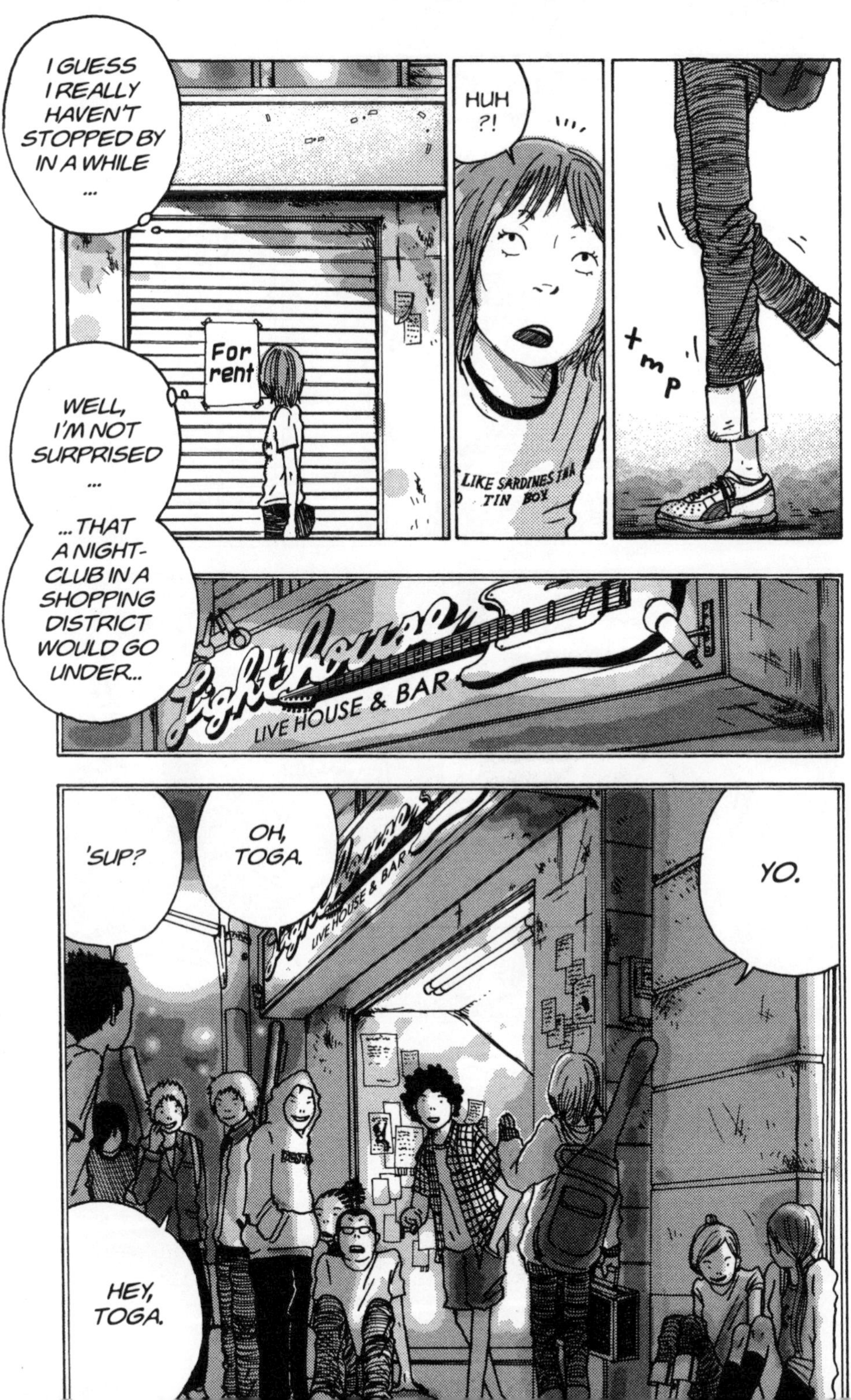
tmp
HUH ?!
I GUESS I REALLY HAVEN'T STOPPED BY IN A WHILE ...
For rent
WELL, I'M NOT SURPRISED ...
...THAT A NIGHT-CLUB IN A SHOPPING DISTRICT WOULD GO UNDER...
LIKE SARDINES
TIN BOX
Lighthouse
LIVE HOUSE & BAR
YO.
OH, TOGA.
'SUP?
HEY, TOGA.

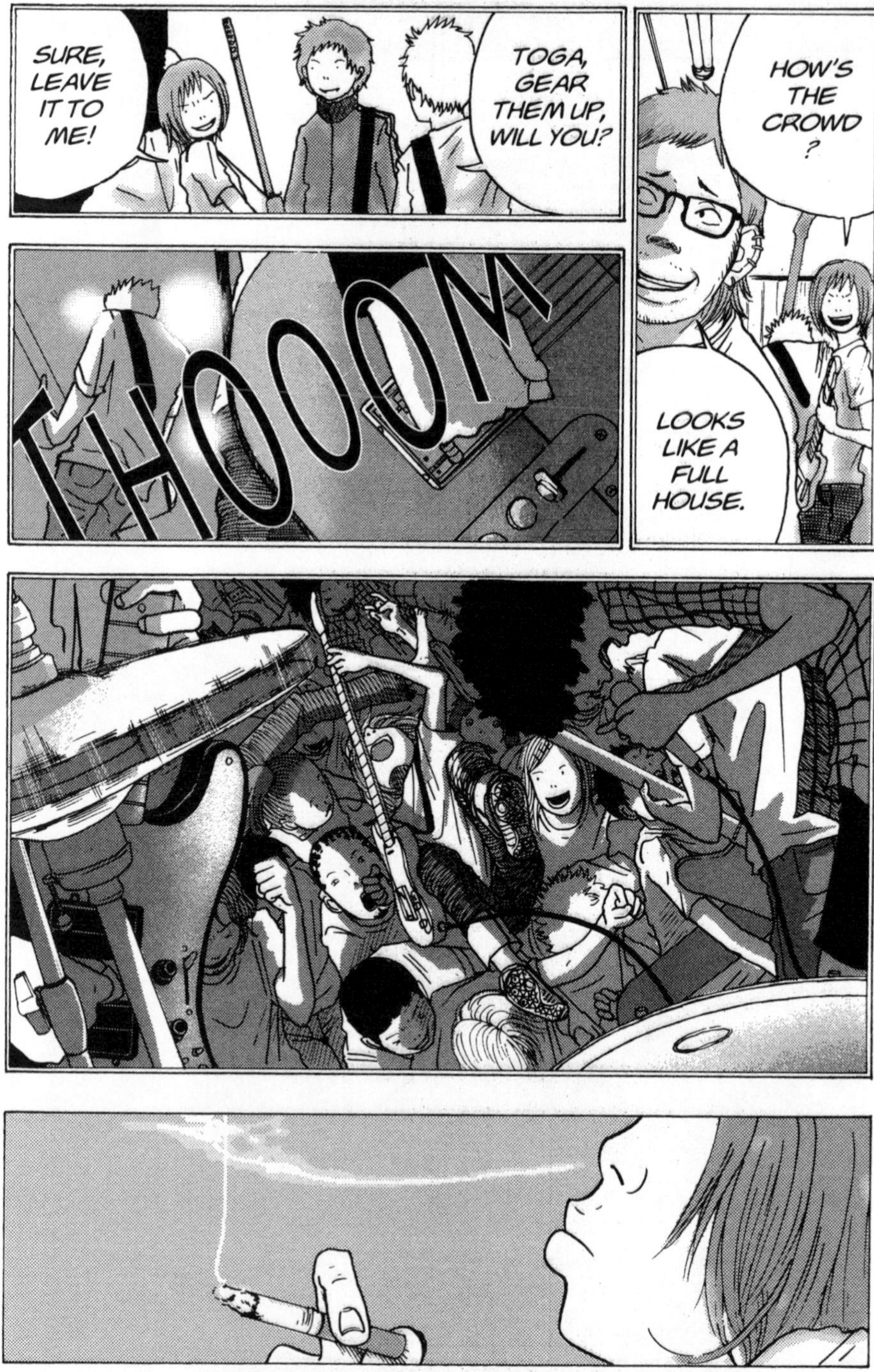
HOW'S THE CROWD?
LOOKS LIKE A FULL HOUSE.
TOGA, GEAR THEM UP, WILL YOU?
SURE, LEAVE IT TO ME!
THOOOM

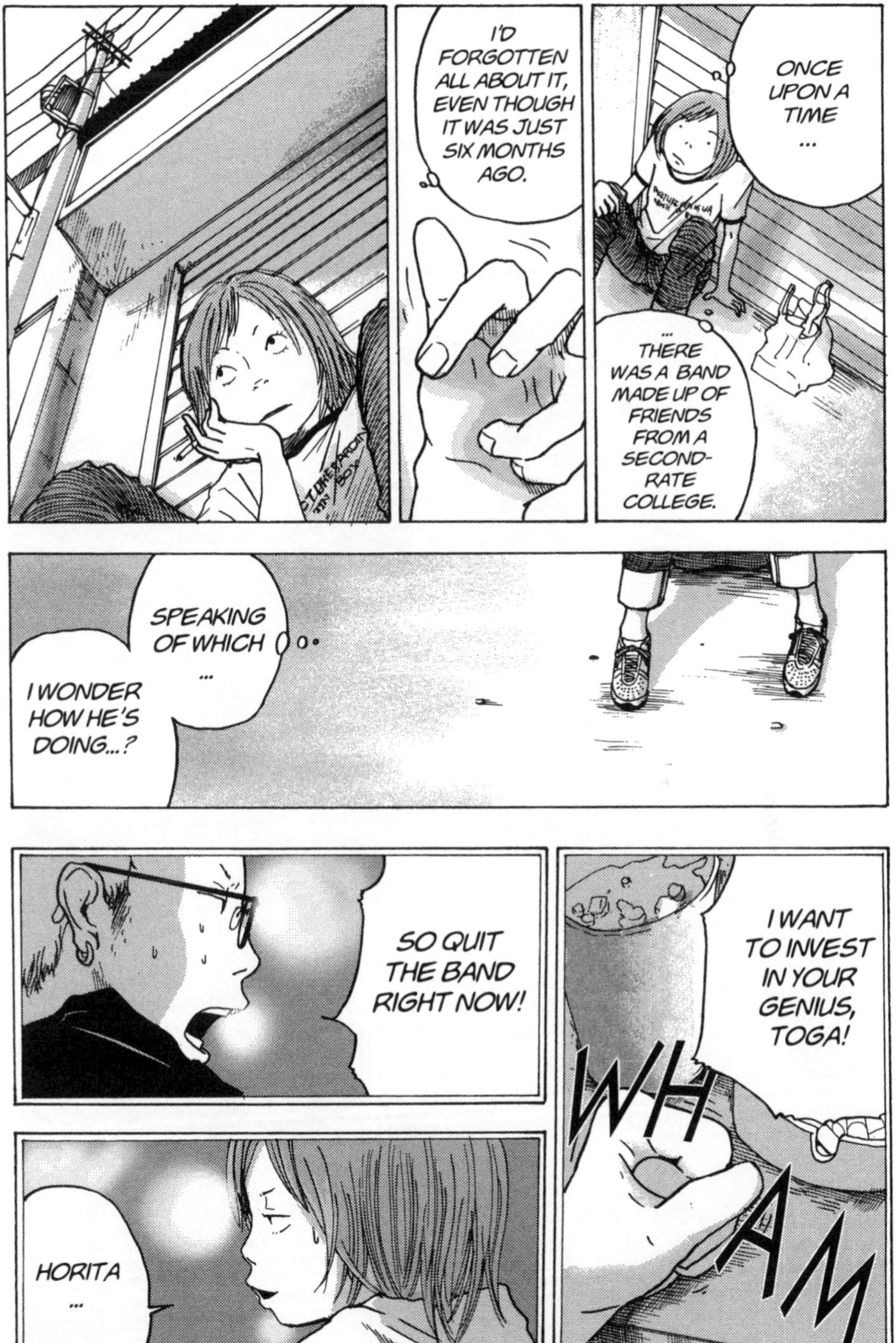
ONCE UPON A TIME ...
... THERE WAS A BAND MADE UP OF FRIENDS FROM A SECOND-RATE COLLEGE.
I'D FORGOTTEN ALL ABOUT IT, EVEN THOUGH IT WAS JUST SIX MONTHS AGO.
SPEAKING OF WHICH ...
I WONDER HOW HE'S DOING...?
I WANT TO INVEST IN YOUR GENIUS, TOGA!
WHAM
SO QUIT THE BAND RIGHT NOW!
HORITA ...

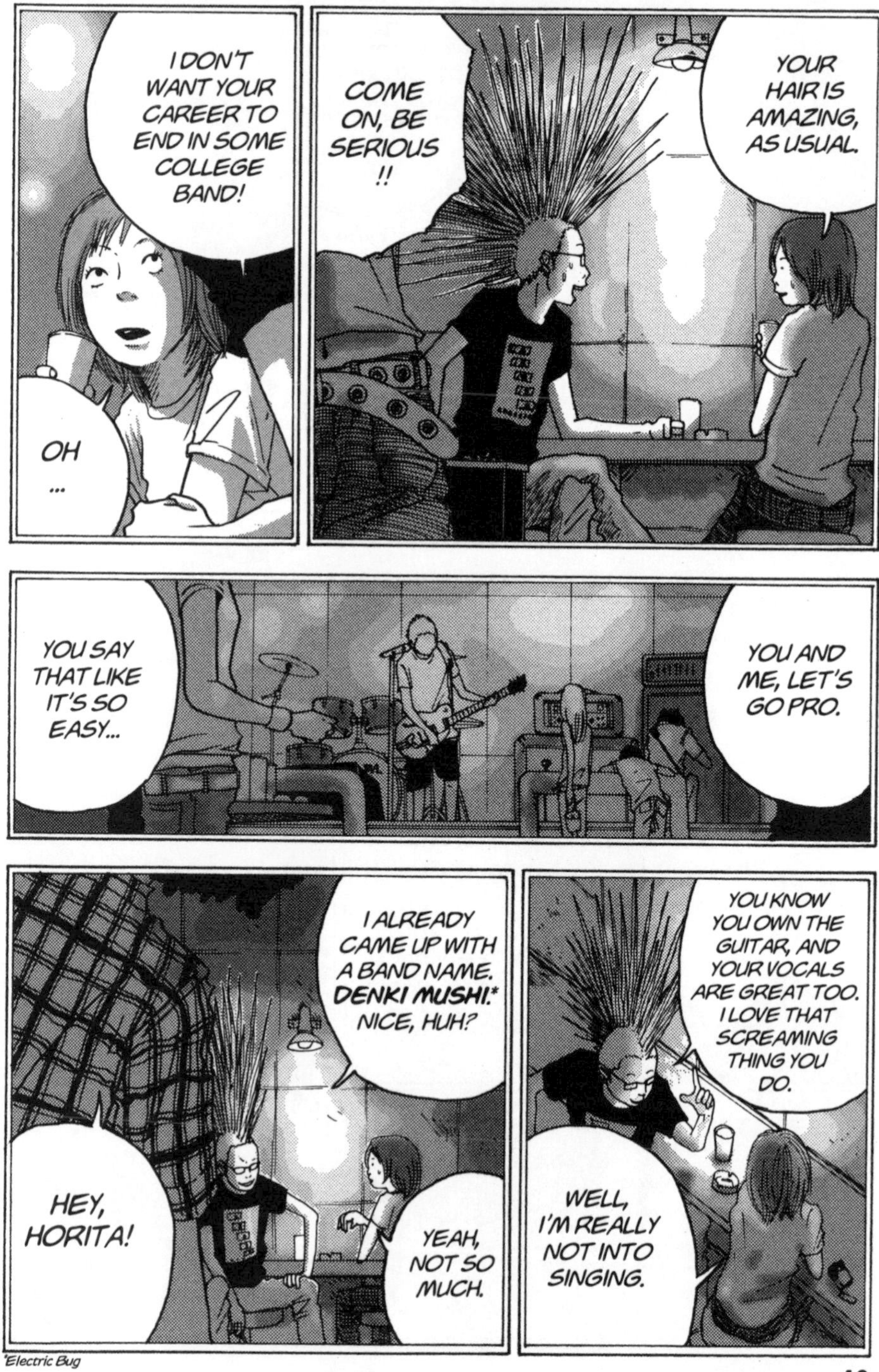
YOUR HAIR IS AMAZING, AS USUAL.
COME ON, BE SERIOUS !!
I DON'T WANT YOUR CAREER TO END IN SOME COLLEGE BAND!
OH ...
YOU AND ME, LET'S GO PRO.
YOU SAY THAT LIKE IT'S SO EASY...
YOU KNOW YOU OWN THE GUITAR, AND YOUR VOCALS ARE GREAT TOO. I LOVE THAT SCREAMING THING YOU DO.
WELL, I'M REALLY NOT INTO SINGING.
I ALREADY CAME UP WITH A BAND NAME. **DENKI MUSHI.*** NICE, HUH?
YEAH, NOT SO MUCH.
HEY, HORITA!

*Electric Bug

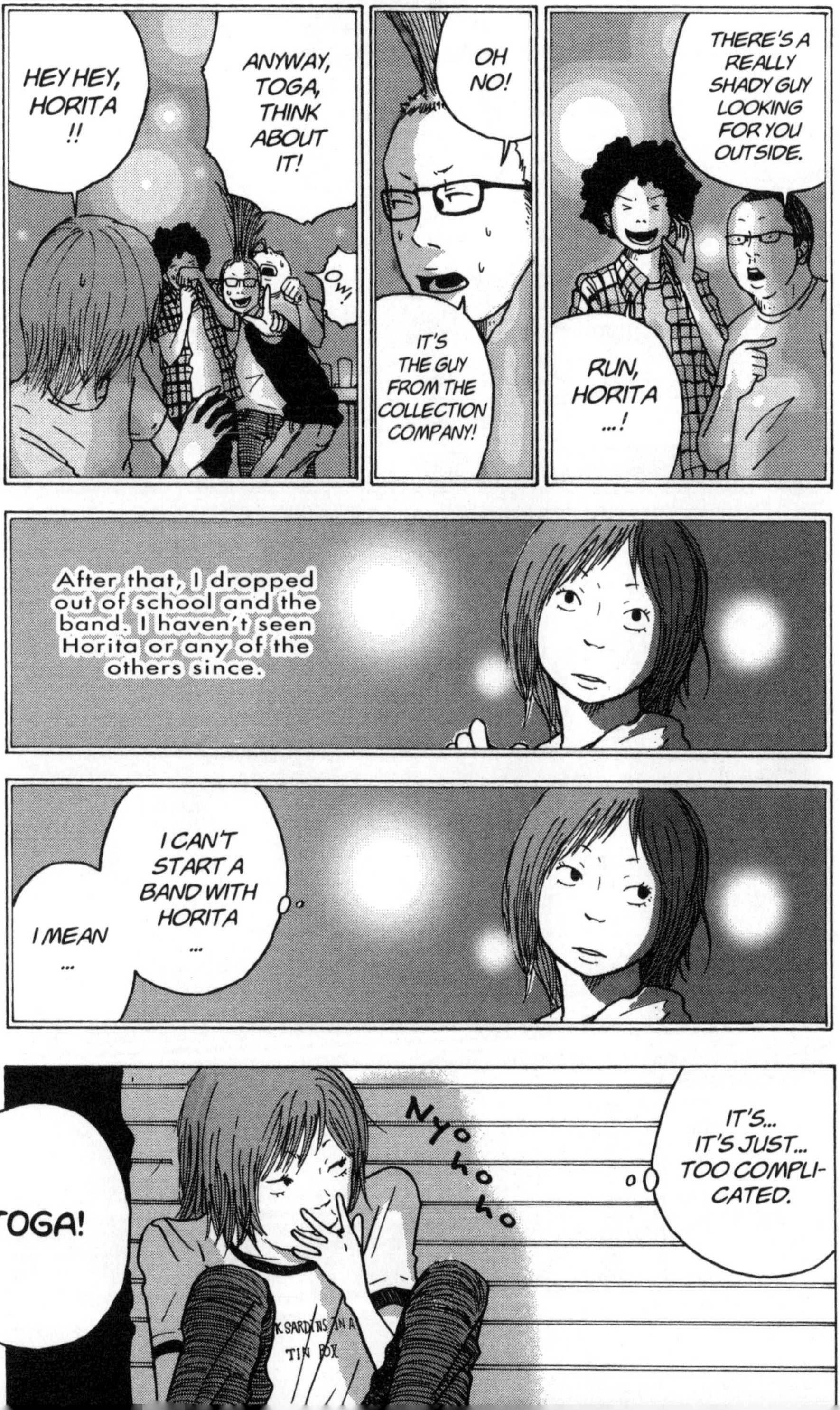
THERE'S A REALLY SHADY GUY LOOKING FOR YOU OUTSIDE.
RUN, HORITA ...!
OH NO!
IT'S THE GUY FROM THE COLLECTION COMPANY!
ANYWAY, TOGA, THINK ABOUT IT!
HEY HEY, HORITA !!
OW!
After that, I dropped out of school and the band. I haven't seen Horita or any of the others since.
I CAN'T START A BAND WITH HORITA ...
I MEAN ...
IT'S... IT'S JUST... TOO COMPLI-CATED.
NYOHOHO
TOGA!

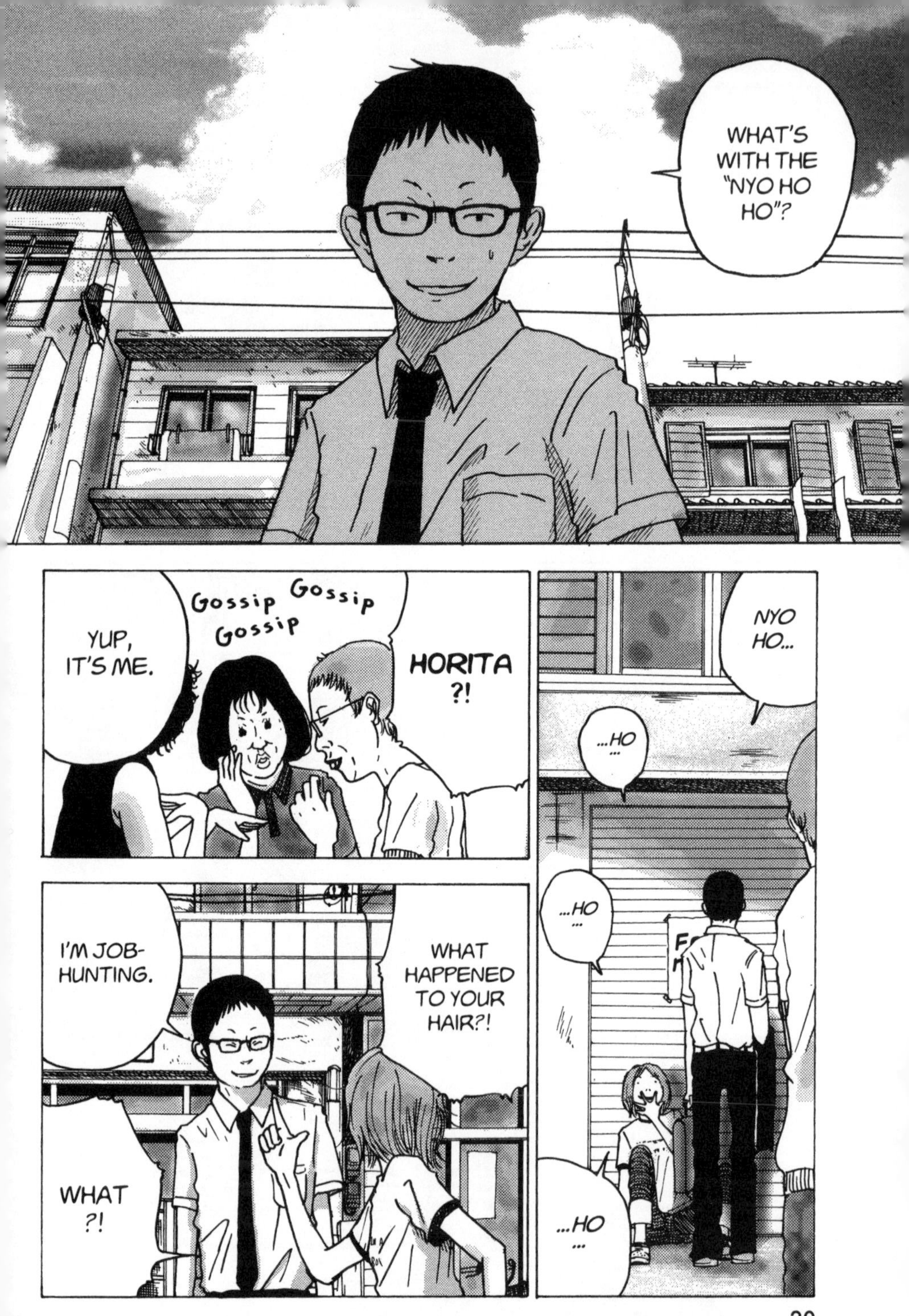
WHAT'S WITH THE "NYO HO HO"?
NYO HO...
...HO ...
...HO ...
...HO ...
HORITA ?!
Gossip Gossip Gossip
YUP, IT'S ME.
WHAT HAPPENED TO YOUR HAIR?!
I'M JOB-HUNTING.
WHAT ?!

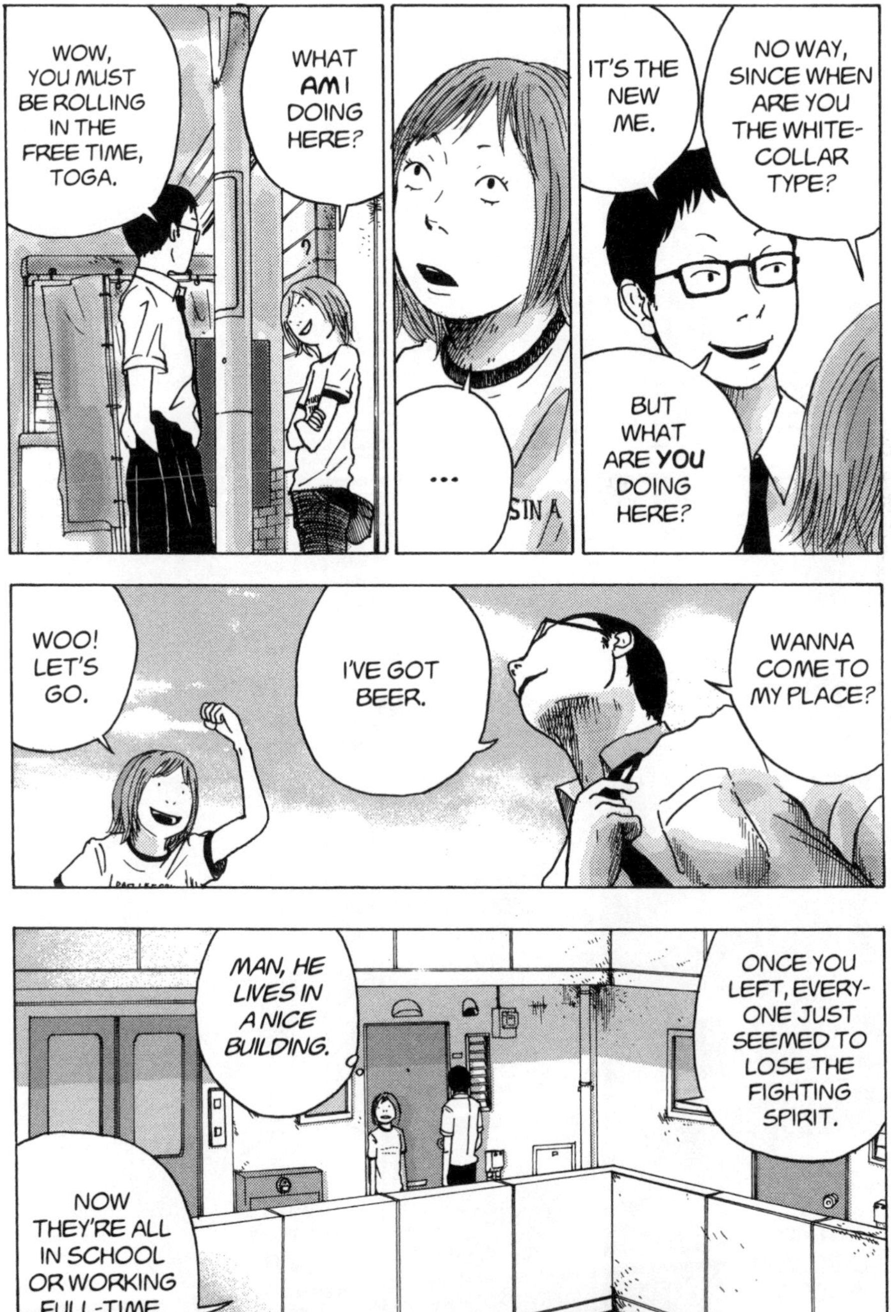
NO WAY, SINCE WHEN ARE YOU THE WHITE-COLLAR TYPE?
IT'S THE NEW ME.
BUT WHAT ARE **YOU** DOING HERE?
...
WHAT **AM** I DOING HERE?
WOW, YOU MUST BE ROLLING IN THE FREE TIME, TOGA.
WANNA COME TO MY PLACE?
I'VE GOT BEER.
WOO! LET'S GO.
ONCE YOU LEFT, EVERY-ONE JUST SEEMED TO LOSE THE FIGHTING SPIRIT.
MAN, HE LIVES IN A NICE BUILDING.
NOW THEY'RE ALL IN SCHOOL OR WORKING FULL-TIME.

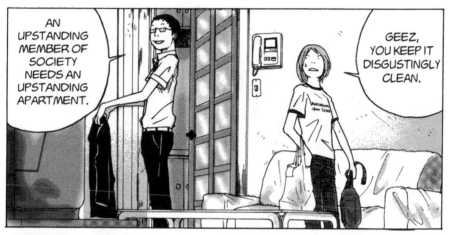

GEEZ, YOU KEEP IT DISGUSTINGLY CLEAN.
AN UPSTANDING MEMBER OF SOCIETY NEEDS AN UPSTANDING APARTMENT.
OH ?!
I SEE YOU HAVEN'T ABANDONED MUSIC ALTOGETHER.
OH, I TRIED TO SELL IT, BUT THE OFFERS WERE WAY LOW...
TOGA, YOU WANTED THAT SG, DIDN'T YOU? YOU CAN HAVE IT.
NO... THAT'S OKAY. YOU KEEP IT.

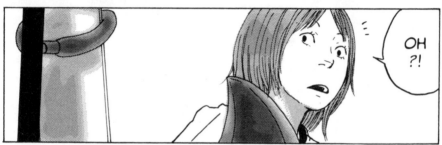

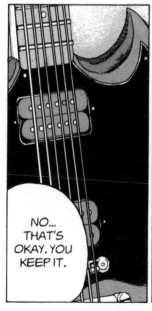

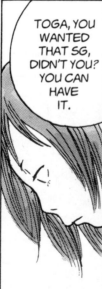

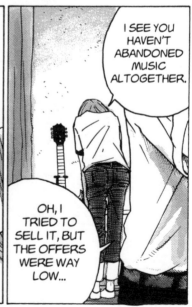

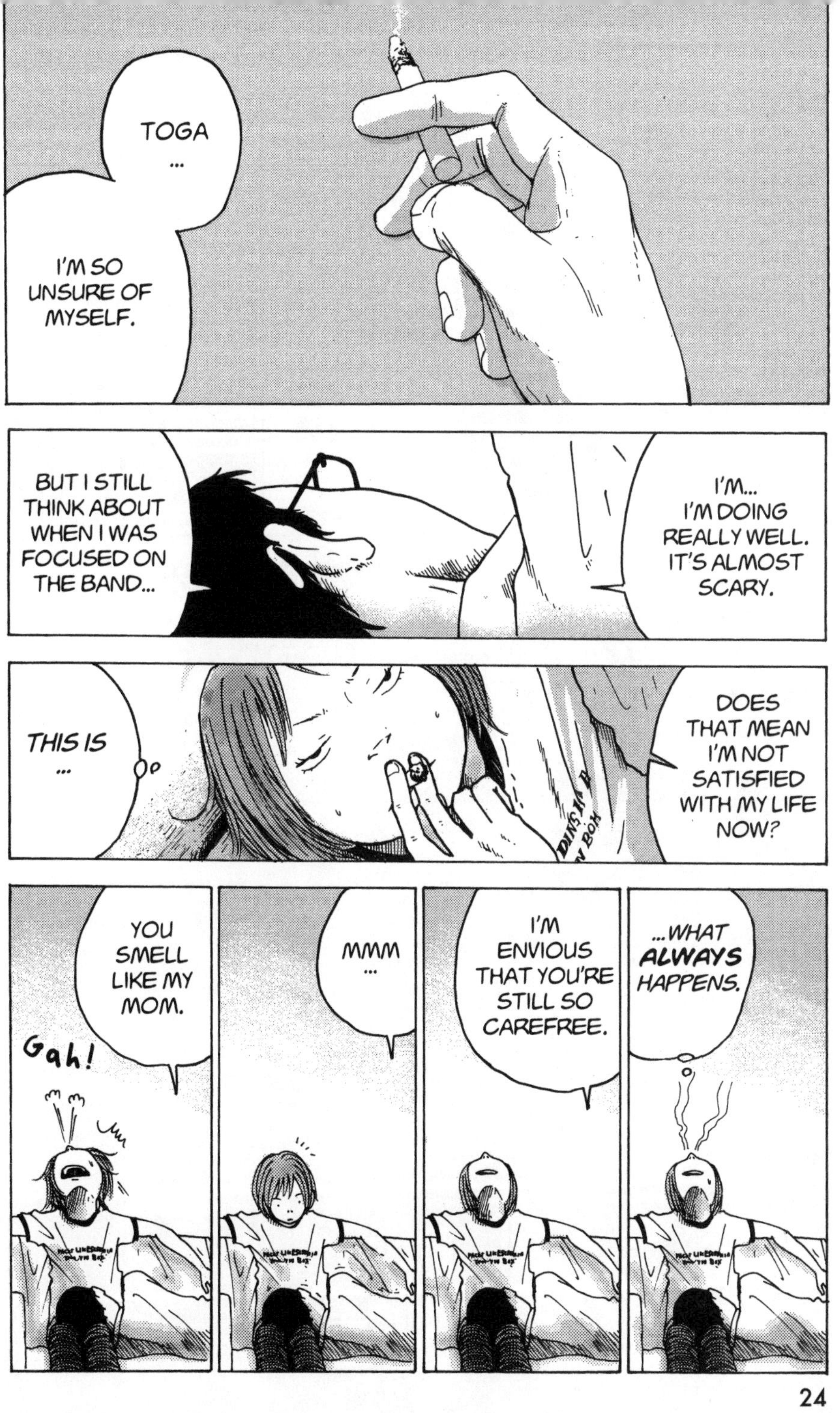
TOGA ...
I'M SO UNSURE OF MYSELF.
I'M... I'M DOING REALLY WELL. IT'S ALMOST SCARY.
BUT I STILL THINK ABOUT WHEN I WAS FOCUSED ON THE BAND...
DOES THAT MEAN I'M NOT SATISFIED WITH MY LIFE NOW?
THIS IS ...
...WHAT **ALWAYS** HAPPENS.
I'M ENVIOUS THAT YOU'RE STILL SO CAREFREE.
MMM ...
YOU SMELL LIKE MY MOM.
Gah!

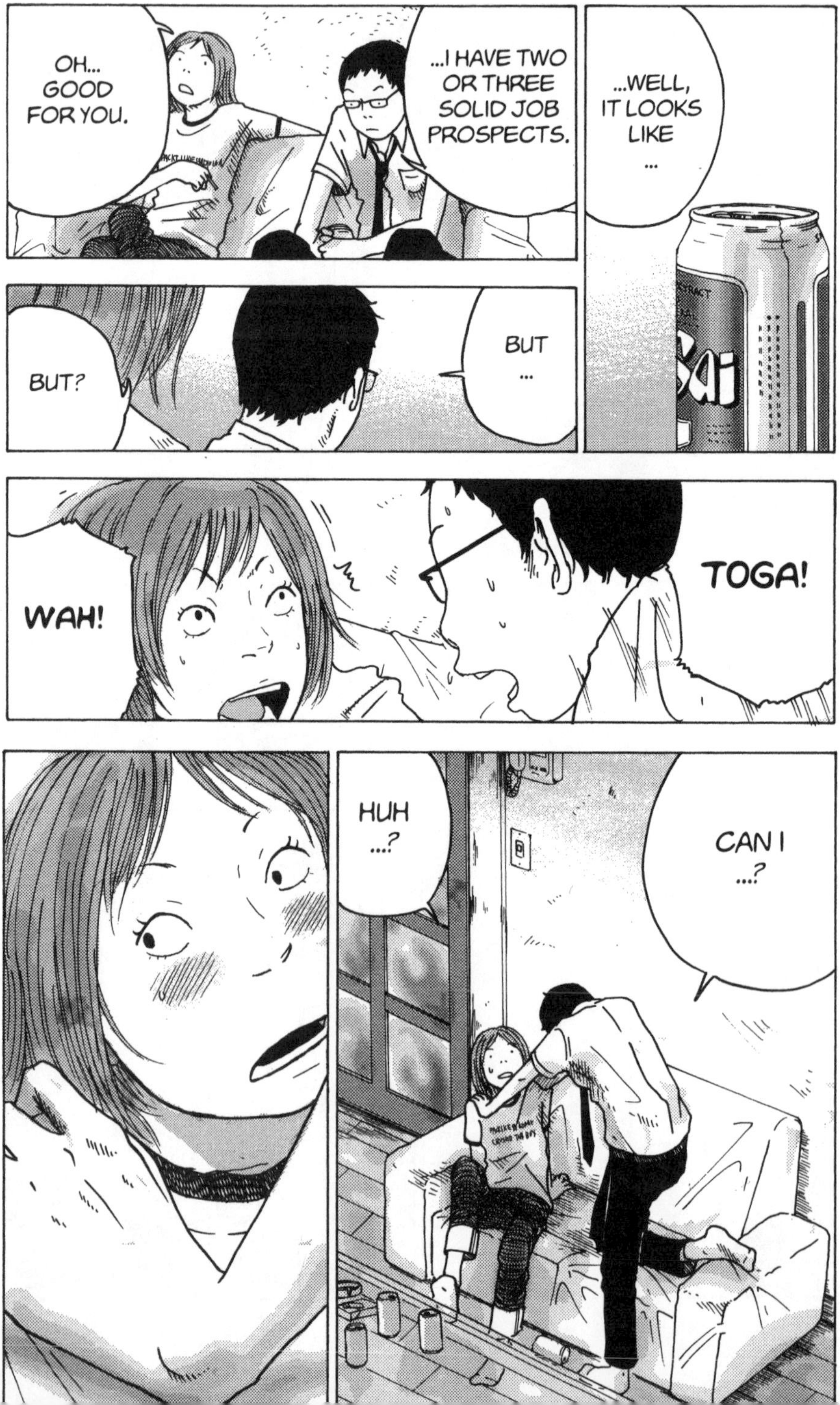
...WELL, IT LOOKS LIKE ...
...I HAVE TWO OR THREE SOLID JOB PROSPECTS.
OH... GOOD FOR YOU.
BUT ...
BUT?
TOGA!
WAH!
CAN I ...?
HUH ...?

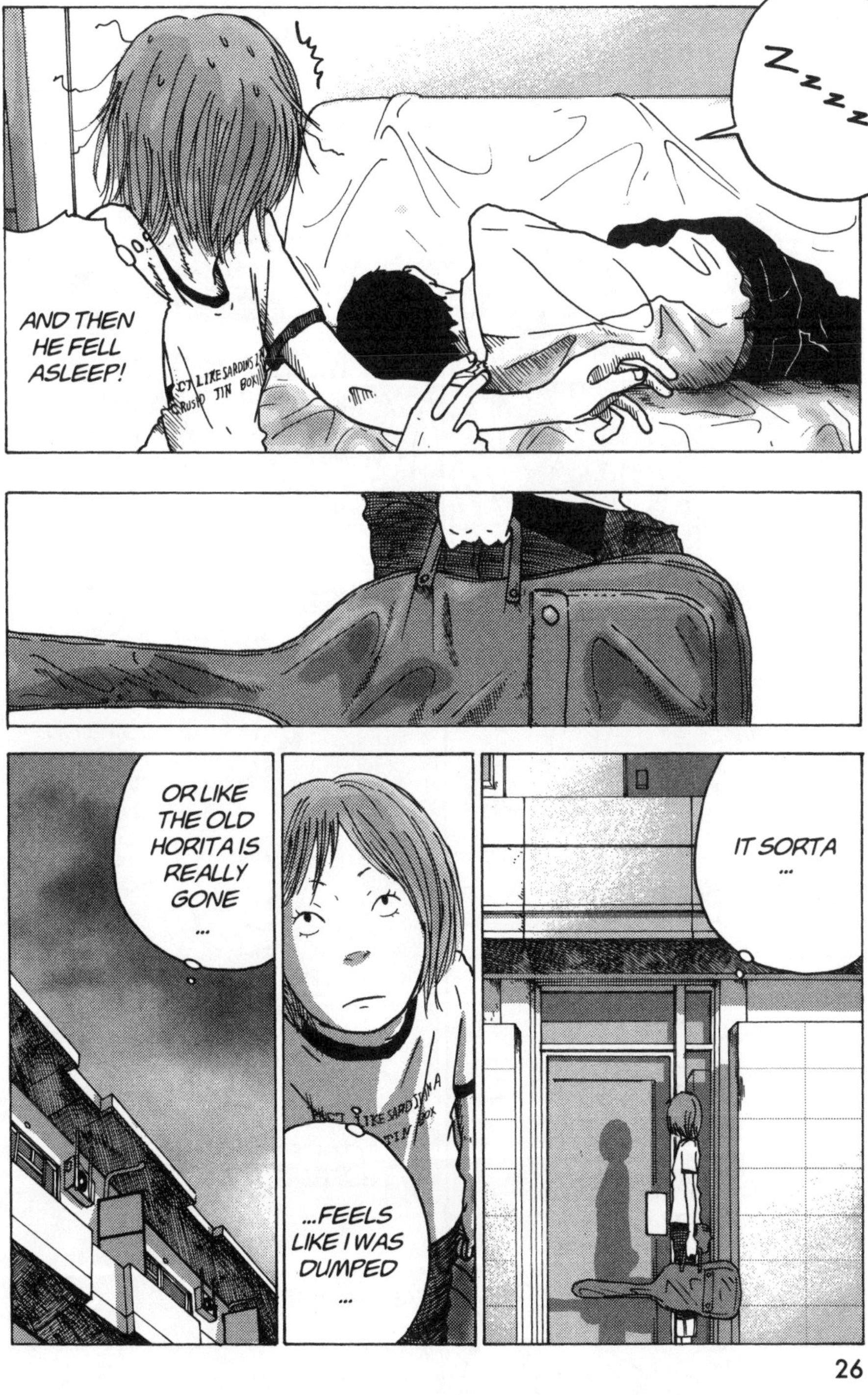
Zzzz
AND THEN HE FELL ASLEEP!
IT SORTA ...
...FEELS LIKE I WAS DUMPED ...
OR LIKE THE OLD HORITA IS REALLY GONE ...

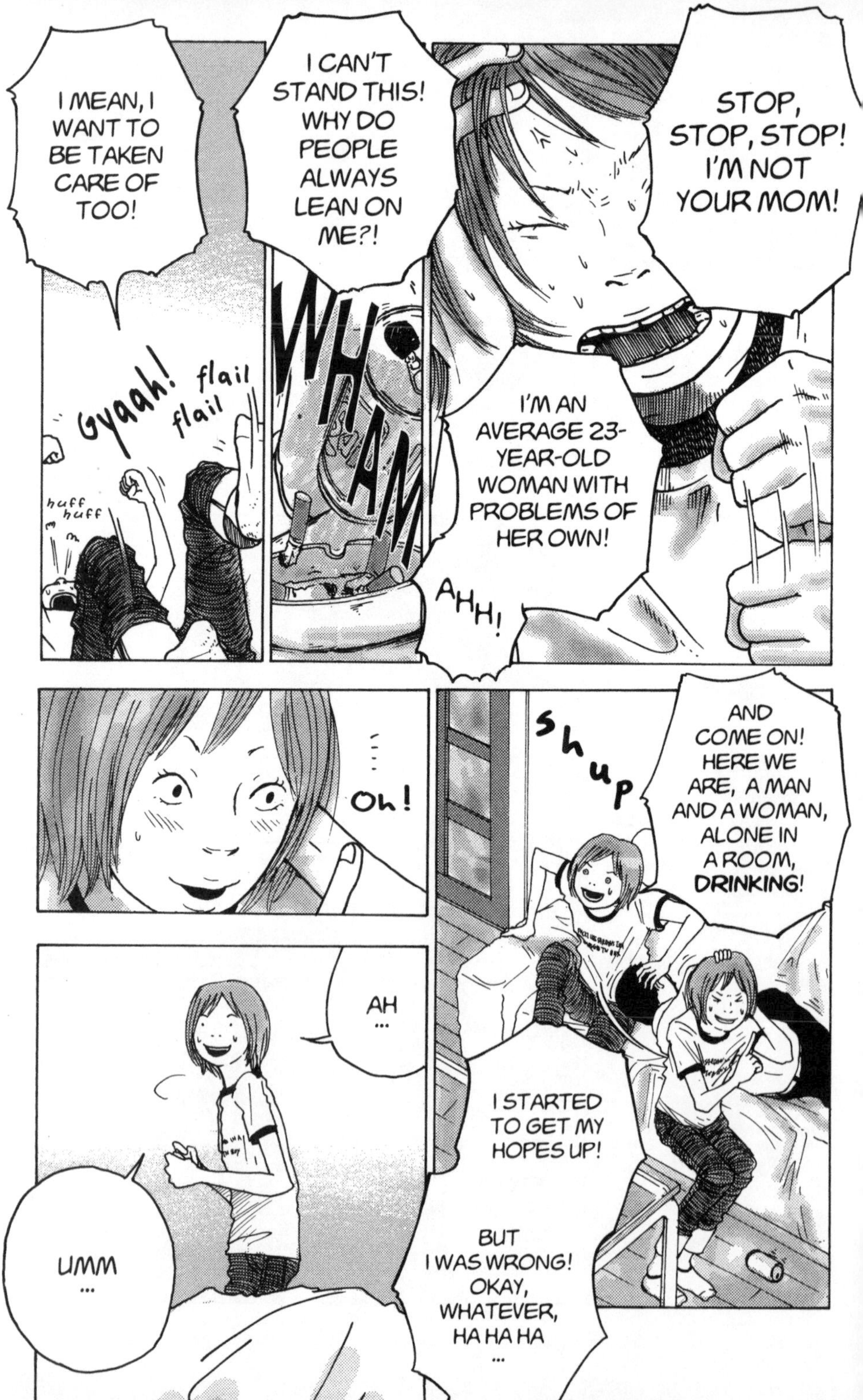
STOP, STOP, STOP! I'M NOT YOUR MOM!
I'M AN AVERAGE 23-YEAR-OLD WOMAN WITH PROBLEMS OF HER OWN!
AHH!
I CAN'T STAND THIS! WHY DO PEOPLE ALWAYS LEAN ON ME?!
WHAM
I MEAN, I WANT TO BE TAKEN CARE OF TOO!
Gyaah!
flail flail
huff huff
shup
AND COME ON! HERE WE ARE, A MAN AND A WOMAN, ALONE IN A ROOM, **DRINKING**!
I STARTED TO GET MY HOPES UP!
BUT I WAS WRONG! OKAY, WHATEVER, HA HA HA ...
Oh!
AH ...
UMM ...

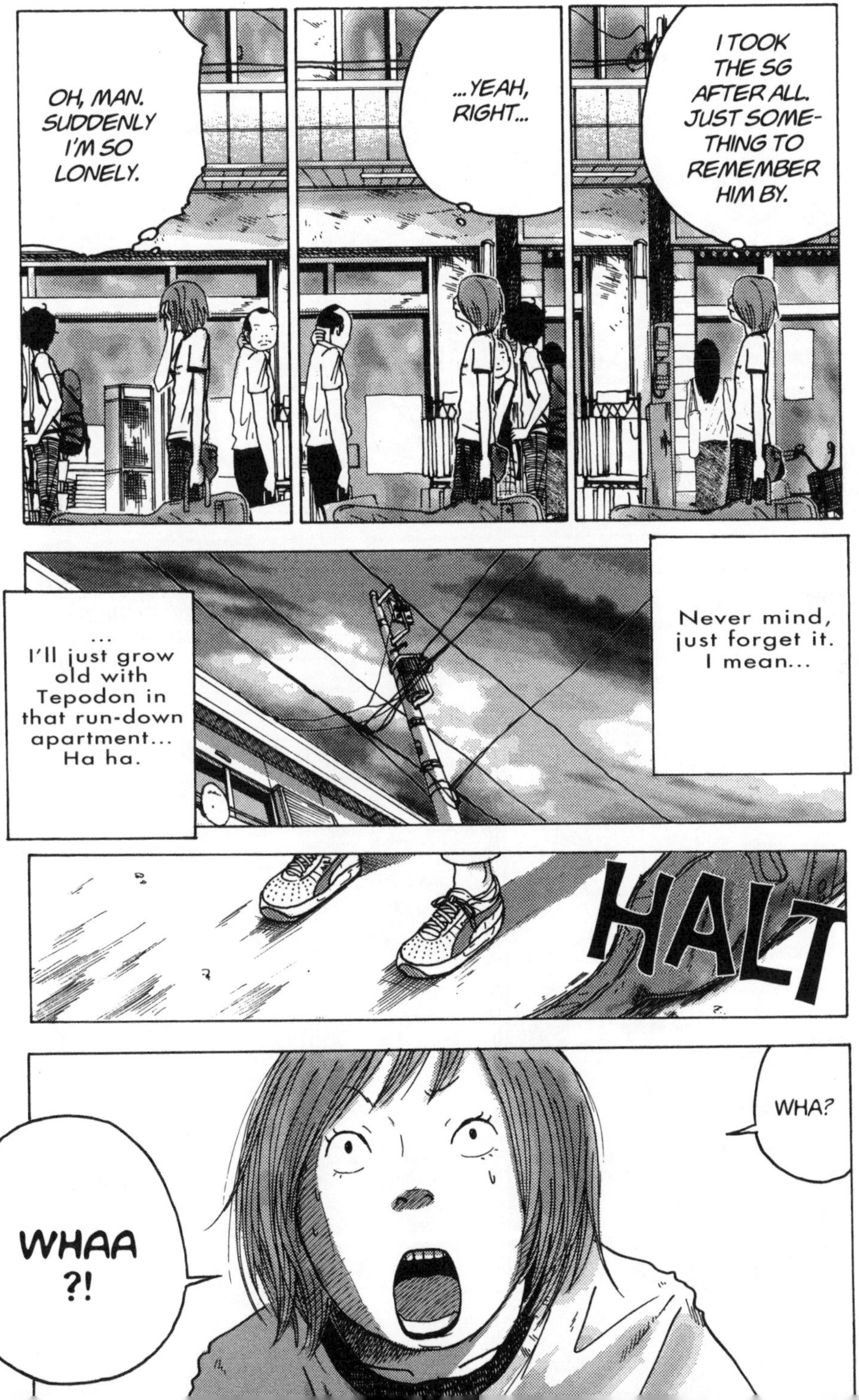
I TOOK THE SG AFTER ALL. JUST SOME-THING TO REMEMBER HIM BY.
...YEAH, RIGHT...
OH, MAN. SUDDENLY I'M SO LONELY.
Never mind, just forget it. I mean...
... I'll just grow old with Tepodon in that run-down apartment... Ha ha.
HALT
WHA?
WHAA ?!

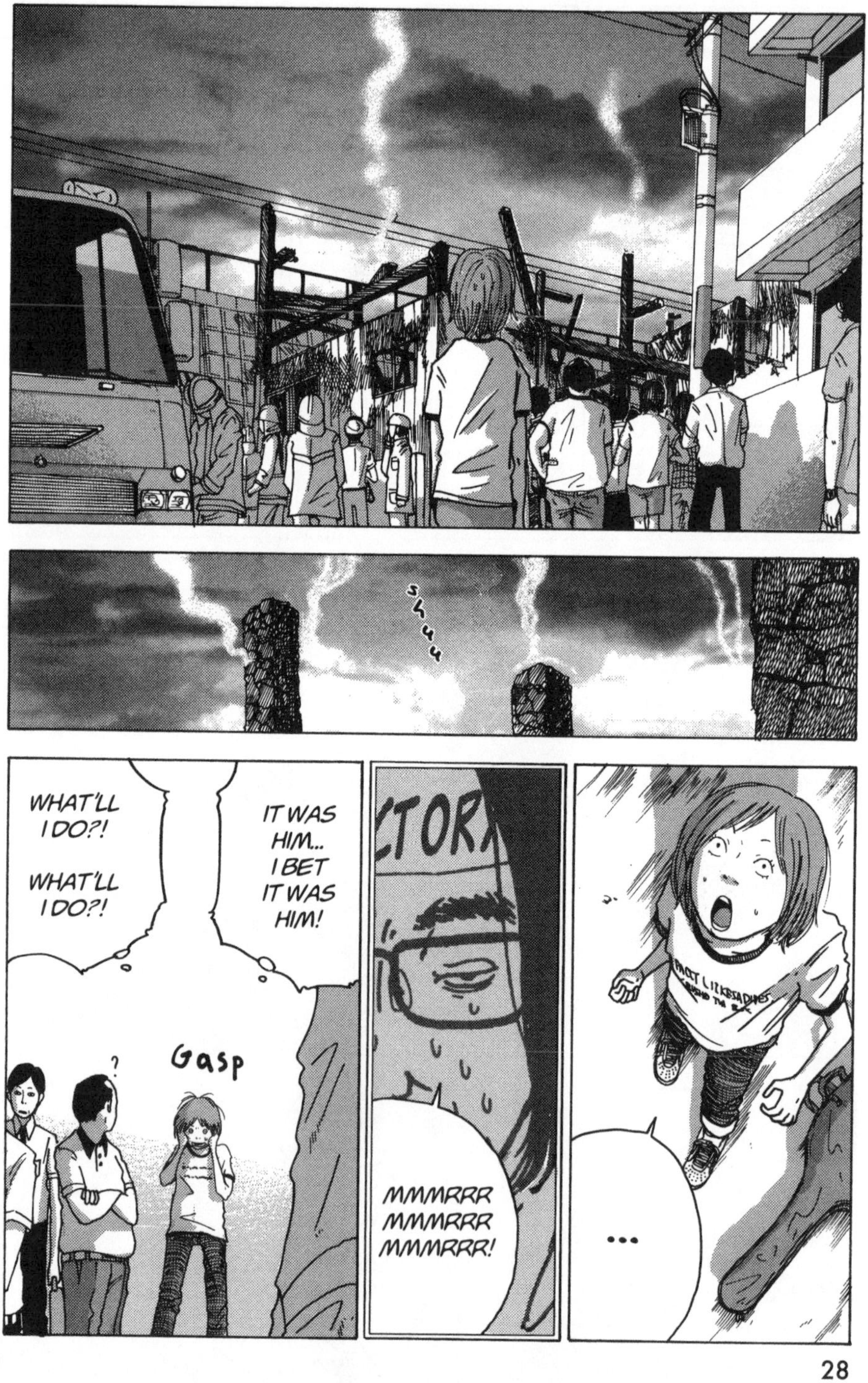
shuu
...
MMMRRR MMMRRR MMMRRR!
IT WAS HIM... I BET IT WAS HIM!
WHAT'LL I DO?! WHAT'LL I DO?!
Gasp

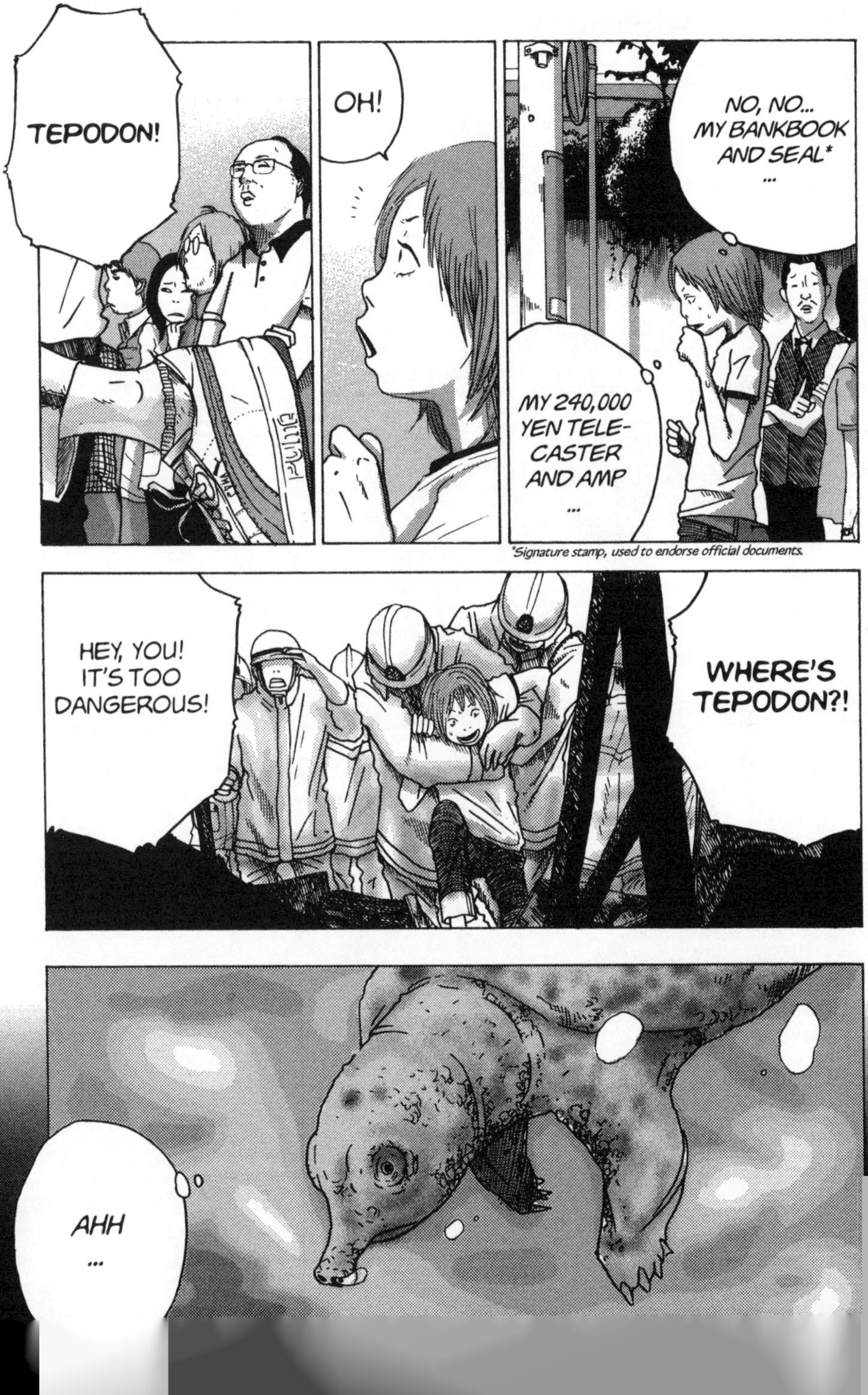
NO, NO... MY BANKBOOK AND SEAL* ...
MY 240,000 YEN TELE-CASTER AND AMP ...
OH!
TEPODON!
WHERE'S TEPODON?!
HEY, YOU! IT'S TOO DANGEROUS!
AHH ...

*Signature stamp, used to endorse official documents.

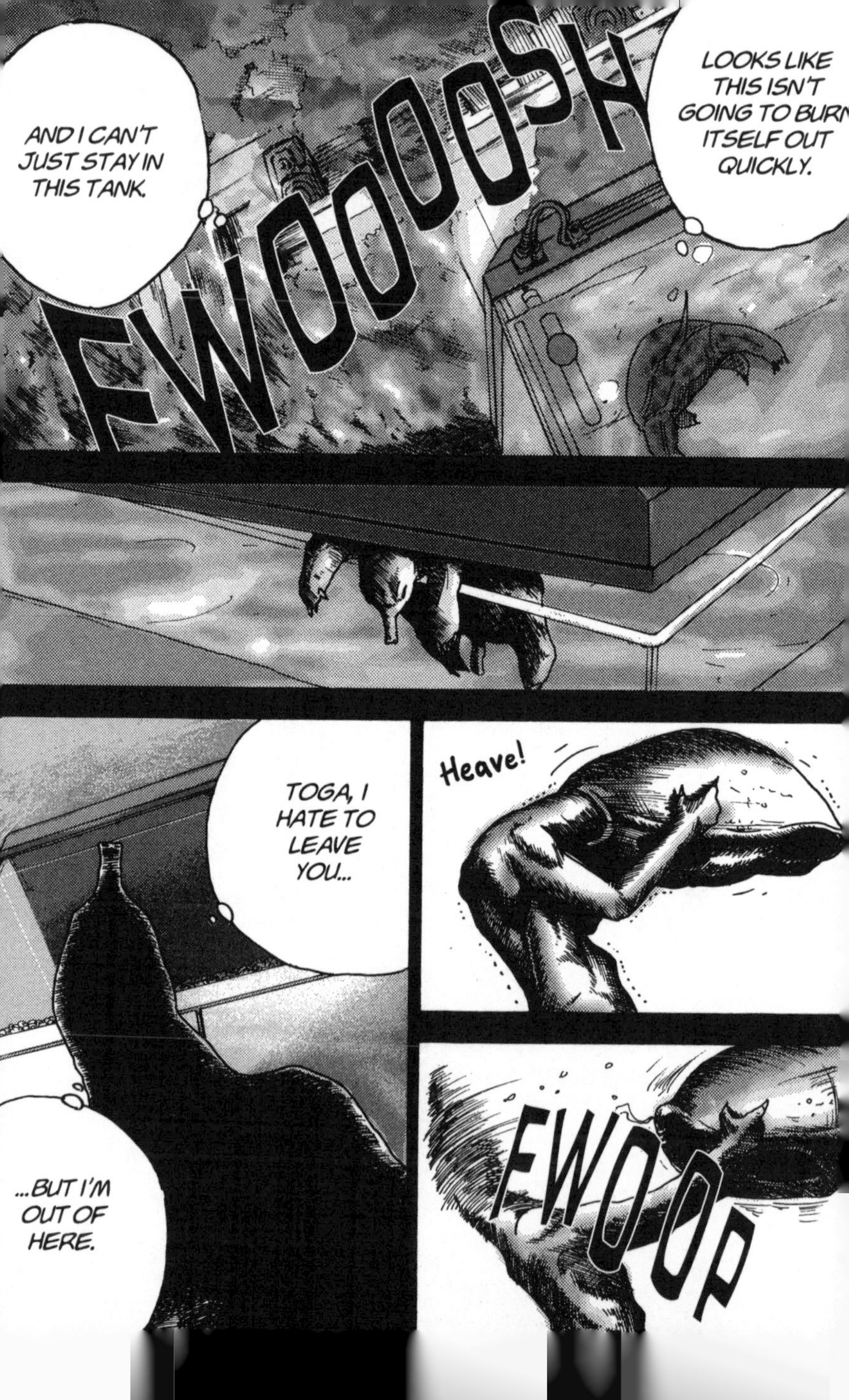
LOOKS LIKE THIS ISN'T GOING TO BURN ITSELF OUT QUICKLY.
FWOOOOSH
AND I CAN'T JUST STAY IN THIS TANK.
Heave!
FWOOP
TOGA, I HATE TO LEAVE YOU...
...BUT I'M OUT OF HERE.

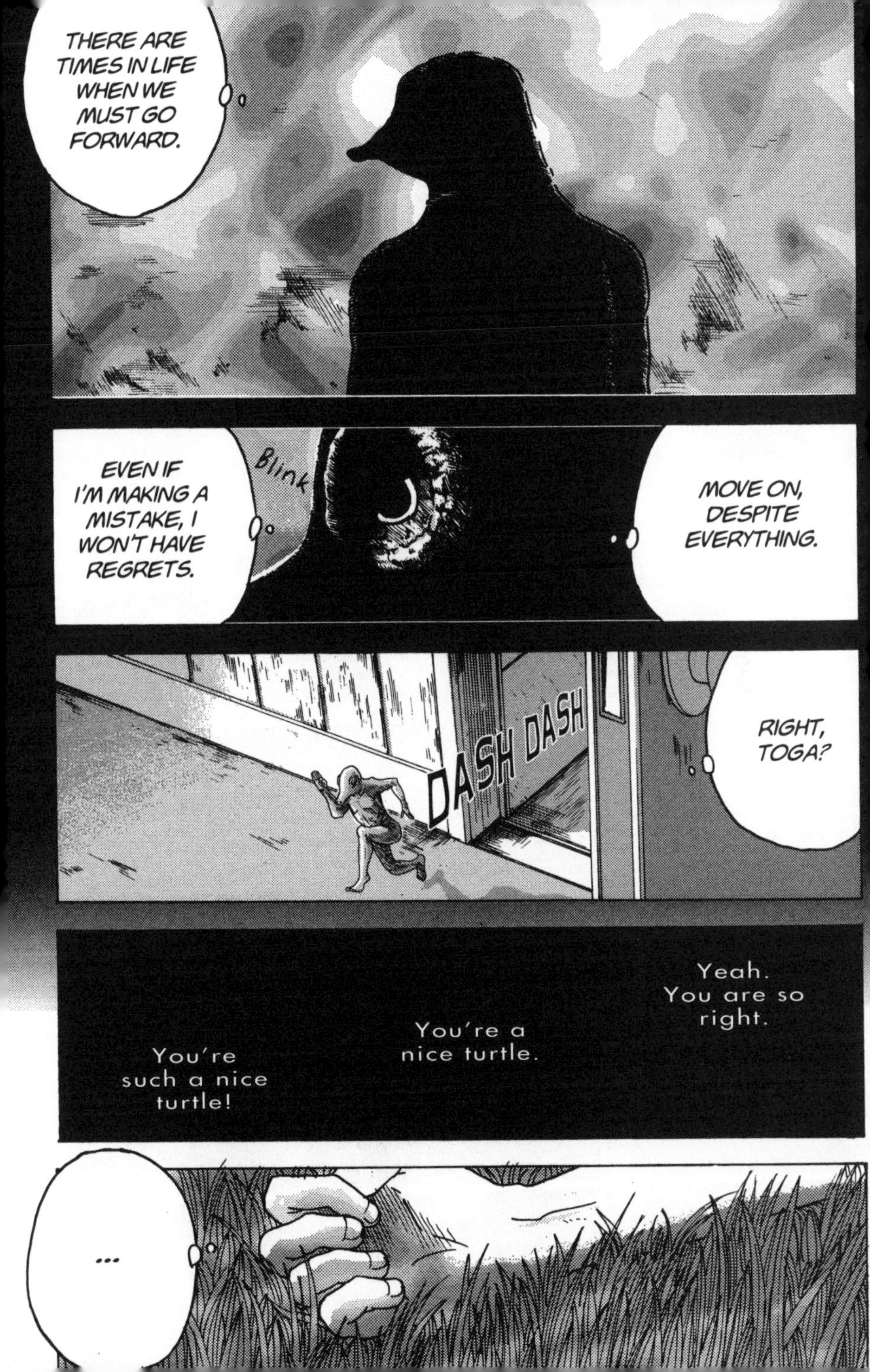
THERE ARE TIMES IN LIFE WHEN WE MUST GO FORWARD.
MOVE ON, DESPITE EVERYTHING.
Blink
EVEN IF I'M MAKING A MISTAKE, I WON'T HAVE REGRETS.
RIGHT, TOGA?
DASH DASH
Yeah. You are so right.
You're a nice turtle.
You're such a nice turtle!
...

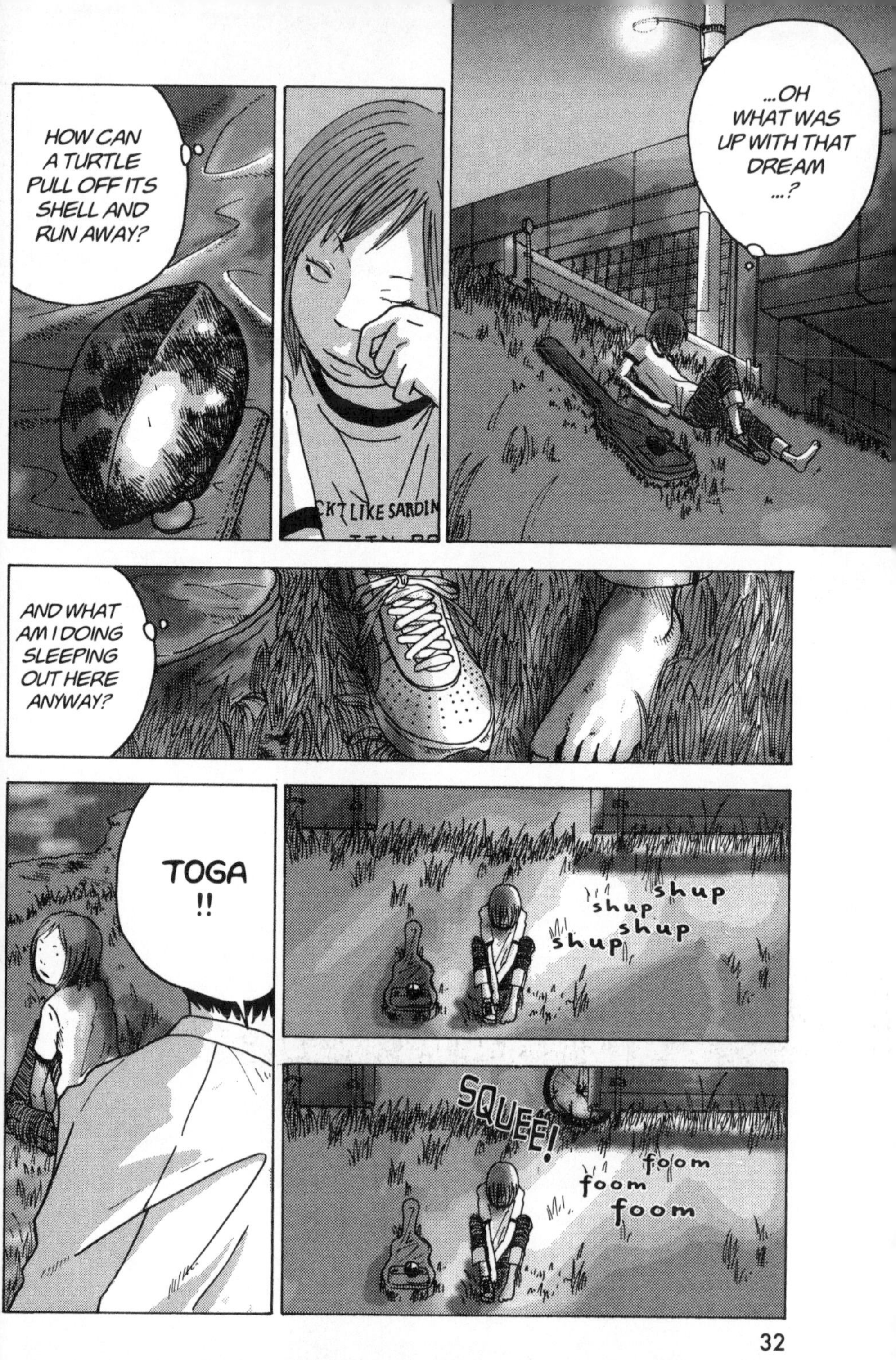
...OH WHAT WAS UP WITH THAT DREAM ...?
HOW CAN A TURTLE PULL OFF ITS SHELL AND RUN AWAY?
AND WHAT AM I DOING SLEEPING OUT HERE ANYWAY?
shup shup shup shup
SQUEE!
foom foom foom
TOGA !!

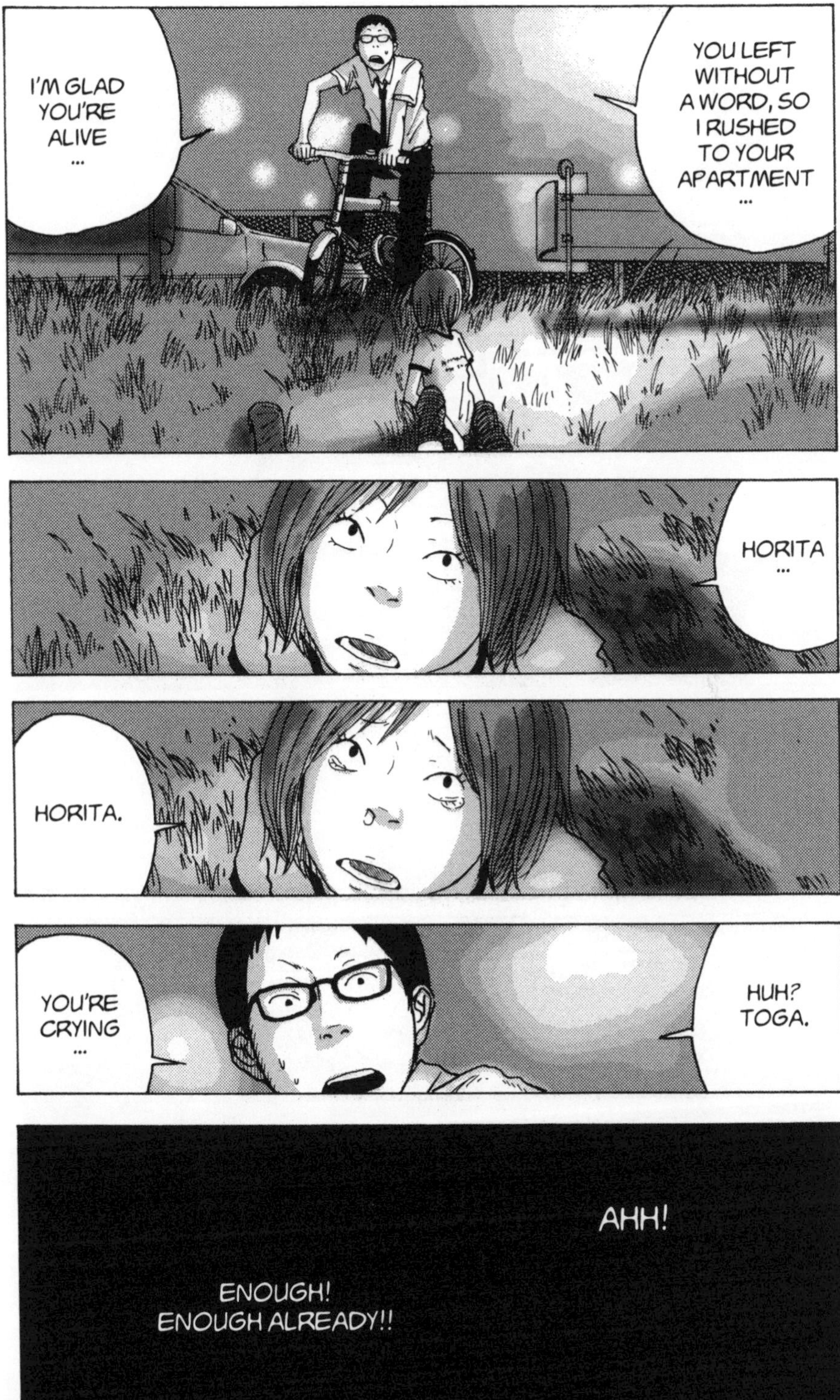
YOU LEFT WITHOUT A WORD, SO I RUSHED TO YOUR APARTMENT ...
I'M GLAD YOU'RE ALIVE ...
HORITA ...
HORITA.
HUH? TOGA.
YOU'RE CRYING ...
AHH!
ENOUGH! ENOUGH ALREADY!!

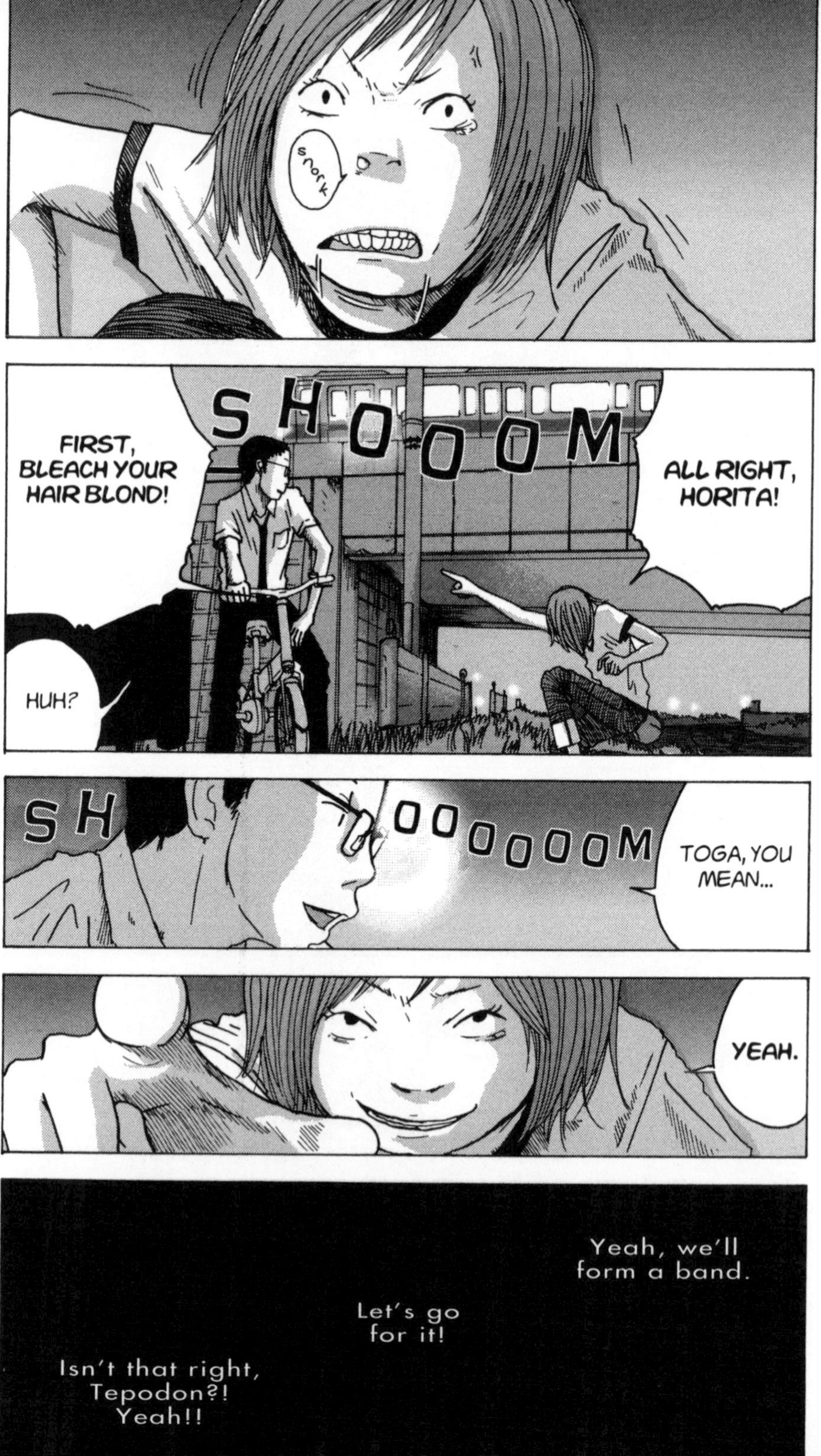
snork
SHOOOM
ALL RIGHT, HORITA!
FIRST, BLEACH YOUR HAIR BLOND!
HUH?
TOGA, YOU MEAN...
SHOOOOOOOM
YEAH.
Yeah, we'll form a band.
Let's go for it!
Isn't that right, Tepodon?! Yeah!!

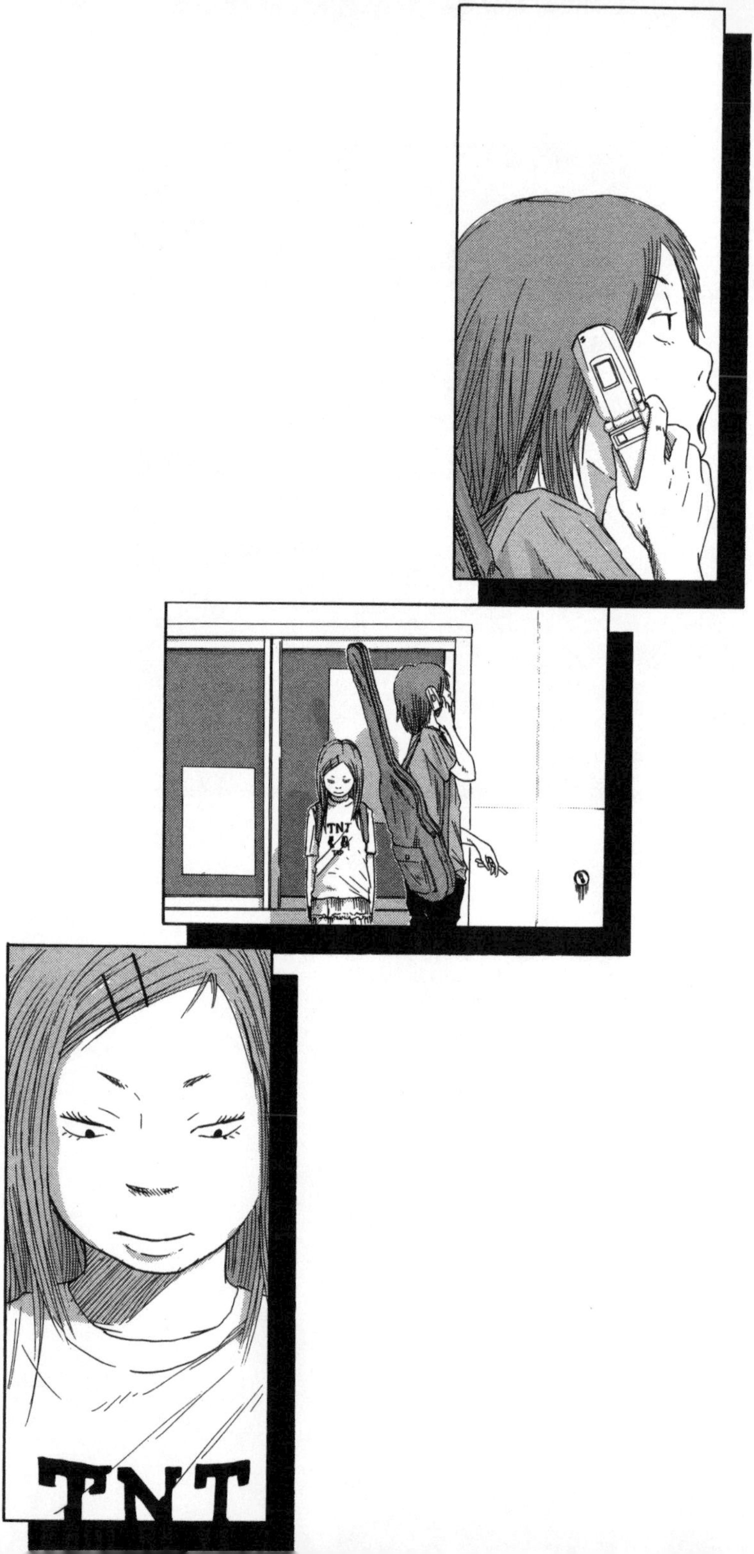
TNT

2nd track A Town of Many Hills

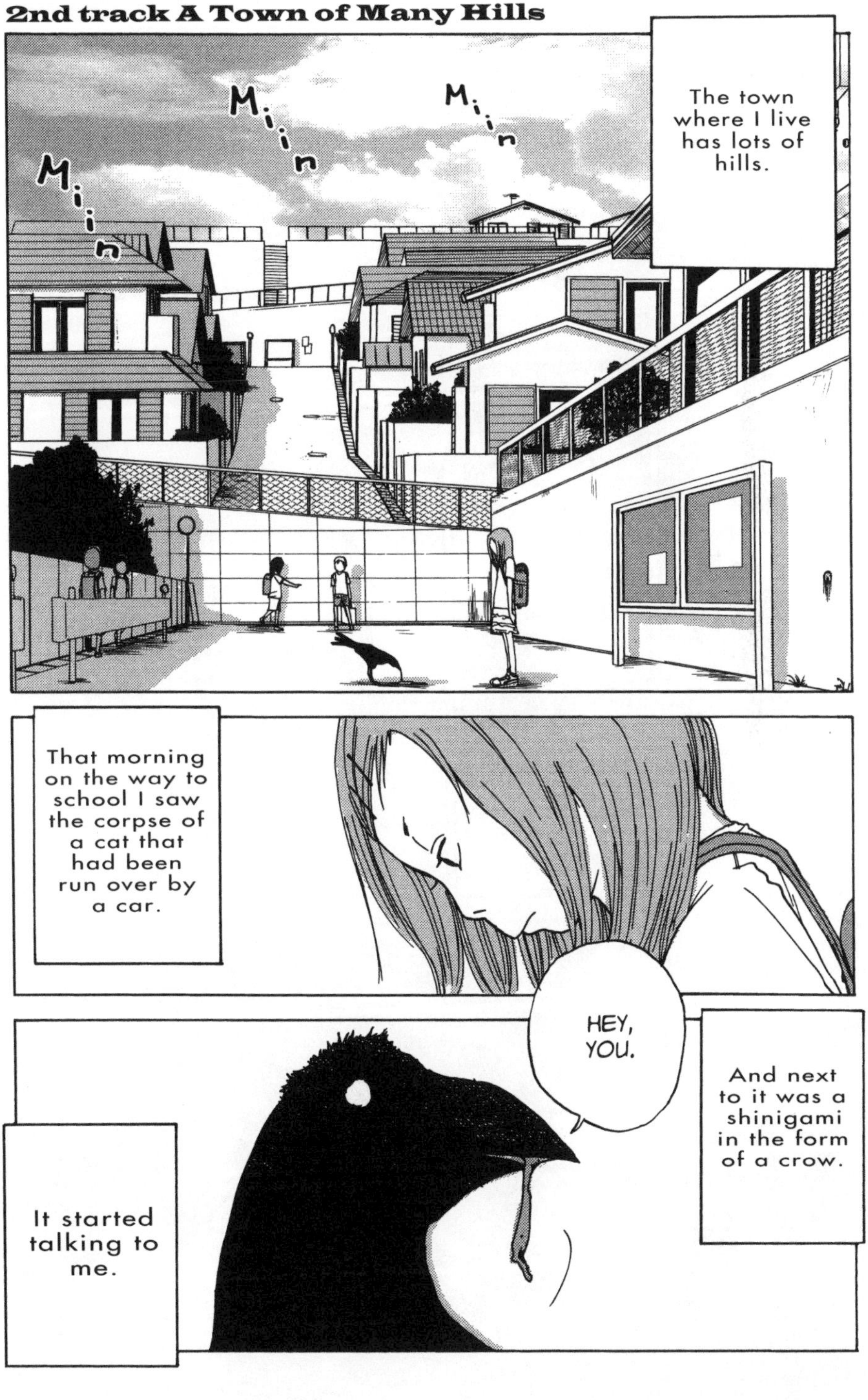
The town where I live has lots of hills.
Miin
Miin
Miin
That morning on the way to school I saw the corpse of a cat that had been run over by a car.
And next to it was a shinigami in the form of a crow.
HEY, YOU.
It started talking to me.

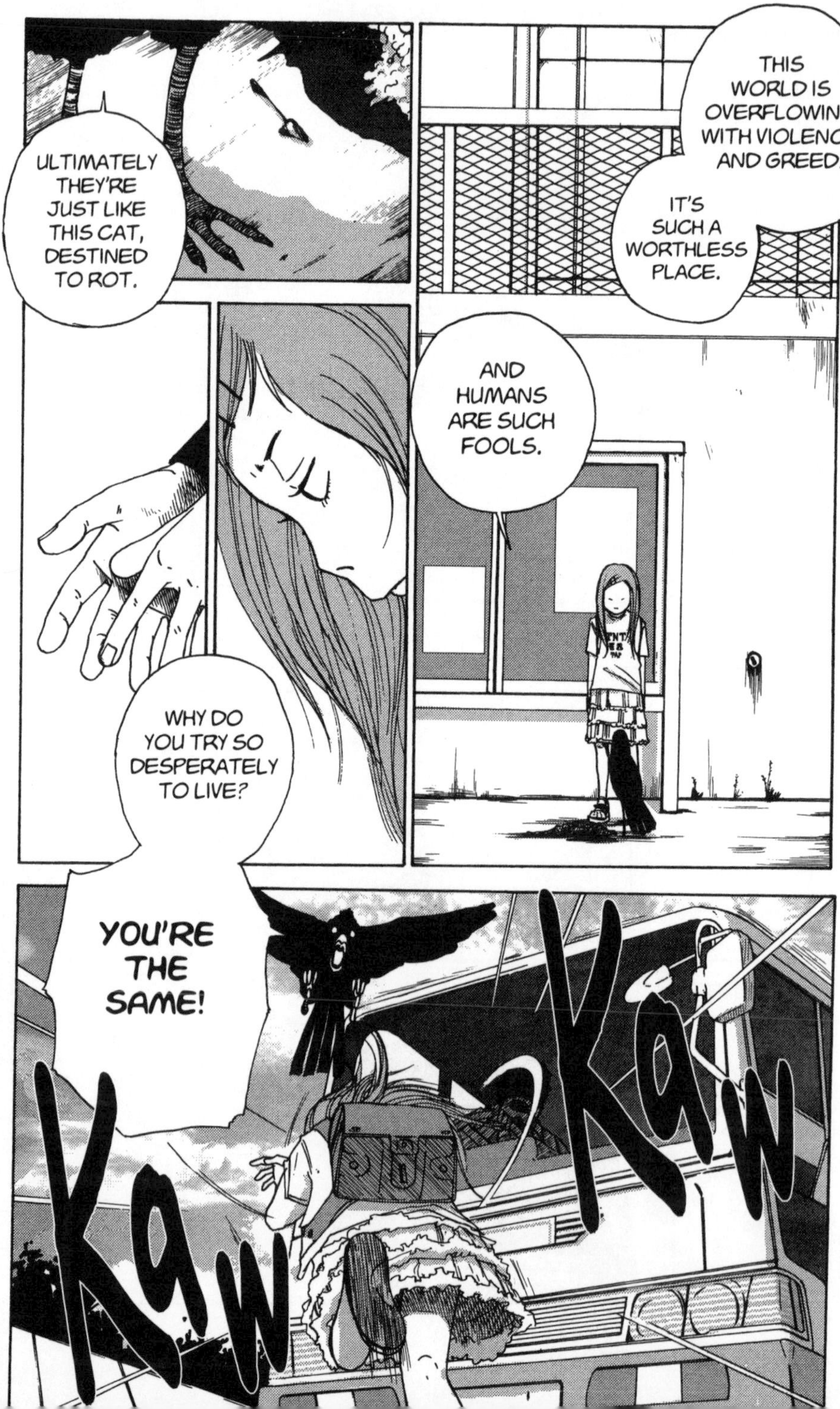
THIS WORLD IS OVERFLOWING WITH VIOLENCE AND GREED.
IT'S SUCH A WORTHLESS PLACE.
ULTIMATELY THEY'RE JUST LIKE THIS CAT, DESTINED TO ROT.
AND HUMANS ARE SUCH FOOLS.
WHY DO YOU TRY SO DESPERATELY TO LIVE?
YOU'RE THE SAME!
Kaw
Kaw

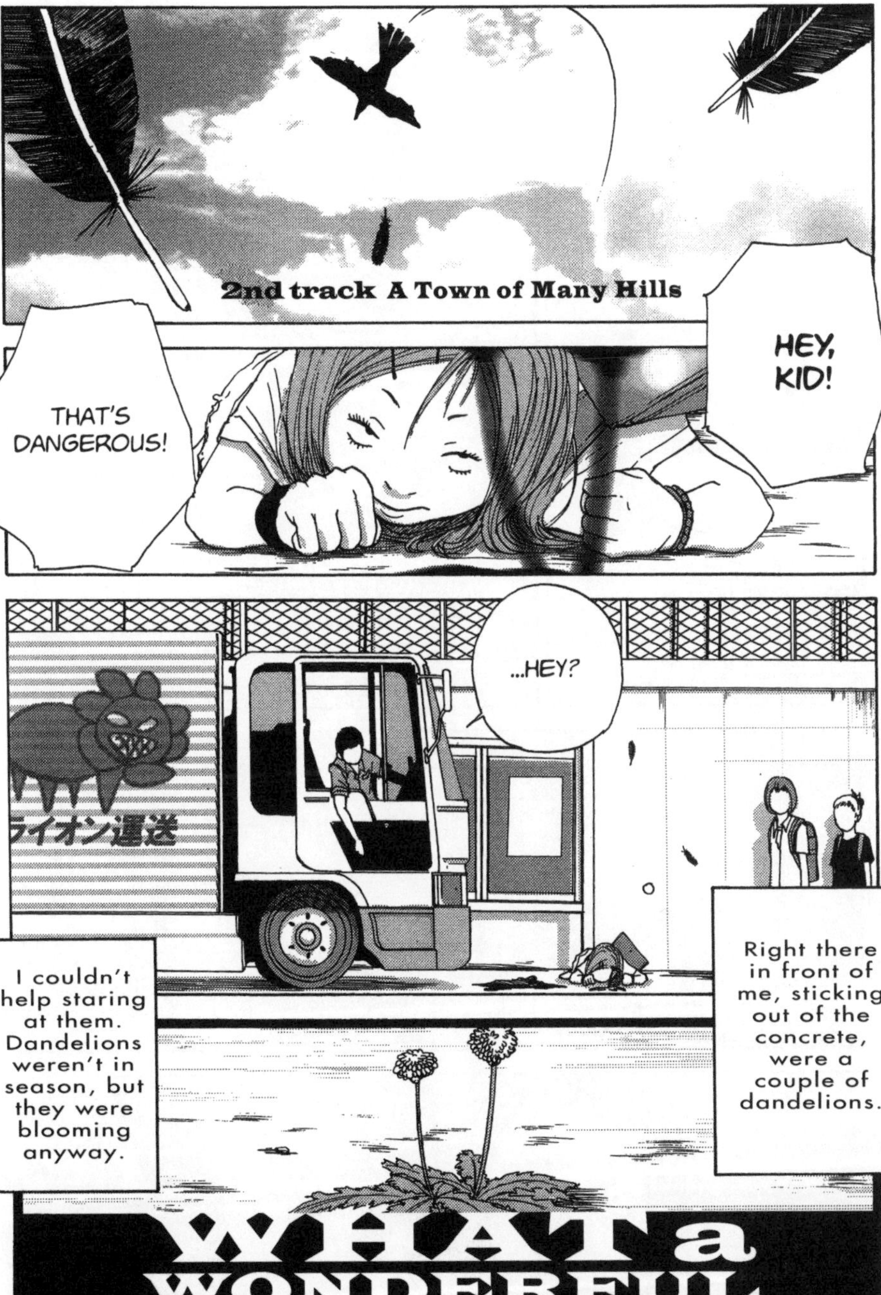
2nd track A Town of Many Hills
HEY, KID!
THAT'S DANGEROUS!
...HEY?
ライオン運送
Right there in front of me, sticking out of the concrete, were a couple of dandelions.
I couldn't help staring at them. Dandelions weren't in season, but they were blooming anyway.
WHAT a WONDERFUL WORLD!

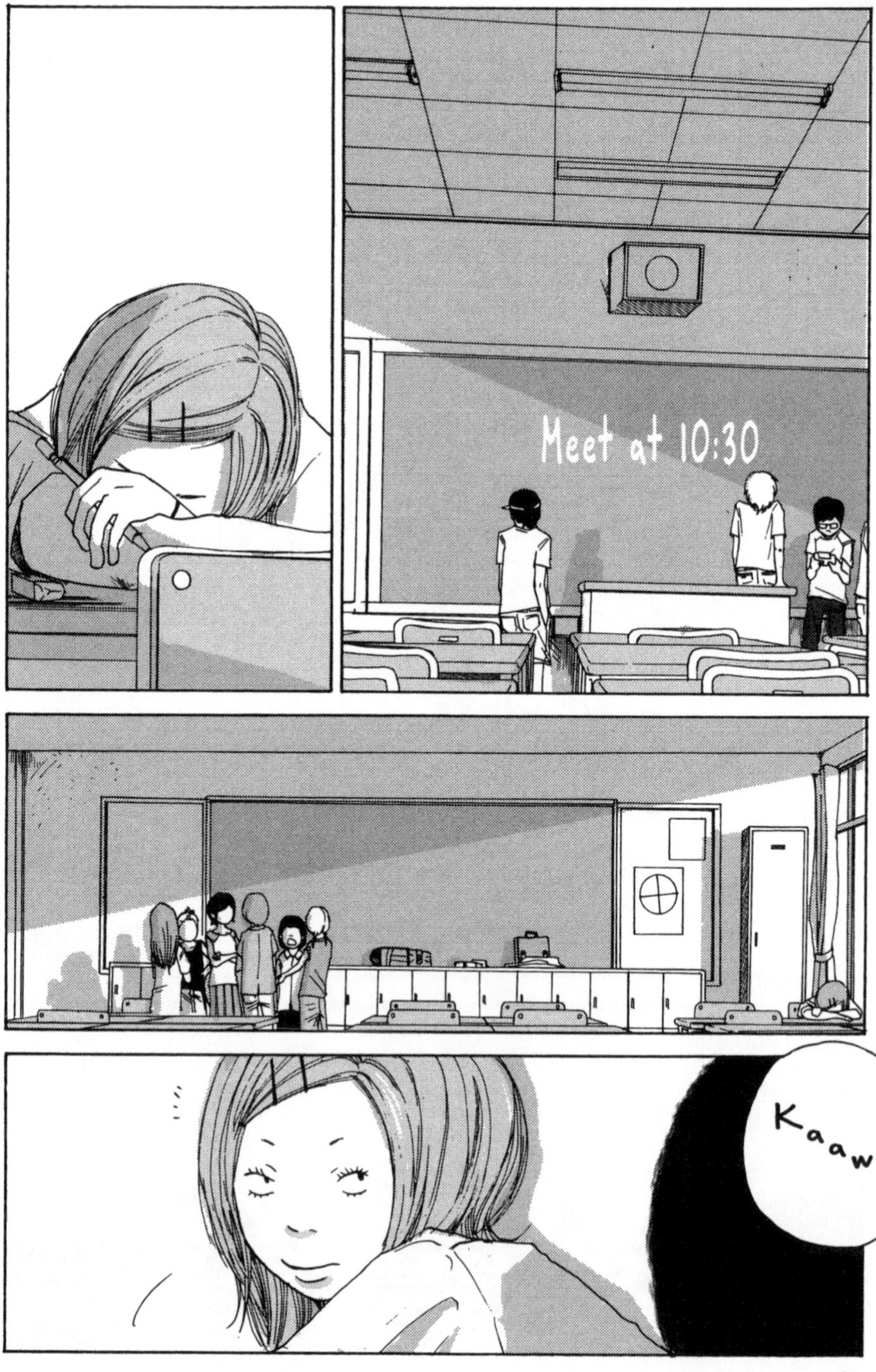
Meet at 10:30
Kaaw!

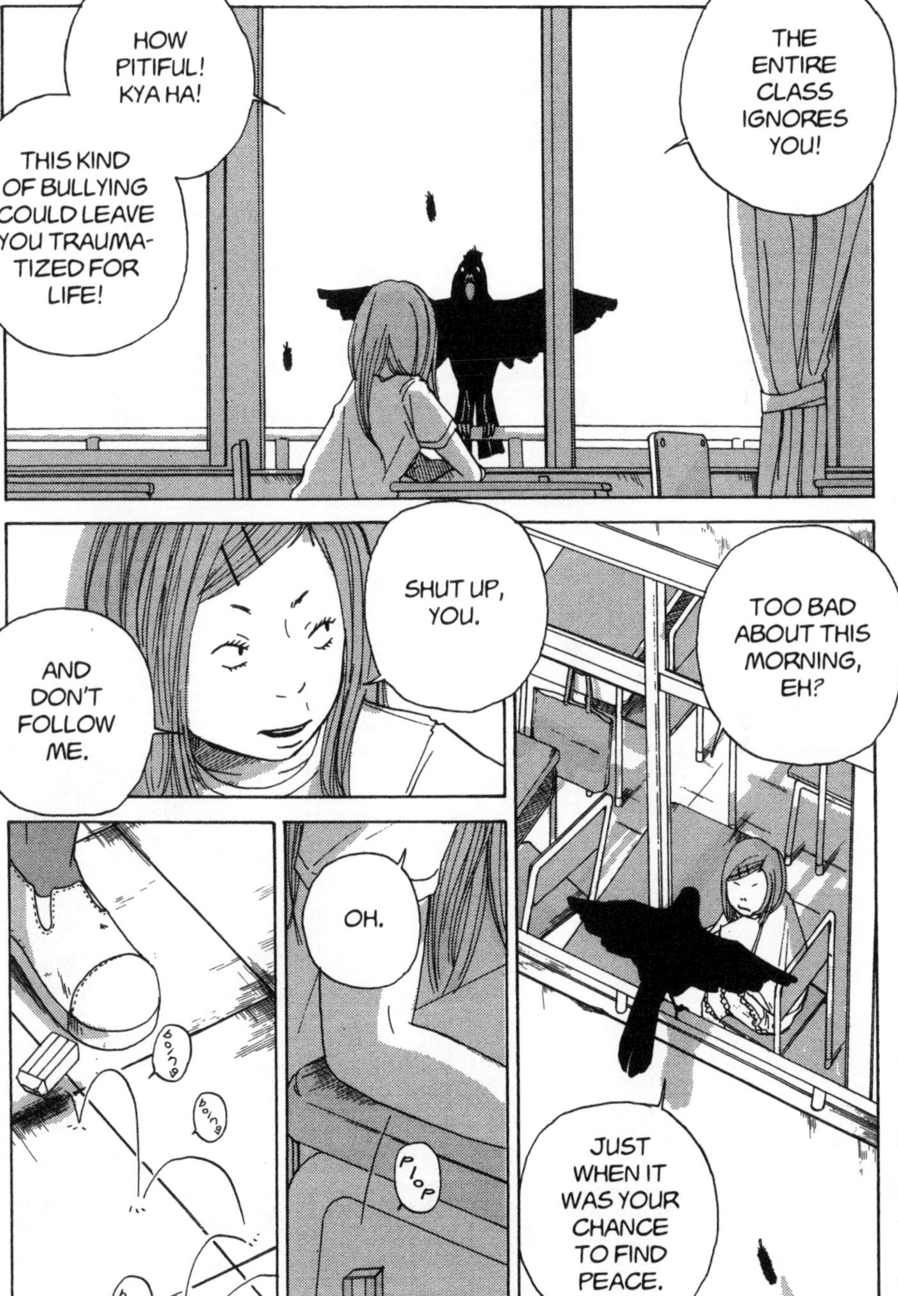
THE ENTIRE CLASS IGNORES YOU!
HOW PITIFUL! KYA HA!
THIS KIND OF BULLYING COULD LEAVE YOU TRAUMA-TIZED FOR LIFE!
TOO BAD ABOUT THIS MORNING, EH?
JUST WHEN IT WAS YOUR CHANCE TO FIND PEACE.
SHUT UP, YOU.
AND DON'T FOLLOW ME.
OH.
Plop
boing
boing
boing

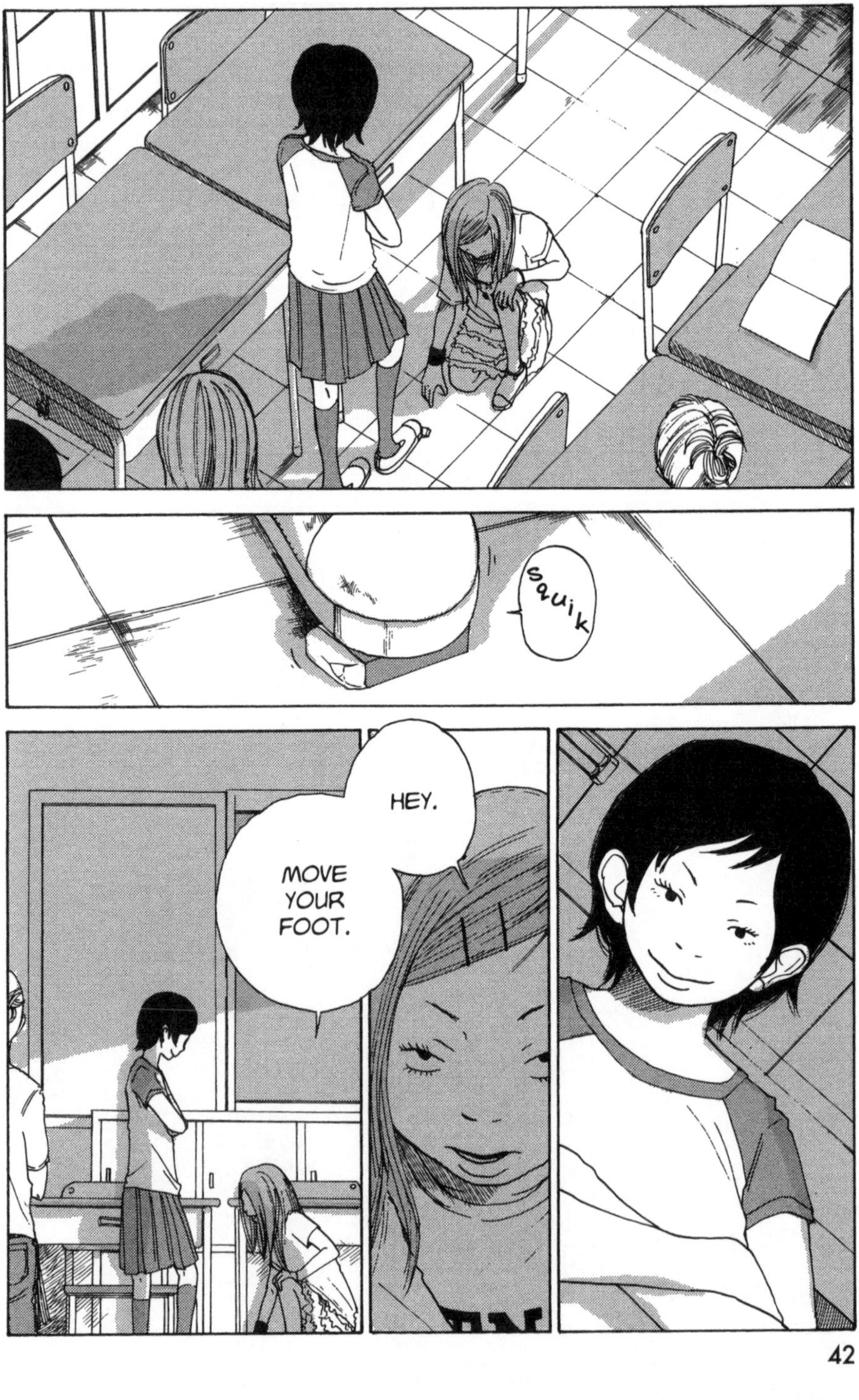
squik
HEY.
MOVE YOUR FOOT.

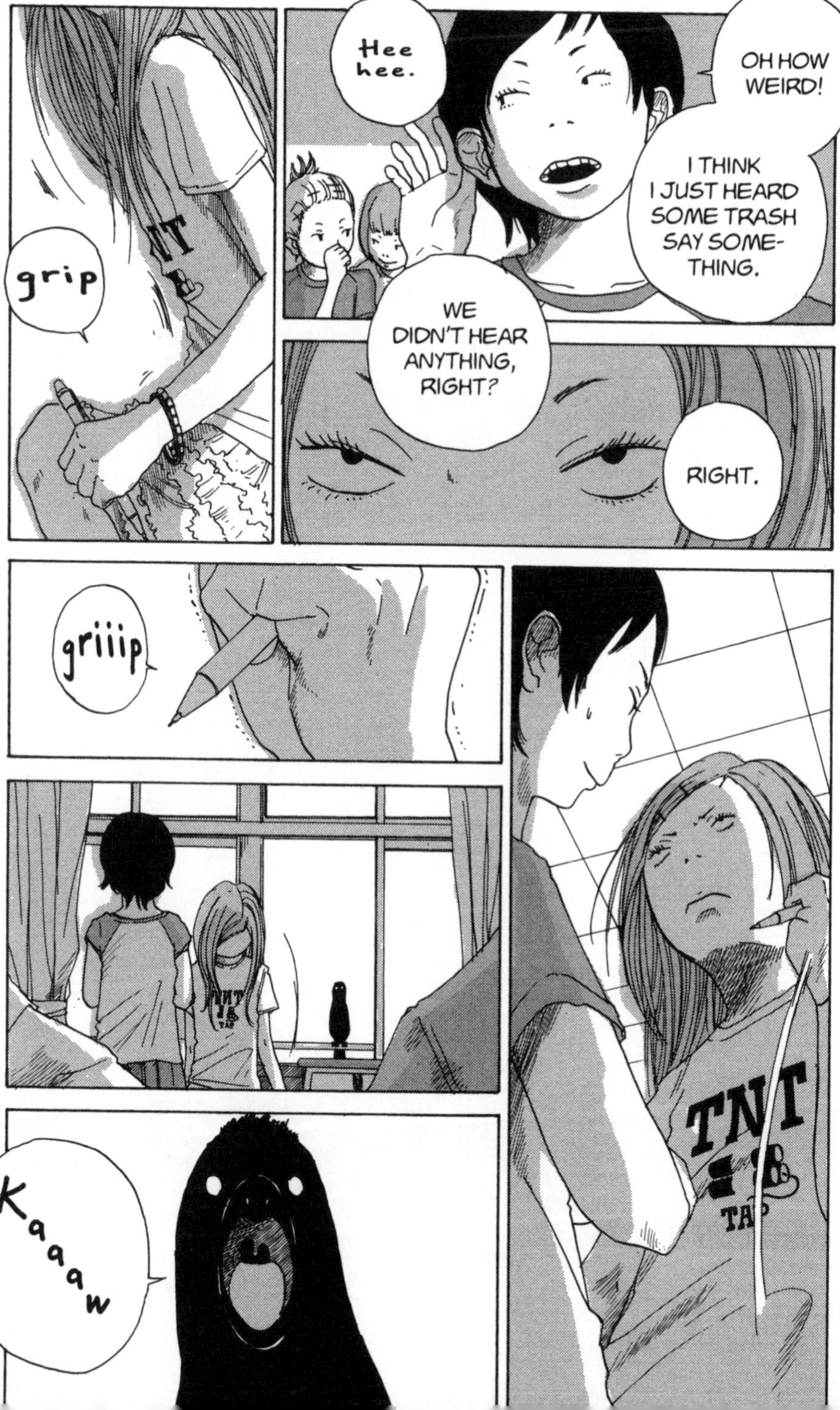
OH HOW WEIRD!
I THINK I JUST HEARD SOME TRASH SAY SOME-THING.
Hee hee.
WE DIDN'T HEAR ANYTHING, RIGHT?
RIGHT.
grip
griiip
Kaaaw

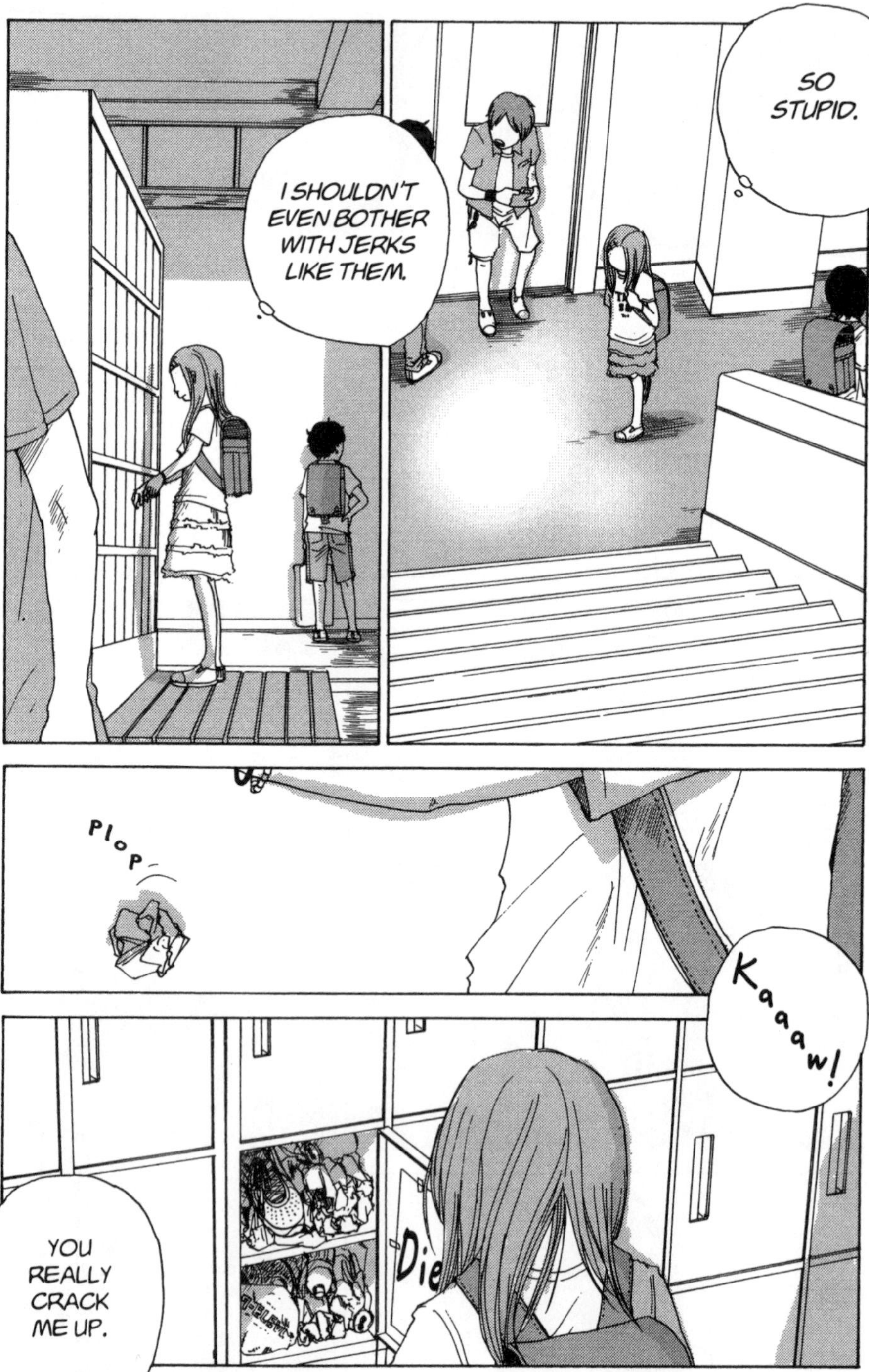
SO STUPID.
I SHOULDN'T EVEN BOTHER WITH JERKS LIKE THEM.
PLOP
Kaaaw!
Die
YOU REALLY CRACK ME UP.

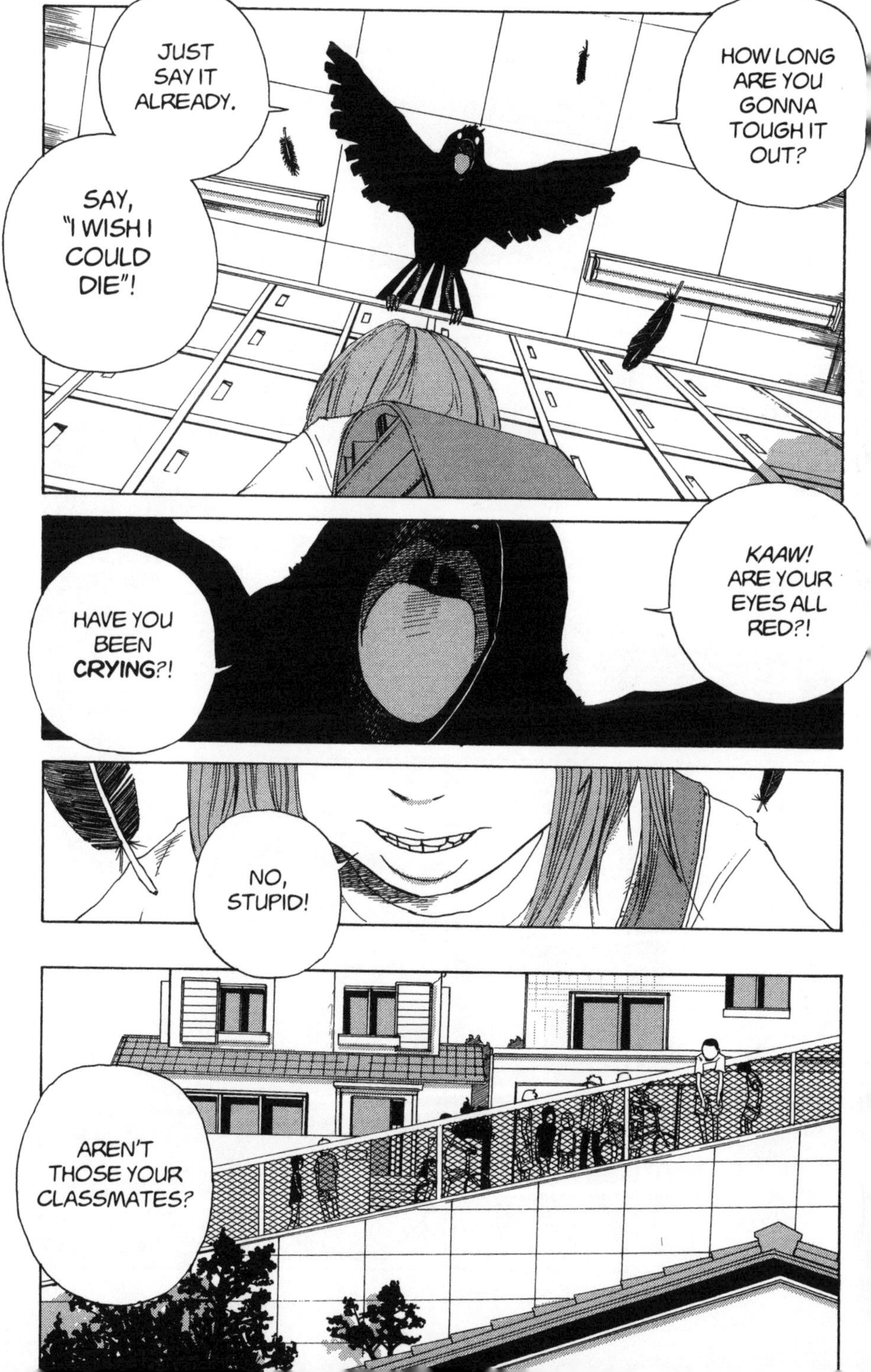
HOW LONG ARE YOU GONNA TOUGH IT OUT?
JUST SAY IT ALREADY.
SAY, "I WISH I COULD DIE"!
KAAW! ARE YOUR EYES ALL RED?!
HAVE YOU BEEN **CRYING**?!
NO, STUPID!
AREN'T THOSE YOUR CLASSMATES?

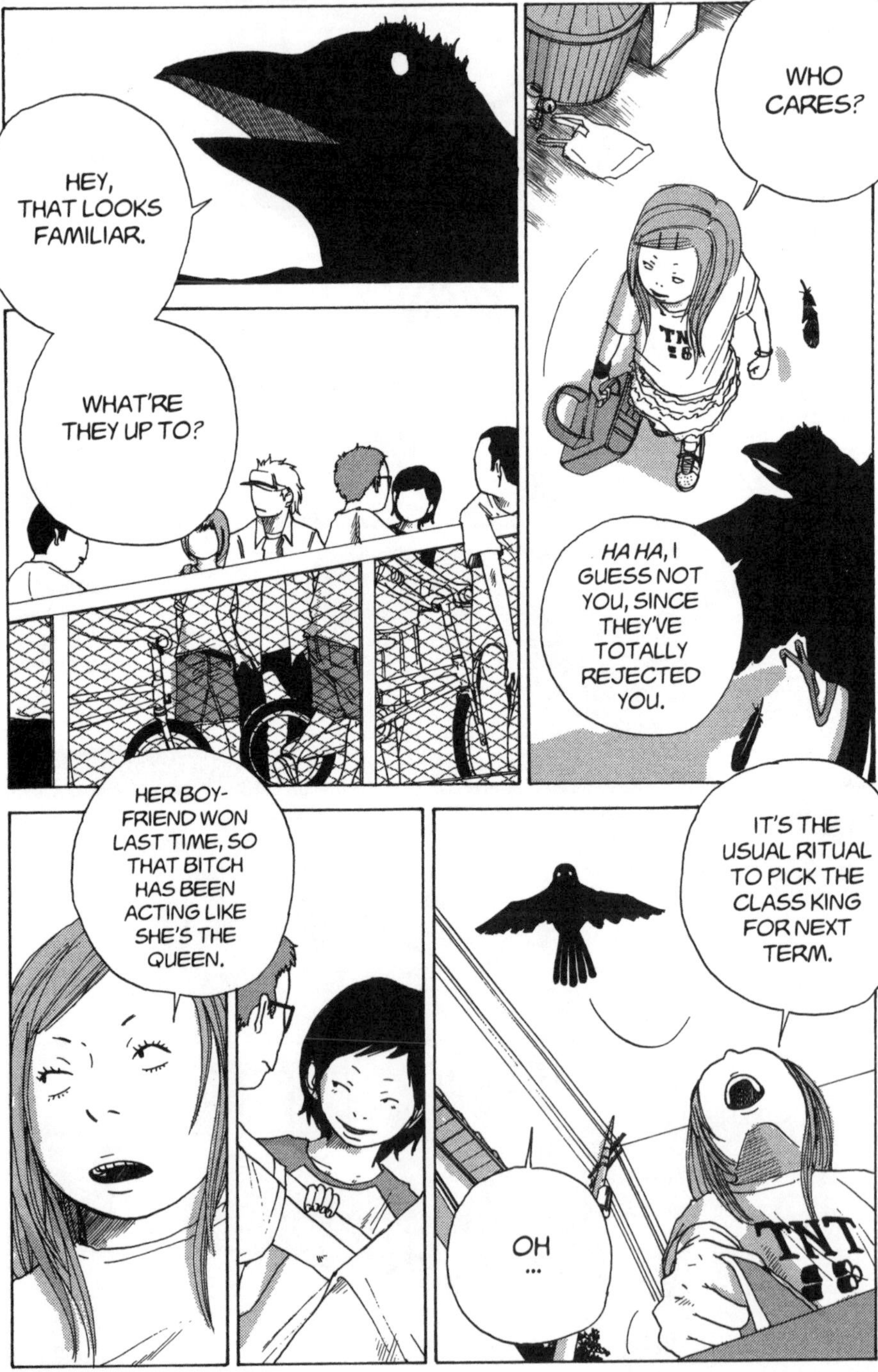
WHO CARES?
HA HA, I GUESS NOT YOU, SINCE THEY'VE TOTALLY REJECTED YOU.
HEY, THAT LOOKS FAMILIAR.
WHAT'RE THEY UP TO?
IT'S THE USUAL RITUAL TO PICK THE CLASS KING FOR NEXT TERM.
OH ...
HER BOY-FRIEND WON LAST TIME, SO THAT BITCH HAS BEEN ACTING LIKE SHE'S THE QUEEN.

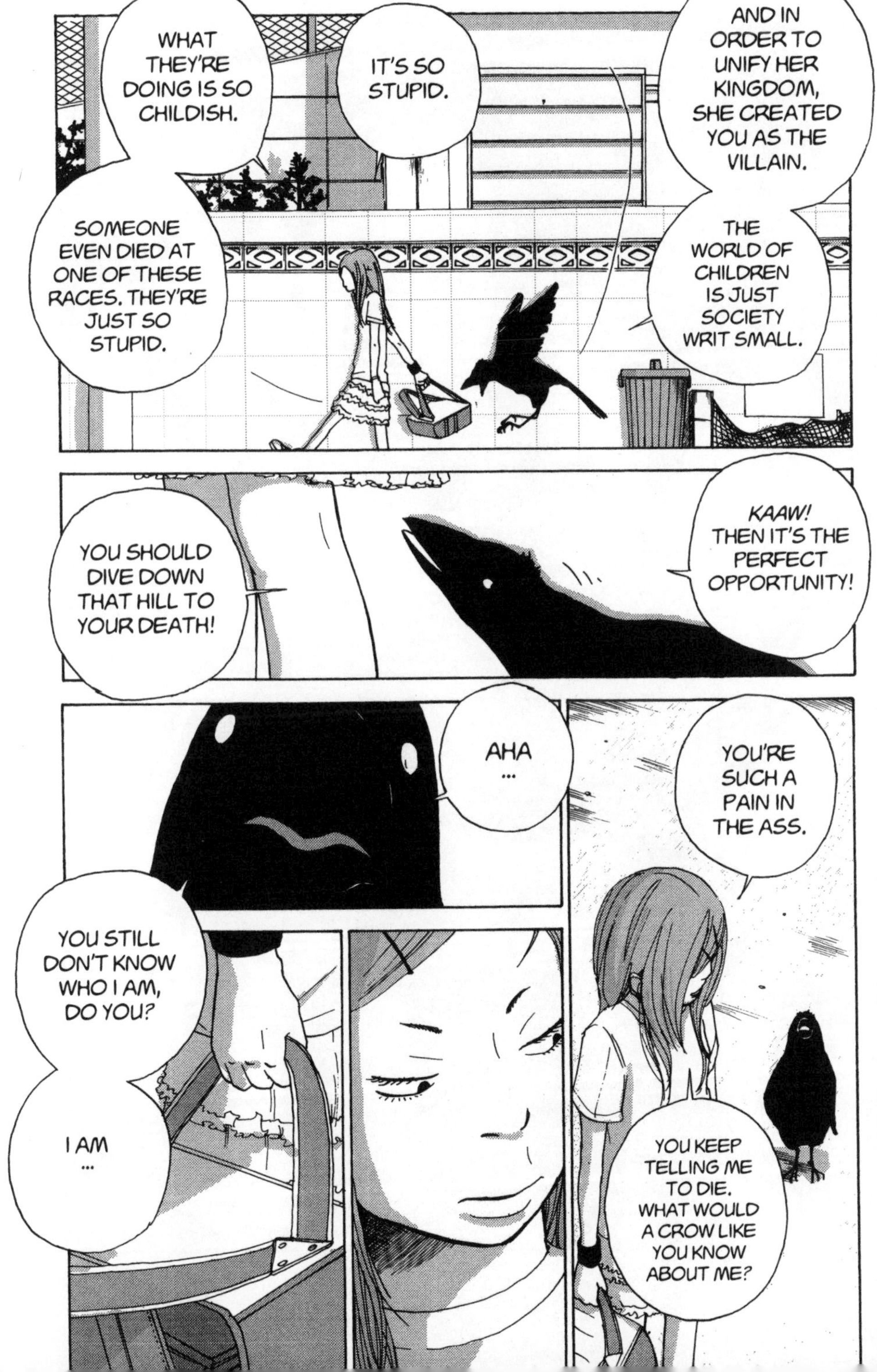
AND IN ORDER TO UNIFY HER KINGDOM, SHE CREATED YOU AS THE VILLAIN.
THE WORLD OF CHILDREN IS JUST SOCIETY WRIT SMALL.
IT'S SO STUPID.
WHAT THEY'RE DOING IS SO CHILDISH.
SOMEONE EVEN DIED AT ONE OF THESE RACES. THEY'RE JUST SO STUPID.
KAAW! THEN IT'S THE PERFECT OPPORTUNITY!
YOU SHOULD DIVE DOWN THAT HILL TO YOUR DEATH!
YOU'RE SUCH A PAIN IN THE ASS.
YOU KEEP TELLING ME TO DIE. WHAT WOULD A CROW LIKE YOU KNOW ABOUT ME?
AHA ...
YOU STILL DON'T KNOW WHO I AM, DO YOU?
I AM ...

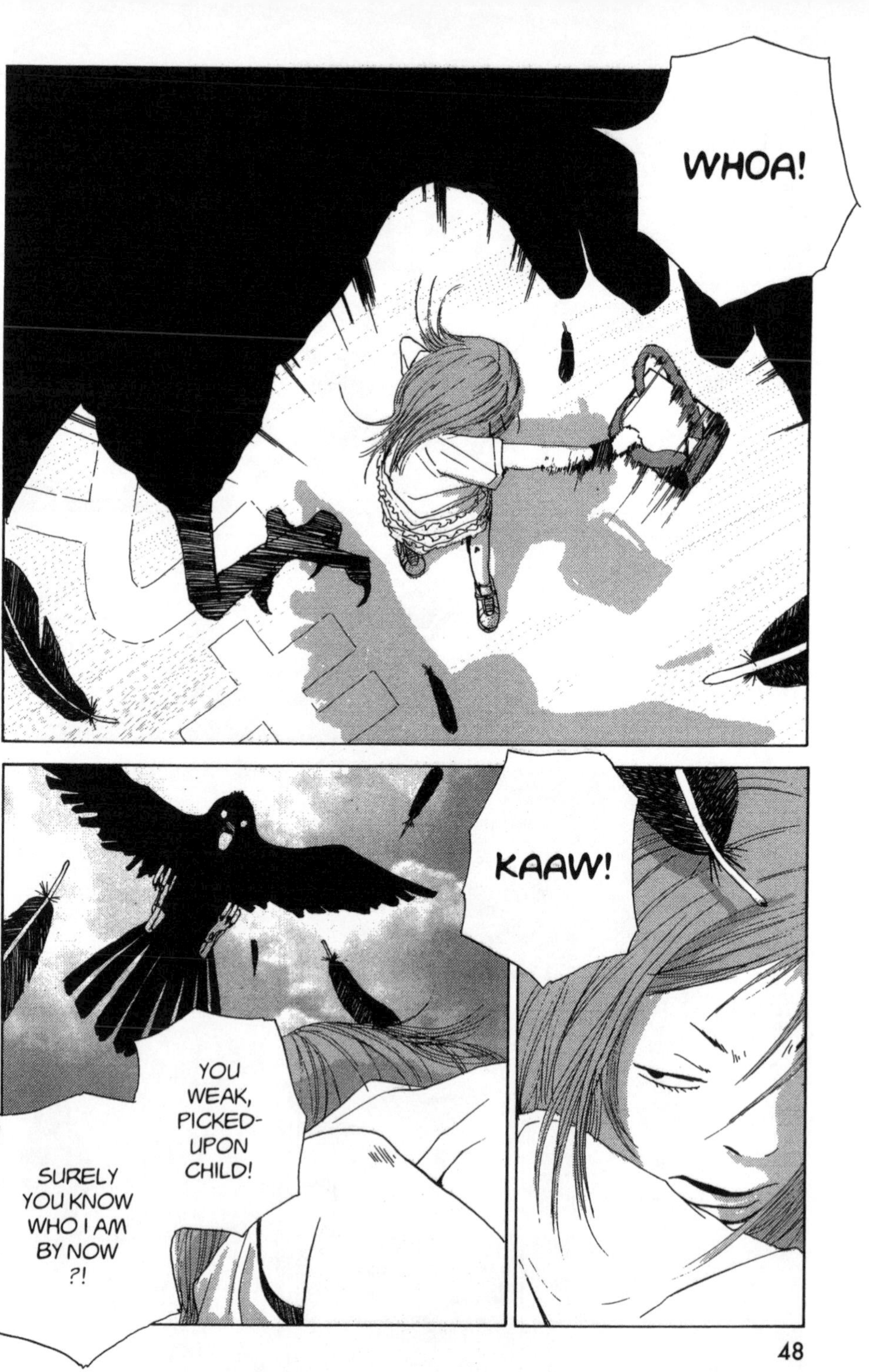
WHOA!
KAAW!
YOU WEAK, PICKED-UPON CHILD!
SURELY YOU KNOW WHO I AM BY NOW?!

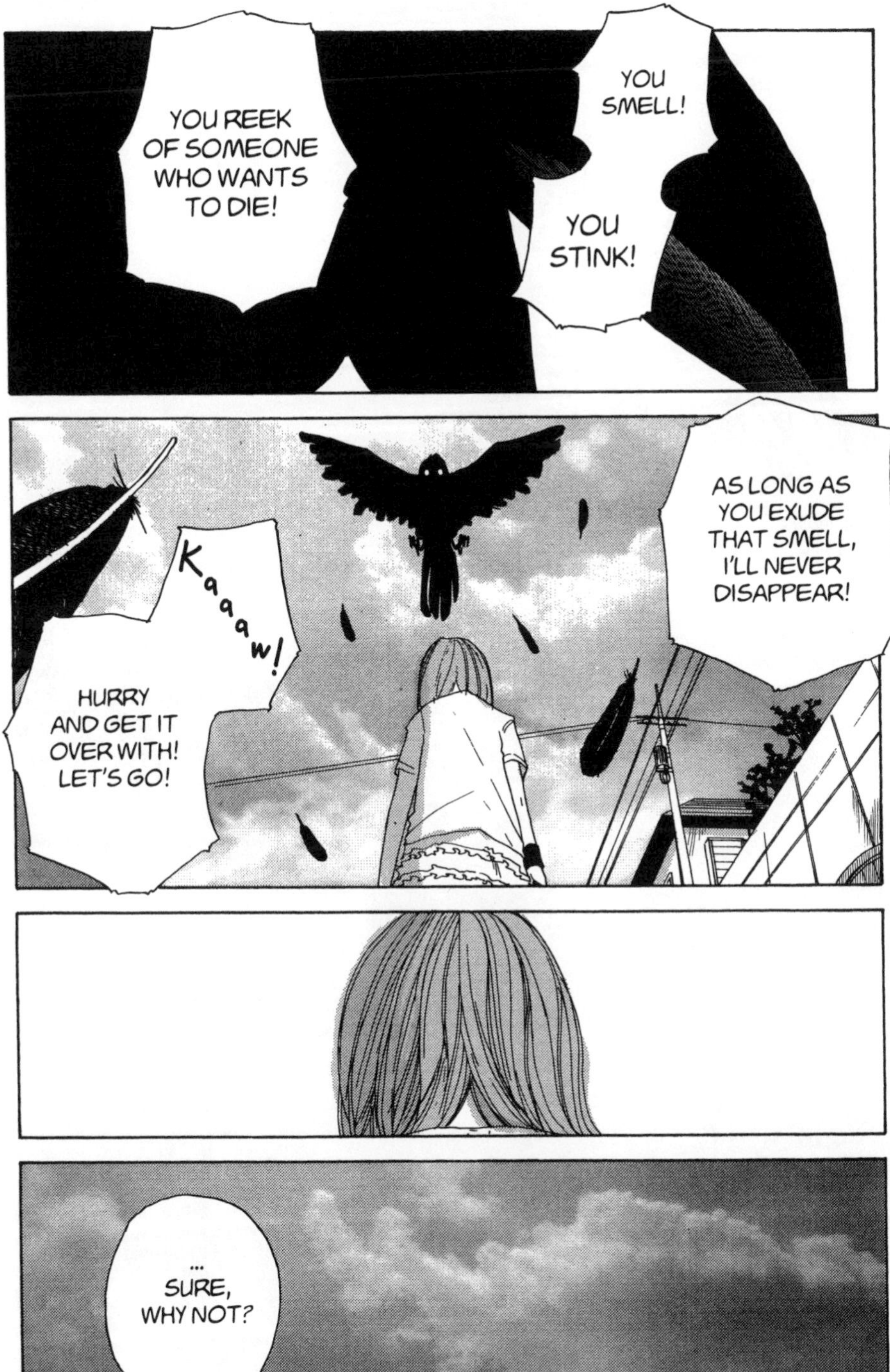
YOU SMELL!
YOU STINK!
YOU REEK OF SOMEONE WHO WANTS TO DIE!
AS LONG AS YOU EXUDE THAT SMELL, I'LL NEVER DISAPPEAR!
Kaaaw!
HURRY AND GET IT OVER WITH! LET'S GO!
... SURE, WHY NOT?

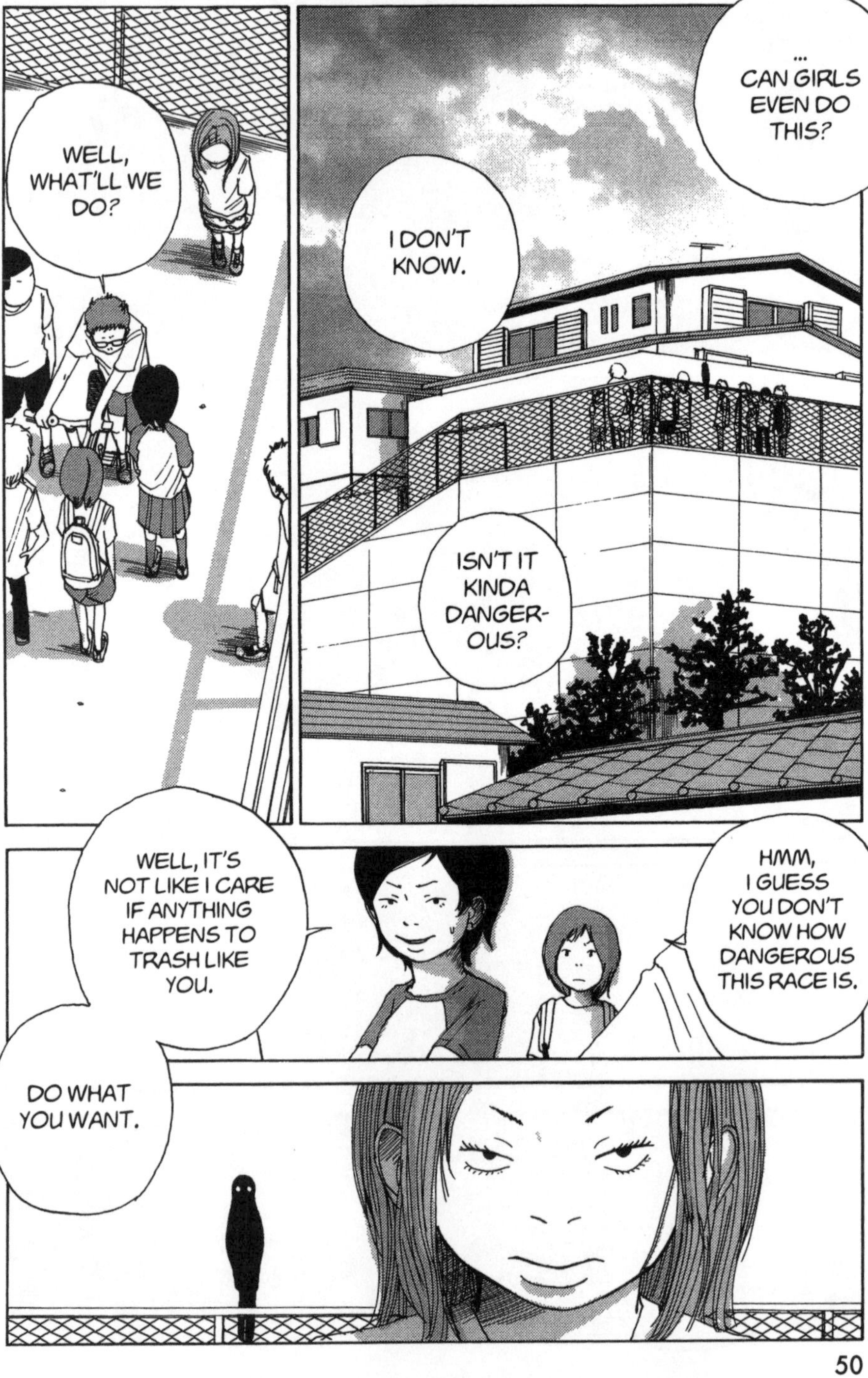

... CAN GIRLS EVEN DO THIS?
I DON'T KNOW.
ISN'T IT KINDA DANGER-OUS?
WELL, WHAT'LL WE DO?
HMM, I GUESS YOU DON'T KNOW HOW DANGEROUS THIS RACE IS.
WELL, IT'S NOT LIKE I CARE IF ANYTHING HAPPENS TO TRASH LIKE YOU.
DO WHAT YOU WANT.

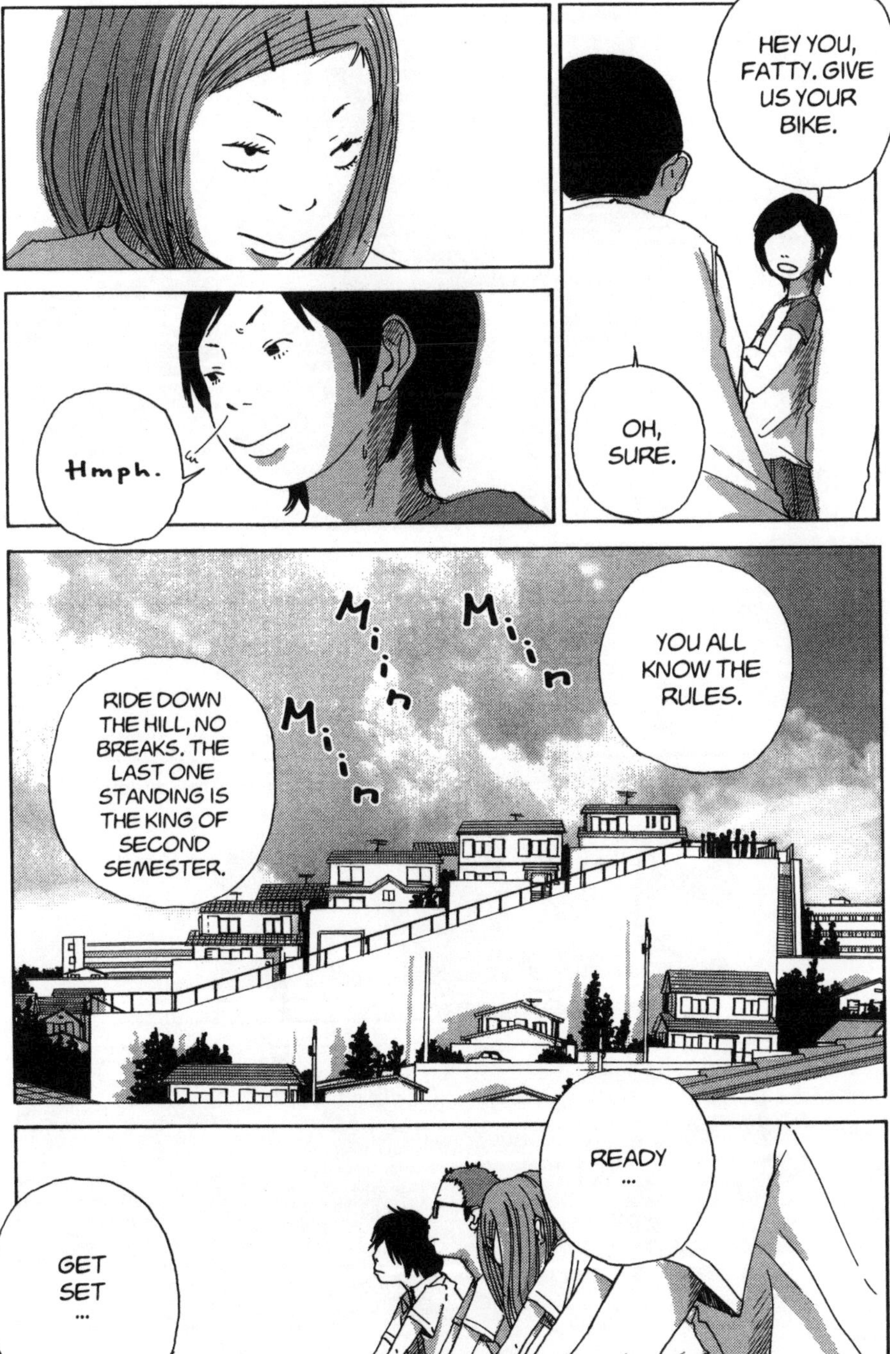
HEY YOU, FATTY. GIVE US YOUR BIKE.
OH, SURE.
Hmph.
YOU ALL KNOW THE RULES.
Miin
Miin
Miin
RIDE DOWN THE HILL, NO BREAKS. THE LAST ONE STANDING IS THE KING OF SECOND SEMESTER.
READY ...
GET SET ...

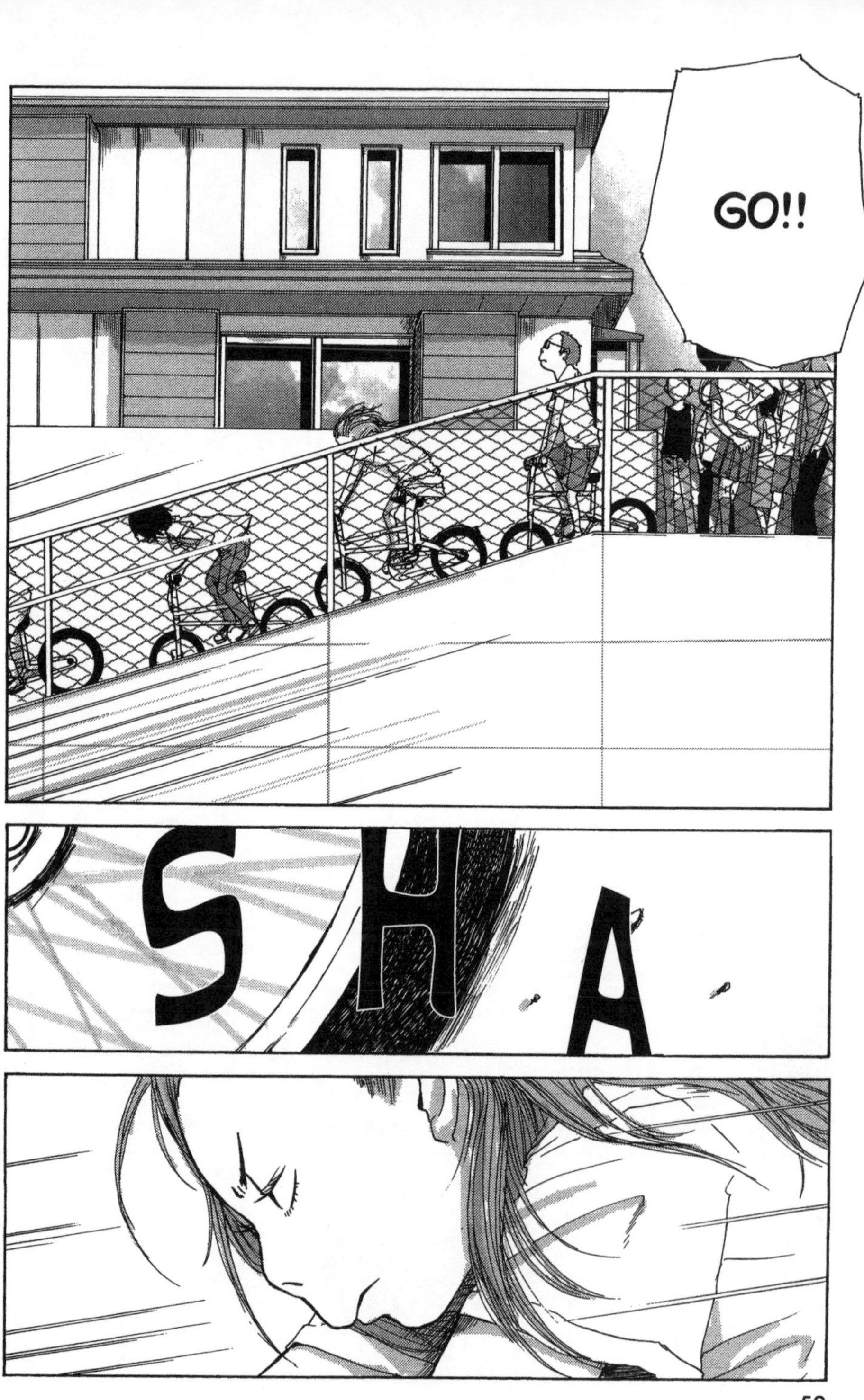
GO!!
SHA

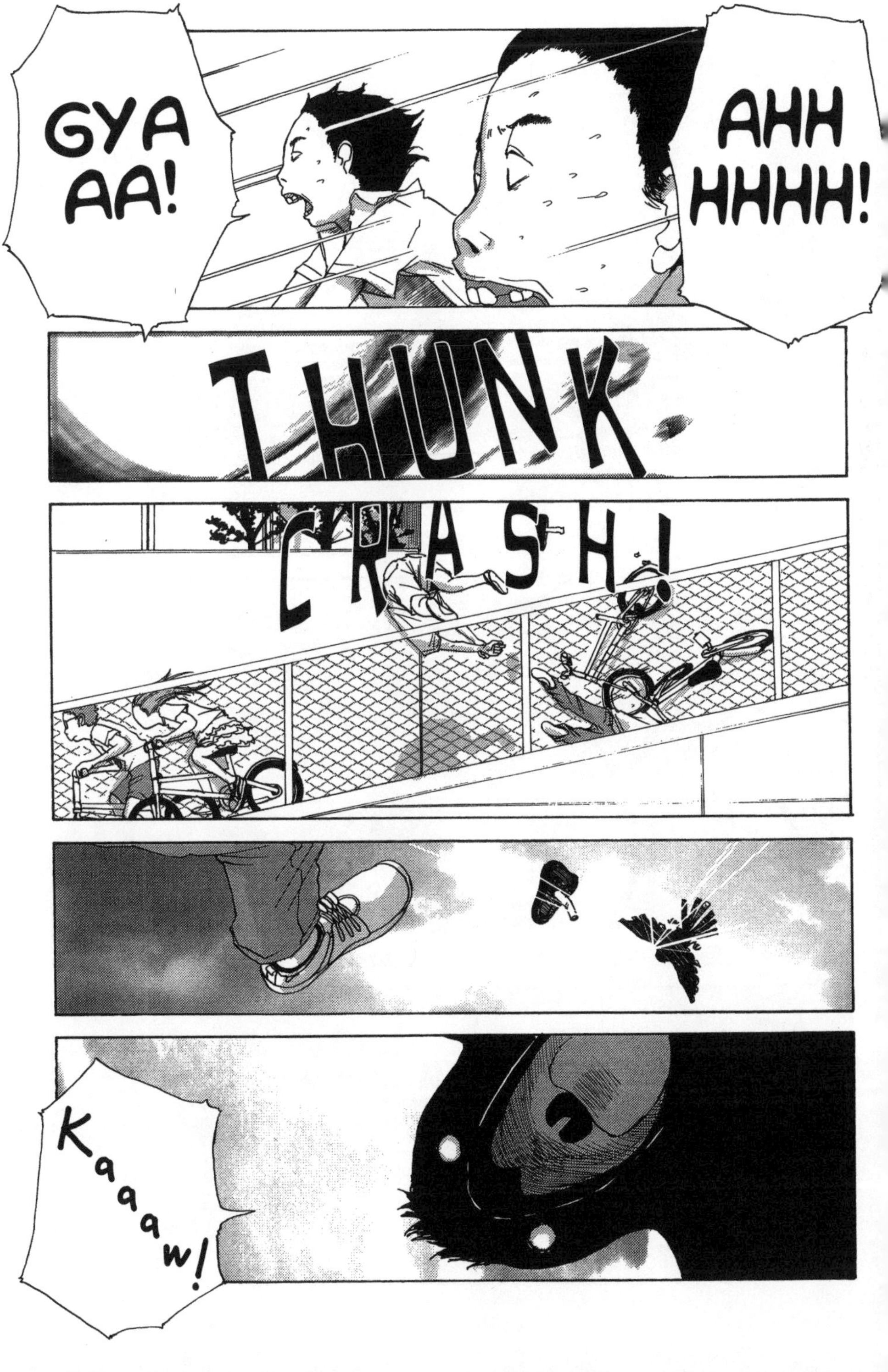
AHH HHHH!
GYA AA!
THUNK
CRASH!
Kaaaw!

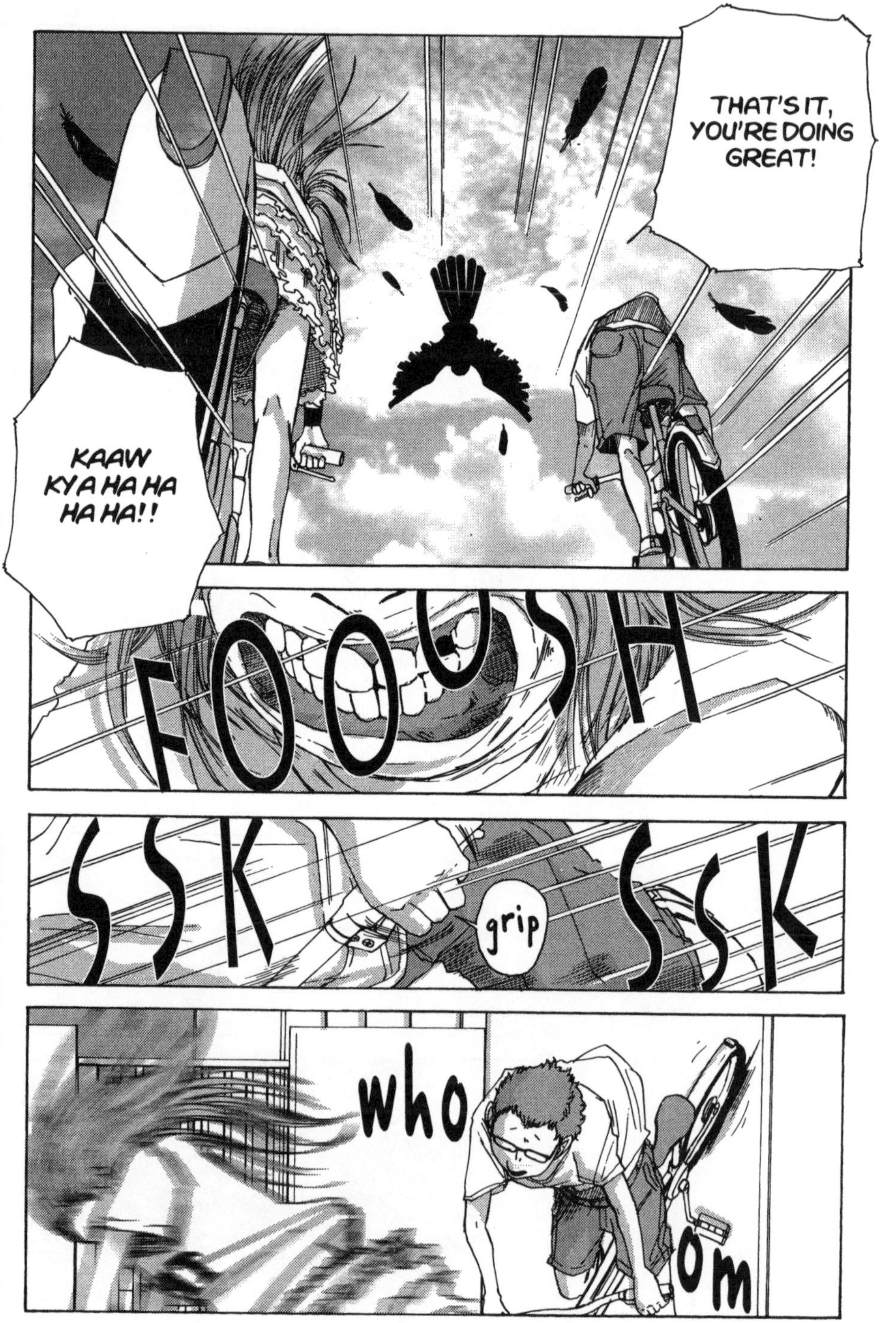
THAT'S IT, YOU'RE DOING GREAT!
KAAW KYA HA HA HA HA!!
FOOOSH
SSK
grip
SSK
whooom

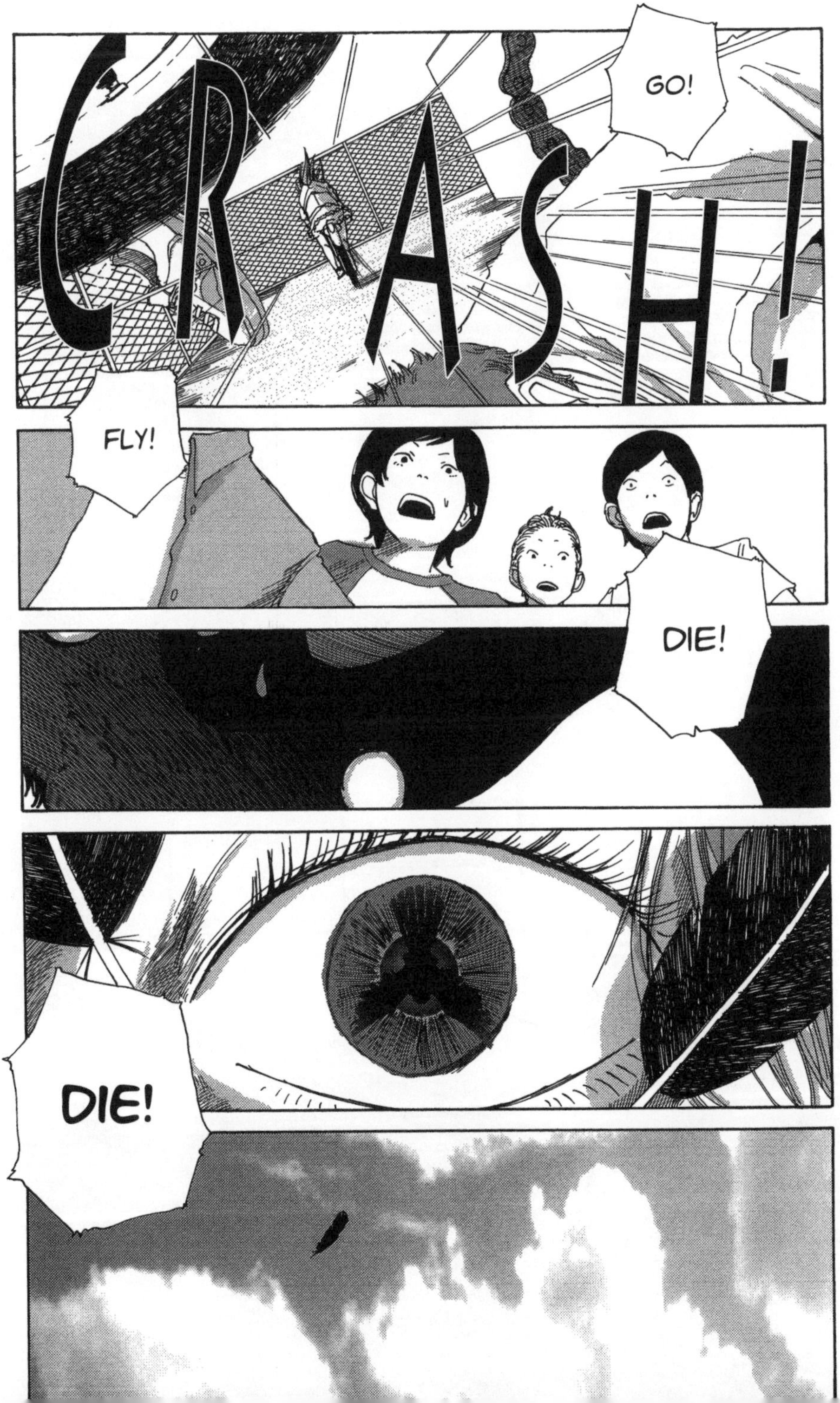
GO!
CRASH!
FLY!
DIE!
DIE!

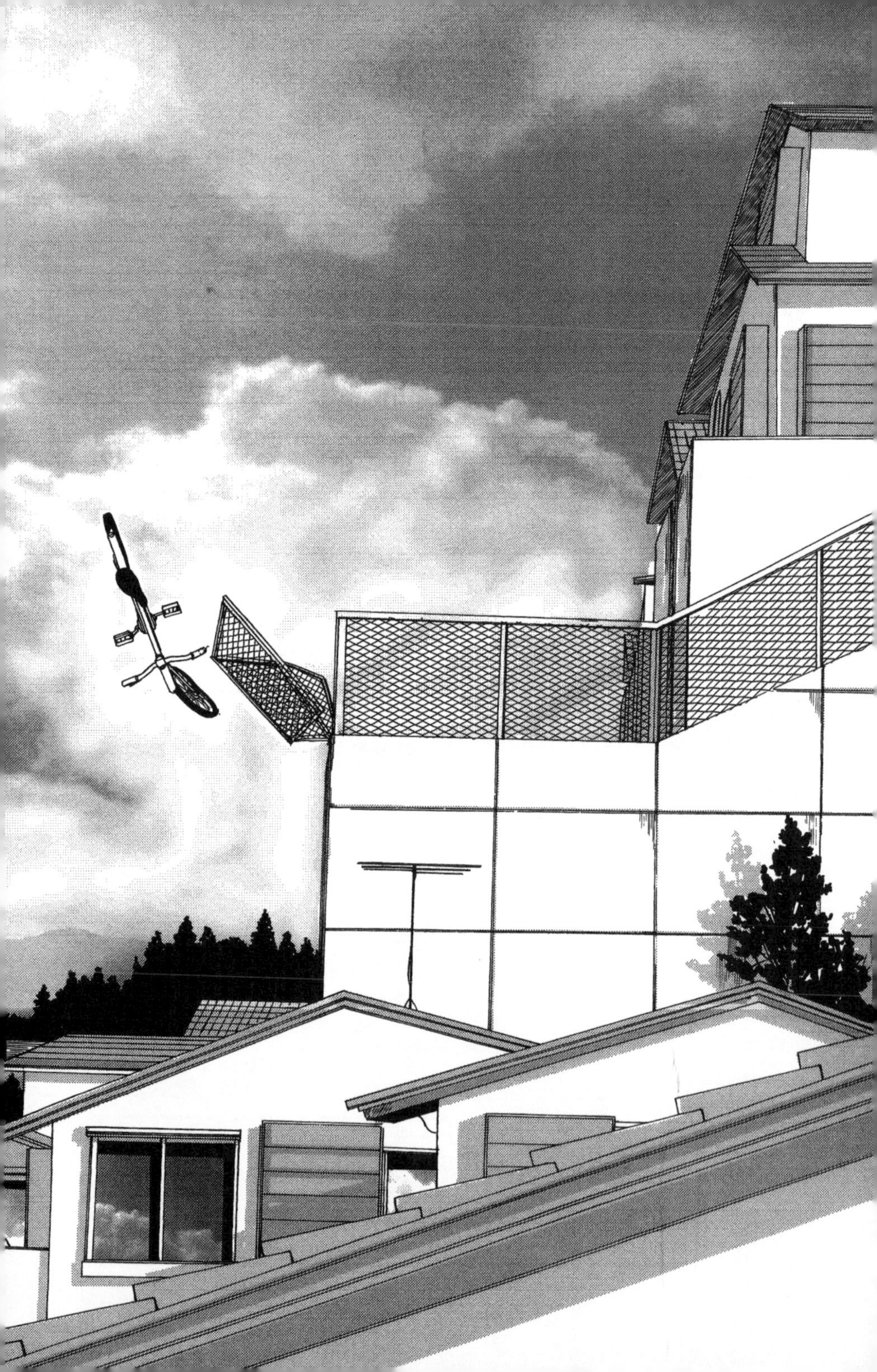

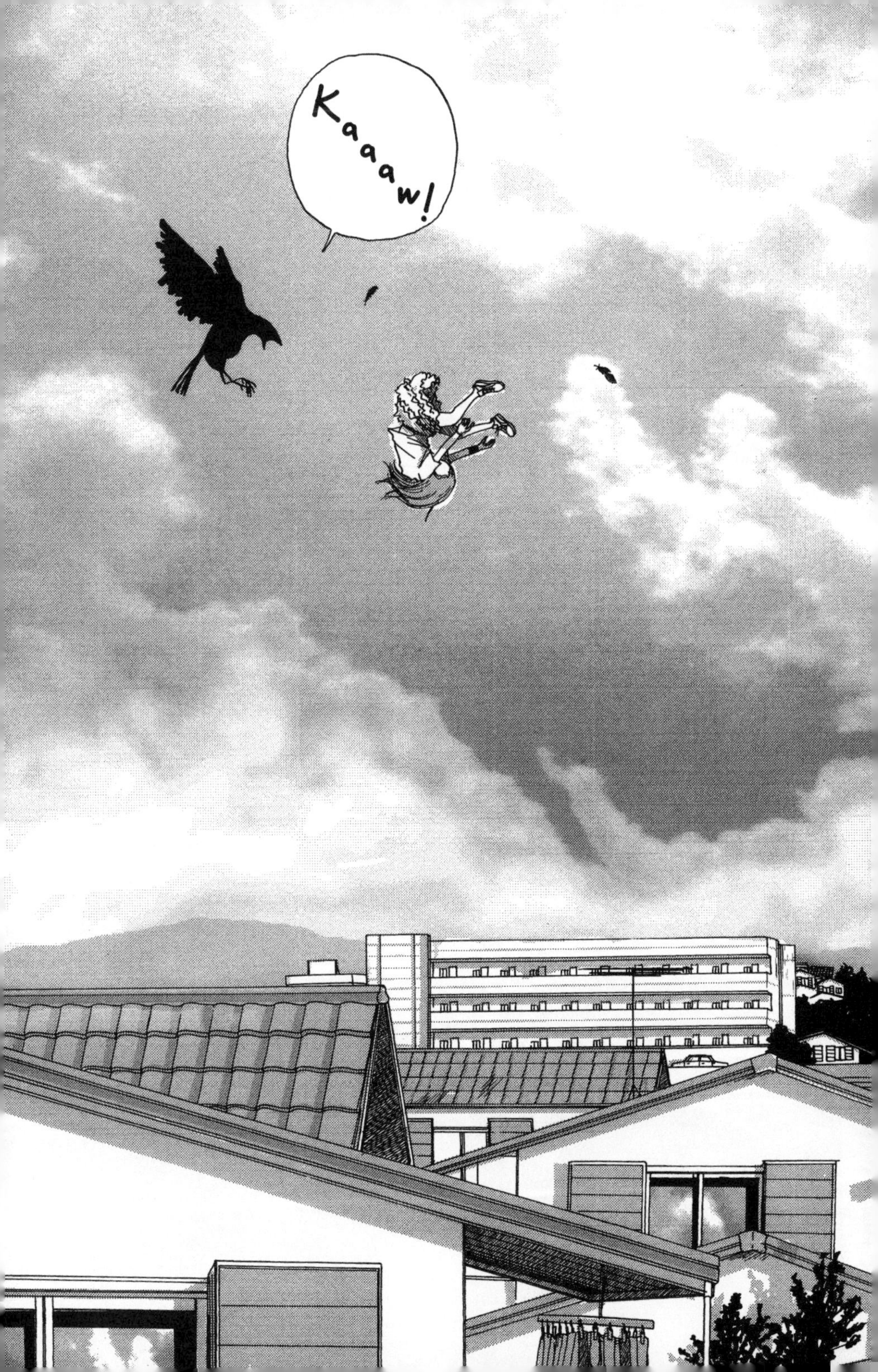
Kaaaw!

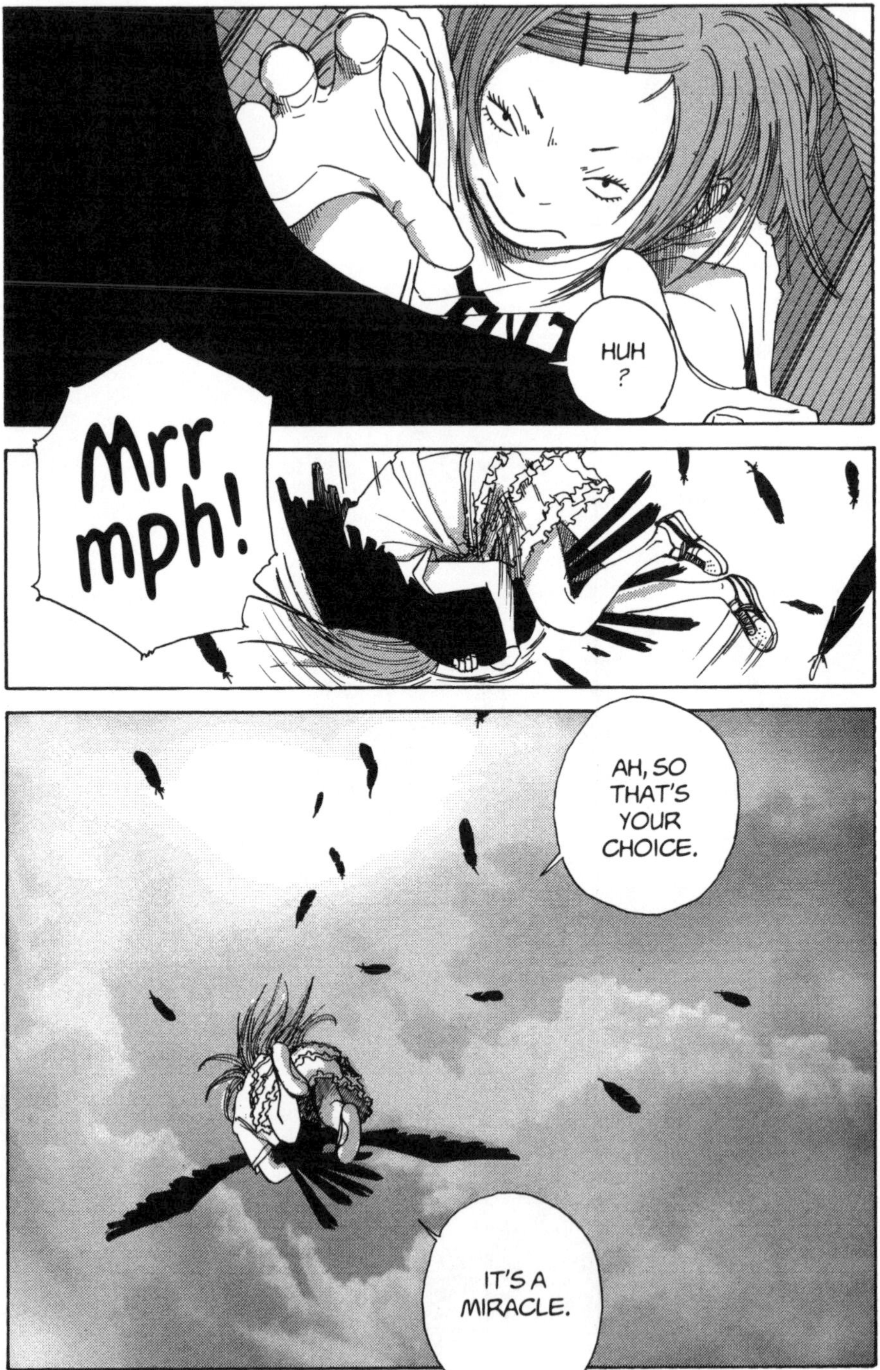
HUH ?
Mrr mph!
AH, SO THAT'S YOUR CHOICE.
IT'S A MIRACLE.

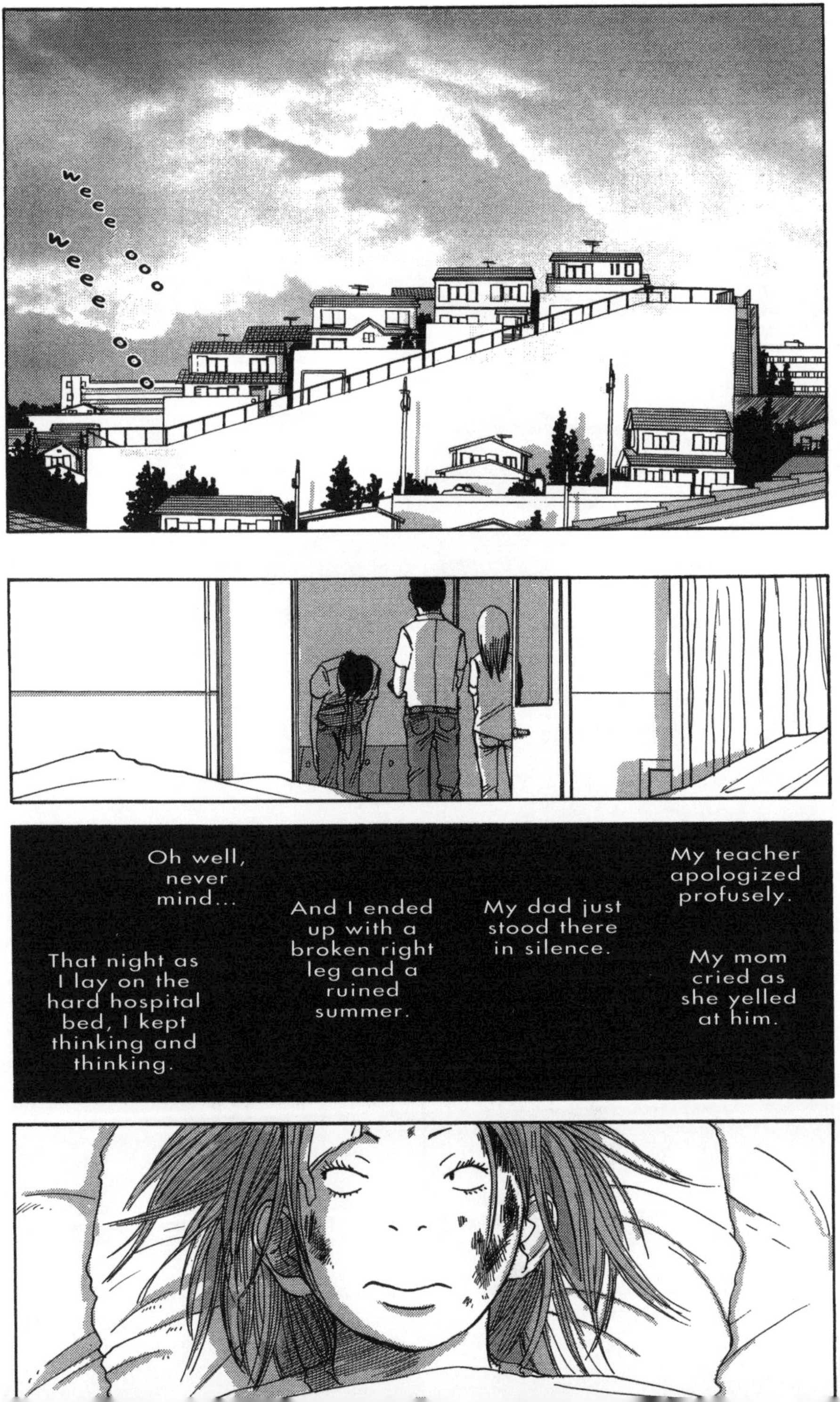
weee ooo weee ooo
My teacher apologized profusely.
My mom cried as she yelled at him.
My dad just stood there in silence.
And I ended up with a broken right leg and a ruined summer.
Oh well, never mind...
That night as I lay on the hard hospital bed, I kept thinking and thinking.

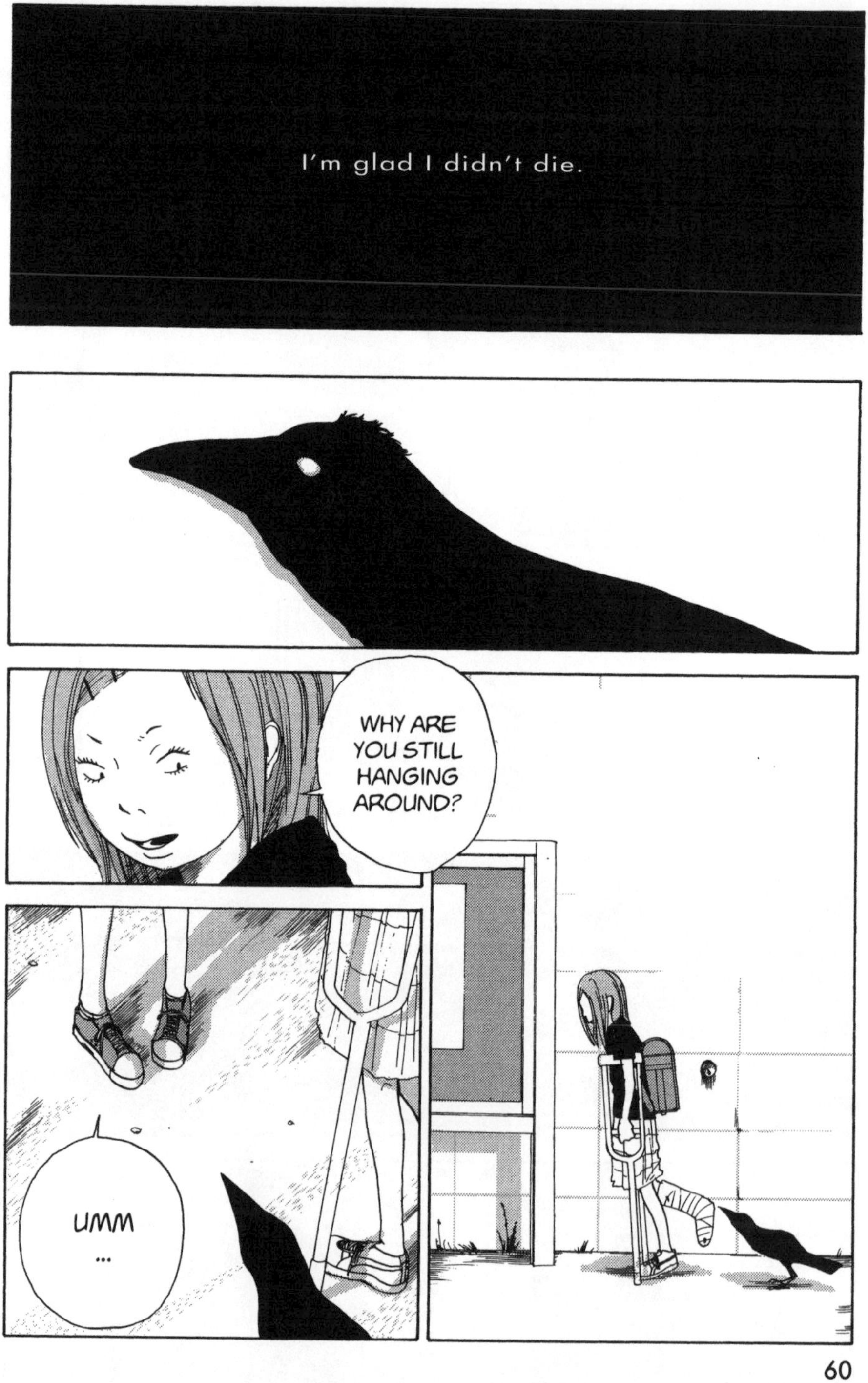
I'm glad I didn't die.
WHY ARE YOU STILL HANGING AROUND?
UMM ...

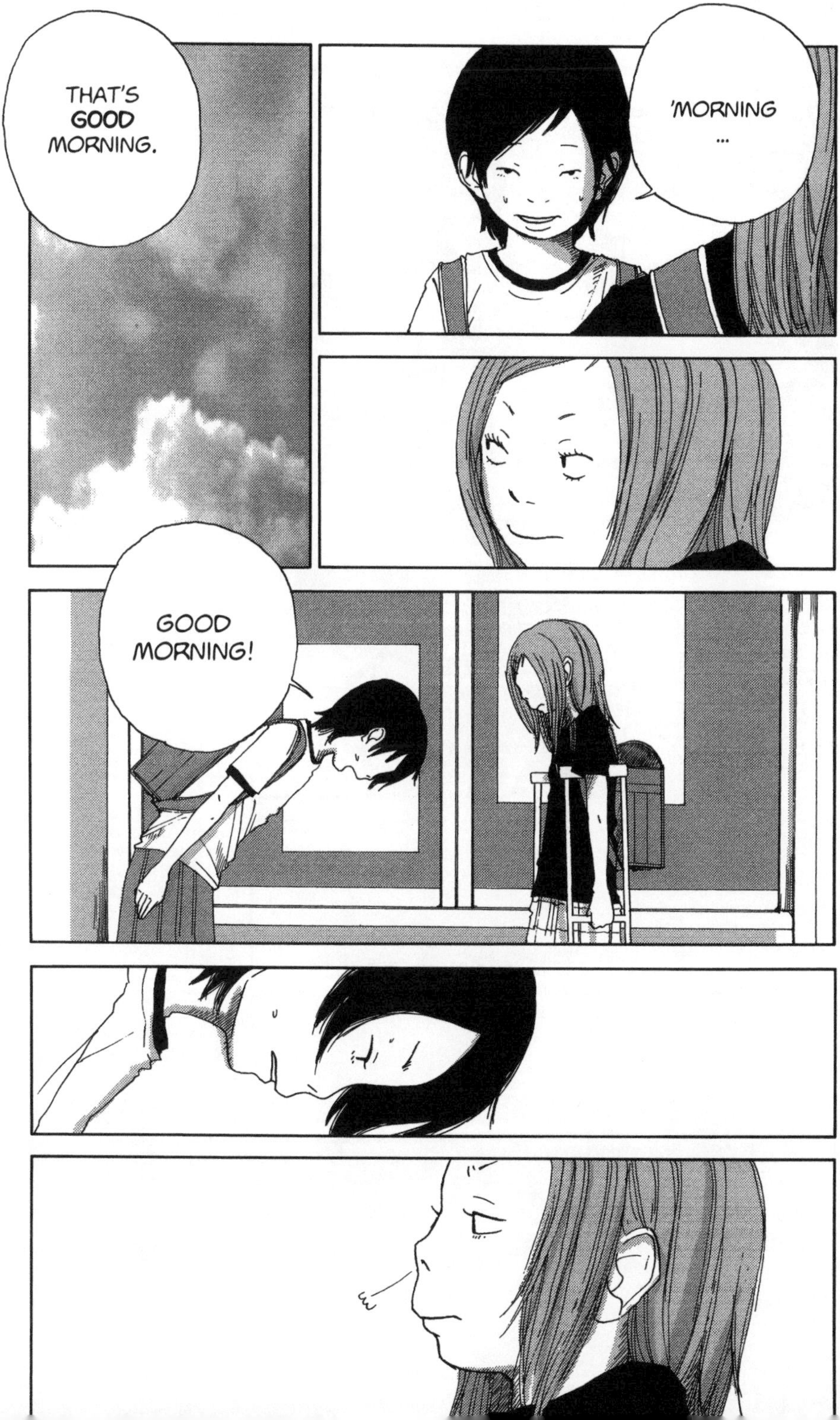
'MORNING ...
THAT'S **GOOD** MORNING.
GOOD MORNING!

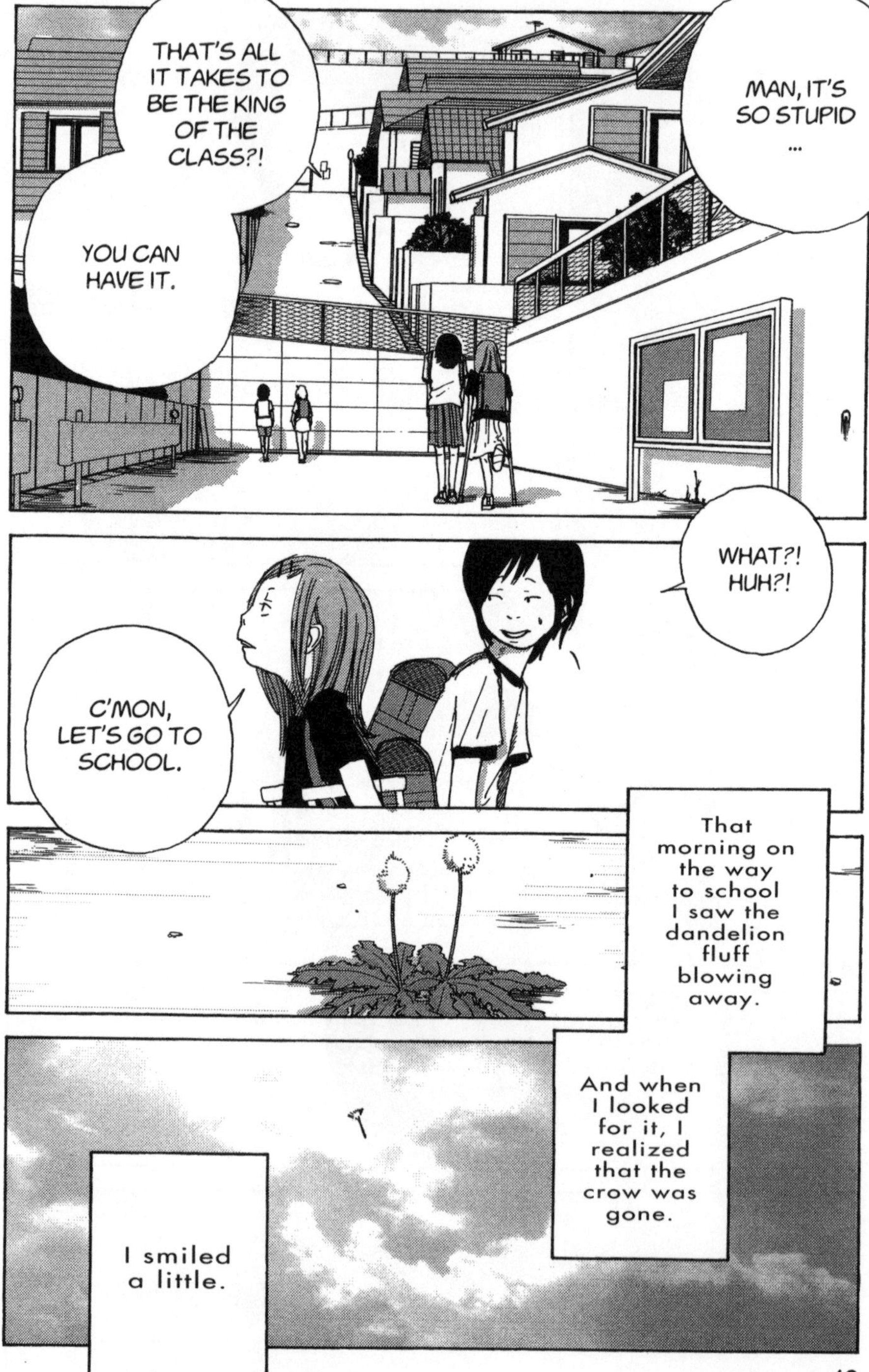
MAN, IT'S SO STUPID ...
THAT'S ALL IT TAKES TO BE THE KING OF THE CLASS?!
YOU CAN HAVE IT.
WHAT?! HUH?!
C'MON, LET'S GO TO SCHOOL.
That morning on the way to school I saw the dandelion fluff blowing away.
And when I looked for it, I realized that the crow was gone.
I smiled a little.

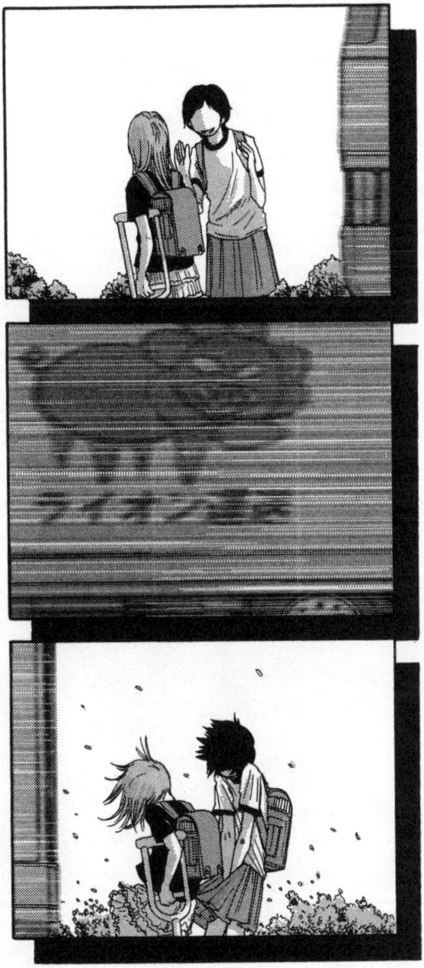
ライオン

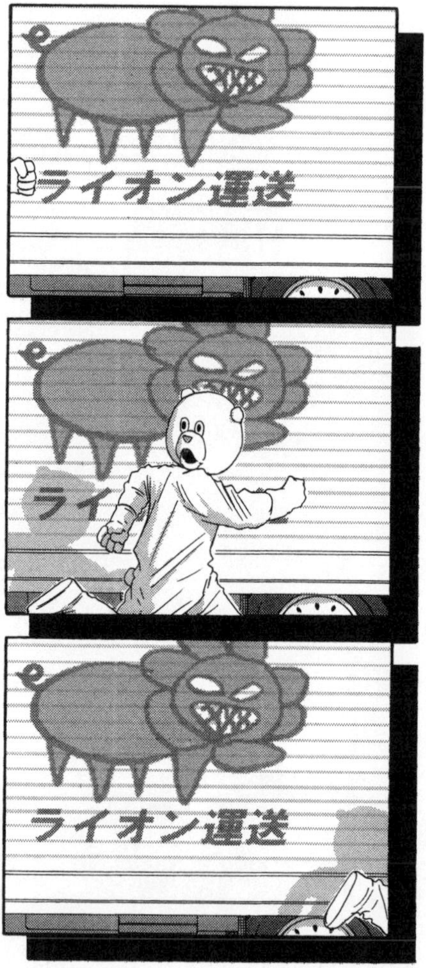
ライオン運送
ライ
ライオン運送

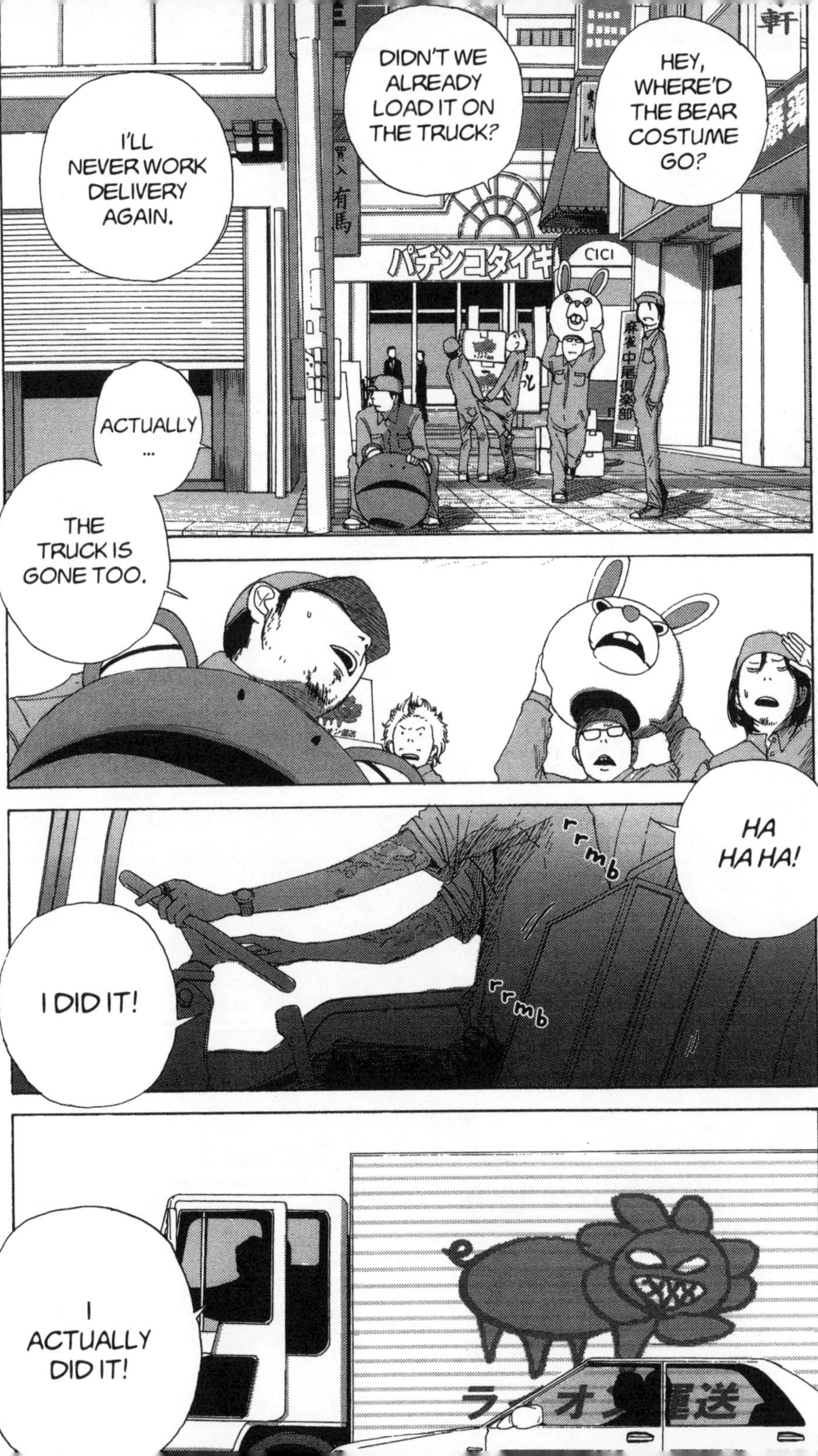
HEY, WHERE'D THE BEAR COSTUME GO?
DIDN'T WE ALREADY LOAD IT ON THE TRUCK?
I'LL NEVER WORK DELIVERY AGAIN.
パチンコタイキ
CICI
ACTUALLY ...
THE TRUCK IS GONE TOO.
HA HA HA!
rrmb
rrmb
I DID IT!
I ACTUALLY DID IT!

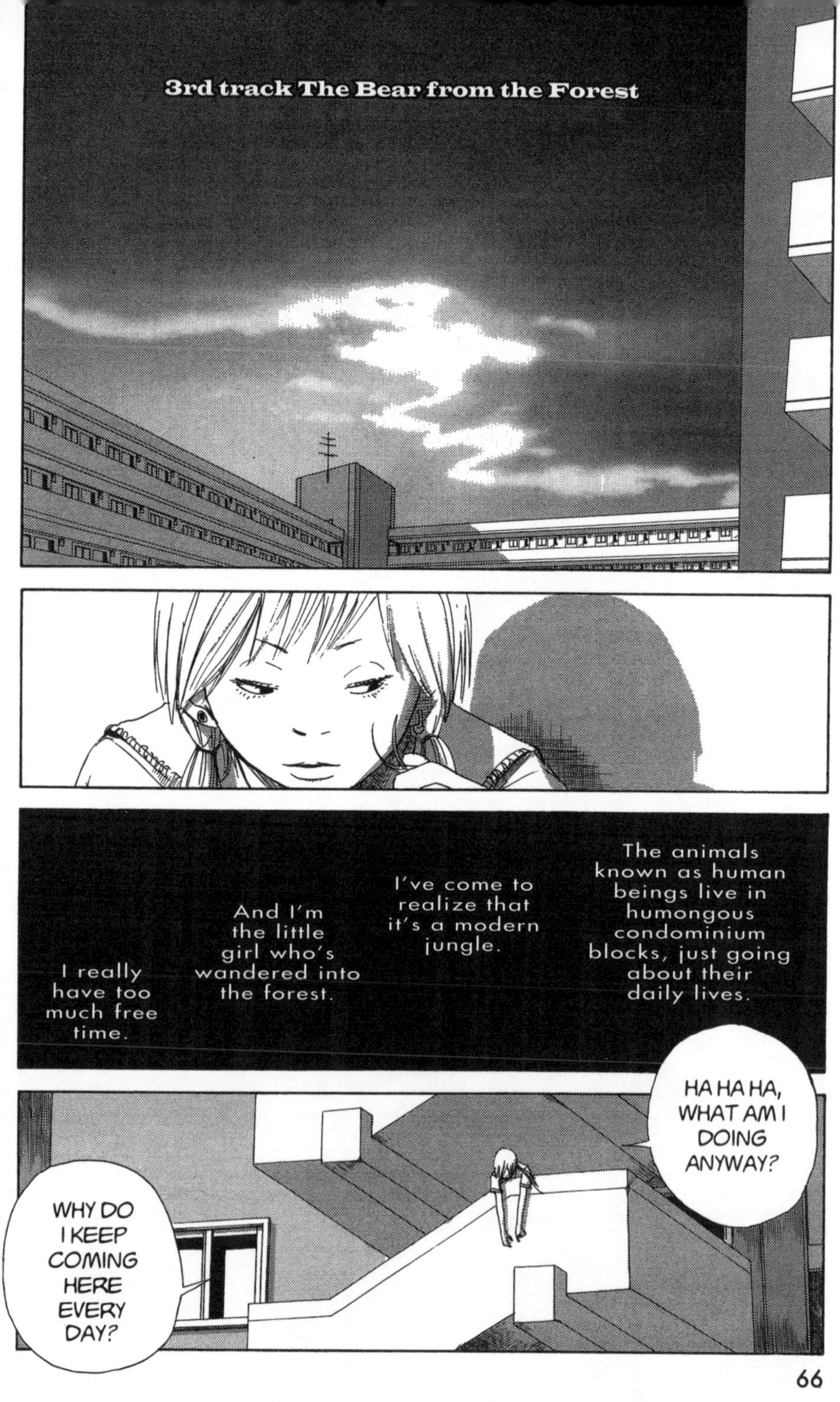
3rd track The Bear from the Forest
The animals known as human beings live in humongous condominium blocks, just going about their daily lives.
I've come to realize that it's a modern jungle.
And I'm the little girl who's wandered into the forest.
I really have too much free time.
HA HA HA, WHAT AM I DOING ANYWAY?
WHY DO I KEEP COMING HERE EVERY DAY?

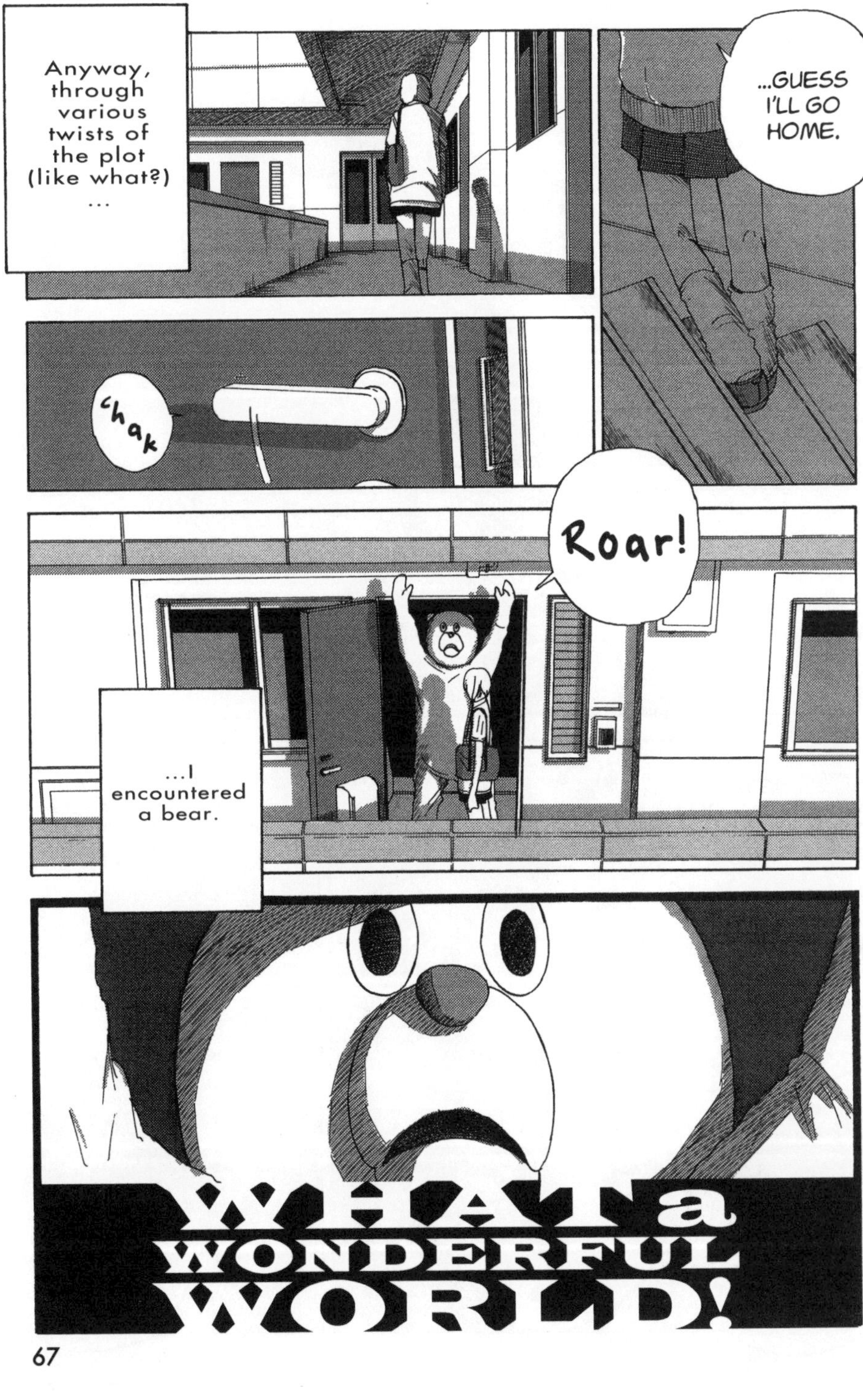
...GUESS I'LL GO HOME.
Anyway, through various twists of the plot (like what?) ...
chak
Roar!
...I encountered a bear.
WHAT a WONDERFUL WORLD!

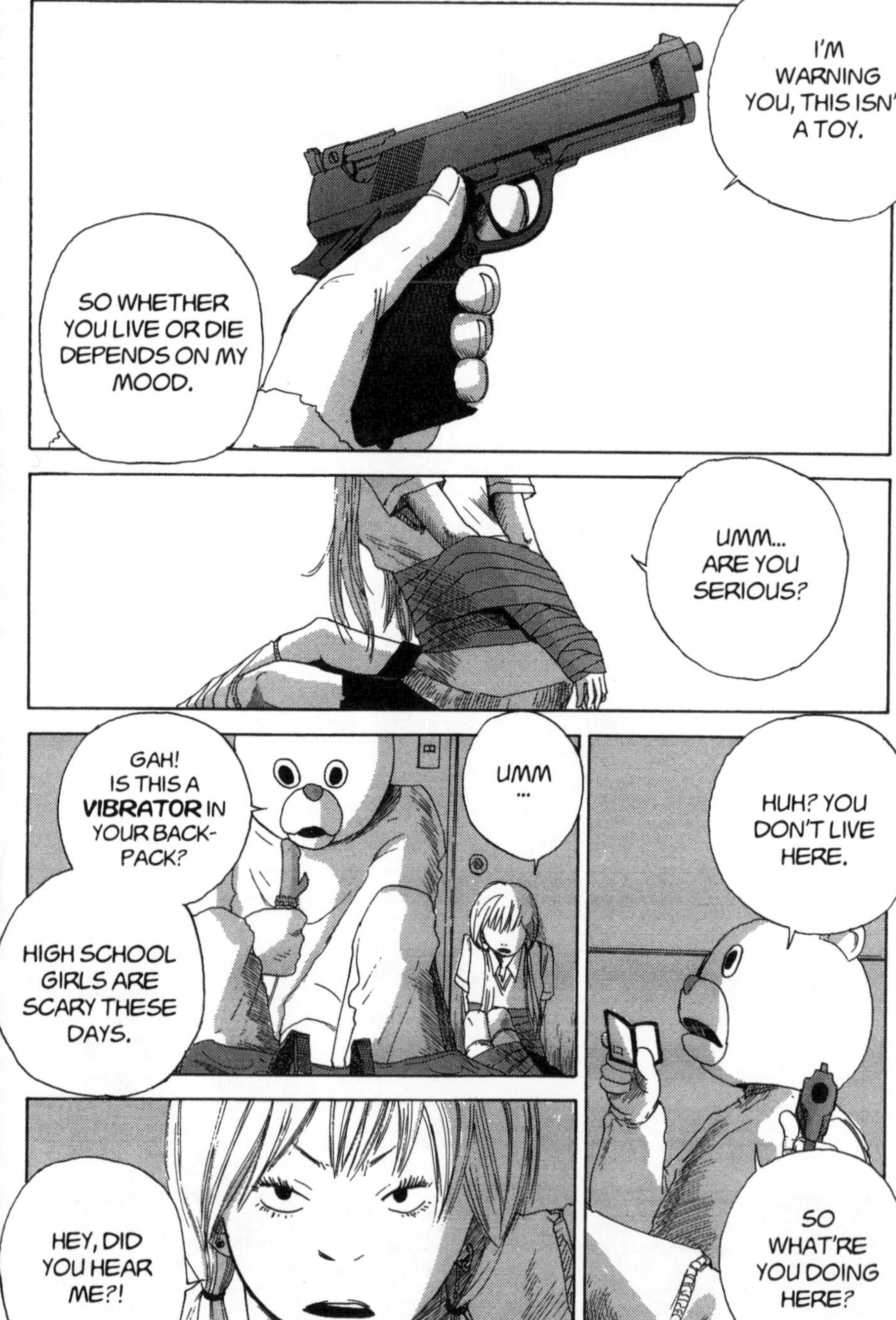
I'M WARNING YOU, THIS ISN'T A TOY.
SO WHETHER YOU LIVE OR DIE DEPENDS ON MY MOOD.
UMM... ARE YOU SERIOUS?
HUH? YOU DON'T LIVE HERE.
SO WHAT'RE YOU DOING HERE?
UMM ...
GAH! IS THIS A **VIBRATOR** IN YOUR BACK-PACK?
HIGH SCHOOL GIRLS ARE SCARY THESE DAYS.
HEY, DID YOU HEAR ME?!

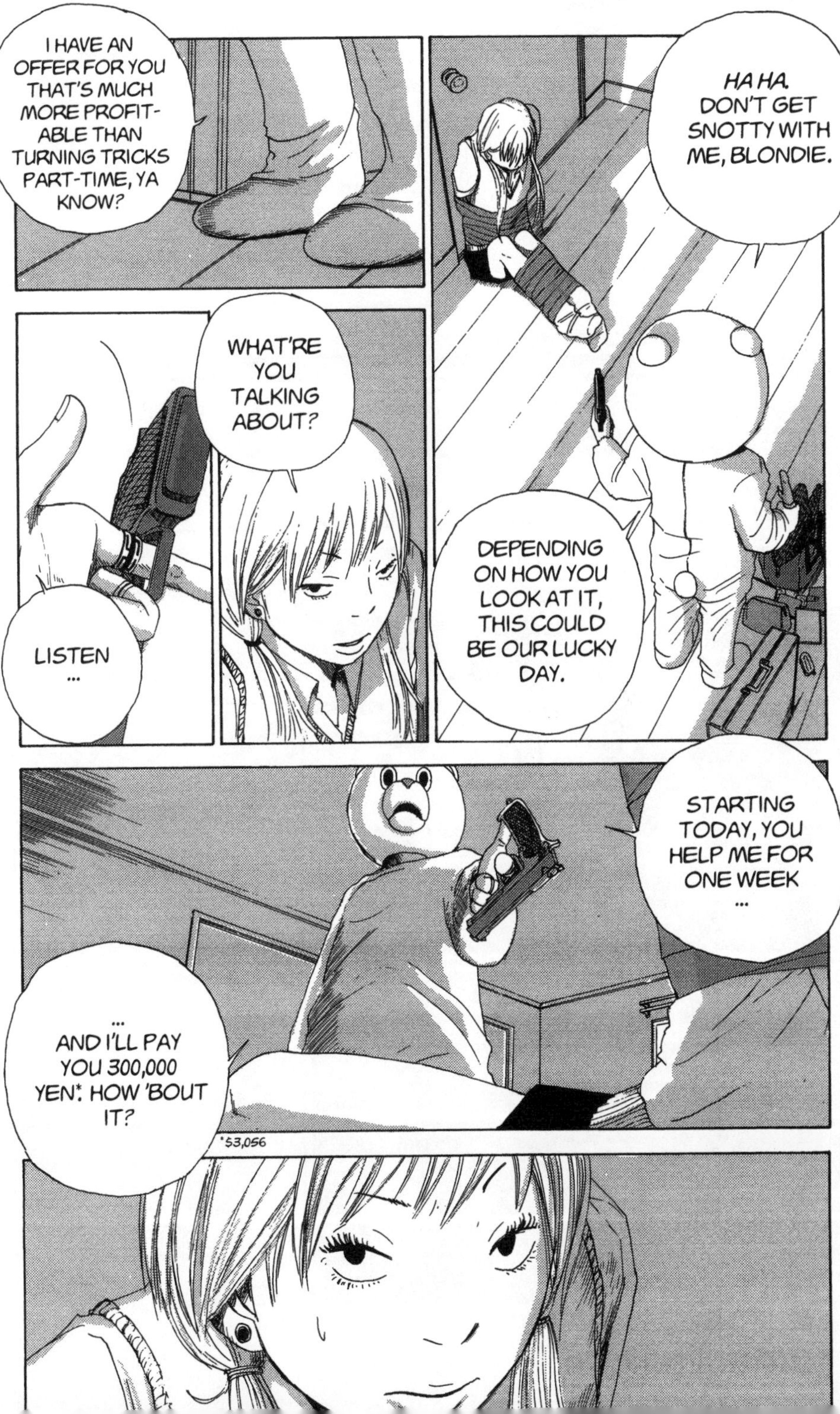
HA HA. DON'T GET SNOTTY WITH ME, BLONDIE.
DEPENDING ON HOW YOU LOOK AT IT, THIS COULD BE OUR LUCKY DAY.
I HAVE AN OFFER FOR YOU THAT'S MUCH MORE PROFIT-ABLE THAN TURNING TRICKS PART-TIME, YA KNOW?
WHAT'RE YOU TALKING ABOUT?
LISTEN ...
STARTING TODAY, YOU HELP ME FOR ONE WEEK ...
... AND I'LL PAY YOU 300,000 YEN*. HOW 'BOUT IT?

*$3,056

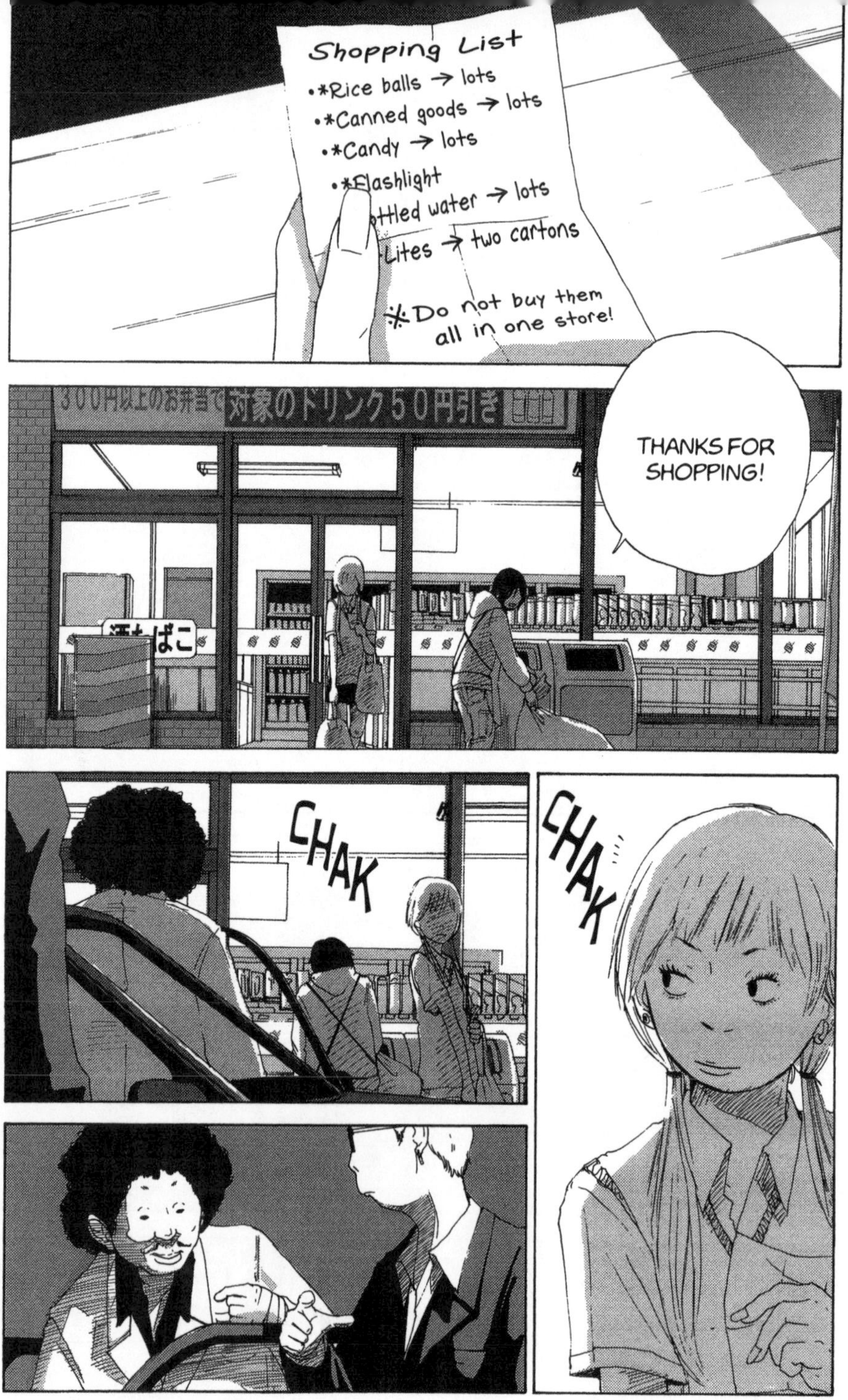

Shopping List
•*Rice balls → lots
•*Canned goods → lots
•*Candy → lots
•*Flashlight
ttled water → lots
Lites → two cartons
※Do not buy them all in one store!
300円以上のお弁当で 対象のドリンク50円引き
THANKS FOR SHOPPING!
CHAK
CHAK

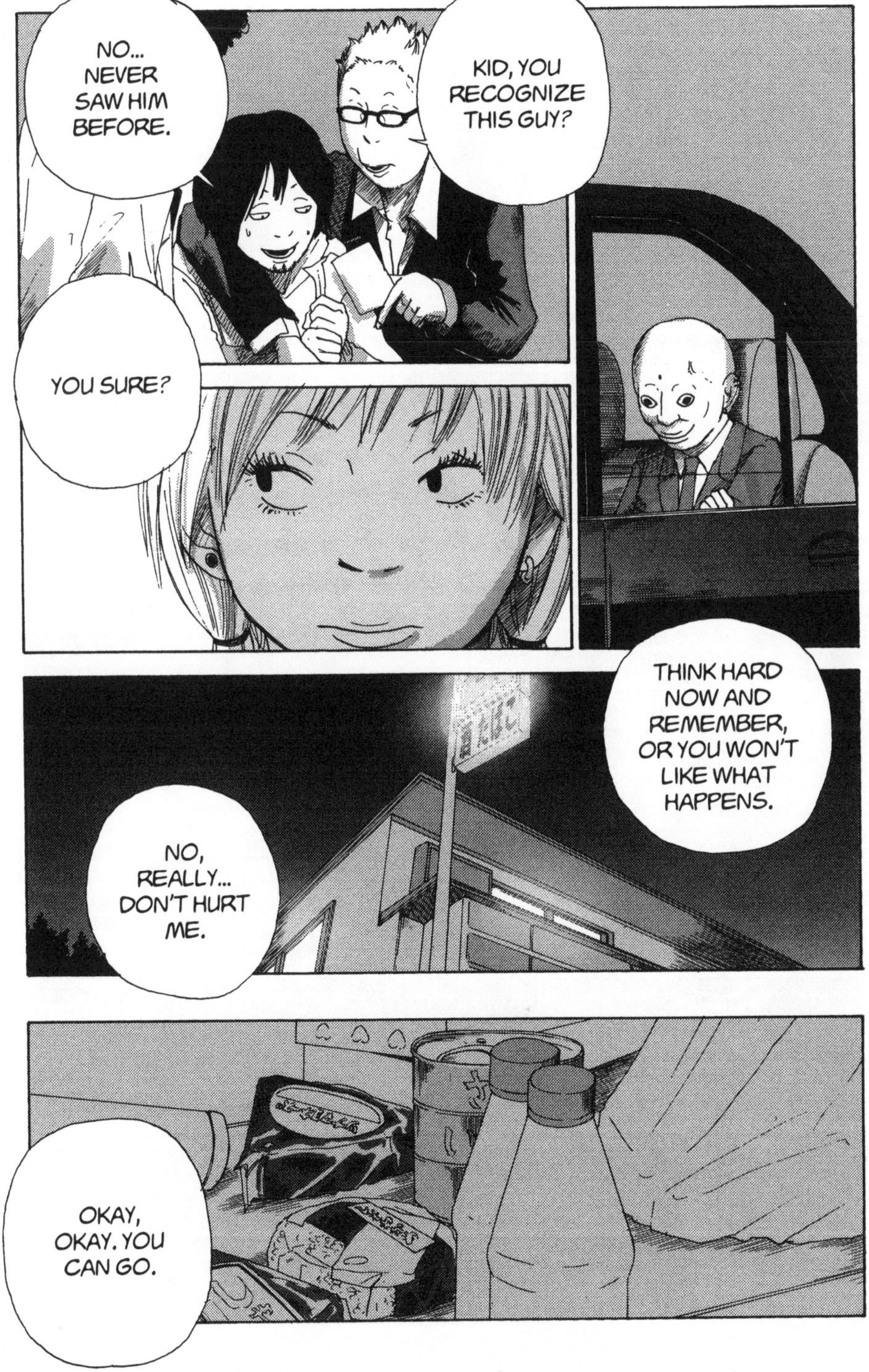
KID, YOU RECOGNIZE THIS GUY?
NO... NEVER SAW HIM BEFORE.
YOU SURE?
THINK HARD NOW AND REMEMBER, OR YOU WON'T LIKE WHAT HAPPENS.
NO, REALLY... DON'T HURT ME.
OKAY, OKAY. YOU CAN GO.

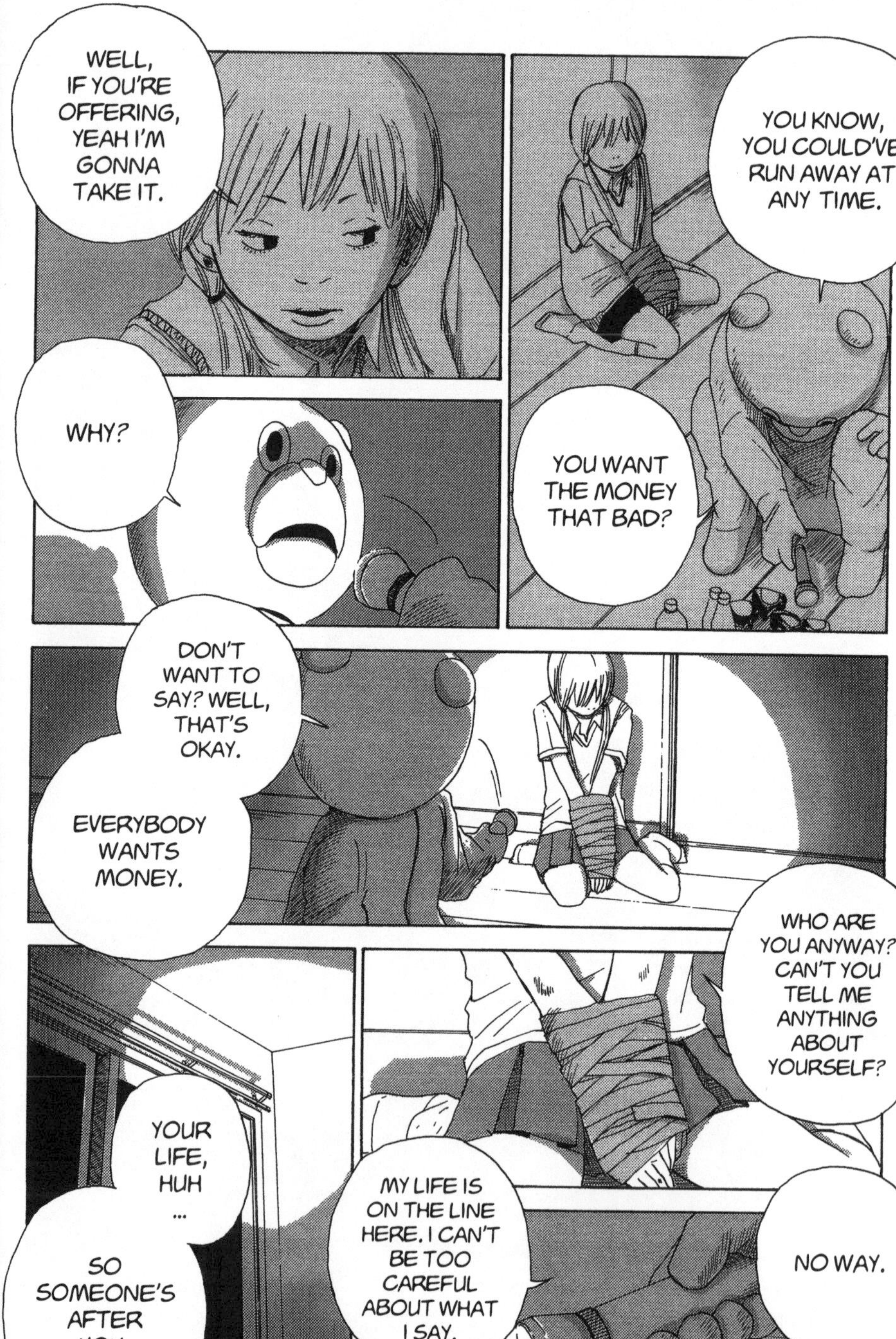
YOU KNOW, YOU COULD'VE RUN AWAY AT ANY TIME.
YOU WANT THE MONEY THAT BAD?
WELL, IF YOU'RE OFFERING, YEAH I'M GONNA TAKE IT.
WHY?
DON'T WANT TO SAY? WELL, THAT'S OKAY.
EVERYBODY WANTS MONEY.
WHO ARE YOU ANYWAY? CAN'T YOU TELL ME ANYTHING ABOUT YOURSELF?
NO WAY.
MY LIFE IS ON THE LINE HERE. I CAN'T BE TOO CAREFUL ABOUT WHAT I SAY.
YOUR LIFE, HUH ...
SO SOMEONE'S AFTER YOU.

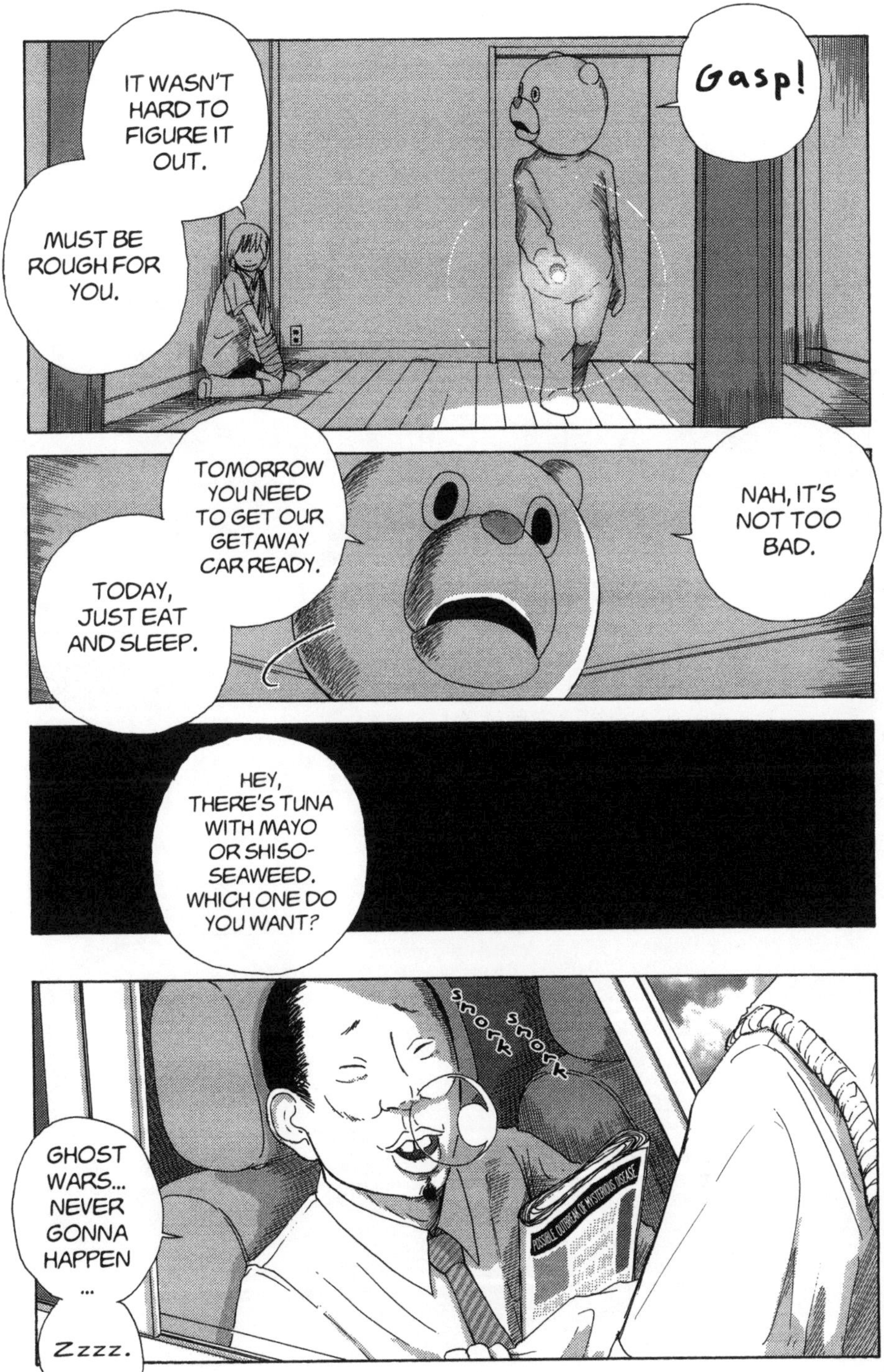
Gasp!
IT WASN'T HARD TO FIGURE IT OUT.
MUST BE ROUGH FOR YOU.
NAH, IT'S NOT TOO BAD.
TOMORROW YOU NEED TO GET OUR GETAWAY CAR READY.
TODAY, JUST EAT AND SLEEP.
HEY, THERE'S TUNA WITH MAYO OR SHISO-SEAWEED. WHICH ONE DO YOU WANT?
snork snork
POSSIBLE OUTBREAK OF MYSTERIOUS DISEASE
GHOST WARS... NEVER GONNA HAPPEN ...
Zzzz.

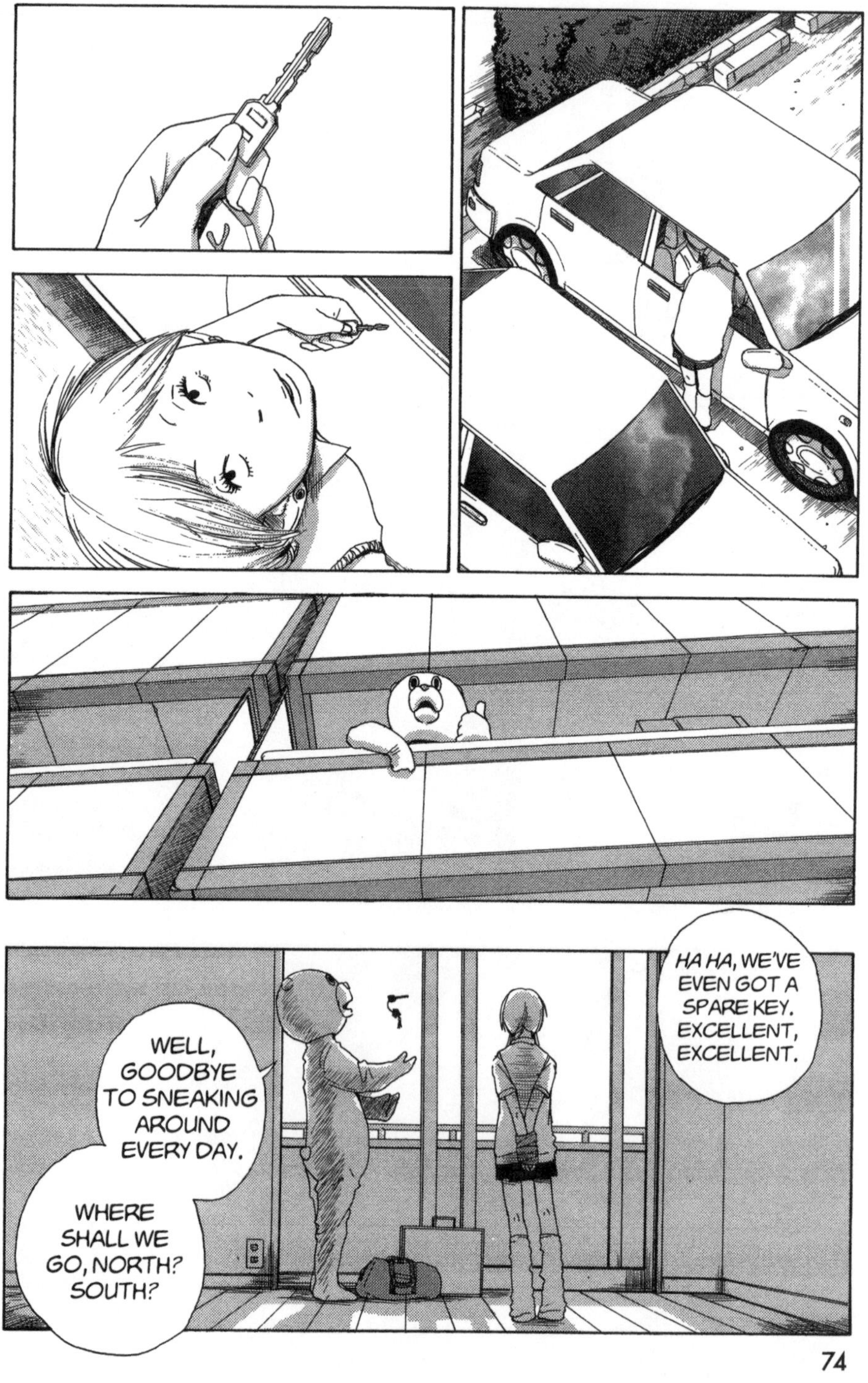
HA HA, WE'VE EVEN GOT A SPARE KEY. EXCELLENT, EXCELLENT.
WELL, GOODBYE TO SNEAKING AROUND EVERY DAY.
WHERE SHALL WE GO, NORTH? SOUTH?

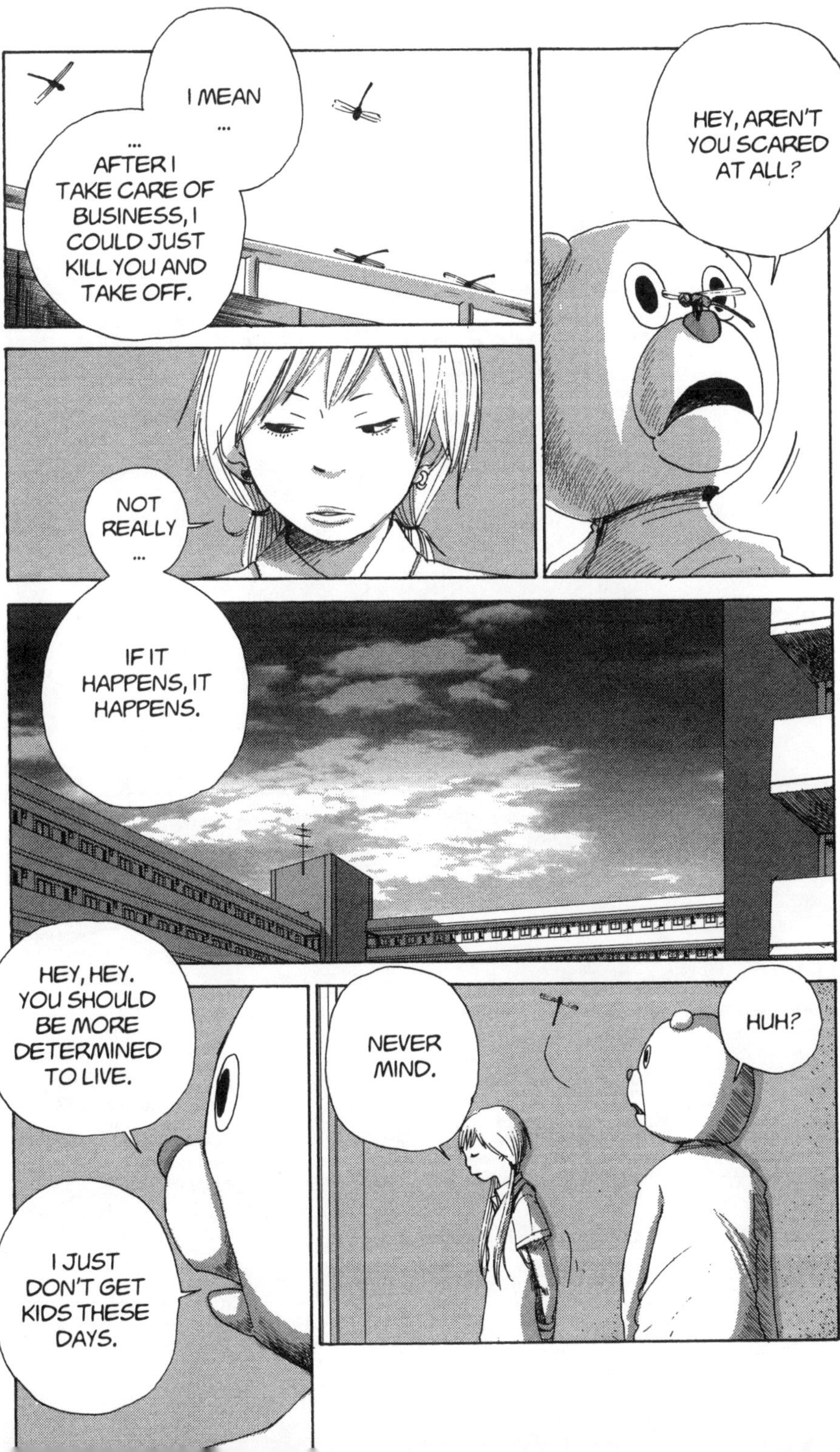
HEY, AREN'T YOU SCARED AT ALL?
I MEAN ...
... AFTER I TAKE CARE OF BUSINESS, I COULD JUST KILL YOU AND TAKE OFF.
NOT REALLY ...
IF IT HAPPENS, IT HAPPENS.
HUH?
NEVER MIND.
HEY, HEY. YOU SHOULD BE MORE DETERMINED TO LIVE.
I JUST DON'T GET KIDS THESE DAYS.

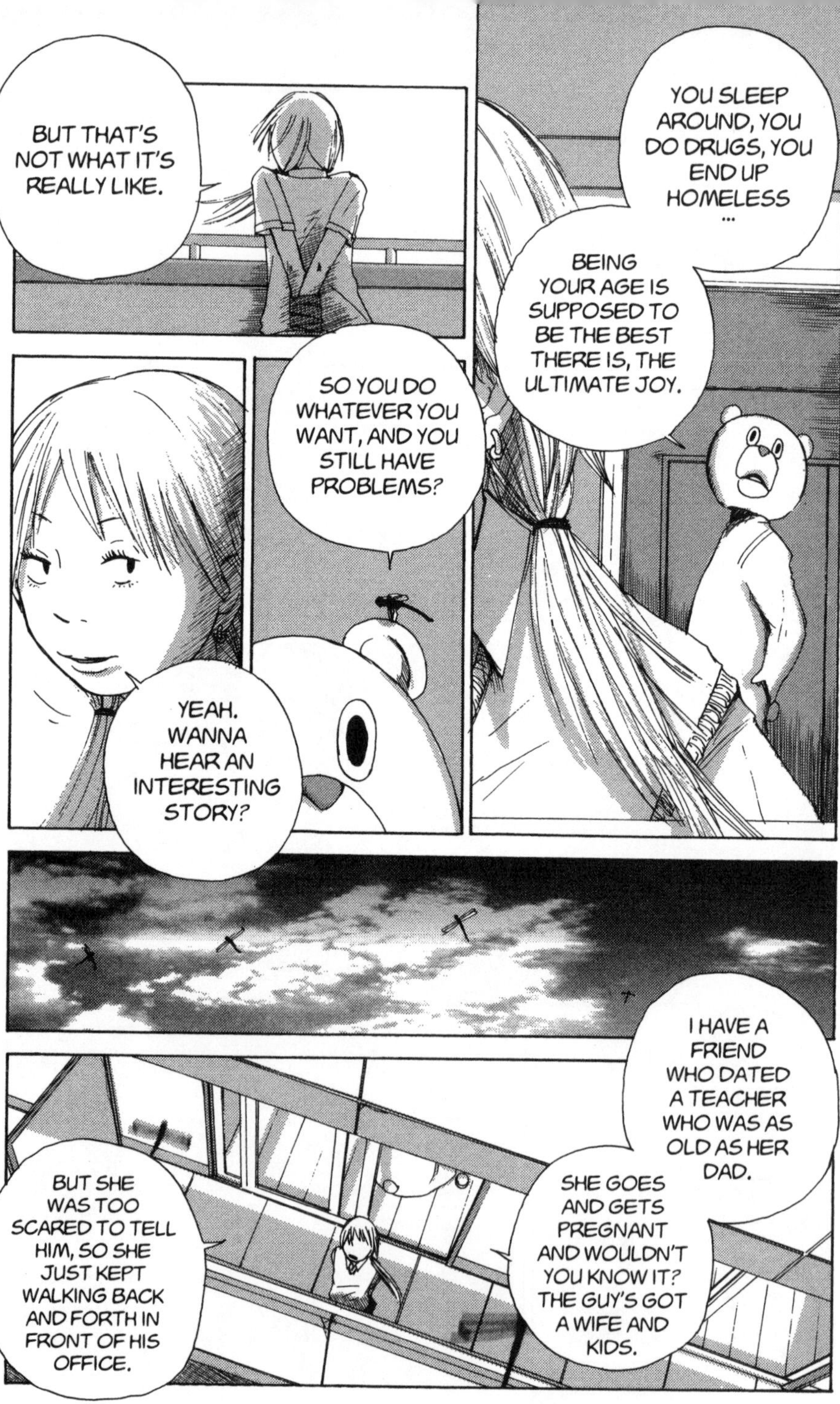
YOU SLEEP AROUND, YOU DO DRUGS, YOU END UP HOMELESS ...
BEING YOUR AGE IS SUPPOSED TO BE THE BEST THERE IS, THE ULTIMATE JOY.
BUT THAT'S NOT WHAT IT'S REALLY LIKE.
SO YOU DO WHATEVER YOU WANT, AND YOU STILL HAVE PROBLEMS?
YEAH. WANNA HEAR AN INTERESTING STORY?
I HAVE A FRIEND WHO DATED A TEACHER WHO WAS AS OLD AS HER DAD.
SHE GOES AND GETS PREGNANT AND WOULDN'T YOU KNOW IT? THE GUY'S GOT A WIFE AND KIDS.
BUT SHE WAS TOO SCARED TO TELL HIM, SO SHE JUST KEPT WALKING BACK AND FORTH IN FRONT OF HIS OFFICE.

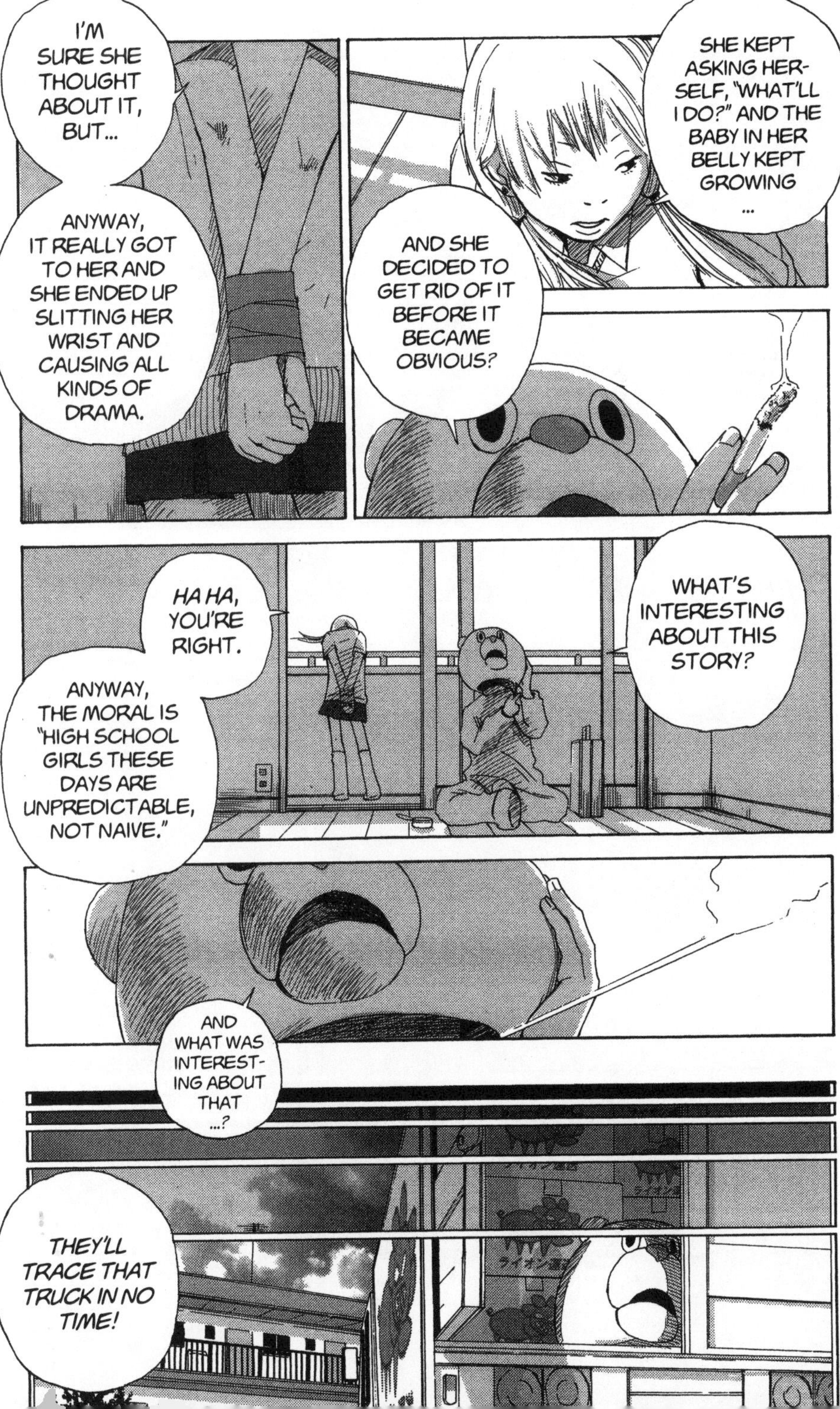
SHE KEPT ASKING HER-SELF, "WHAT'LL I DO?" AND THE BABY IN HER BELLY KEPT GROWING ...
AND SHE DECIDED TO GET RID OF IT BEFORE IT BECAME OBVIOUS?
I'M SURE SHE THOUGHT ABOUT IT, BUT...
ANYWAY, IT REALLY GOT TO HER AND SHE ENDED UP SLITTING HER WRIST AND CAUSING ALL KINDS OF DRAMA.
WHAT'S INTERESTING ABOUT THIS STORY?
HA HA, YOU'RE RIGHT.
ANYWAY, THE MORAL IS "HIGH SCHOOL GIRLS THESE DAYS ARE UNPREDICTABLE, NOT NAIVE."
AND WHAT WAS INTEREST-ING ABOUT THAT ...?
THEY'LL TRACE THAT TRUCK IN NO TIME!

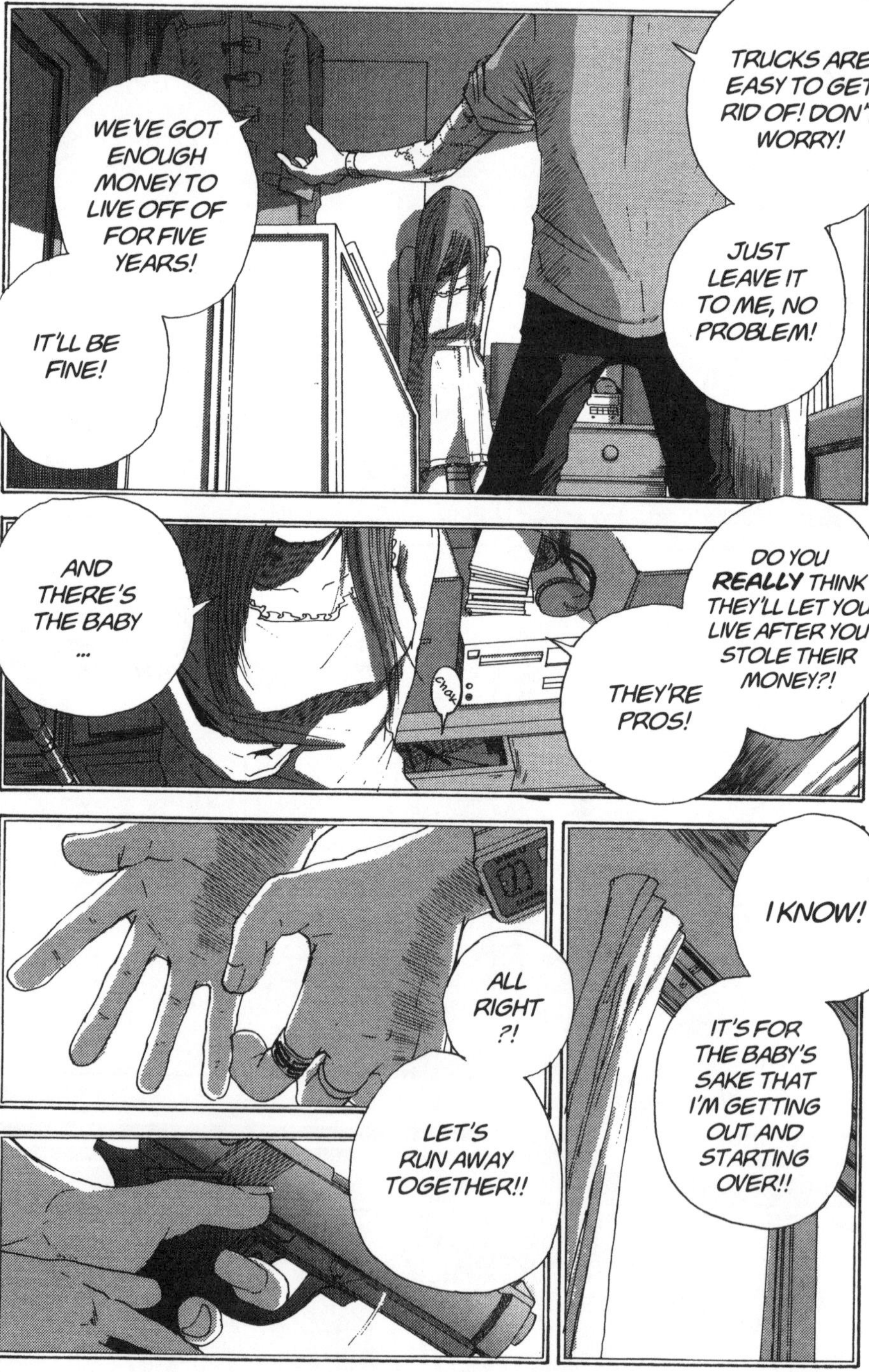
TRUCKS ARE EASY TO GET RID OF! DON'T WORRY!
JUST LEAVE IT TO ME, NO PROBLEM!
WE'VE GOT ENOUGH MONEY TO LIVE OFF OF FOR FIVE YEARS!
IT'LL BE FINE!
DO YOU **REALLY** THINK THEY'LL LET YOU LIVE AFTER YOU STOLE THEIR MONEY?!
THEY'RE PROS!
CHOK
AND THERE'S THE BABY ...
I KNOW!
IT'S FOR THE BABY'S SAKE THAT I'M GETTING OUT AND STARTING OVER!!
ALL RIGHT ?!
LET'S RUN AWAY TOGETHER!!

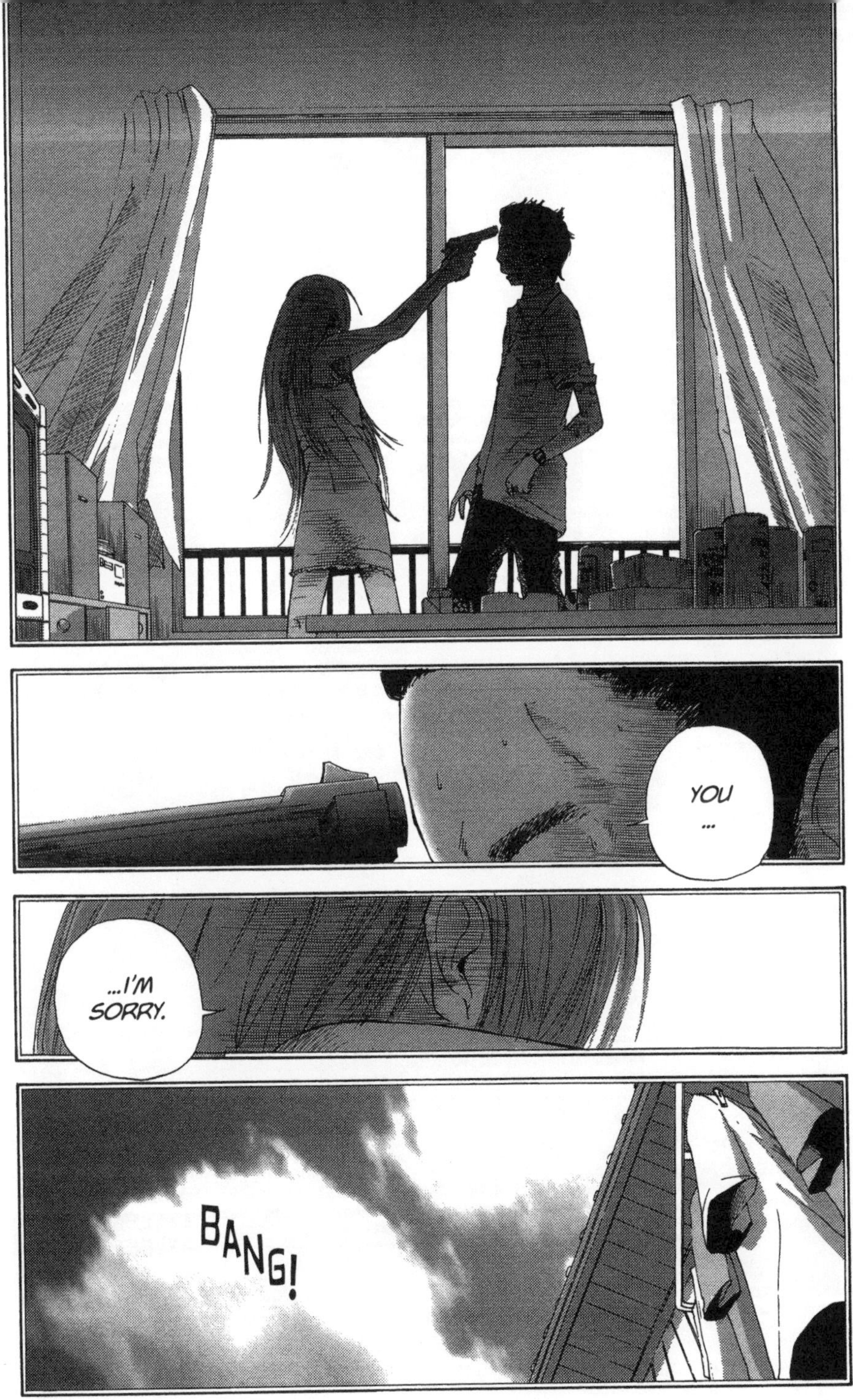
YOU ...
...I'M SORRY.
BANG!

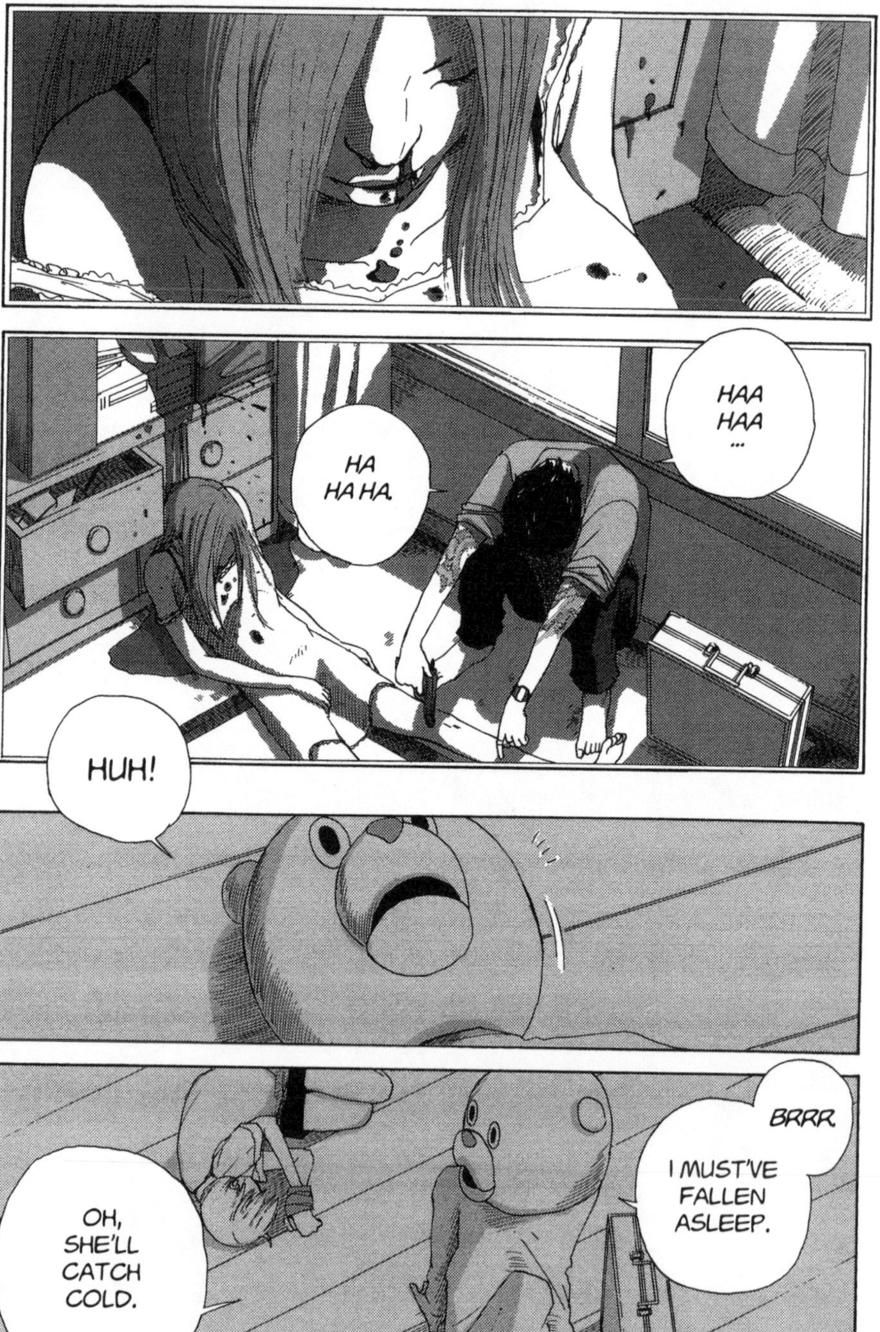
HAA HAA ...
HA HA HA.
HUH!
BRRR.
I MUST'VE FALLEN ASLEEP.
OH, SHE'LL CATCH COLD.

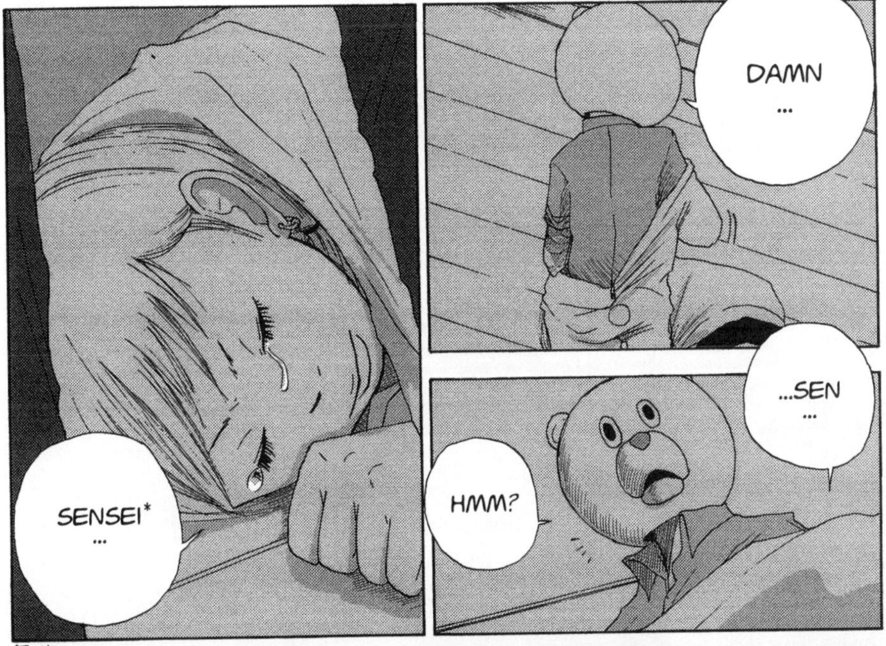
DAMN ...
...SEN ...
HMM?
SENSEI* ...

*Teacher

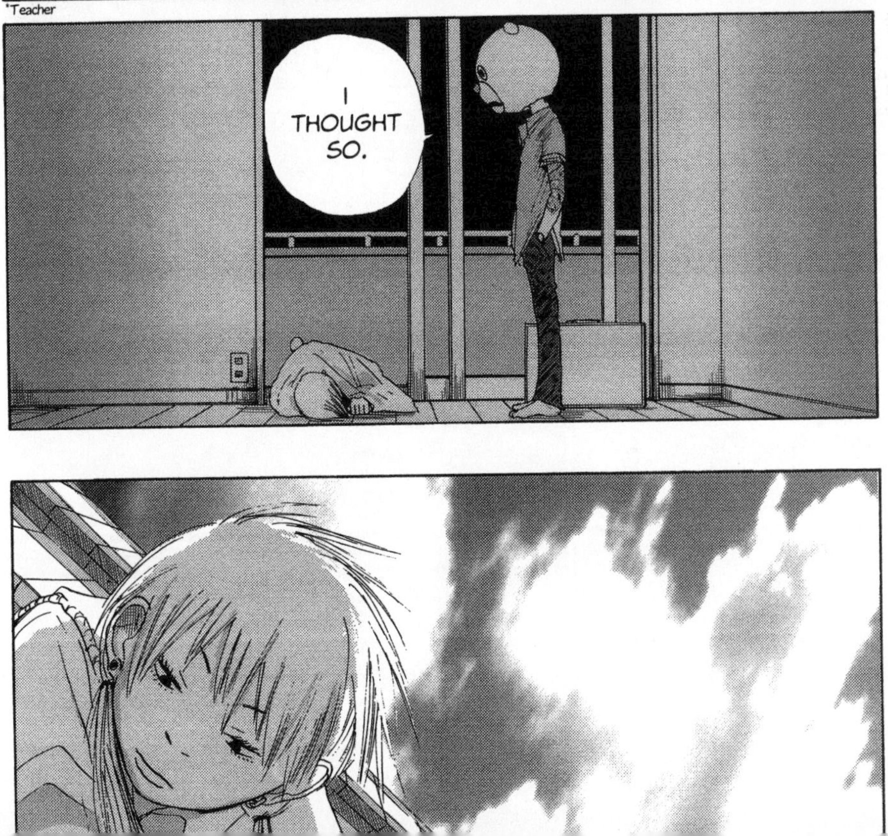
I THOUGHT SO.

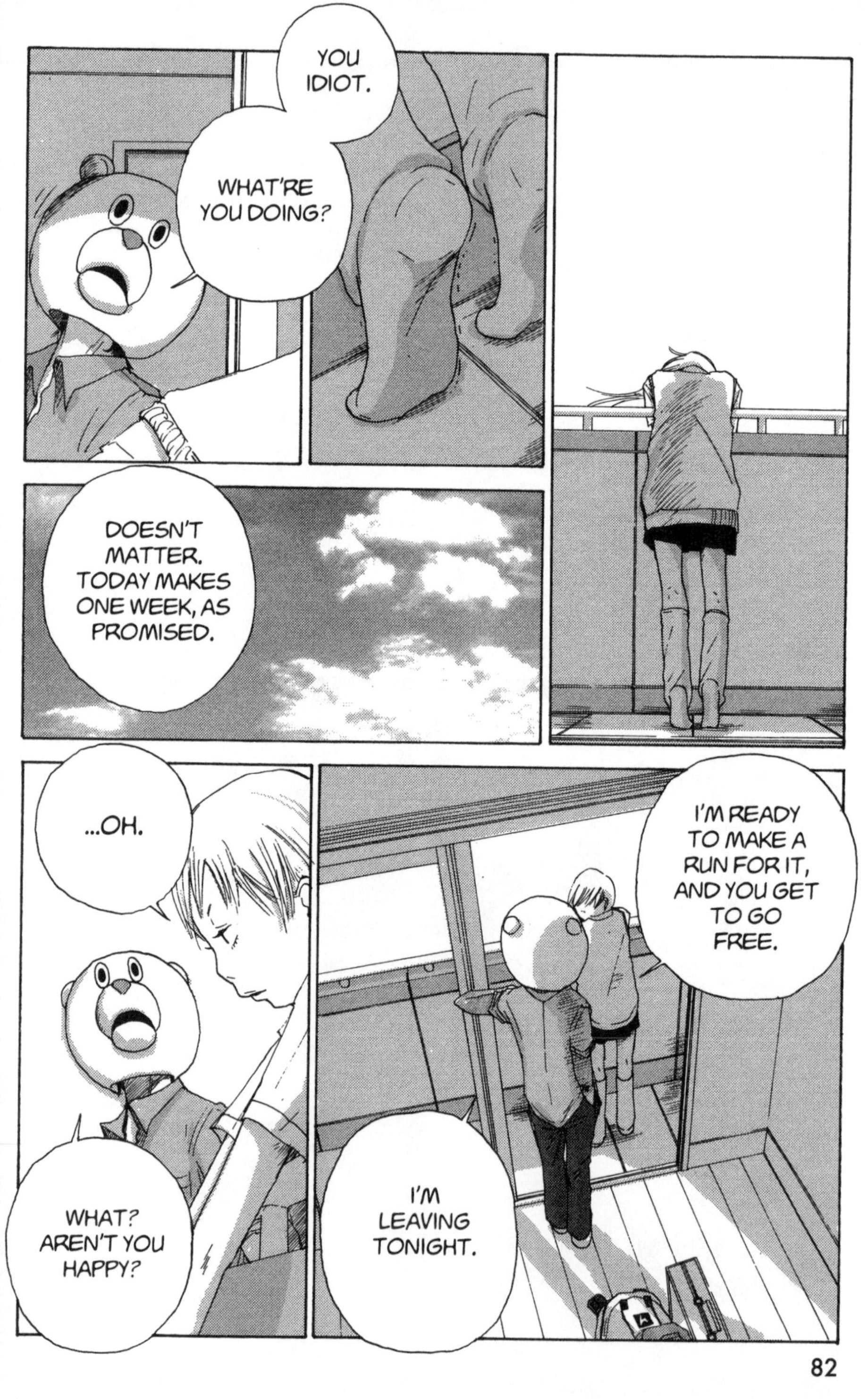
YOU IDIOT.
WHAT'RE YOU DOING?
DOESN'T MATTER. TODAY MAKES ONE WEEK, AS PROMISED.
I'M READY TO MAKE A RUN FOR IT, AND YOU GET TO GO FREE.
I'M LEAVING TONIGHT.
...OH.
WHAT? AREN'T YOU HAPPY?

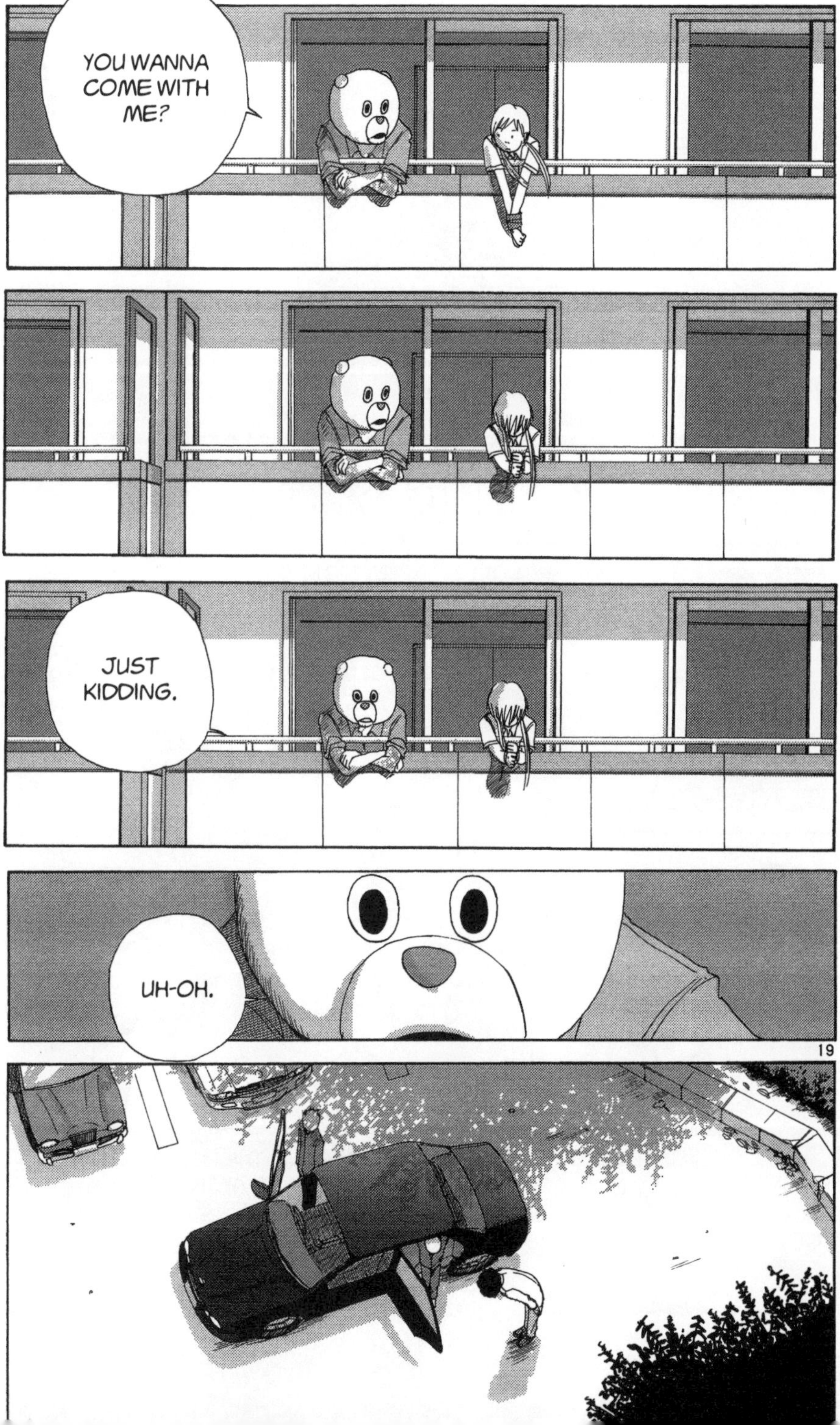
YOU WANNA COME WITH ME?
JUST KIDDING.
UH-OH.

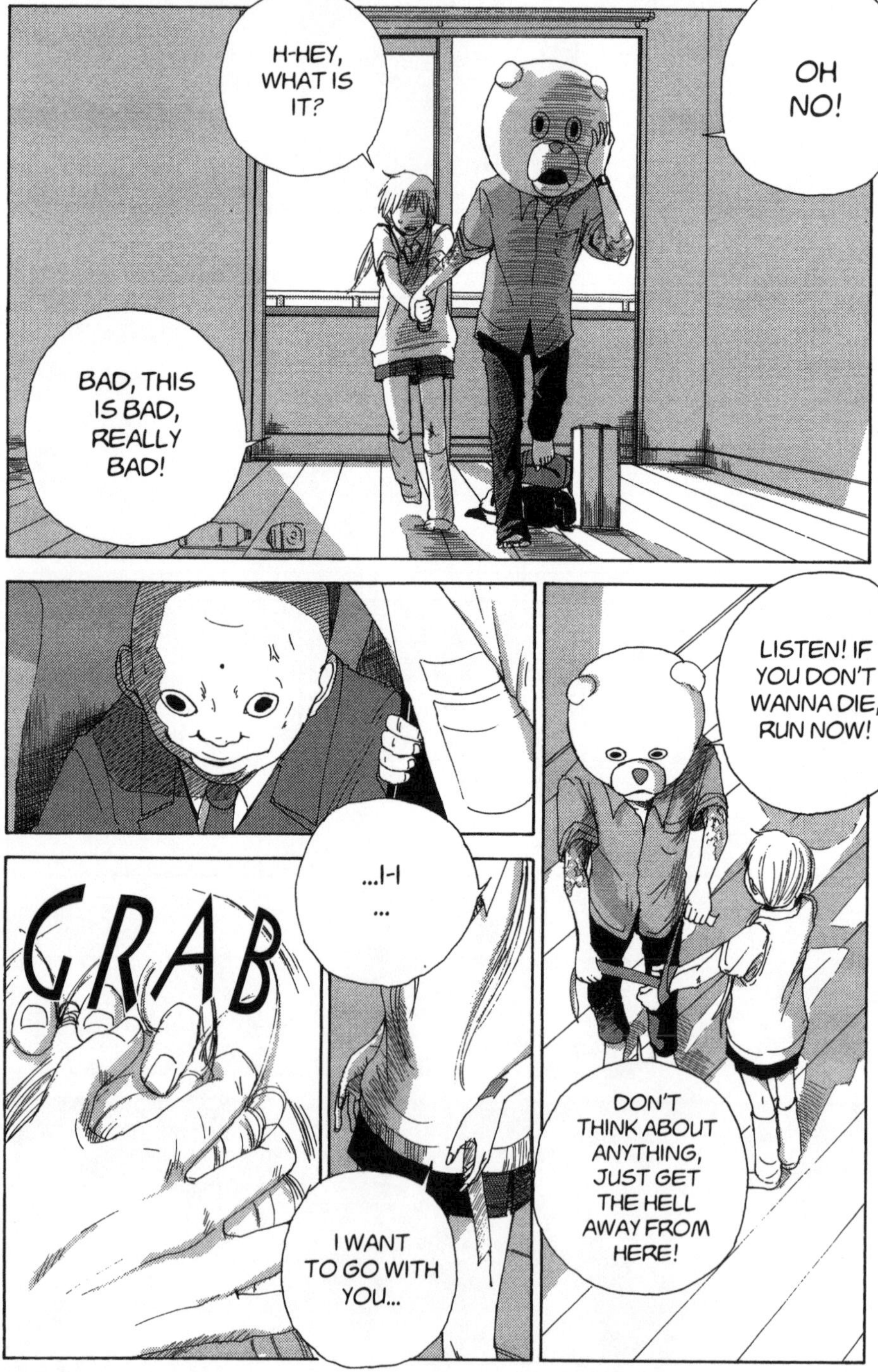
OH NO!
H-HEY, WHAT IS IT?
BAD, THIS IS BAD, REALLY BAD!
LISTEN! IF YOU DON'T WANNA DIE, RUN NOW!
DON'T THINK ABOUT ANYTHING, JUST GET THE HELL AWAY FROM HERE!
...I-I ...
I WANT TO GO WITH YOU...
GRAB

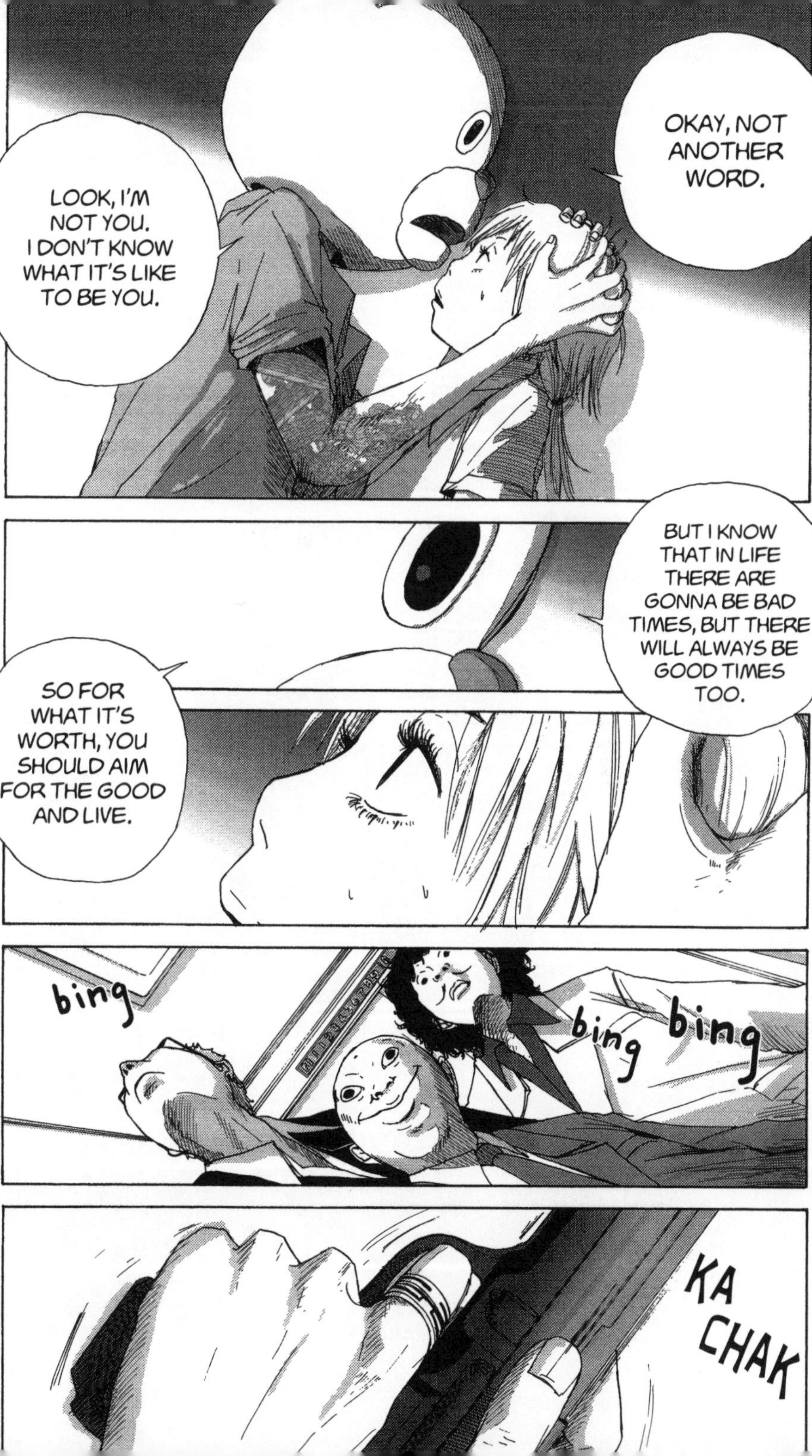
OKAY, NOT ANOTHER WORD.
LOOK, I'M NOT YOU. I DON'T KNOW WHAT IT'S LIKE TO BE YOU.
BUT I KNOW THAT IN LIFE THERE ARE GONNA BE BAD TIMES, BUT THERE WILL ALWAYS BE GOOD TIMES TOO.
SO FOR WHAT IT'S WORTH, YOU SHOULD AIM FOR THE GOOD AND LIVE.
bing
bing
bing
KA CHAK

RUN!

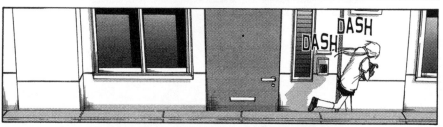

DASH

DASH

SHIT.

I FORGOT TO GIVE HER THE MONEY.

86

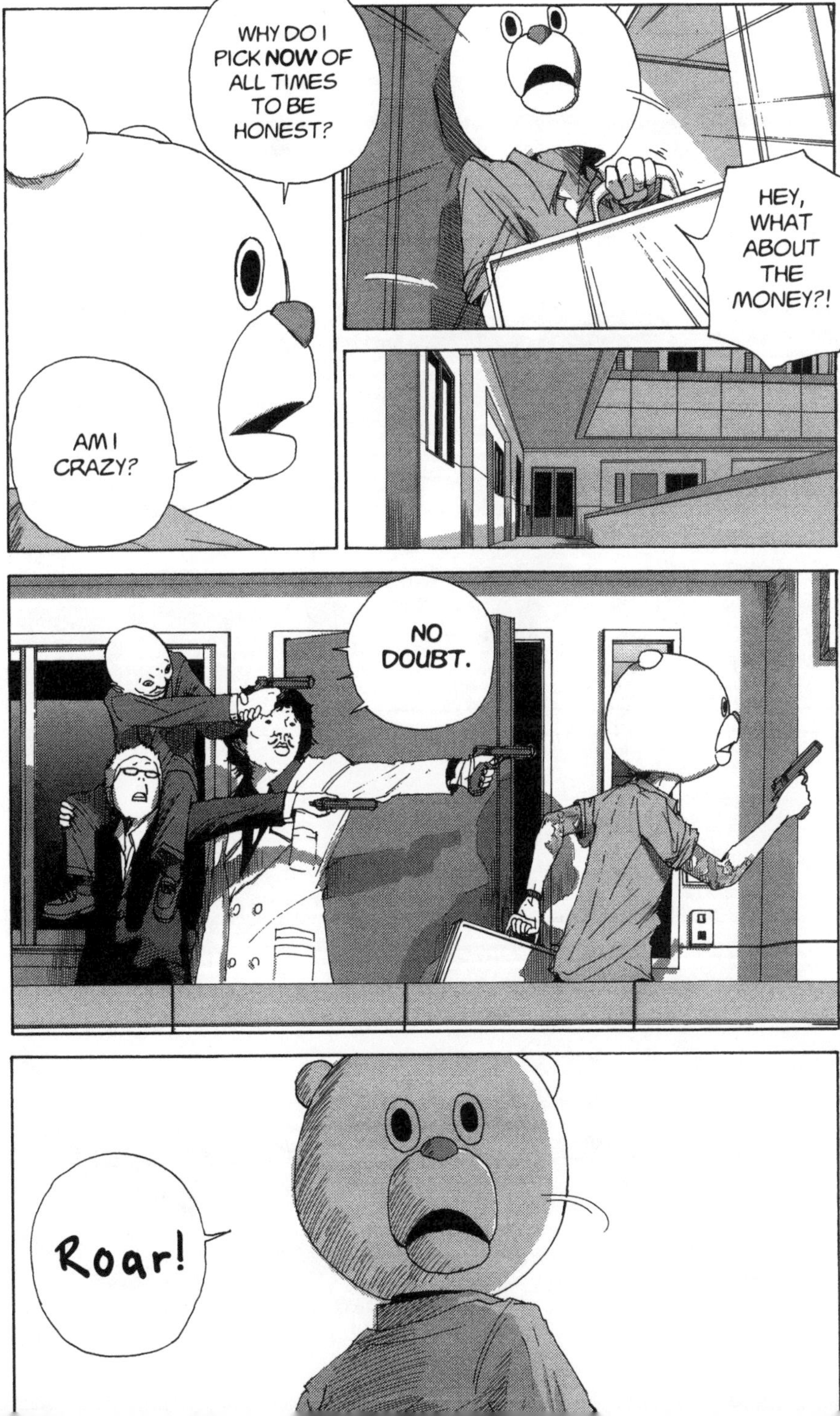
HEY, WHAT ABOUT THE MONEY?!
WHY DO I PICK NOW OF ALL TIMES TO BE HONEST?
AM I CRAZY?
NO DOUBT.
Roar!

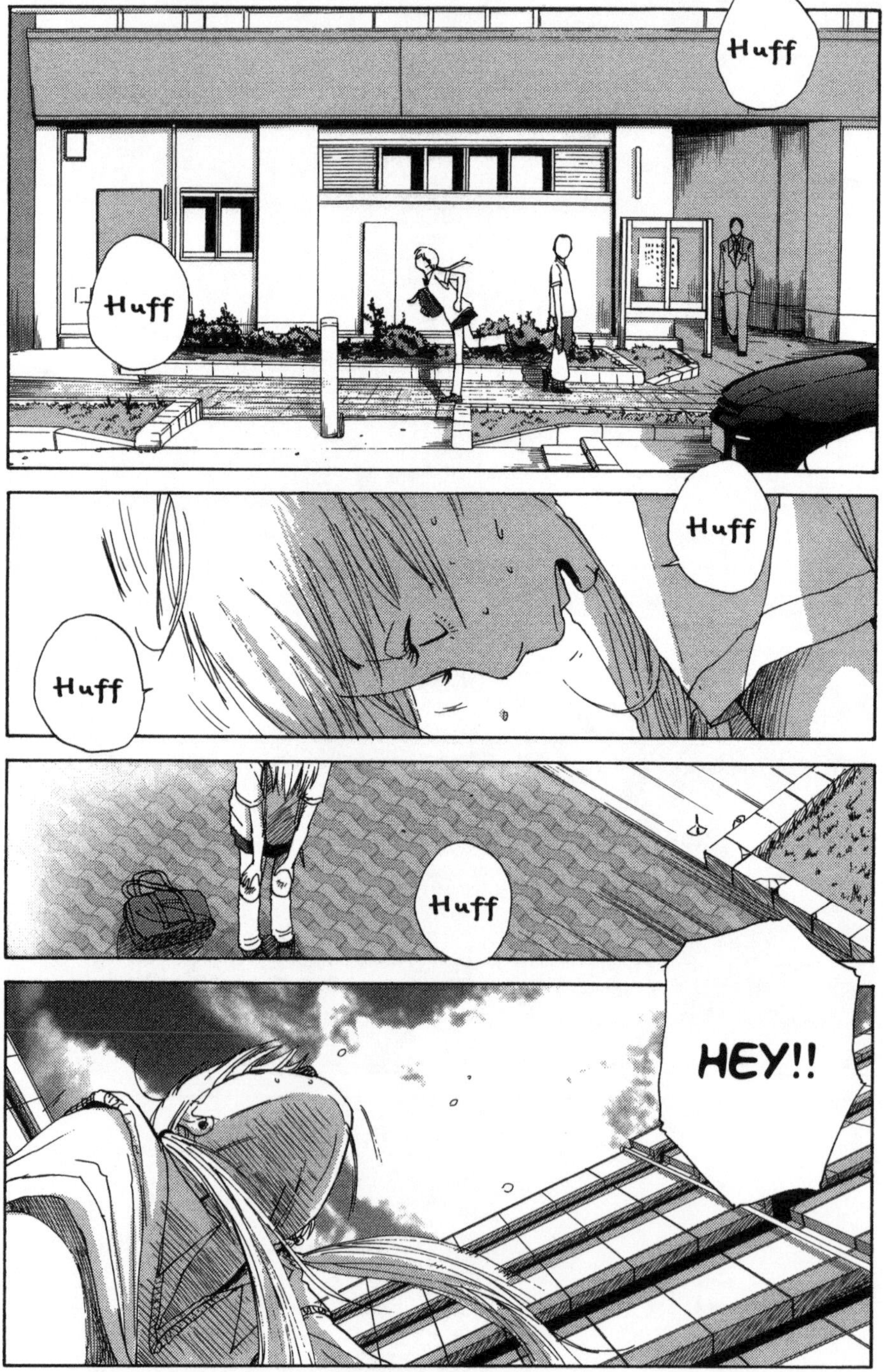
Huff
Huff
Huff
Huff
Huff
HEY!!

IF YOU
WANT IT,
TAKE IT!!

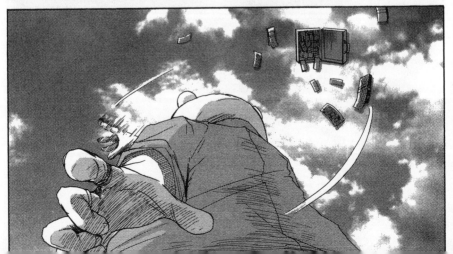

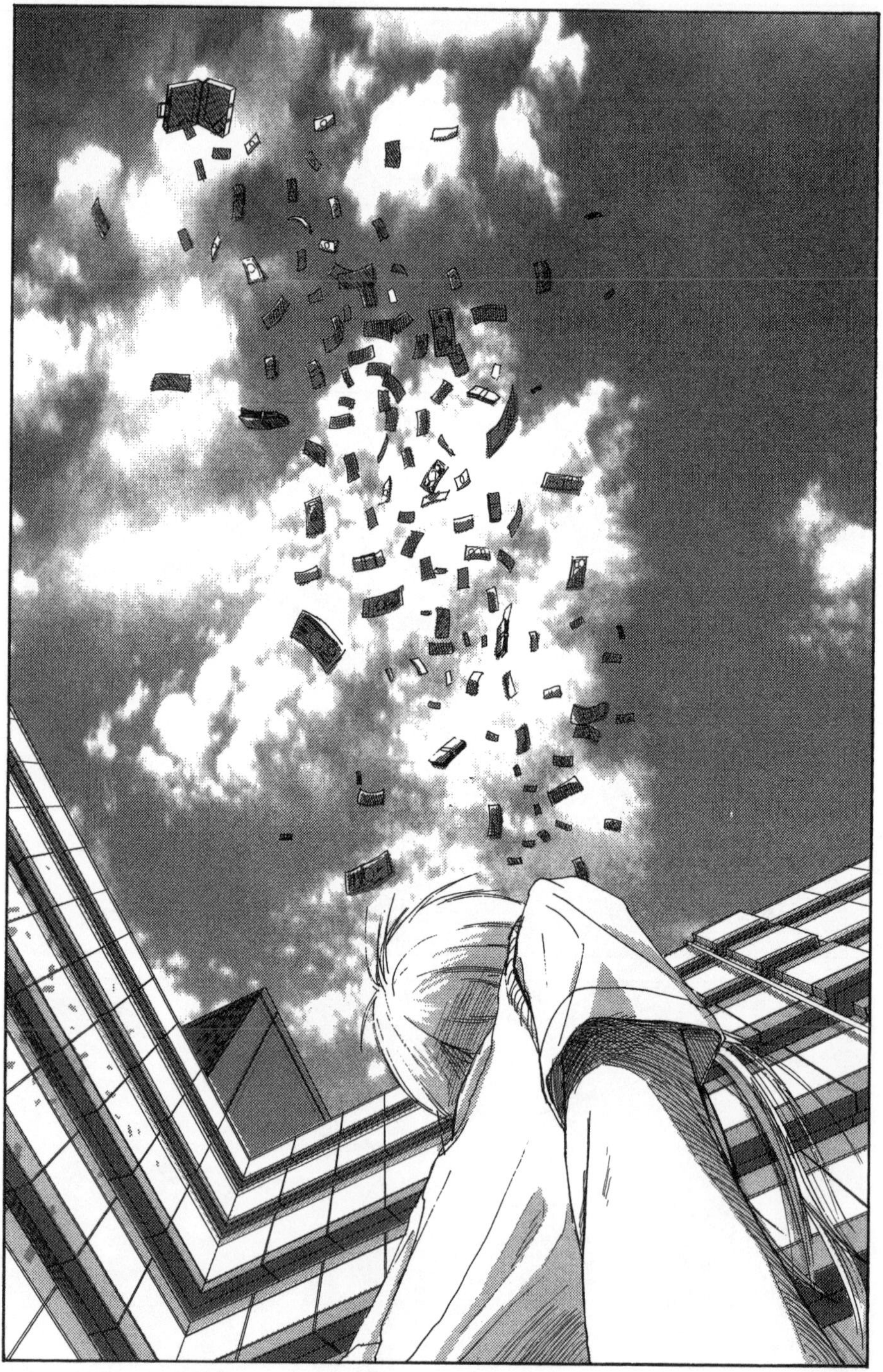

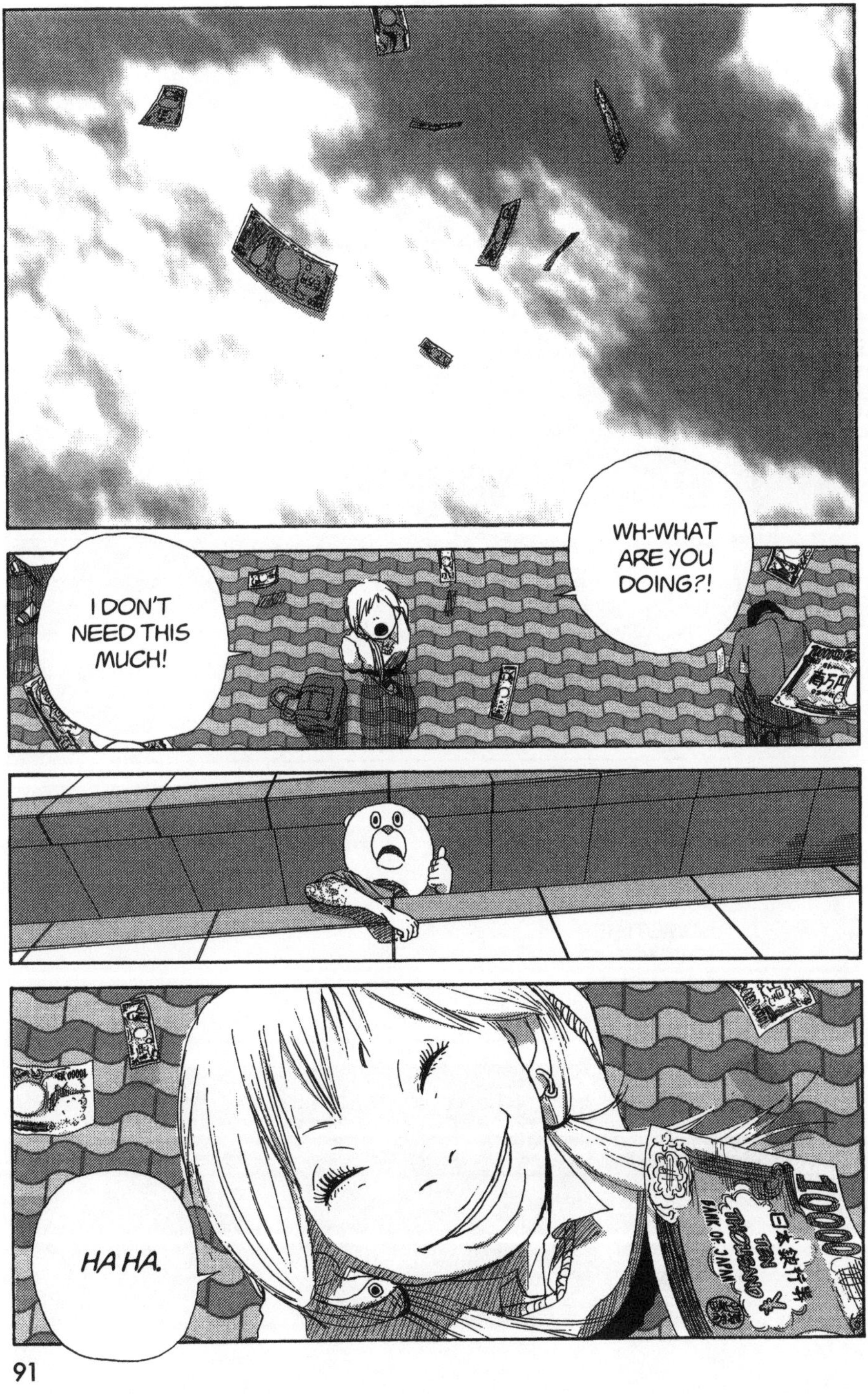
WH-WHAT ARE YOU DOING?!
I DON'T NEED THIS MUCH!
HA HA.
10000
日本銀行券
BANK OF JAPAN

WHAT'S SHE LAUGHING ABOUT?
WELL, I DON'T GET IT...
BUT HANG IN THERE, KID.
SOMETIMES THIS IS THE WAY IT ENDS.

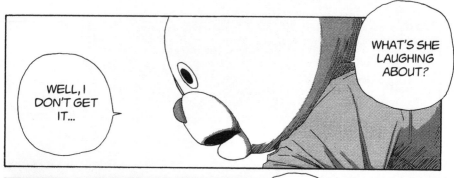

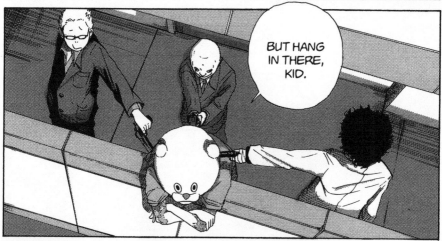

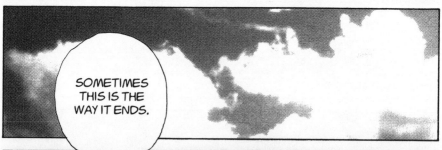

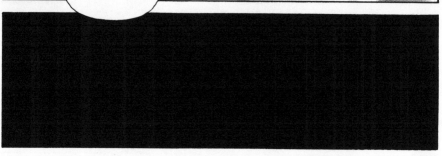

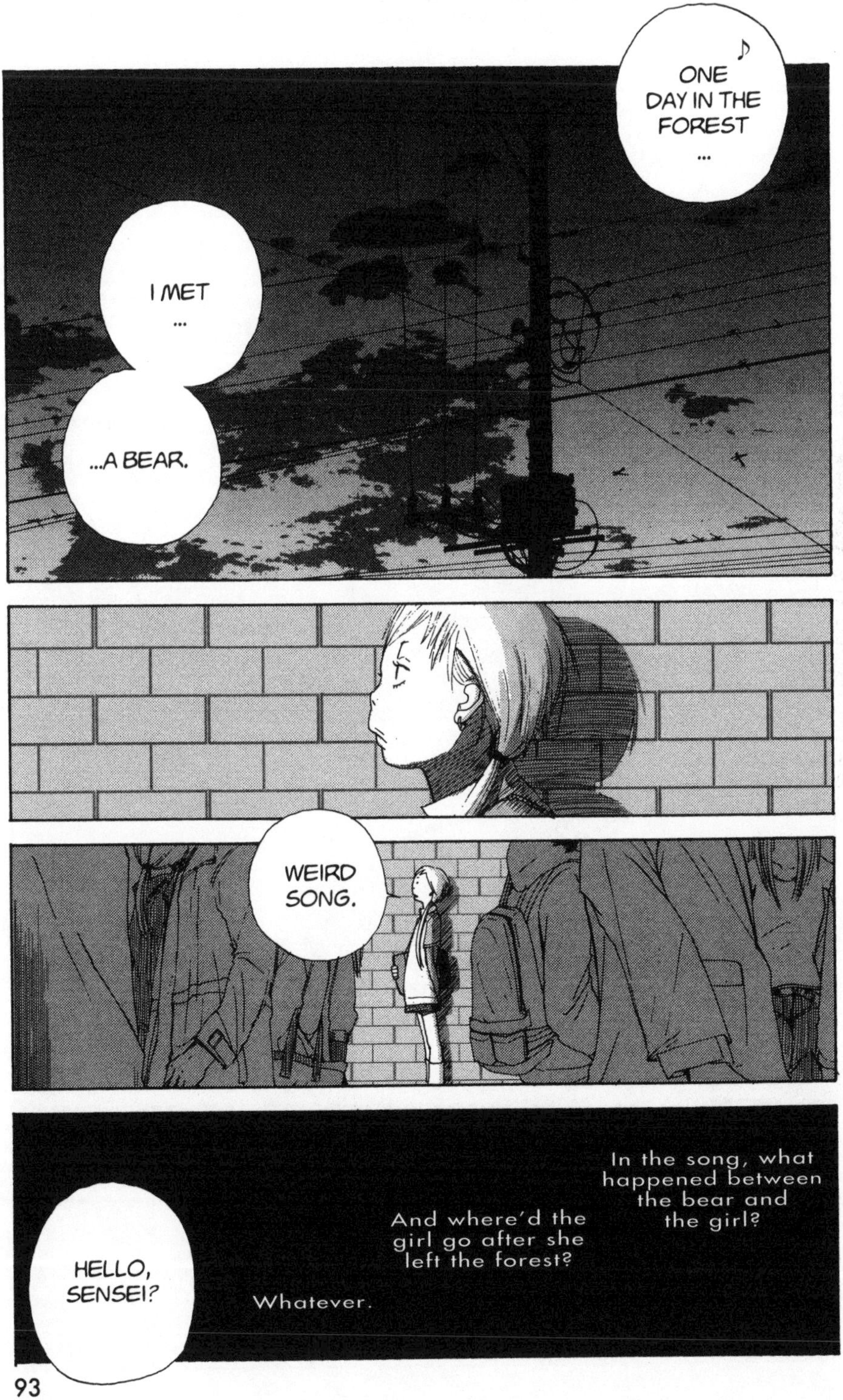
ONE DAY IN THE FOREST ...
I MET ...
...A BEAR.
WEIRD SONG.
In the song, what happened between the bear and the girl?
And where'd the girl go after she left the forest?
Whatever.
HELLO, SENSEI?

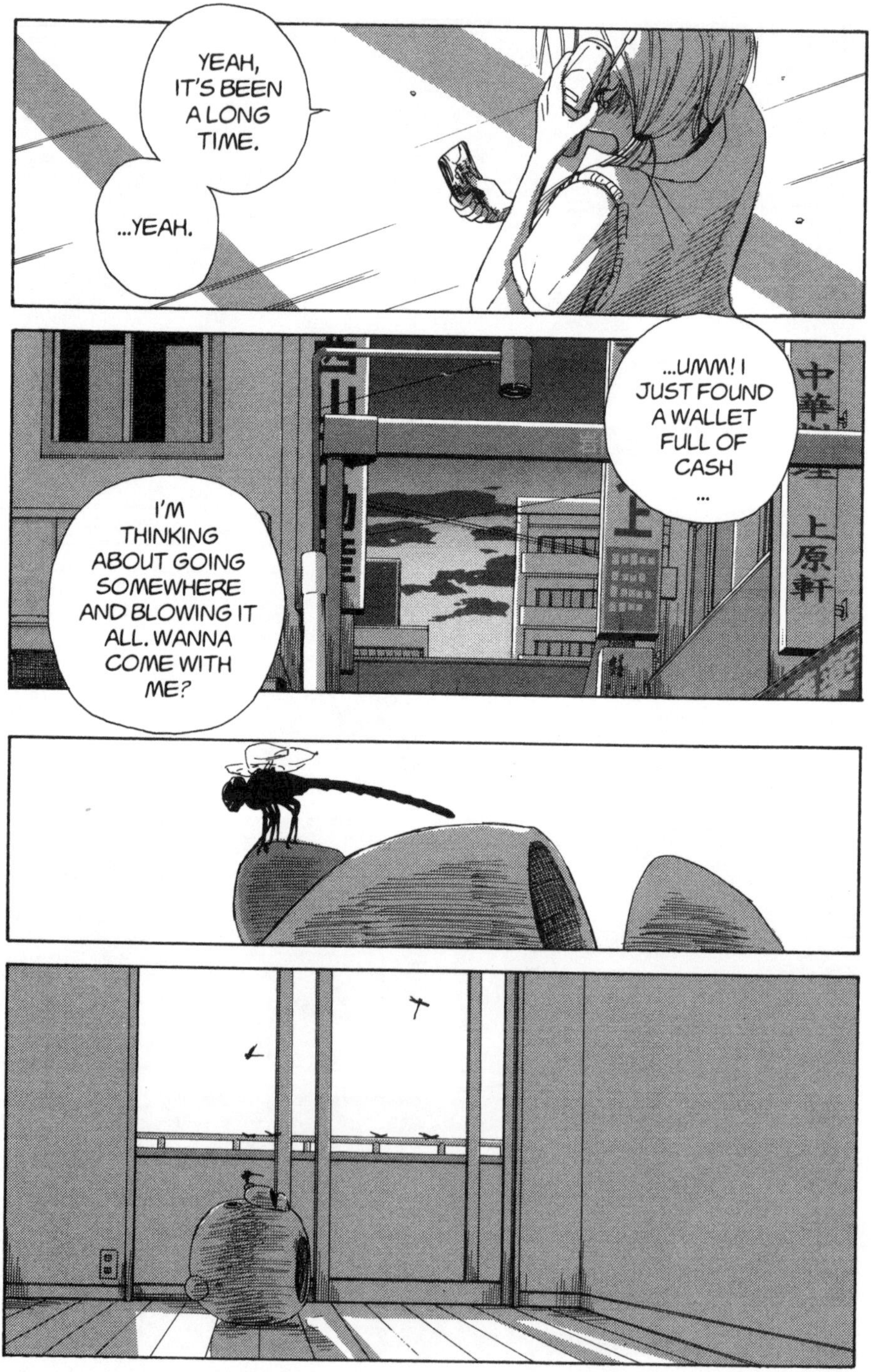
YEAH, IT'S BEEN A LONG TIME.
...YEAH.
...UMM! I JUST FOUND A WALLET FULL OF CASH ...
上原軒
I'M THINKING ABOUT GOING SOMEWHERE AND BLOWING IT ALL. WANNA COME WITH ME?

4th track Wandervogel*

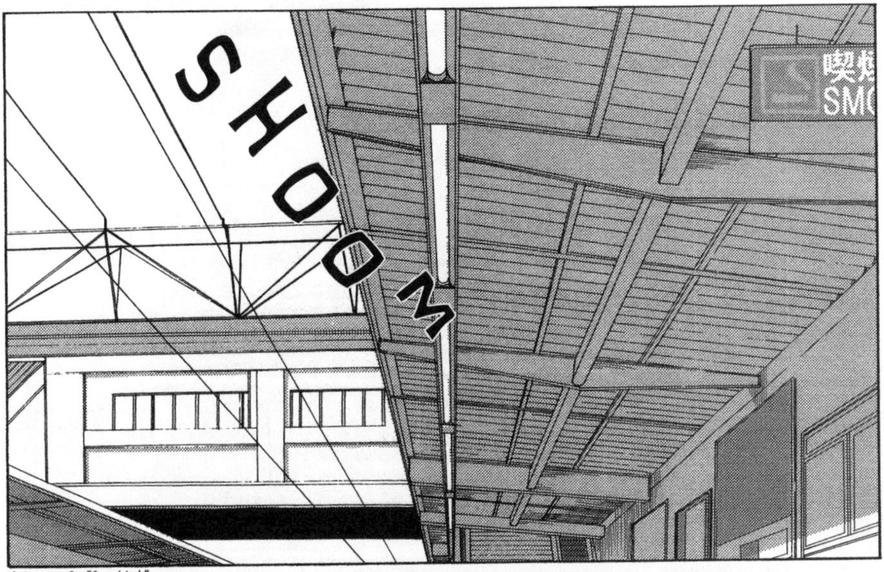
SHOOM

*German for "free bird."

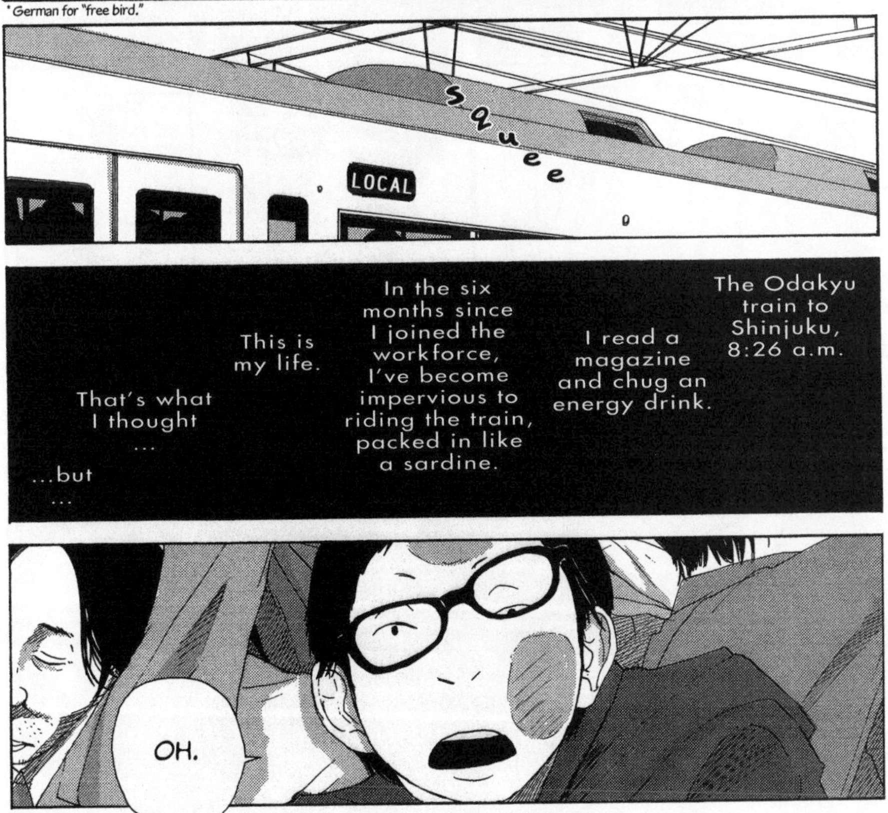
squeee
LOCAL
The Odakyu train to Shinjuku, 8:26 a.m.
I read a magazine and chug an energy drink.
In the six months since I joined the workforce, I've become impervious to riding the train, packed in like a sardine.
This is my life.
That's what I thought...
...but...
OH.

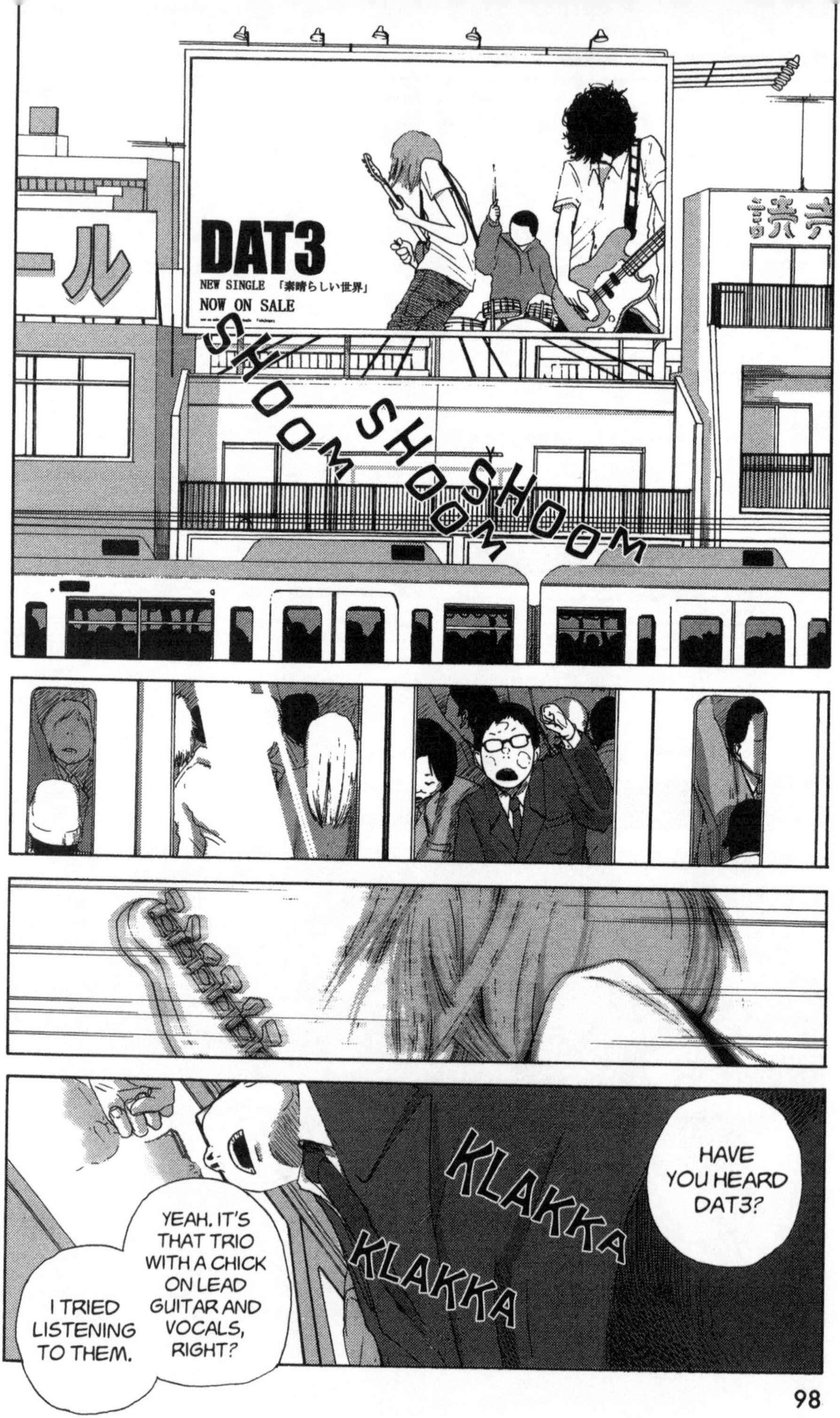
DAT3
NEW SINGLE 「素晴らしい世界」
NOW ON SALE
ール
読売
SHOOM SHOOM
SHOOM SHOOM
HAVE YOU HEARD DAT3?
KLAKKA KLAKKA
YEAH. IT'S THAT TRIO WITH A CHICK ON LEAD GUITAR AND VOCALS, RIGHT?
I TRIED LISTENING TO THEM.

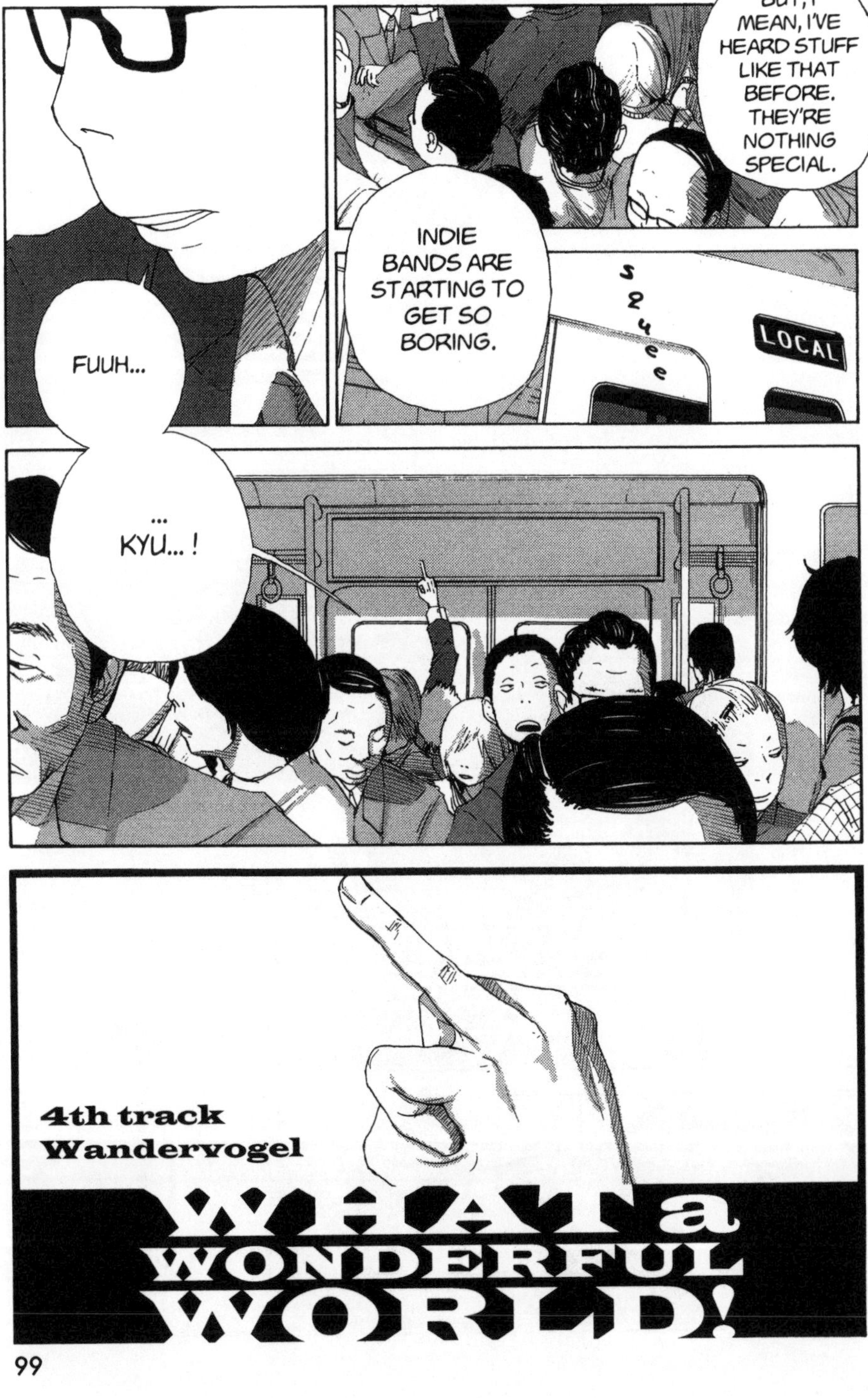
BUT, I MEAN, I'VE HEARD STUFF LIKE THAT BEFORE. THEY'RE NOTHING SPECIAL.
INDIE BANDS ARE STARTING TO GET SO BORING.
squee
LOCAL
FUUH...
... KYU... !
4th track
Wandervogel
WHAT a WONDERFUL WORLD!

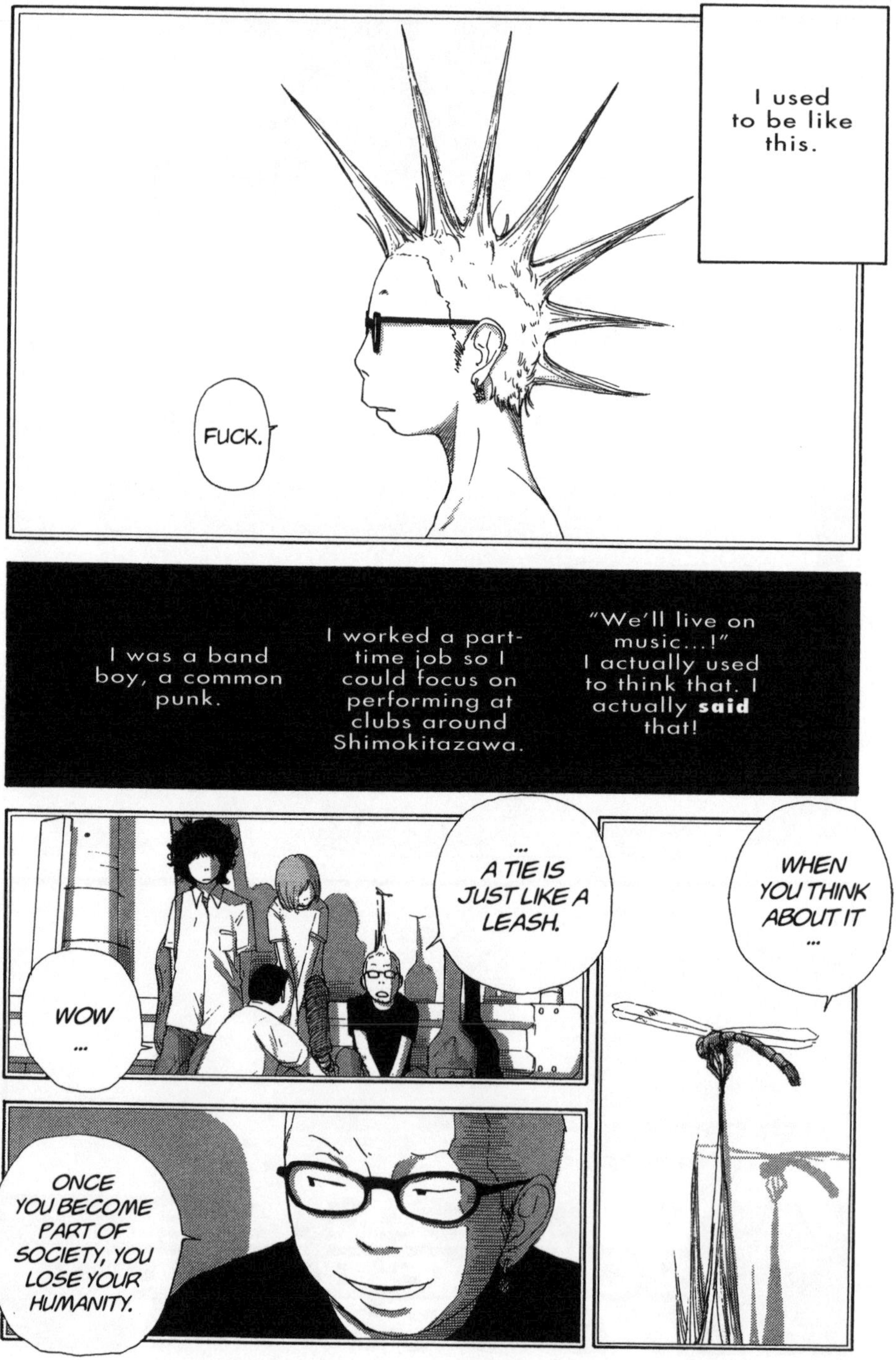
I used to be like this.
FUCK.
"We'll live on music...!" I actually used to think that. I actually **said** that!
I worked a part-time job so I could focus on performing at clubs around Shimokitazawa.
I was a band boy, a common punk.
WHEN YOU THINK ABOUT IT ...
... A TIE IS JUST LIKE A LEASH.
WOW ...
ONCE YOU BECOME PART OF SOCIETY, YOU LOSE YOUR HUMANITY.

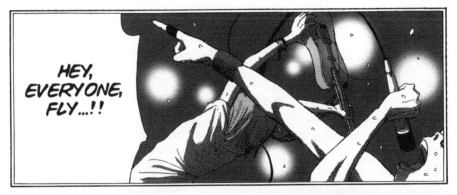

HEY,
EVERYONE,
FLY...!!

I chose reality over my dream.

It wasn't because I didn't have what it took to be a musician or whatever... It's that my parents' connections landed me a job.

But I got over it. Quickly.

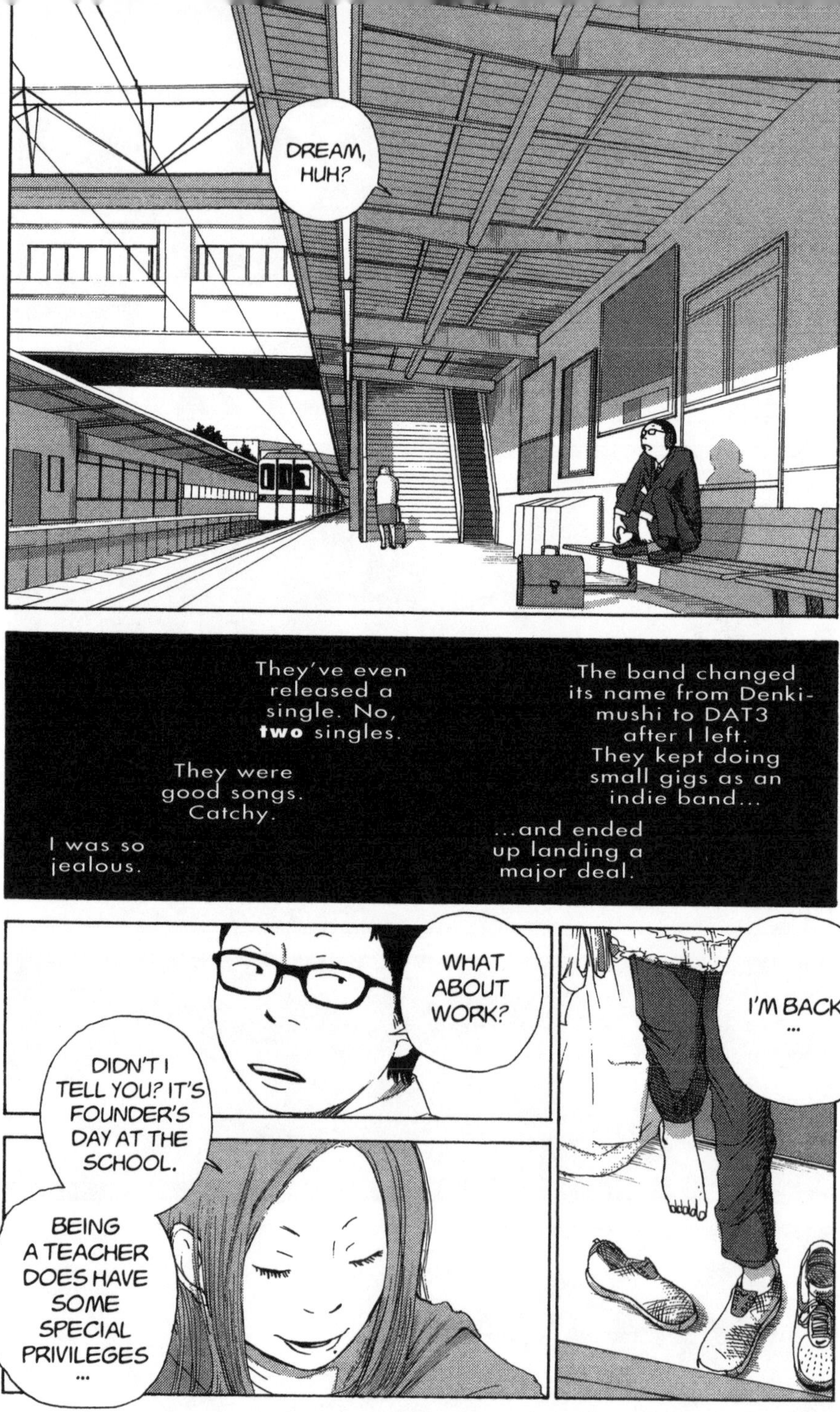
DREAM, HUH?
The band changed its name from Denki-mushi to DAT3 after I left. They kept doing small gigs as an indie band...
...and ended up landing a major deal.
They've even released a single. No, **two** singles.
They were good songs. Catchy.
I was so jealous.
I'M BACK ...
WHAT ABOUT WORK?
DIDN'T I TELL YOU? IT'S FOUNDER'S DAY AT THE SCHOOL.
BEING A TEACHER DOES HAVE SOME SPECIAL PRIVILEGES ...

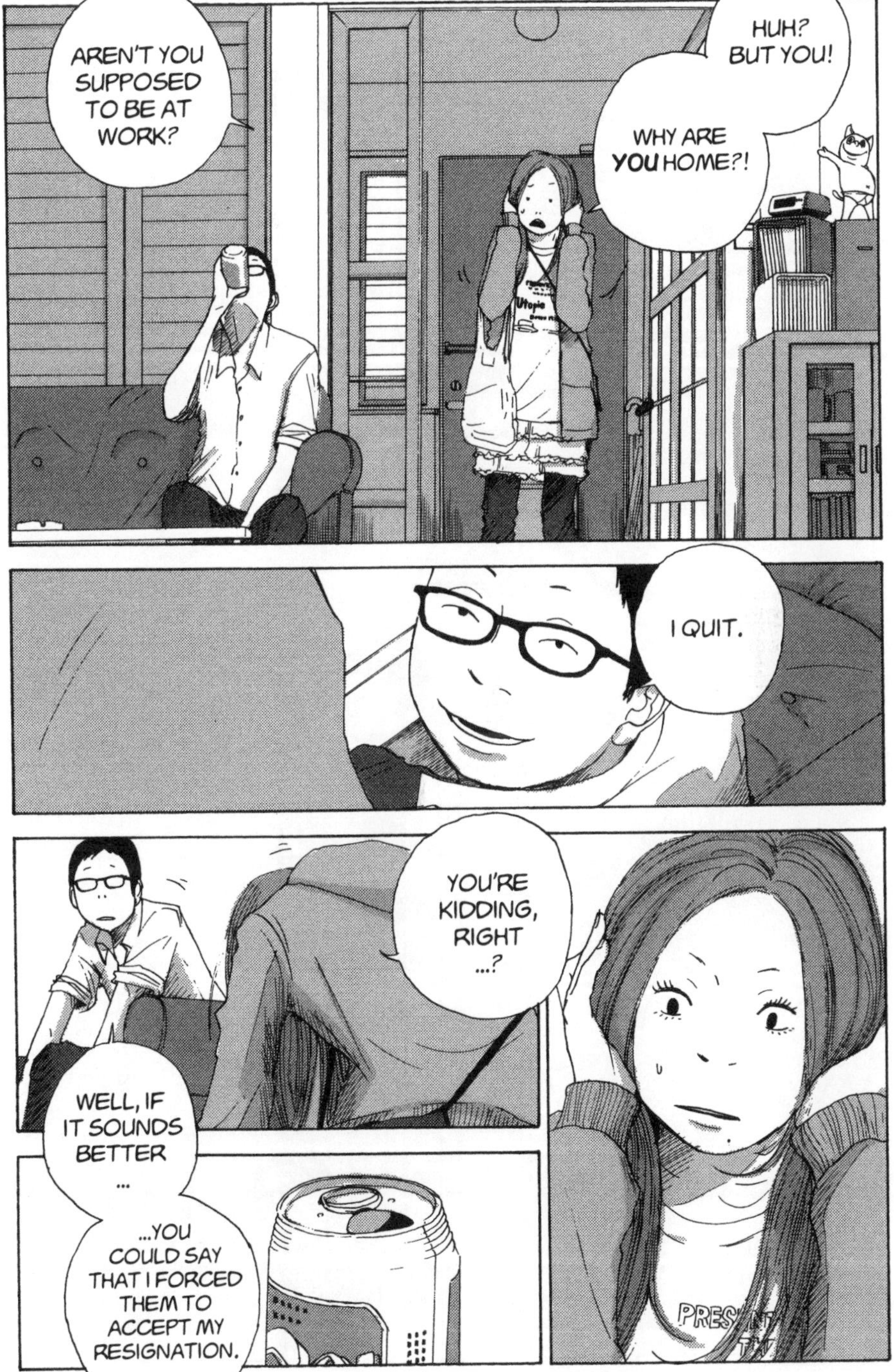
HUH? BUT YOU!
WHY ARE YOU HOME?!
AREN'T YOU SUPPOSED TO BE AT WORK?
I QUIT.
YOU'RE KIDDING, RIGHT ...?
WELL, IF IT SOUNDS BETTER ...
...YOU COULD SAY THAT I FORCED THEM TO ACCEPT MY RESIGNATION.

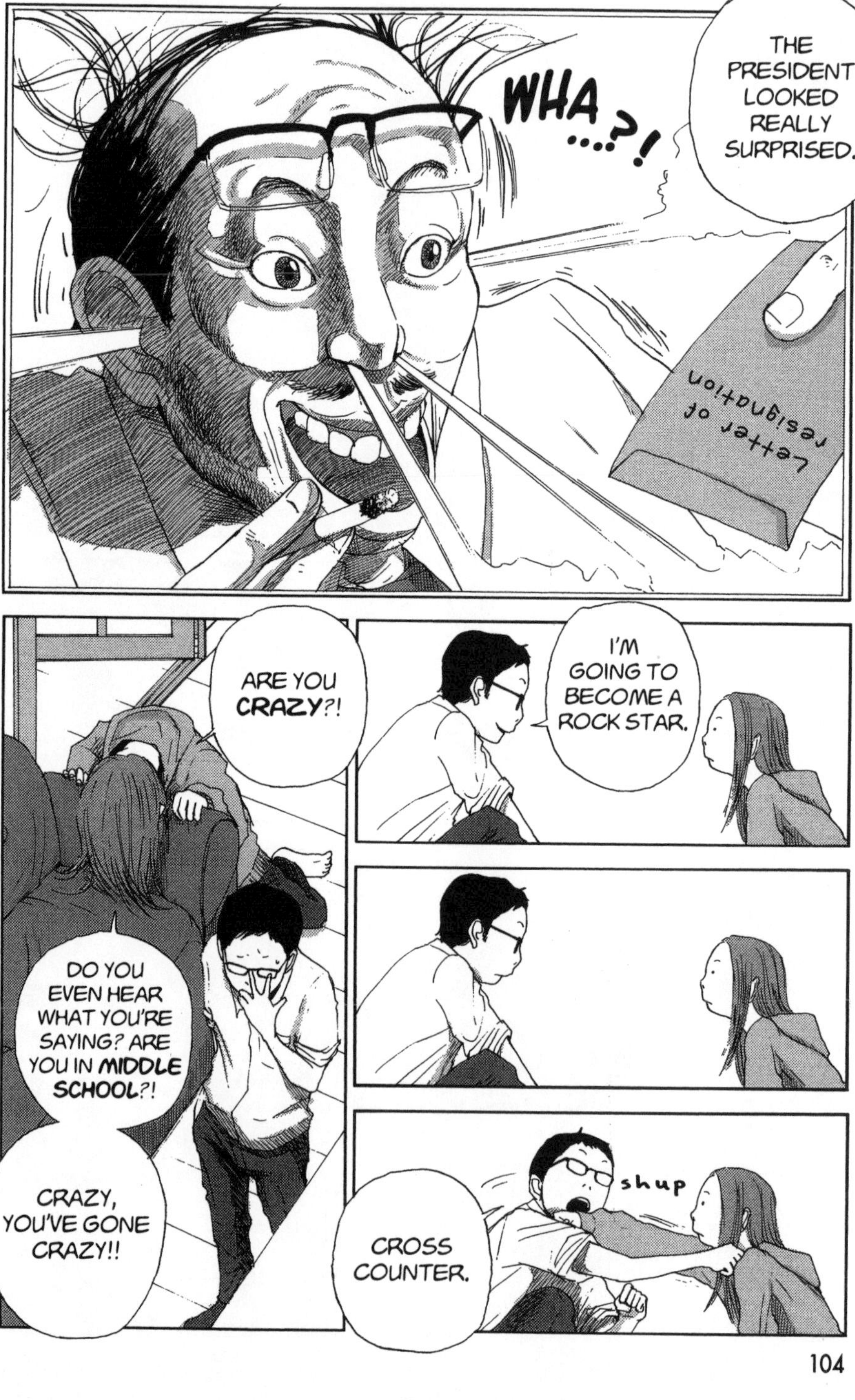
THE PRESIDENT LOOKED REALLY SURPRISED.
WHA...?!
Letter of resignation
I'M GOING TO BECOME A ROCK STAR.
shup
CROSS COUNTER.
ARE YOU **CRAZY**?!
DO YOU EVEN HEAR WHAT YOU'RE SAYING? ARE YOU IN **MIDDLE SCHOOL**?!
CRAZY, YOU'VE GONE CRAZY!!

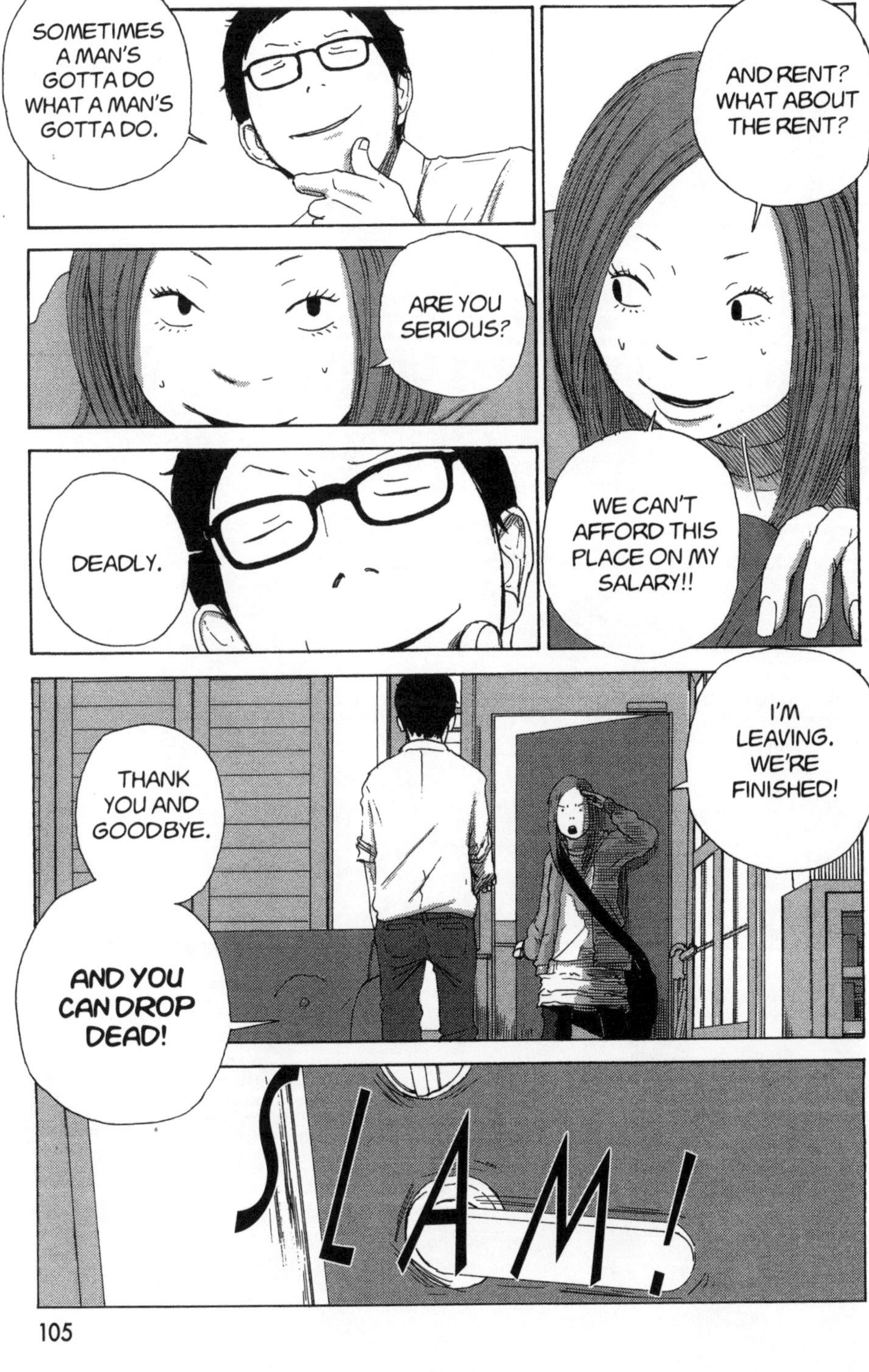
SOMETIMES A MAN'S GOTTA DO WHAT A MAN'S GOTTA DO.
ARE YOU SERIOUS?
DEADLY.
AND RENT? WHAT ABOUT THE RENT?
WE CAN'T AFFORD THIS PLACE ON MY SALARY!!
I'M LEAVING. WE'RE FINISHED!
THANK YOU AND GOODBYE.
AND YOU CAN DROP DEAD!
SLAM!

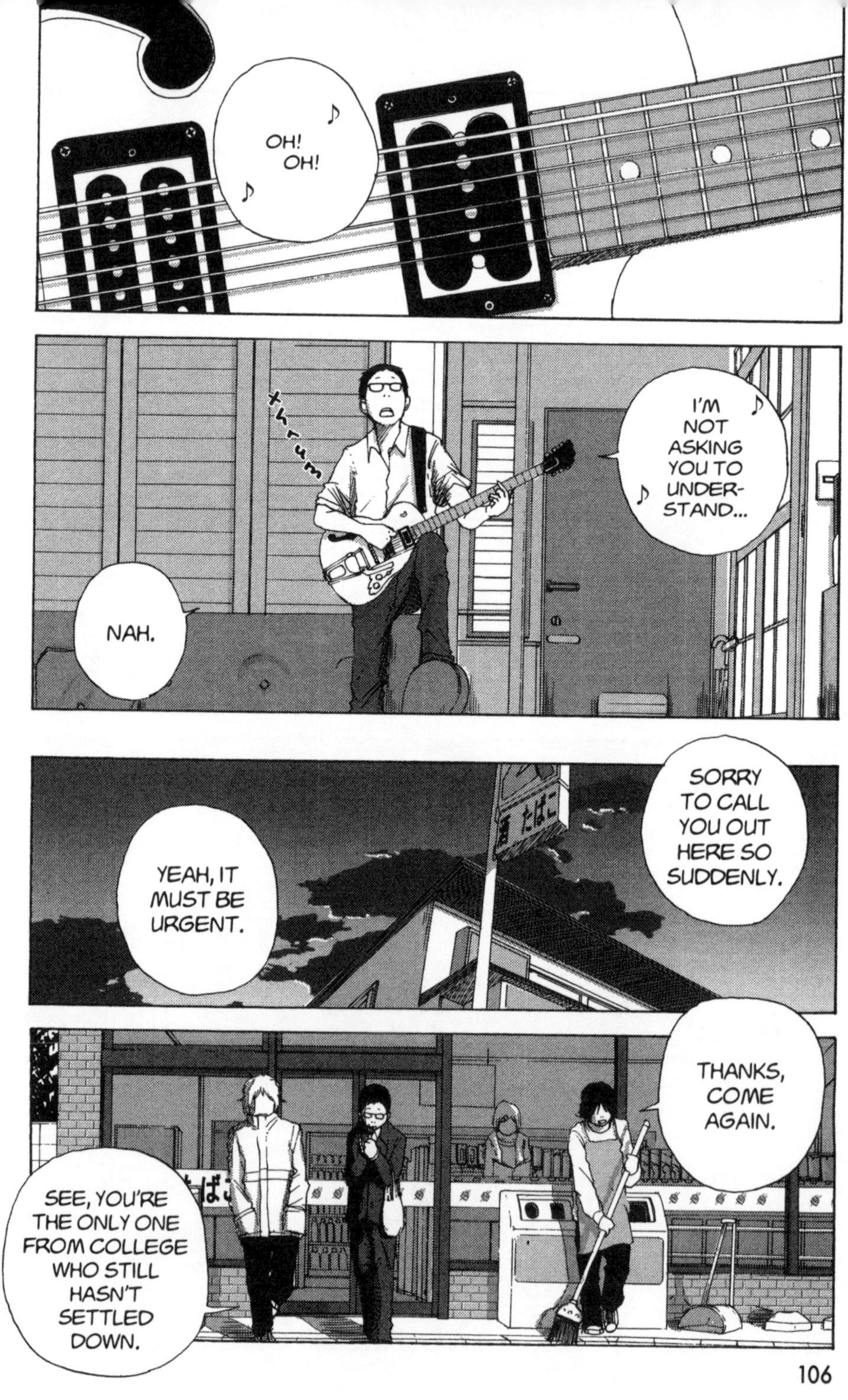
OH! OH!
strum
I'M NOT ASKING YOU TO UNDER-STAND...
NAH.
SORRY TO CALL YOU OUT HERE SO SUDDENLY.
酒 たばこ
YEAH, IT MUST BE URGENT.
THANKS, COME AGAIN.
SEE, YOU'RE THE ONLY ONE FROM COLLEGE WHO STILL HASN'T SETTLED DOWN.

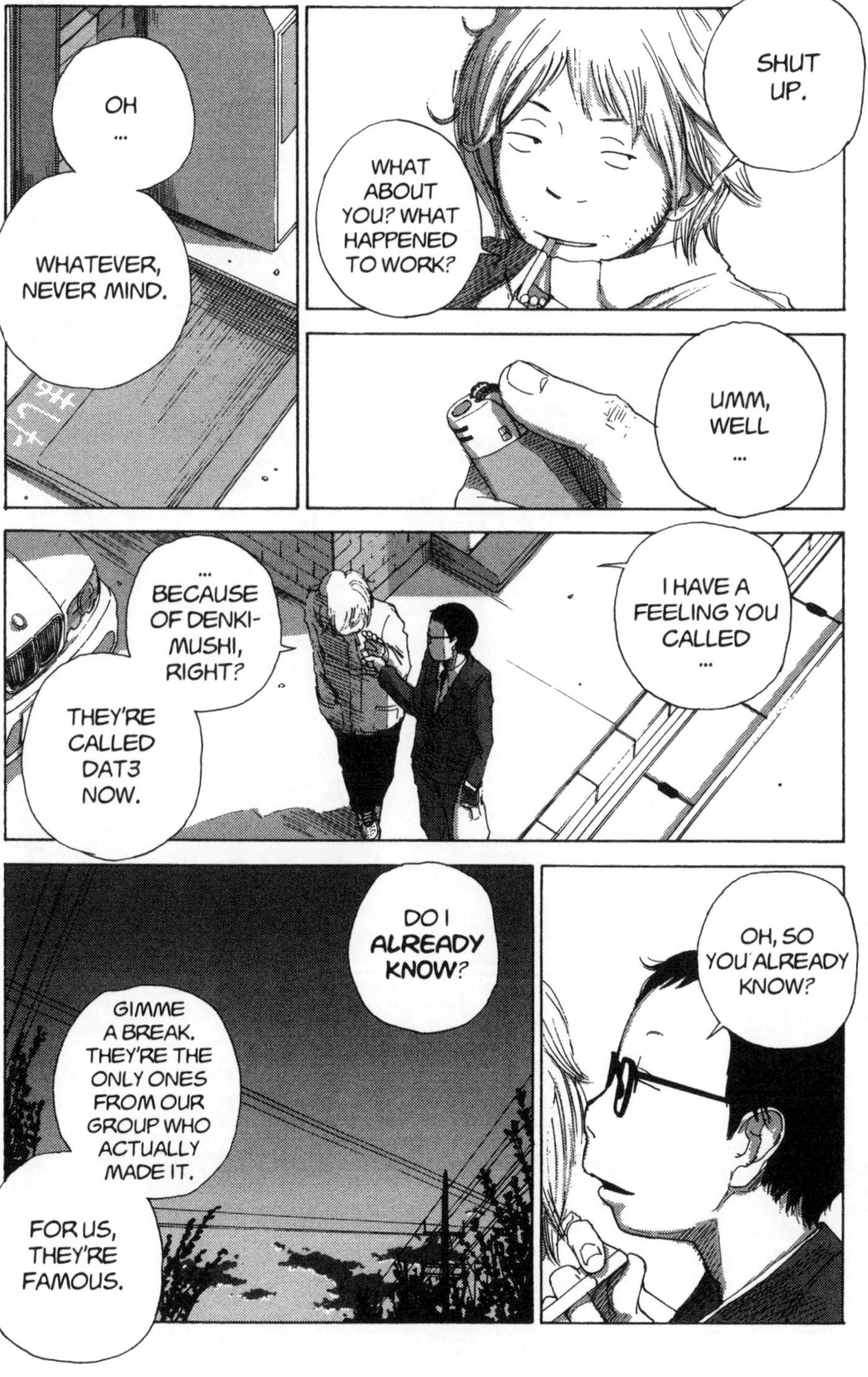
SHUT UP.
WHAT ABOUT YOU? WHAT HAPPENED TO WORK?
UMM, WELL ...
OH ...
WHATEVER, NEVER MIND.
I HAVE A FEELING YOU CALLED ...
... BECAUSE OF DENKI-MUSHI, RIGHT?
THEY'RE CALLED DAT3 NOW.
OH, SO YOU ALREADY KNOW?
DO I **ALREADY KNOW**?
GIMME A BREAK. THEY'RE THE ONLY ONES FROM OUR GROUP WHO ACTUALLY MADE IT.
FOR US, THEY'RE FAMOUS.

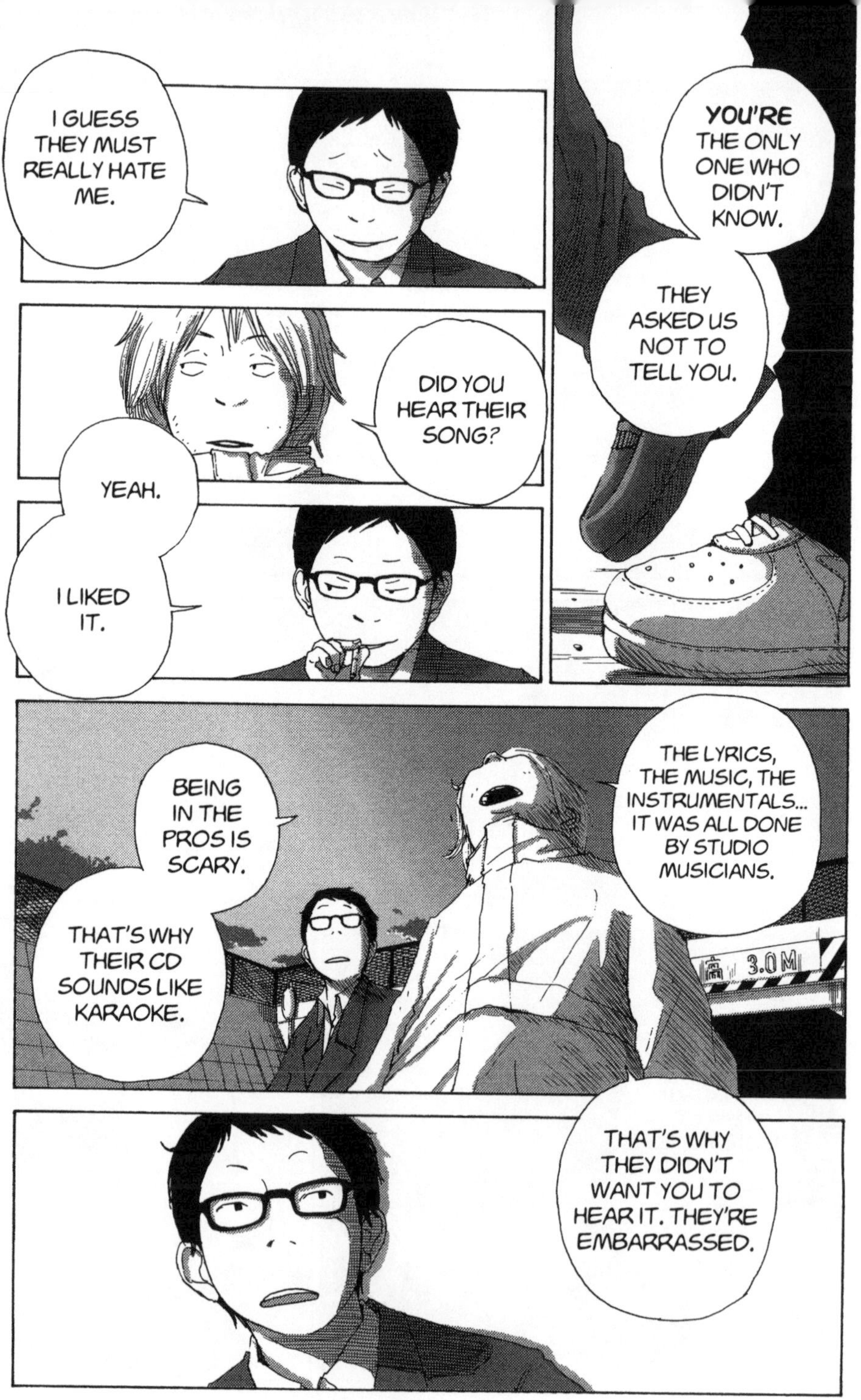
YOU'RE THE ONLY ONE WHO DIDN'T KNOW.
THEY ASKED US NOT TO TELL YOU.
I GUESS THEY MUST REALLY HATE ME.
DID YOU HEAR THEIR SONG?
YEAH.
I LIKED IT.
THE LYRICS, THE MUSIC, THE INSTRUMENTALS... IT WAS ALL DONE BY STUDIO MUSICIANS.
BEING IN THE PROS IS SCARY.
THAT'S WHY THEIR CD SOUNDS LIKE KARAOKE.
THAT'S WHY THEY DIDN'T WANT YOU TO HEAR IT. THEY'RE EMBARRASSED.

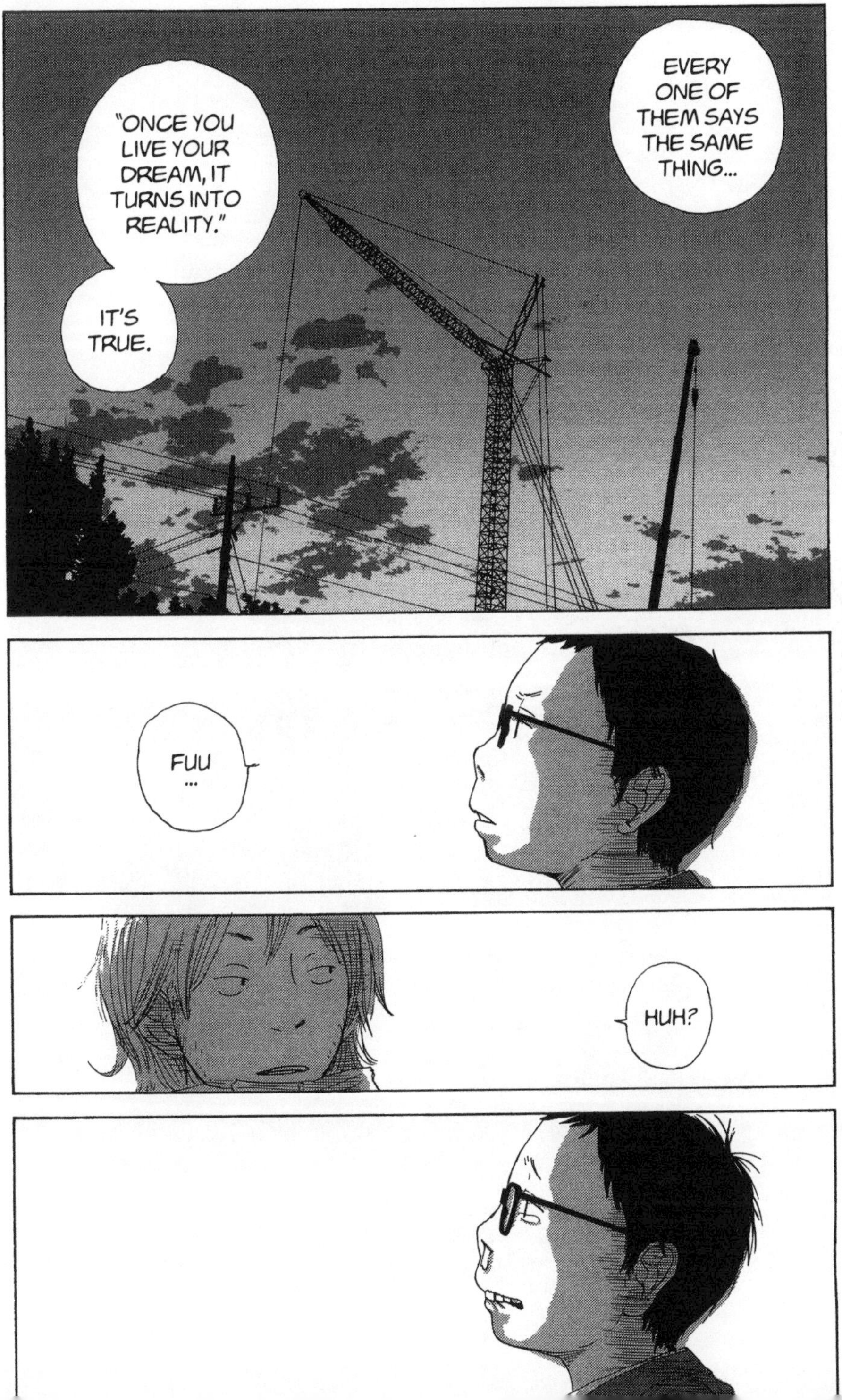
EVERY ONE OF THEM SAYS THE SAME THING...
"ONCE YOU LIVE YOUR DREAM, IT TURNS INTO REALITY."
IT'S TRUE.
FUU ...
HUH?

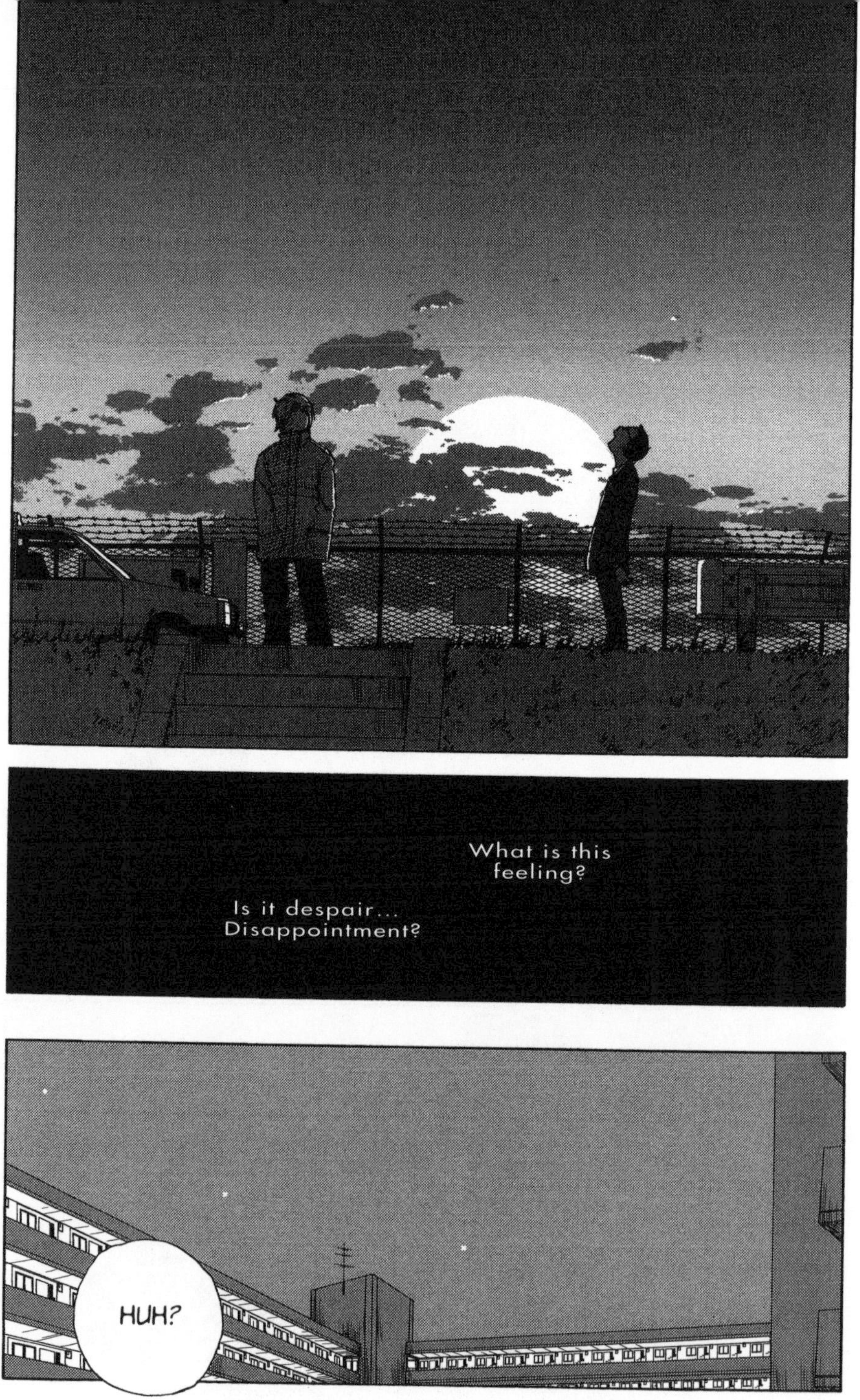
What is this feeling?
Is it despair... Disappointment?
HUH?

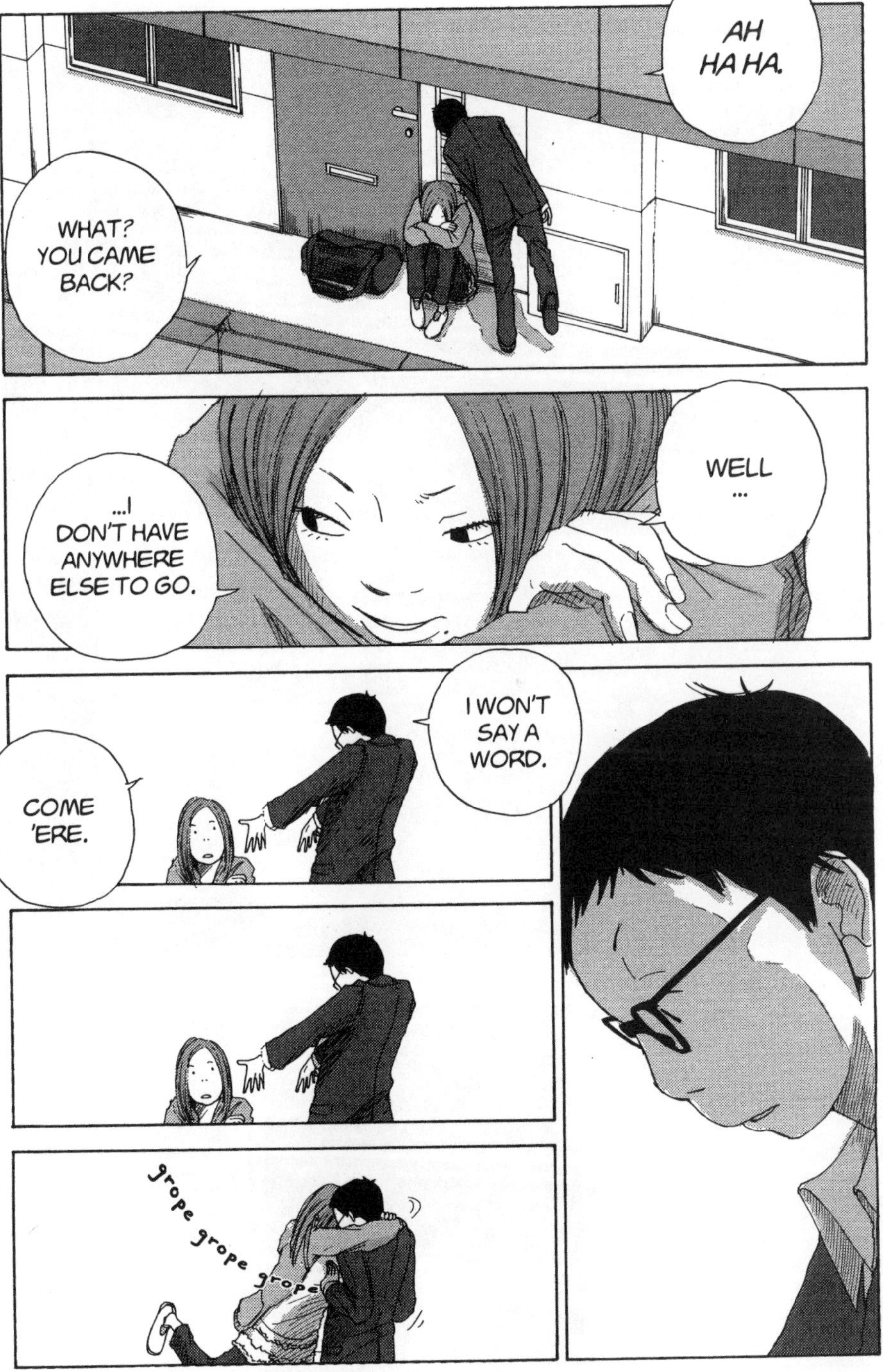
AH HA HA.
WHAT? YOU CAME BACK?
WELL ...
...I DON'T HAVE ANYWHERE ELSE TO GO.
I WON'T SAY A WORD.
COME 'ERE.
grope grope grope

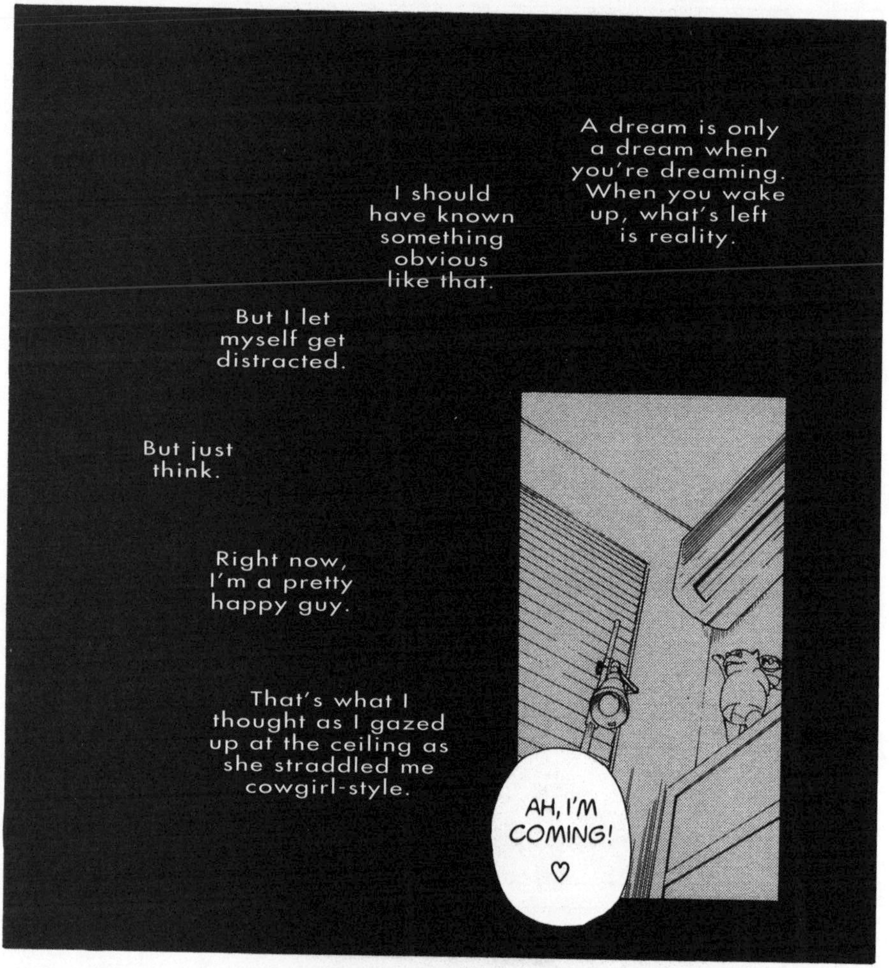
A dream is only a dream when you're dreaming. When you wake up, what's left is reality.
I should have known something obvious like that.
But I let myself get distracted.
But just think.
Right now, I'm a pretty happy guy.
That's what I thought as I gazed up at the ceiling as she straddled me cowgirl-style.
AH, I'M COMING! ♡

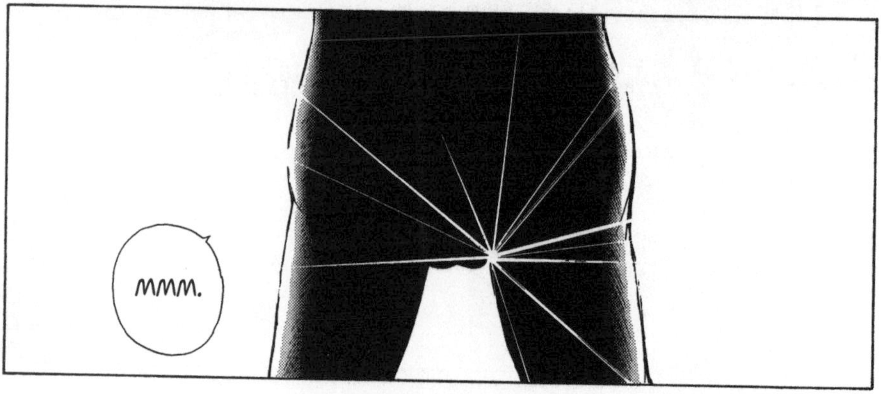
MMM.

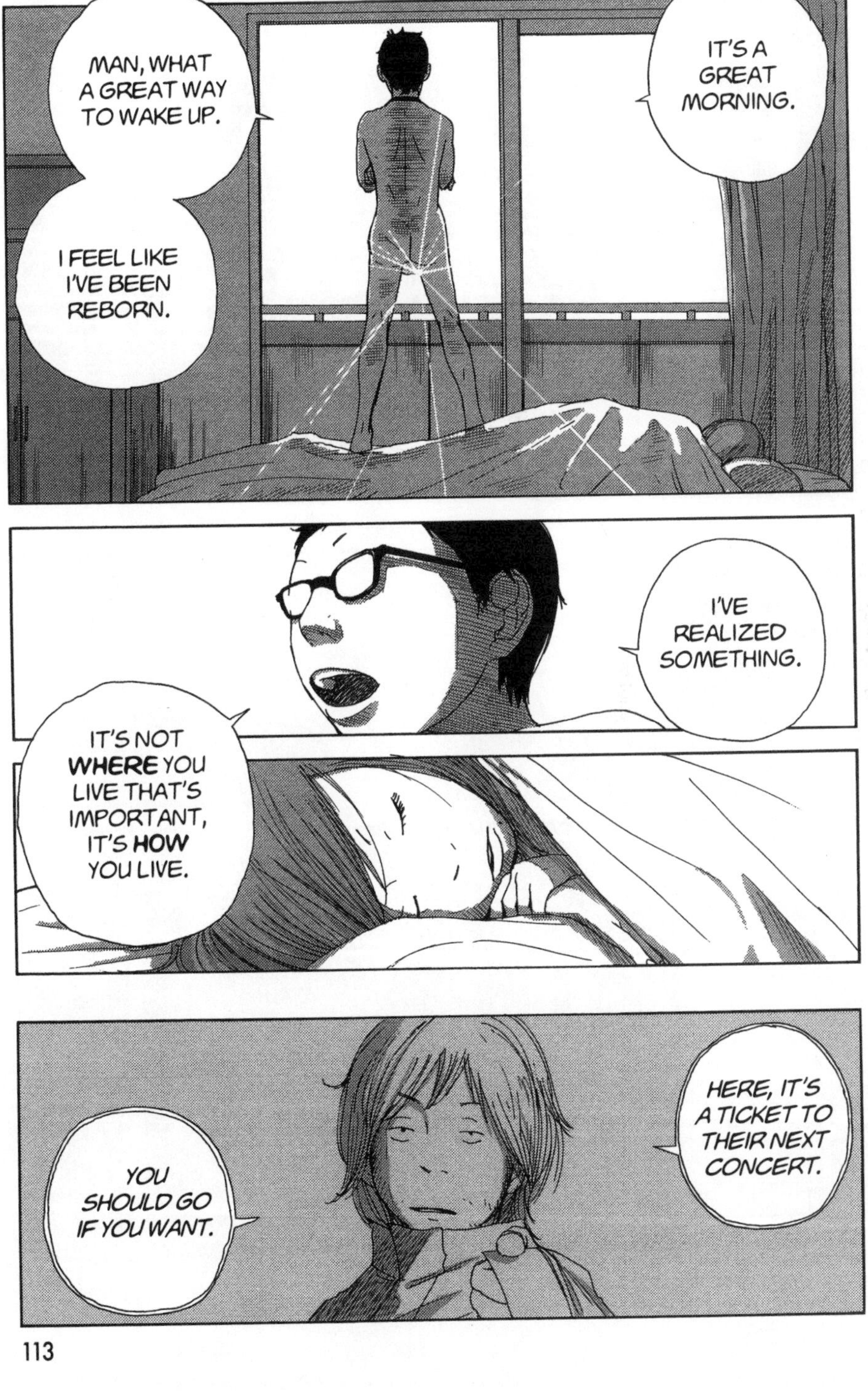
IT'S A GREAT MORNING.
MAN, WHAT A GREAT WAY TO WAKE UP.
I FEEL LIKE I'VE BEEN REBORN.
I'VE REALIZED SOMETHING.
IT'S NOT **WHERE** YOU LIVE THAT'S IMPORTANT, IT'S **HOW** YOU LIVE.
HERE, IT'S A TICKET TO THEIR NEXT CONCERT.
YOU SHOULD GO IF YOU WANT.

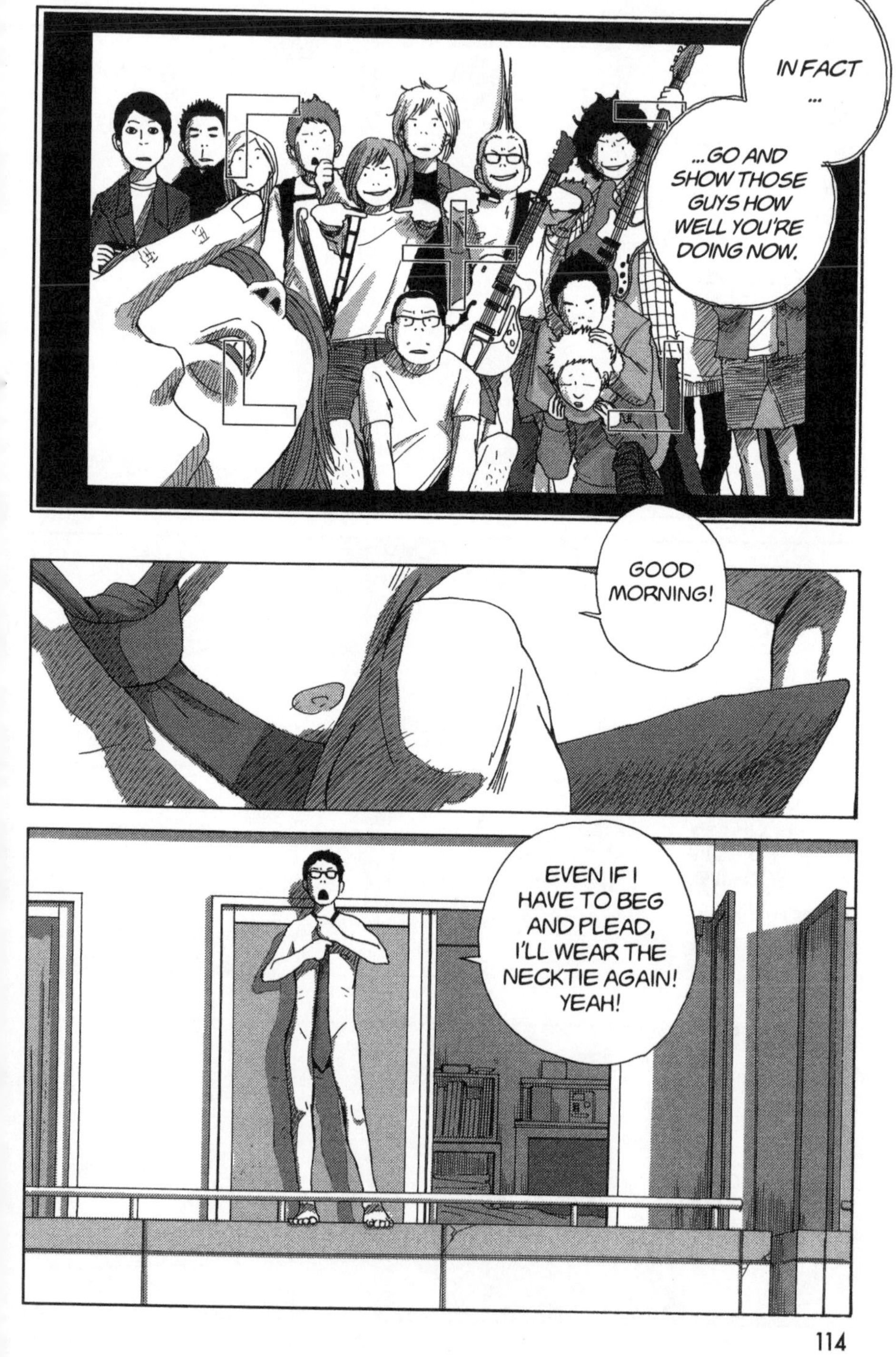
IN FACT ...
...GO AND SHOW THOSE GUYS HOW WELL YOU'RE DOING NOW.
GOOD MORNING!
EVEN IF I HAVE TO BEG AND PLEAD, I'LL WEAR THE NECKTIE AGAIN! YEAH!

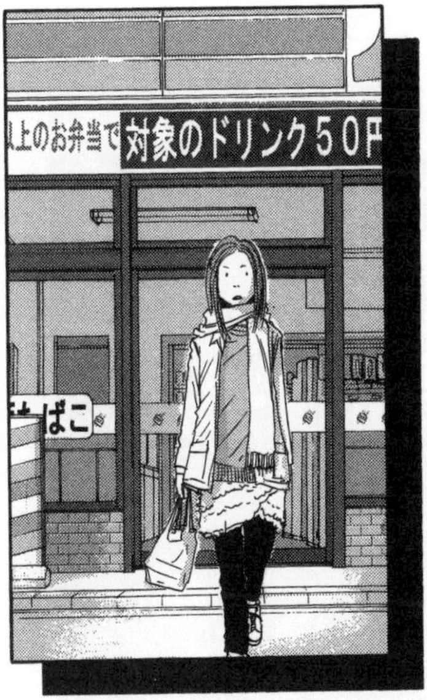

上のお弁当で
対象のドリンク50円
ばこ

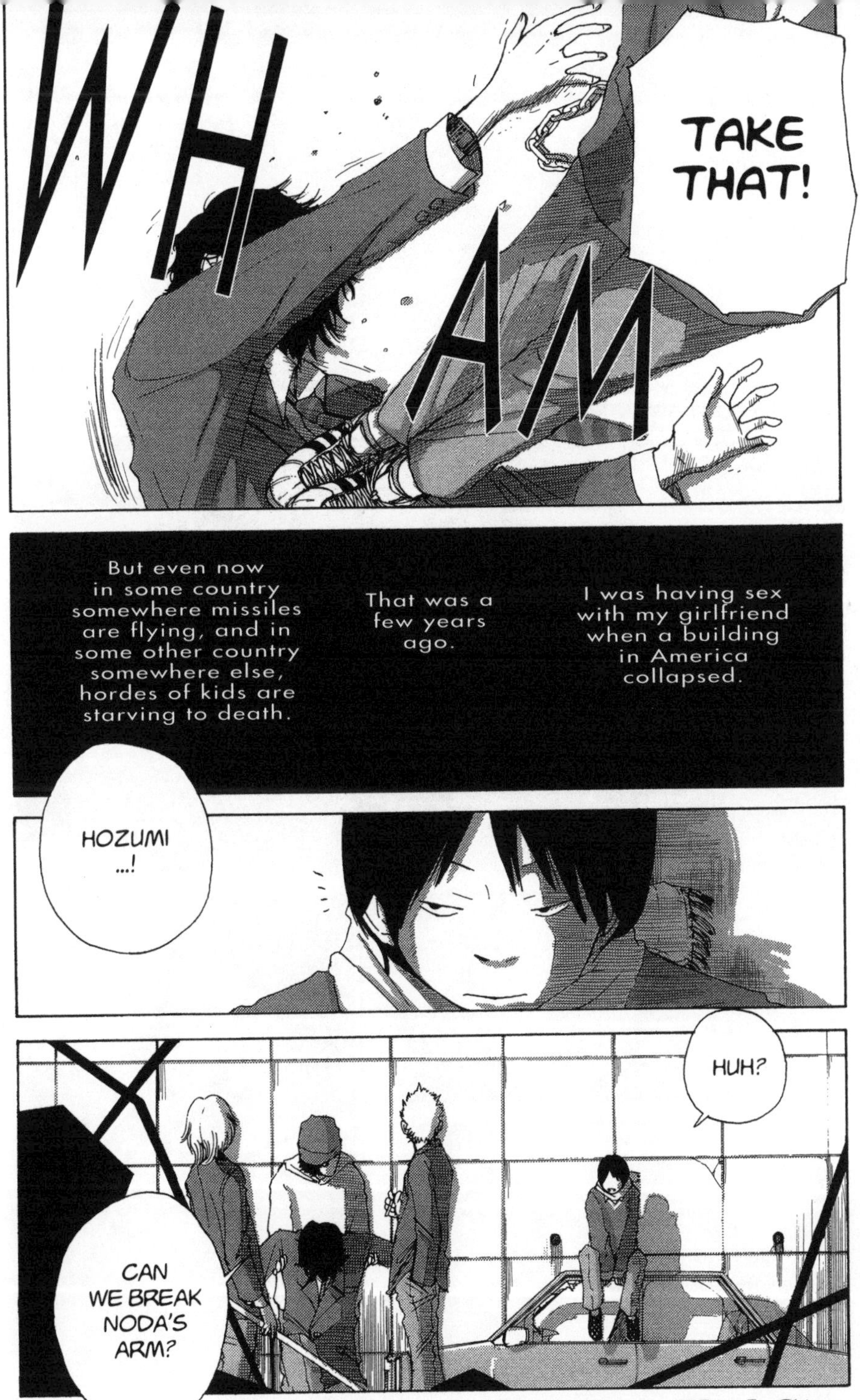
TAKE THAT!
WHAM
I was having sex with my girlfriend when a building in America collapsed.
That was a few years ago.
But even now in some country somewhere missiles are flying, and in some other country somewhere else, hordes of kids are starving to death.
HOZUMI ...!
HUH?
CAN WE BREAK NODA'S ARM?

5th track White Star, Black Star

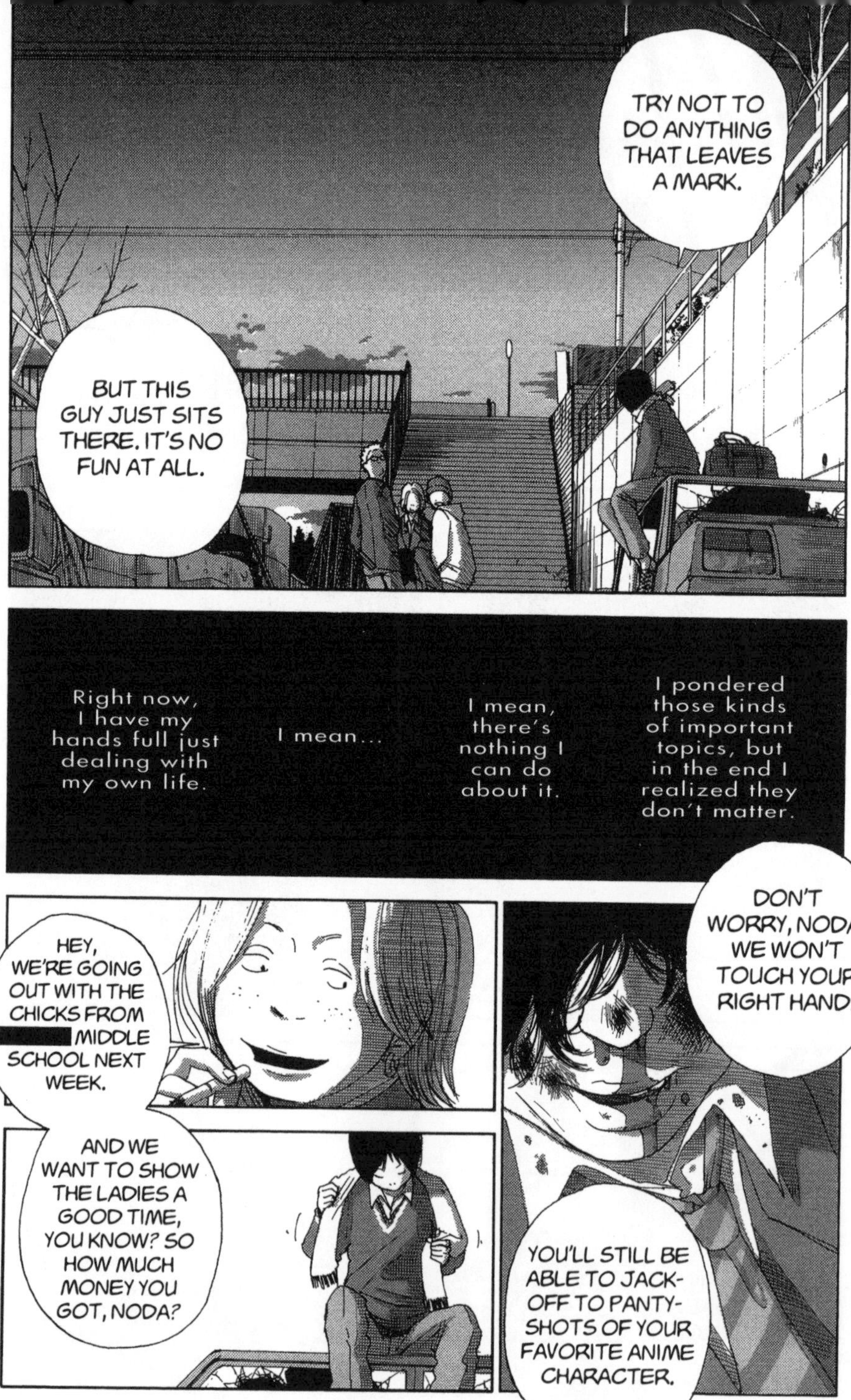
TRY NOT TO DO ANYTHING THAT LEAVES A MARK.
BUT THIS GUY JUST SITS THERE. IT'S NO FUN AT ALL.
I pondered those kinds of important topics, but in the end I realized they don't matter.
I mean, there's nothing I can do about it.
I mean...
Right now, I have my hands full just dealing with my own life.
DON'T WORRY, NODA. WE WON'T TOUCH YOUR RIGHT HAND.
YOU'LL STILL BE ABLE TO JACK-OFF TO PANTY-SHOTS OF YOUR FAVORITE ANIME CHARACTER.
HEY, WE'RE GOING OUT WITH THE CHICKS FROM [redacted] MIDDLE SCHOOL NEXT WEEK.
AND WE WANT TO SHOW THE LADIES A GOOD TIME, YOU KNOW? SO HOW MUCH MONEY YOU GOT, NODA?

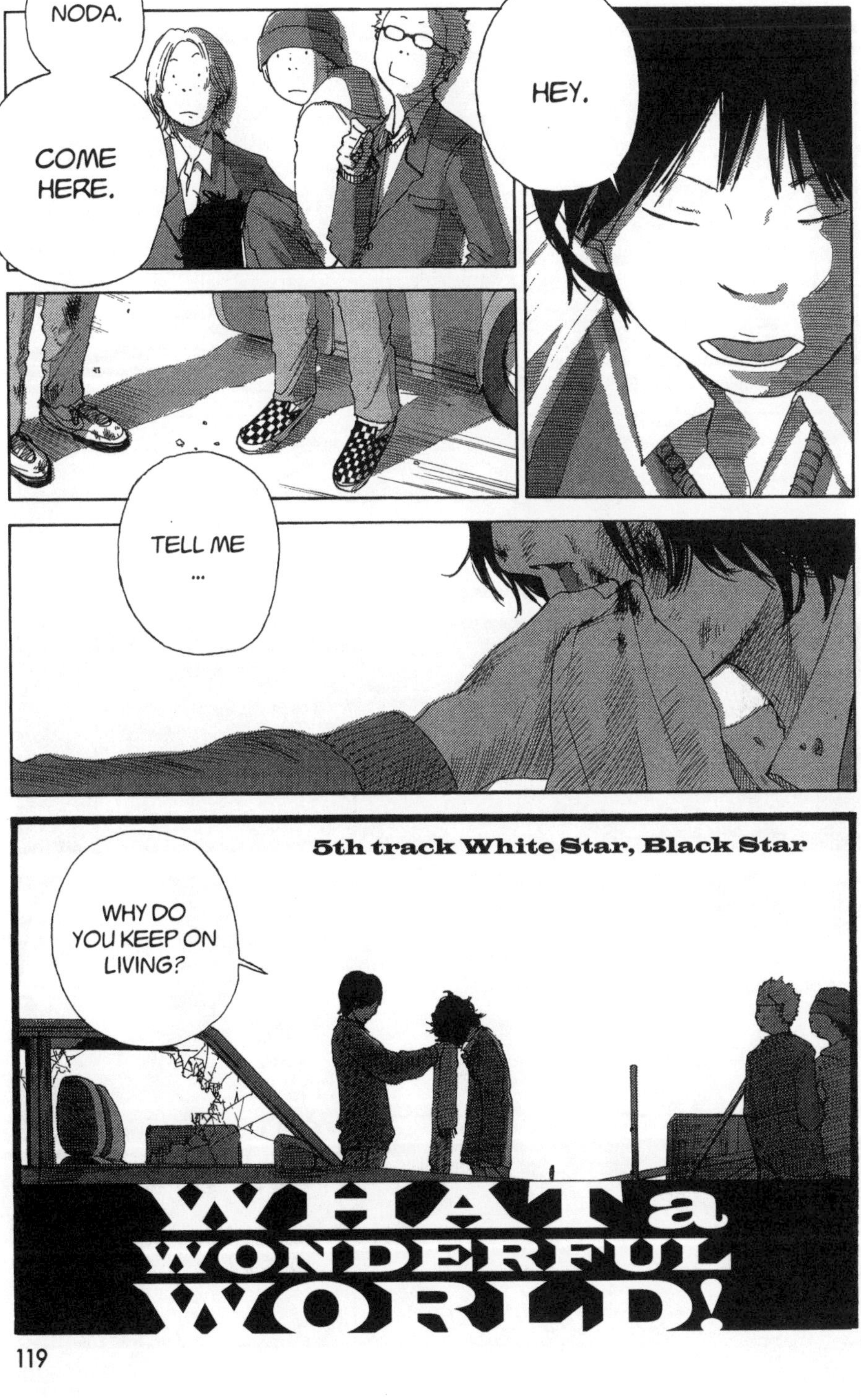
HEY.
NODA.
COME HERE.
TELL ME ...
5th track White Star, Black Star
WHY DO YOU KEEP ON LIVING?
WHAT a WONDERFUL WORLD!

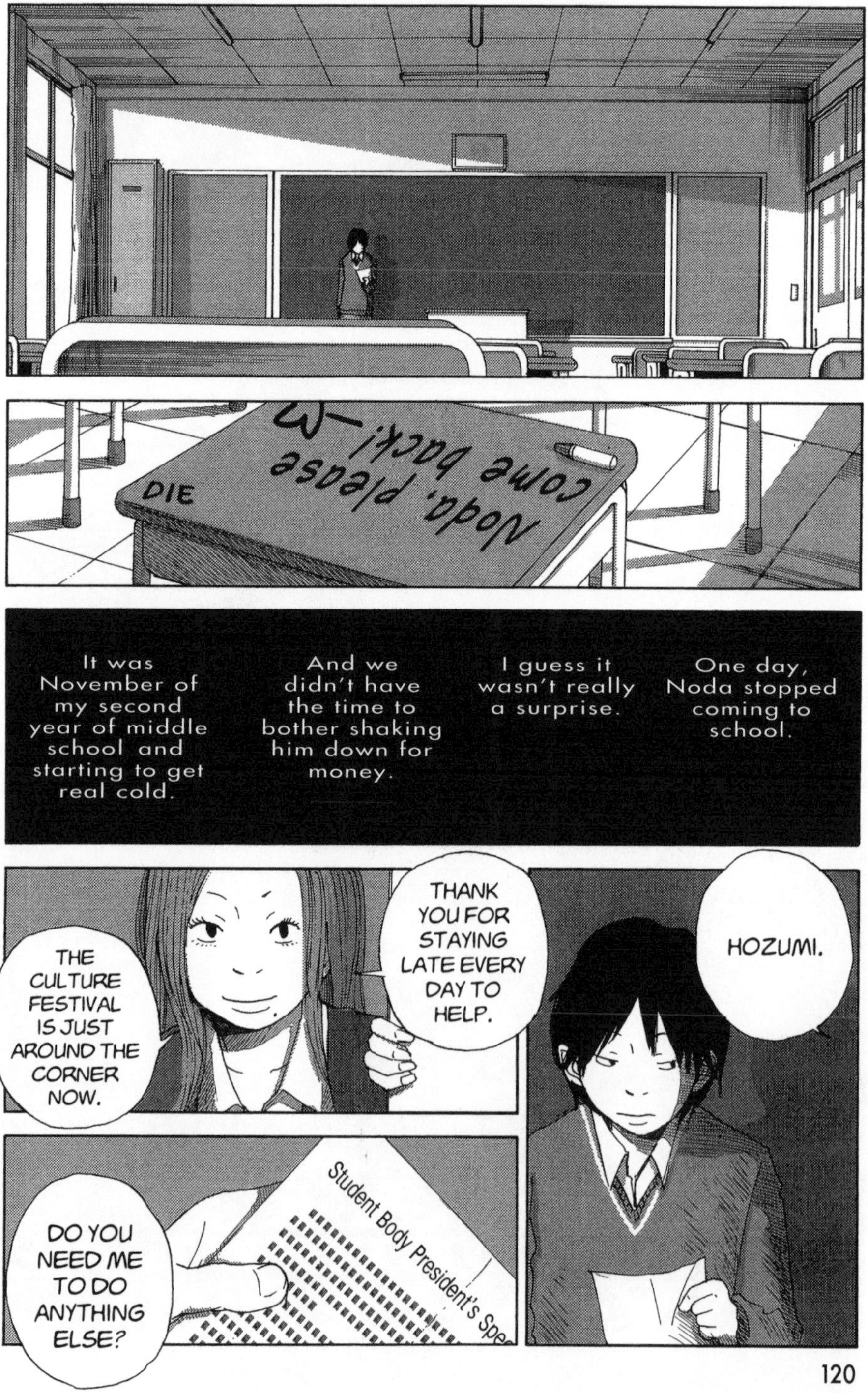
Noda, please come back!
DIE
One day, Noda stopped coming to school.
I guess it wasn't really a surprise.
And we didn't have the time to bother shaking him down for money.
It was November of my second year of middle school and starting to get real cold.
HOZUMI.
THANK YOU FOR STAYING LATE EVERY DAY TO HELP.
THE CULTURE FESTIVAL IS JUST AROUND THE CORNER NOW.
Student Body President's Spe
DO YOU NEED ME TO DO ANYTHING ELSE?

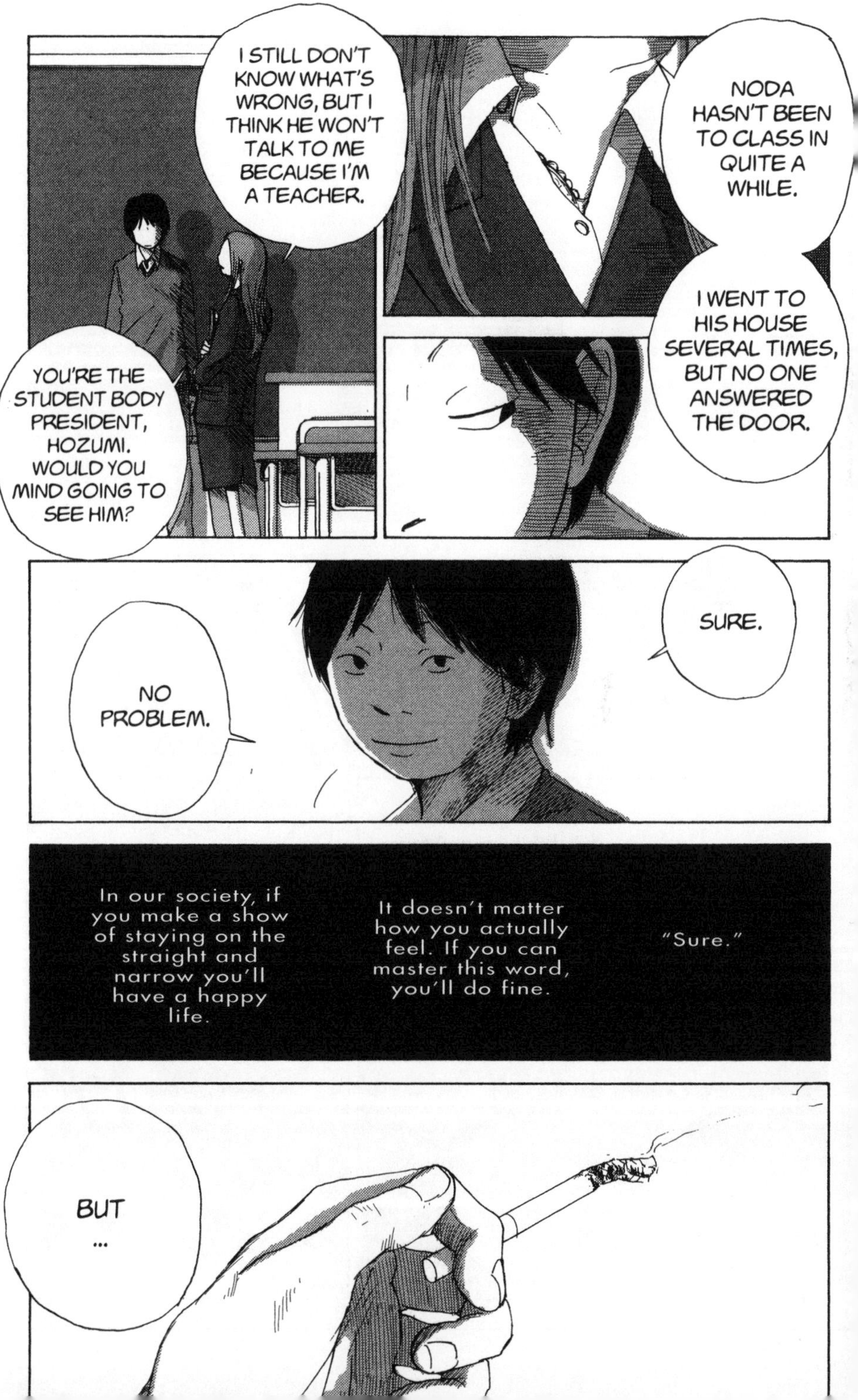
NODA HASN'T BEEN TO CLASS IN QUITE A WHILE.
I WENT TO HIS HOUSE SEVERAL TIMES, BUT NO ONE ANSWERED THE DOOR.
I STILL DON'T KNOW WHAT'S WRONG, BUT I THINK HE WON'T TALK TO ME BECAUSE I'M A TEACHER.
YOU'RE THE STUDENT BODY PRESIDENT, HOZUMI. WOULD YOU MIND GOING TO SEE HIM?
SURE.
NO PROBLEM.
"Sure."
It doesn't matter how you actually feel. If you can master this word, you'll do fine.
In our society, if you make a show of staying on the straight and narrow you'll have a happy life.
BUT ...

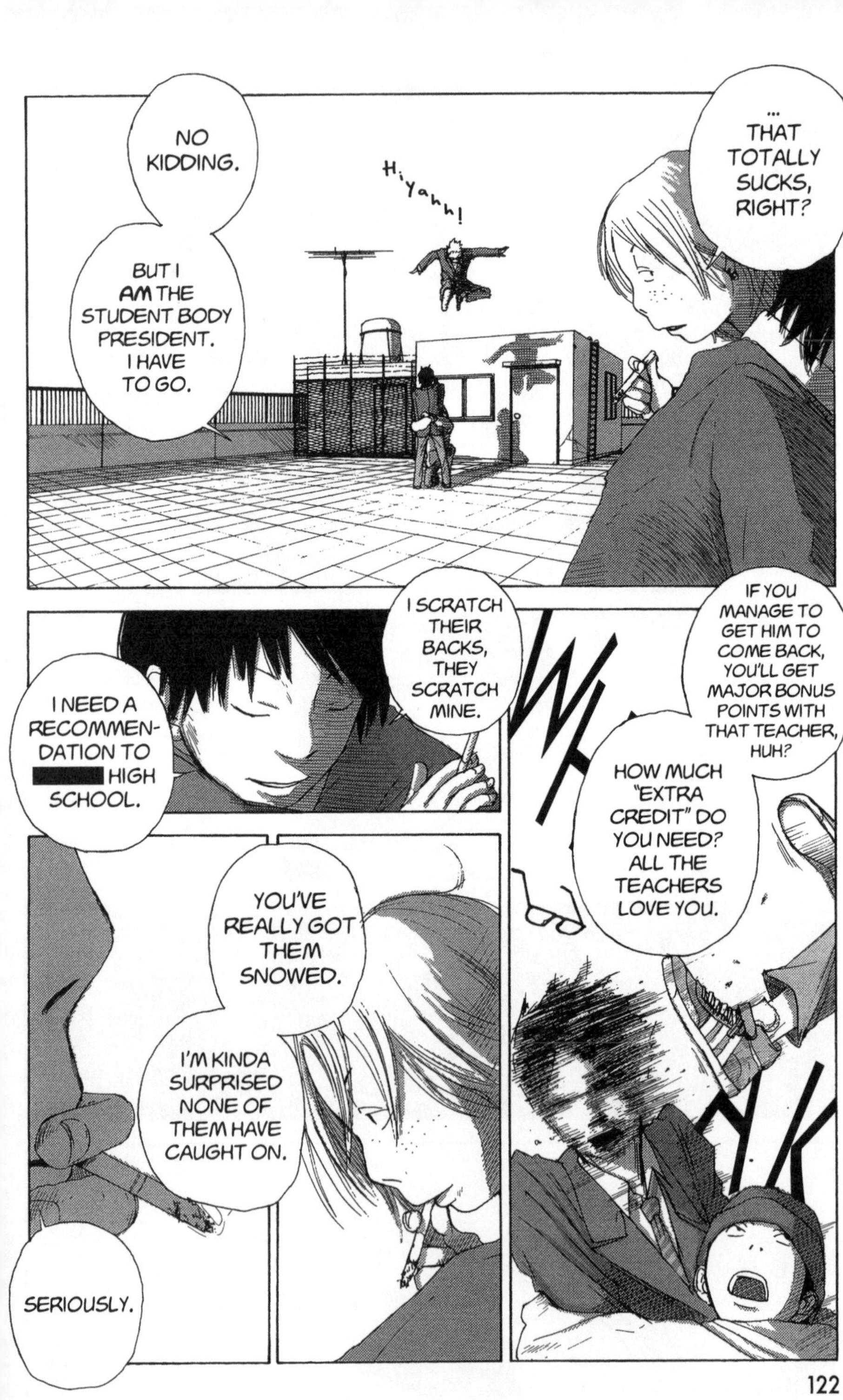
... THAT TOTALLY SUCKS, RIGHT?
Hiyahh!
NO KIDDING.
BUT I **AM** THE STUDENT BODY PRESIDENT. I HAVE TO GO.
IF YOU MANAGE TO GET HIM TO COME BACK, YOU'LL GET MAJOR BONUS POINTS WITH THAT TEACHER, HUH?
HOW MUCH "EXTRA CREDIT" DO YOU NEED? ALL THE TEACHERS LOVE YOU.
WHAK
I SCRATCH THEIR BACKS, THEY SCRATCH MINE.
I NEED A RECOMMENDATION TO [redacted] HIGH SCHOOL.
YOU'VE REALLY GOT THEM SNOWED.
I'M KINDA SURPRISED NONE OF THEM HAVE CAUGHT ON.
SERIOUSLY.

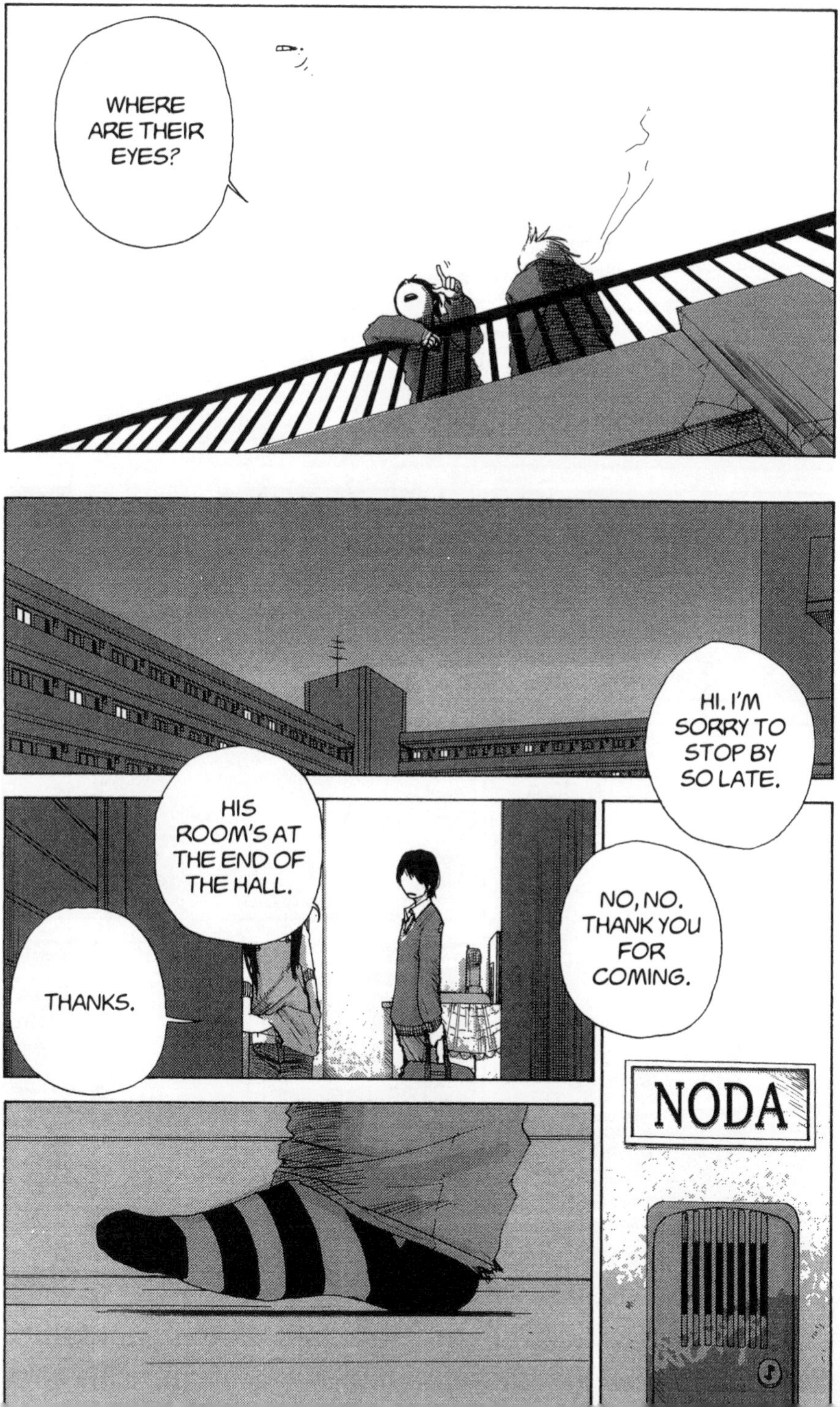
WHERE ARE THEIR EYES?
HI. I'M SORRY TO STOP BY SO LATE.
NO, NO. THANK YOU FOR COMING.
NODA
HIS ROOM'S AT THE END OF THE HALL.
THANKS.

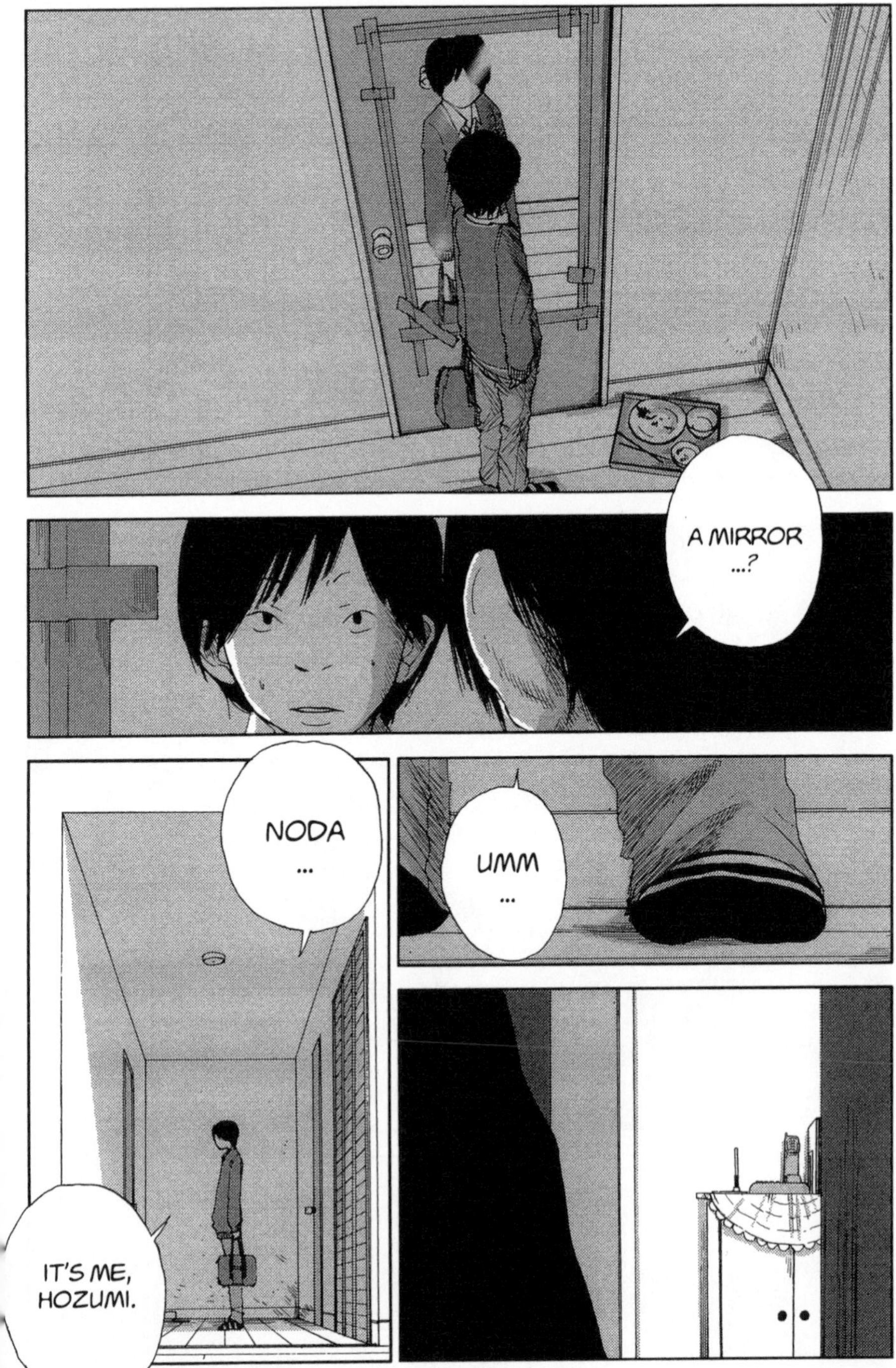
A MIRROR ...?
UMM ...
NODA ...
IT'S ME, HOZUMI.

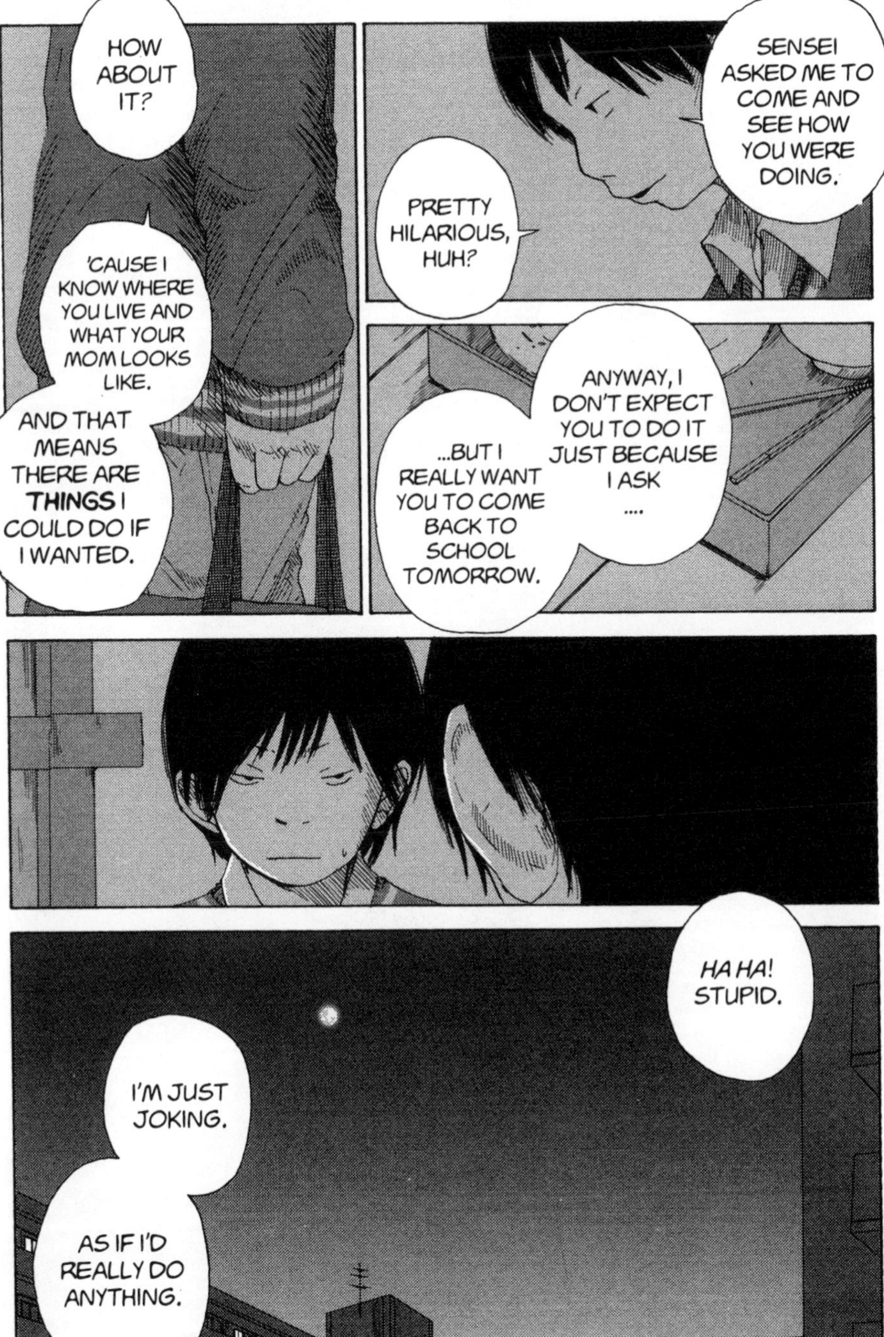
SENSEI ASKED ME TO COME AND SEE HOW YOU WERE DOING.
PRETTY HILARIOUS, HUH?
ANYWAY, I DON'T EXPECT YOU TO DO IT JUST BECAUSE I ASK ....
...BUT I REALLY WANT YOU TO COME BACK TO SCHOOL TOMORROW.
HOW ABOUT IT?
'CAUSE I KNOW WHERE YOU LIVE AND WHAT YOUR MOM LOOKS LIKE.
AND THAT MEANS THERE ARE **THINGS** I COULD DO IF I WANTED.
HA HA! STUPID.
I'M JUST JOKING.
AS IF I'D REALLY DO ANYTHING.

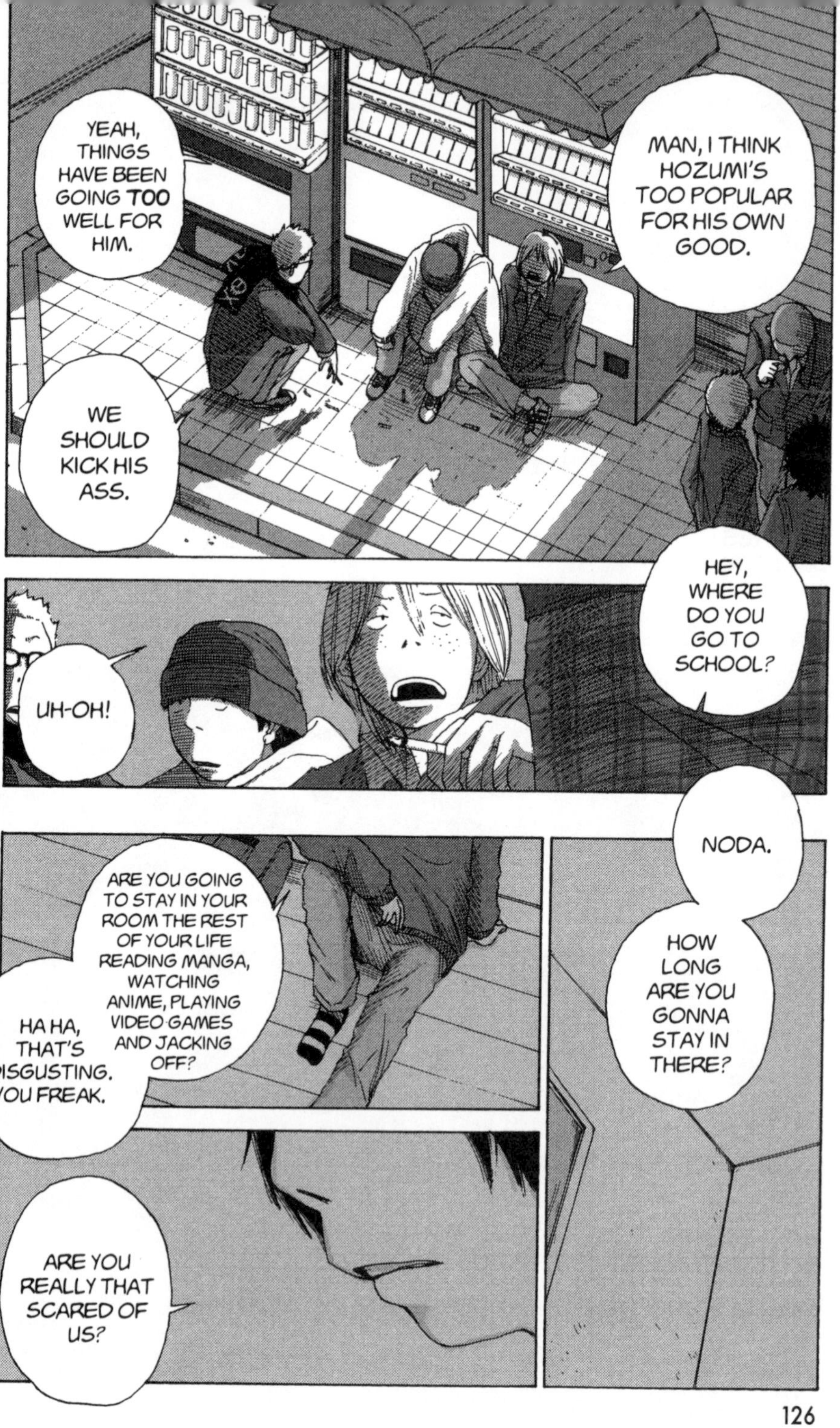
MAN, I THINK HOZUMI'S TOO POPULAR FOR HIS OWN GOOD.
YEAH, THINGS HAVE BEEN GOING **TOO** WELL FOR HIM.
WE SHOULD KICK HIS ASS.
HEY, WHERE DO YOU GO TO SCHOOL?
UH-OH!
NODA.
HOW LONG ARE YOU GONNA STAY IN THERE?
ARE YOU GOING TO STAY IN YOUR ROOM THE REST OF YOUR LIFE READING MANGA, WATCHING ANIME, PLAYING VIDEO GAMES AND JACKING OFF?
HA HA, THAT'S DISGUSTING. YOU FREAK.
ARE YOU REALLY THAT SCARED OF US?

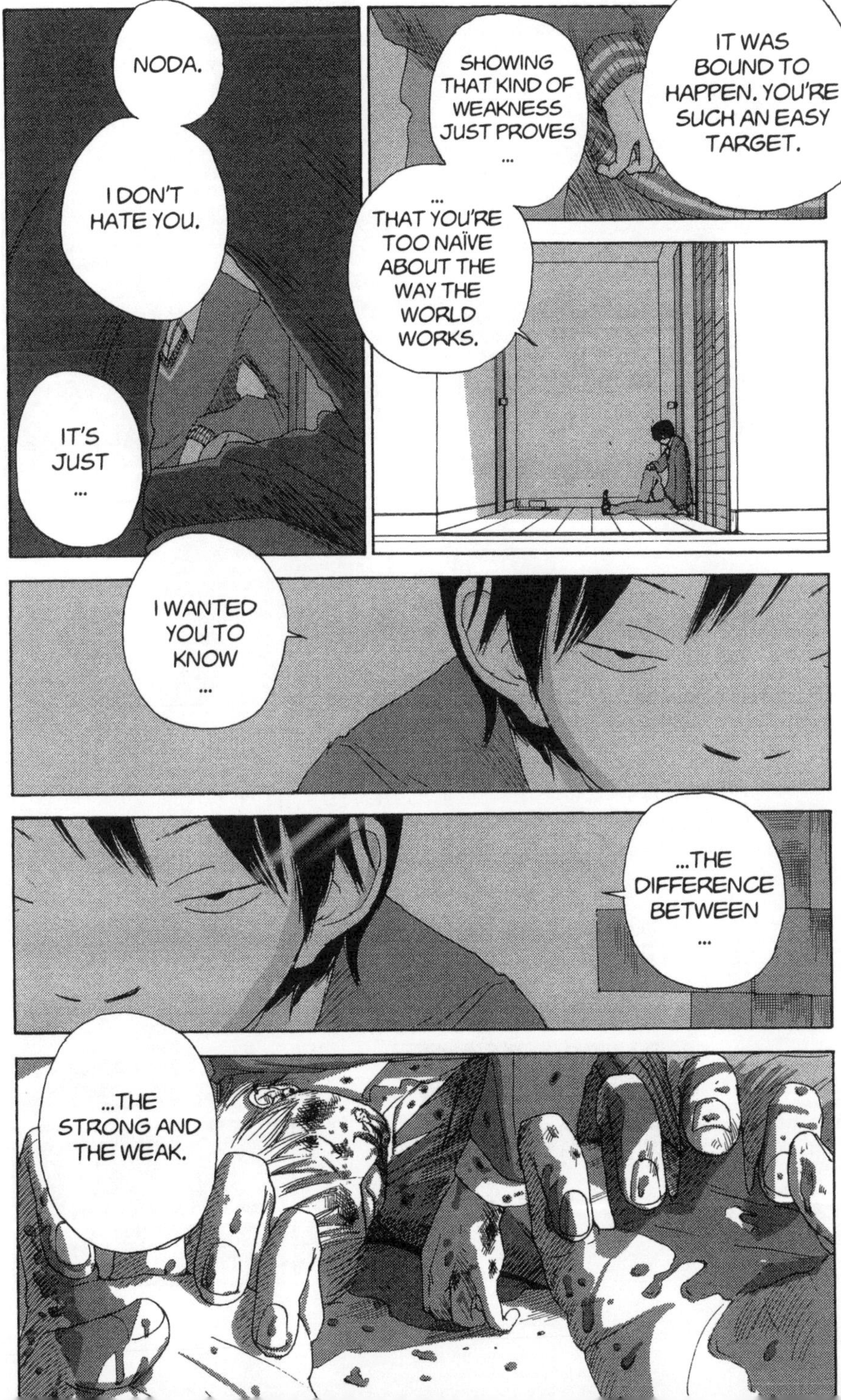
IT WAS BOUND TO HAPPEN. YOU'RE SUCH AN EASY TARGET.
SHOWING THAT KIND OF WEAKNESS JUST PROVES ...
... THAT YOU'RE TOO NAÏVE ABOUT THE WAY THE WORLD WORKS.
NODA.
I DON'T HATE YOU.
IT'S JUST ...
I WANTED YOU TO KNOW ...
...THE DIFFERENCE BETWEEN ...
...THE STRONG AND THE WEAK.

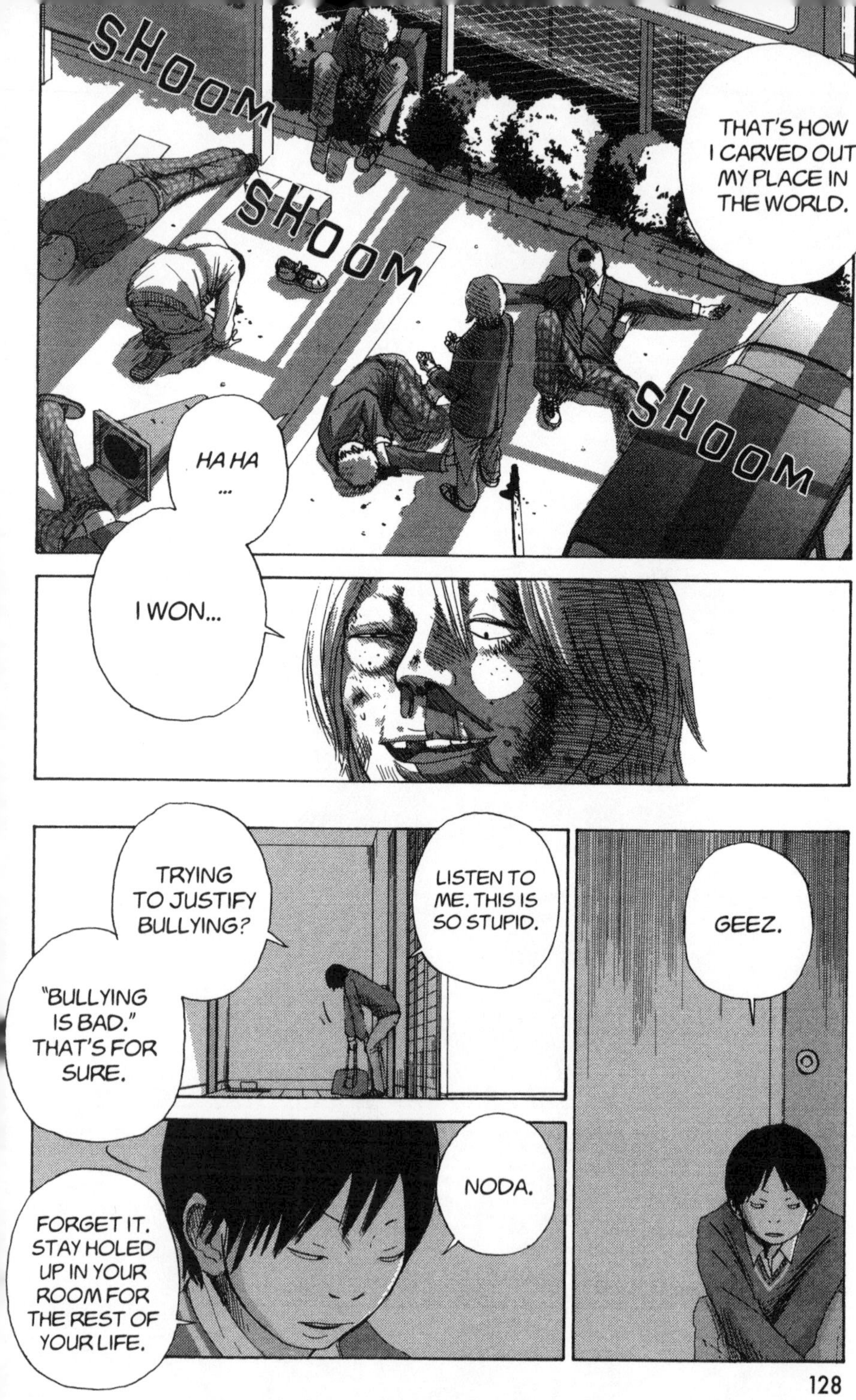
THAT'S HOW I CARVED OUT MY PLACE IN THE WORLD.
SHOOM
SHOOM
SHOOM
SHOOM
HA HA ...
I WON...
GEEZ.
LISTEN TO ME. THIS IS SO STUPID.
TRYING TO JUSTIFY BULLYING?
"BULLYING IS BAD." THAT'S FOR SURE.
NODA.
FORGET IT. STAY HOLED UP IN YOUR ROOM FOR THE REST OF YOUR LIFE.

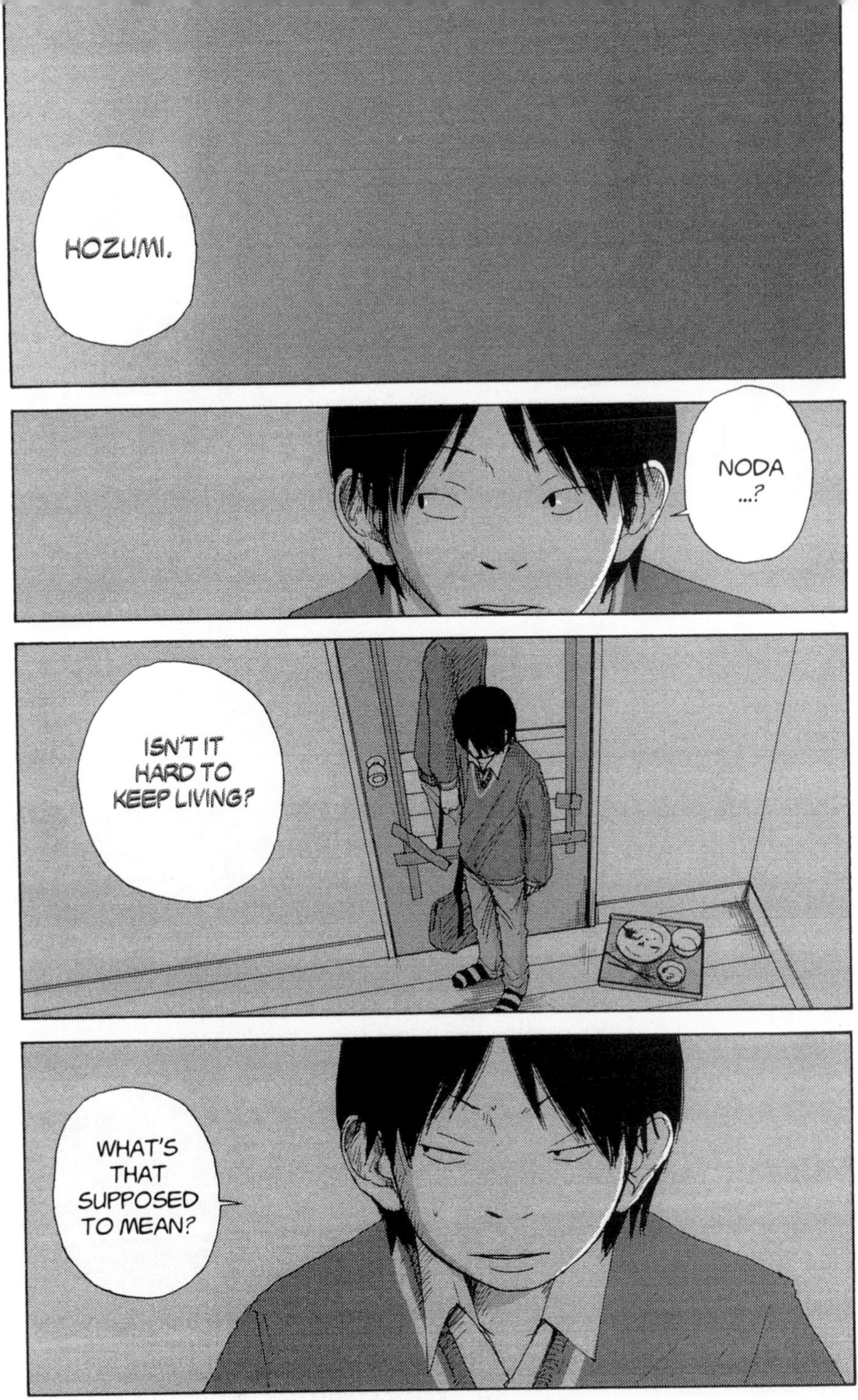
HOZUMI.
NODA ...?
ISN'T IT HARD TO KEEP LIVING?
WHAT'S THAT SUPPOSED TO MEAN?

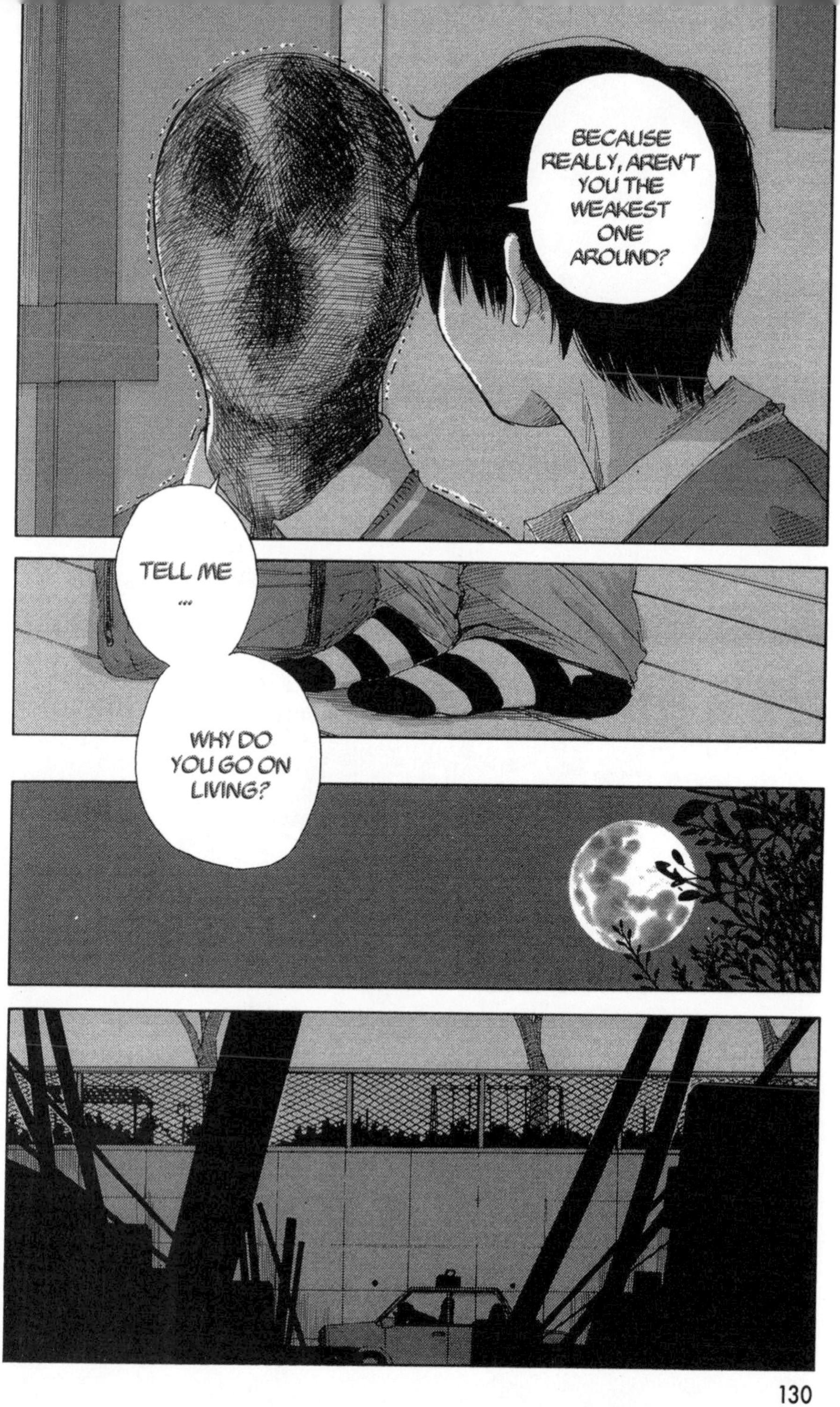

BECAUSE REALLY, AREN'T YOU THE WEAKEST ONE AROUND?
TELL ME ...
WHY DO YOU GO ON LIVING?

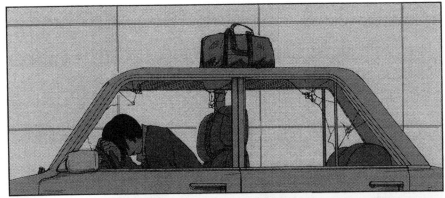

BRR...

OH, HOZUMI!

WHAT HAPPENED? IT'S SO UNUSUAL FOR YOU TO BE LATE.

YEAH...

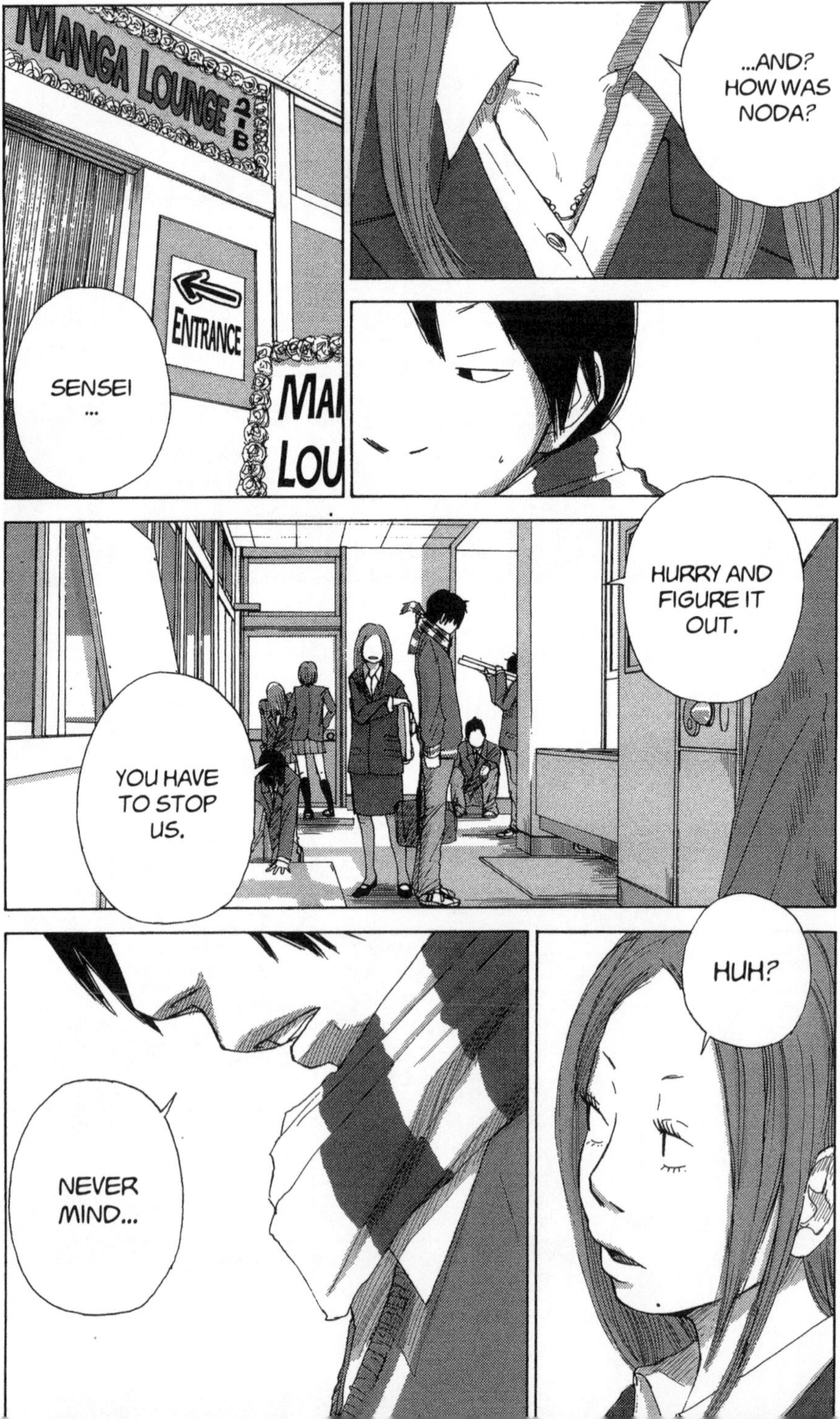
...AND? HOW WAS NODA?
MANGA LOUNGE 2-B
ENTRANCE
SENSEI ...
HURRY AND FIGURE IT OUT.
YOU HAVE TO STOP US.
HUH?
NEVER MIND...

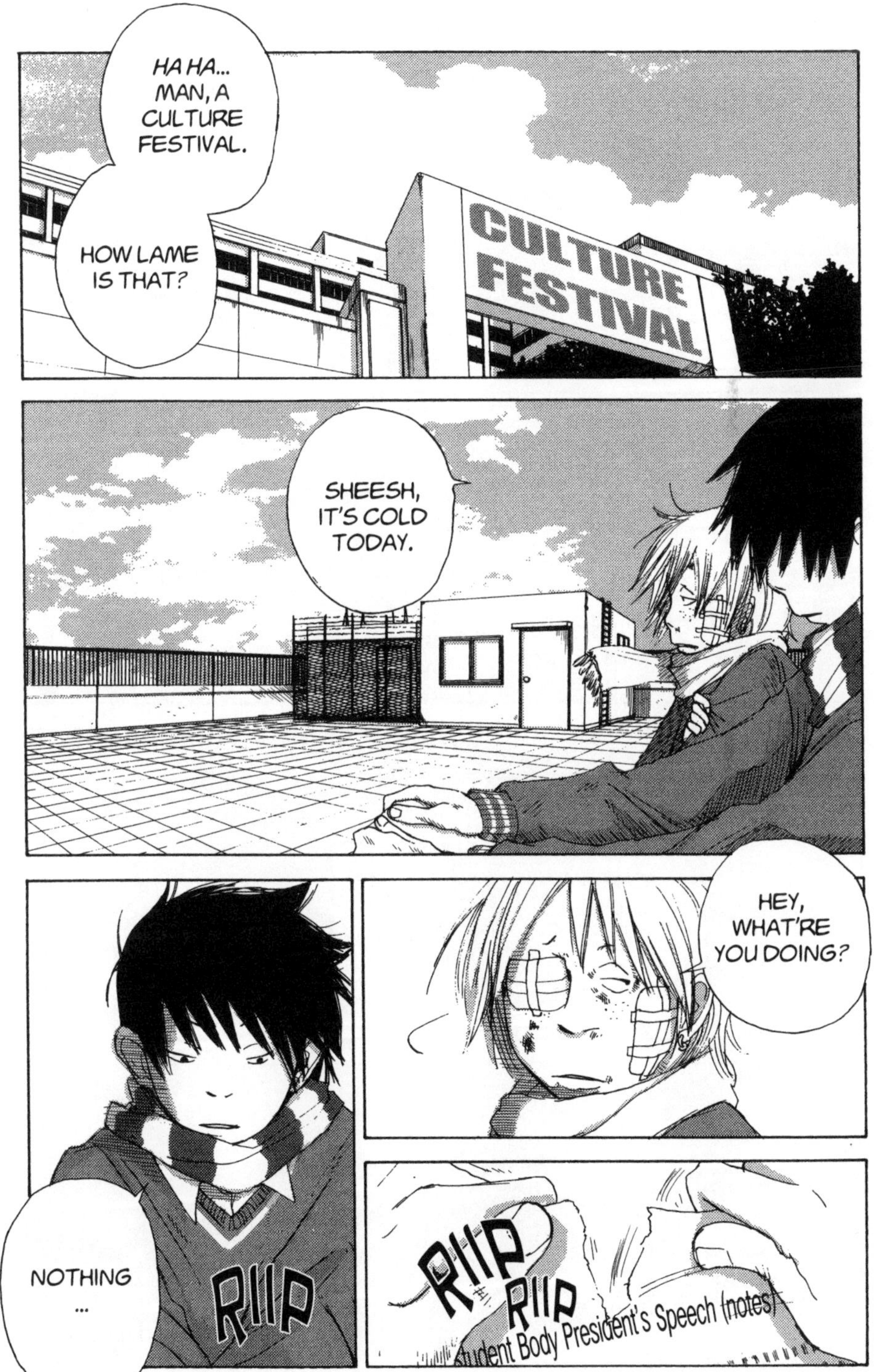
HA HA... MAN, A CULTURE FESTIVAL.
HOW LAME IS THAT?
CULTURE FESTIVAL
SHEESH, IT'S COLD TODAY.
HEY, WHAT'RE YOU DOING?
RIIP
RIIP
Student Body President's Speech (notes)
NOTHING ...
RIIP

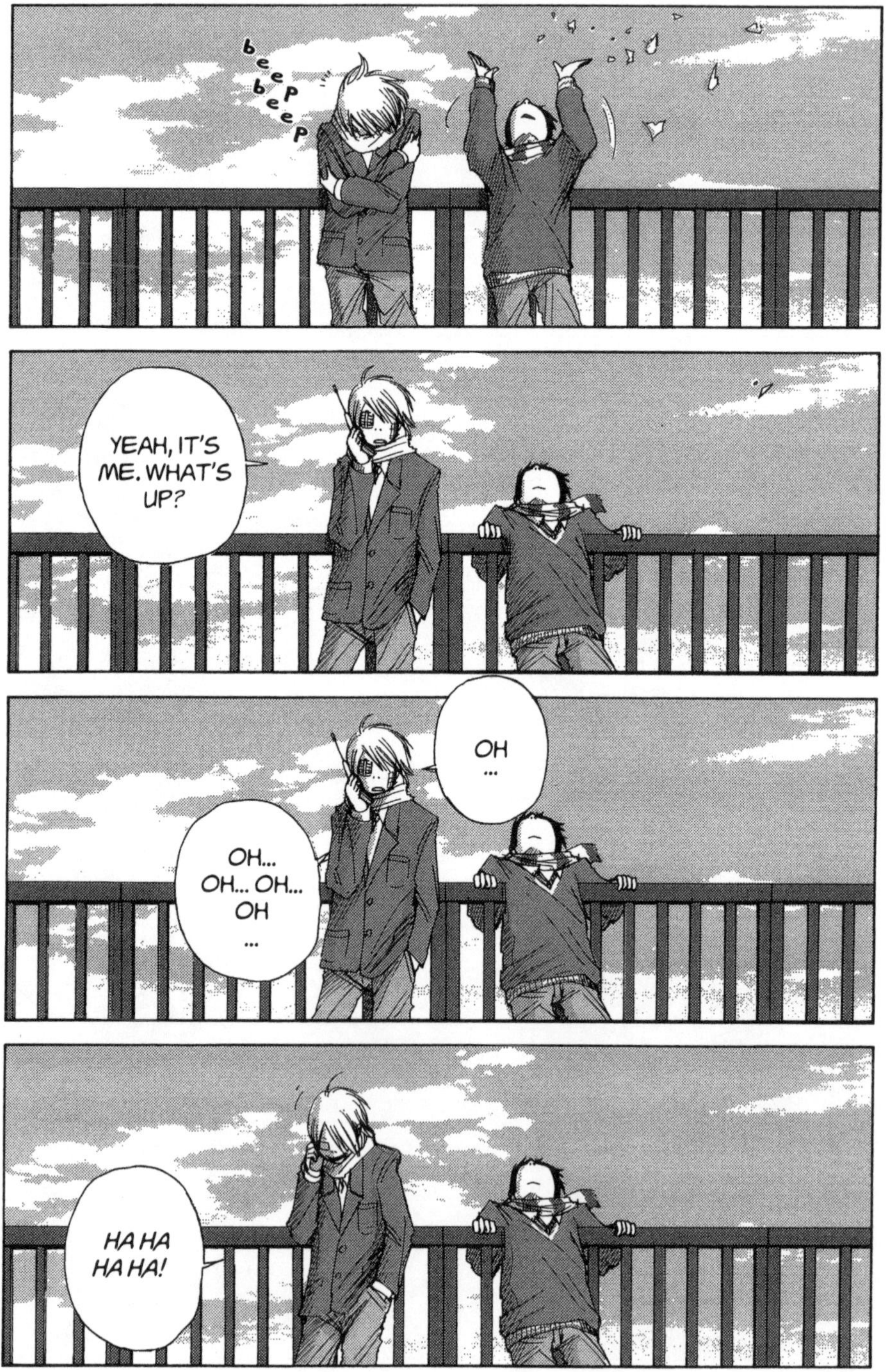
beep beep
YEAH, IT'S ME. WHAT'S UP?
OH ...
OH... OH... OH... OH ...
HA HA HA HA!

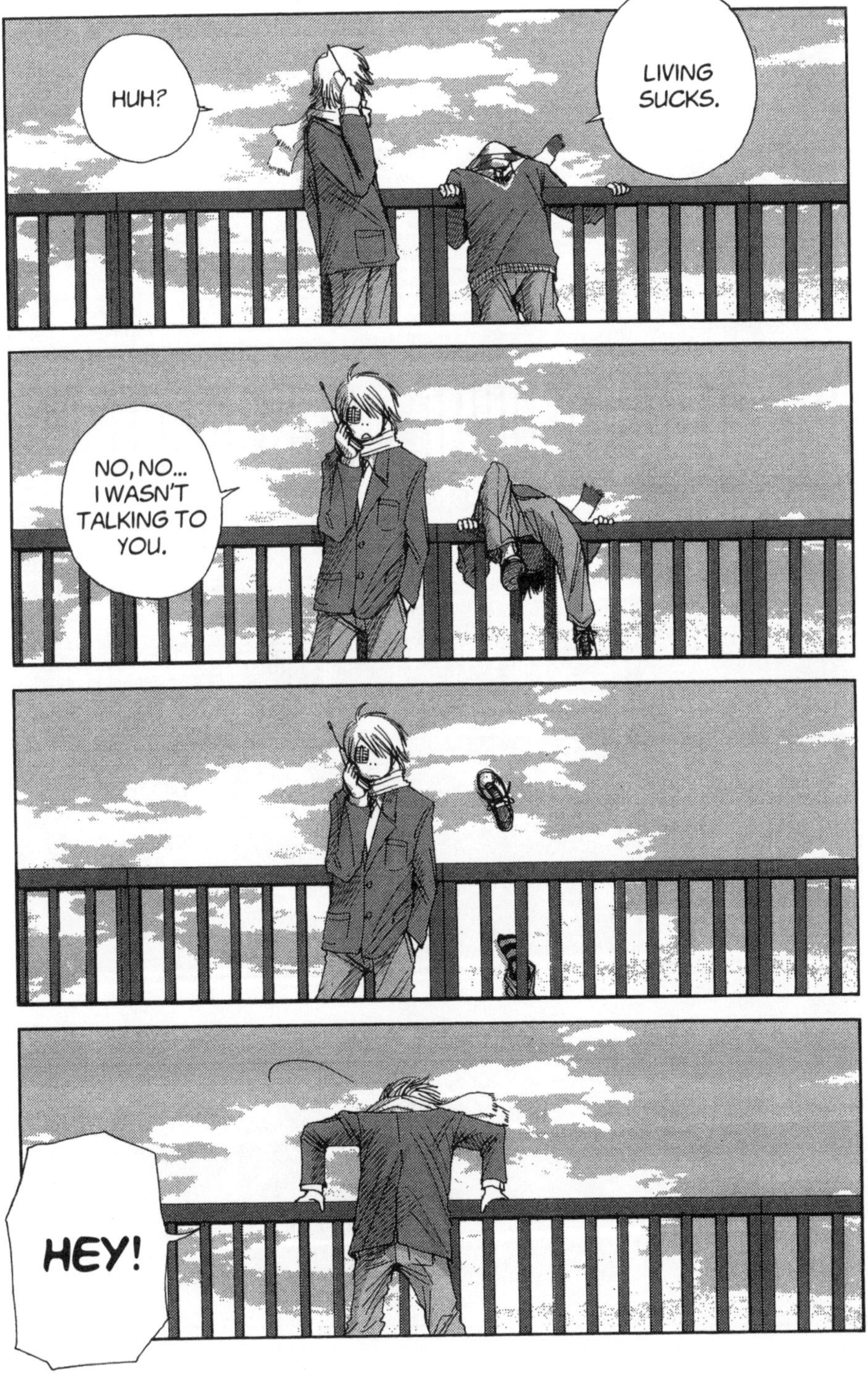
LIVING SUCKS.
HUH?
NO, NO... I WASN'T TALKING TO YOU.
HEY!

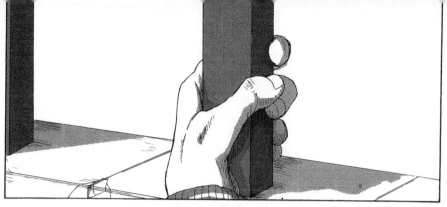

CULTURE FESTIV... DREAMS & HOPE

AND YET, I STILL WANNA LIVE.

BRR!

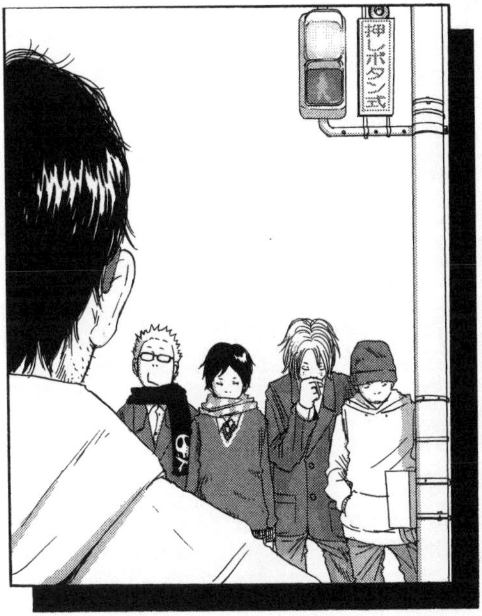
押しボタン式

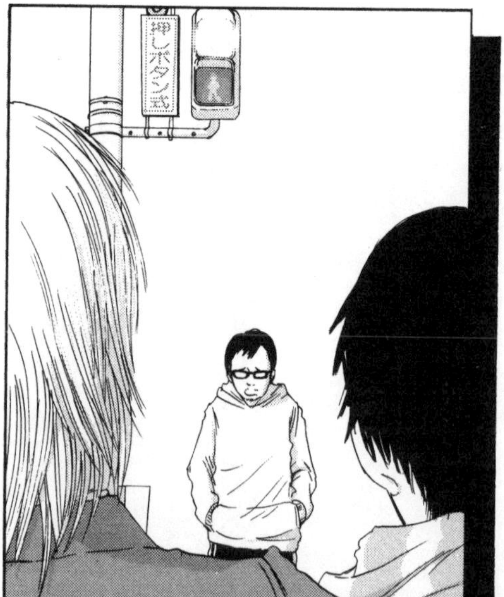
押しボタン式

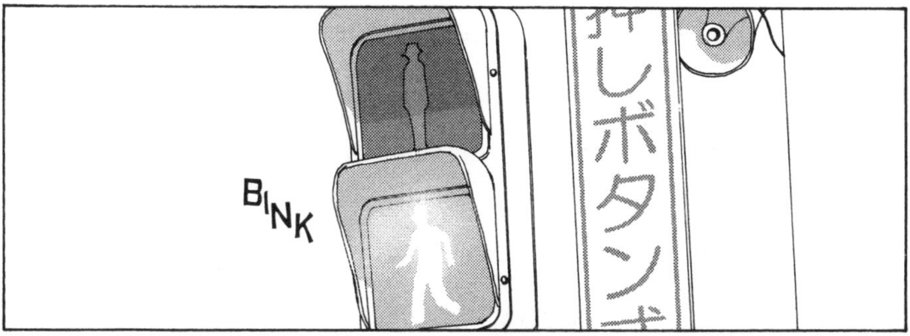
BINK
押しボタン

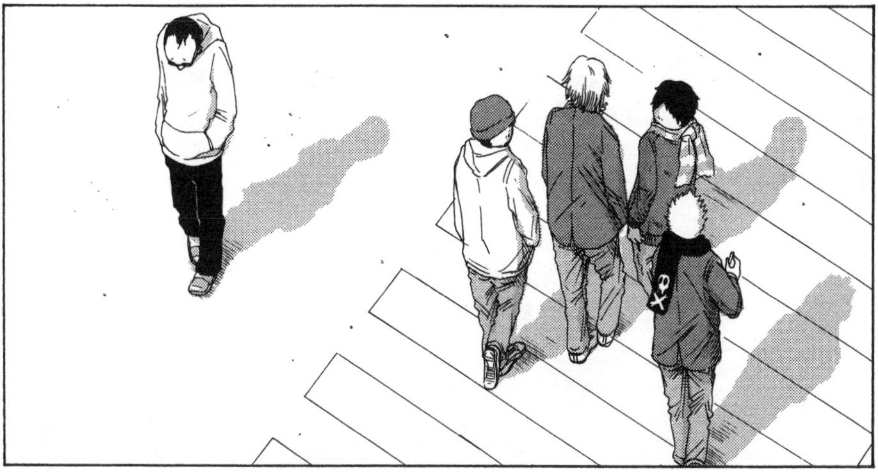

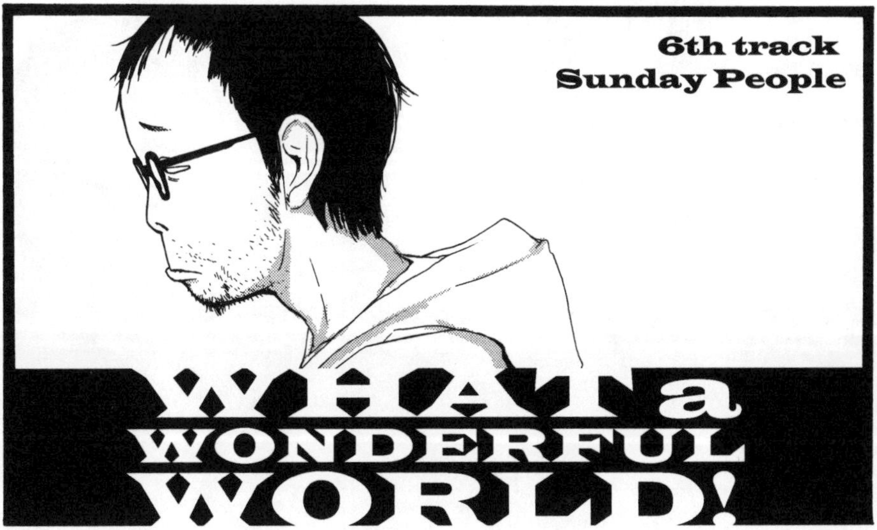
6th track
Sunday People
WHAT a
WONDERFUL
WORLD!

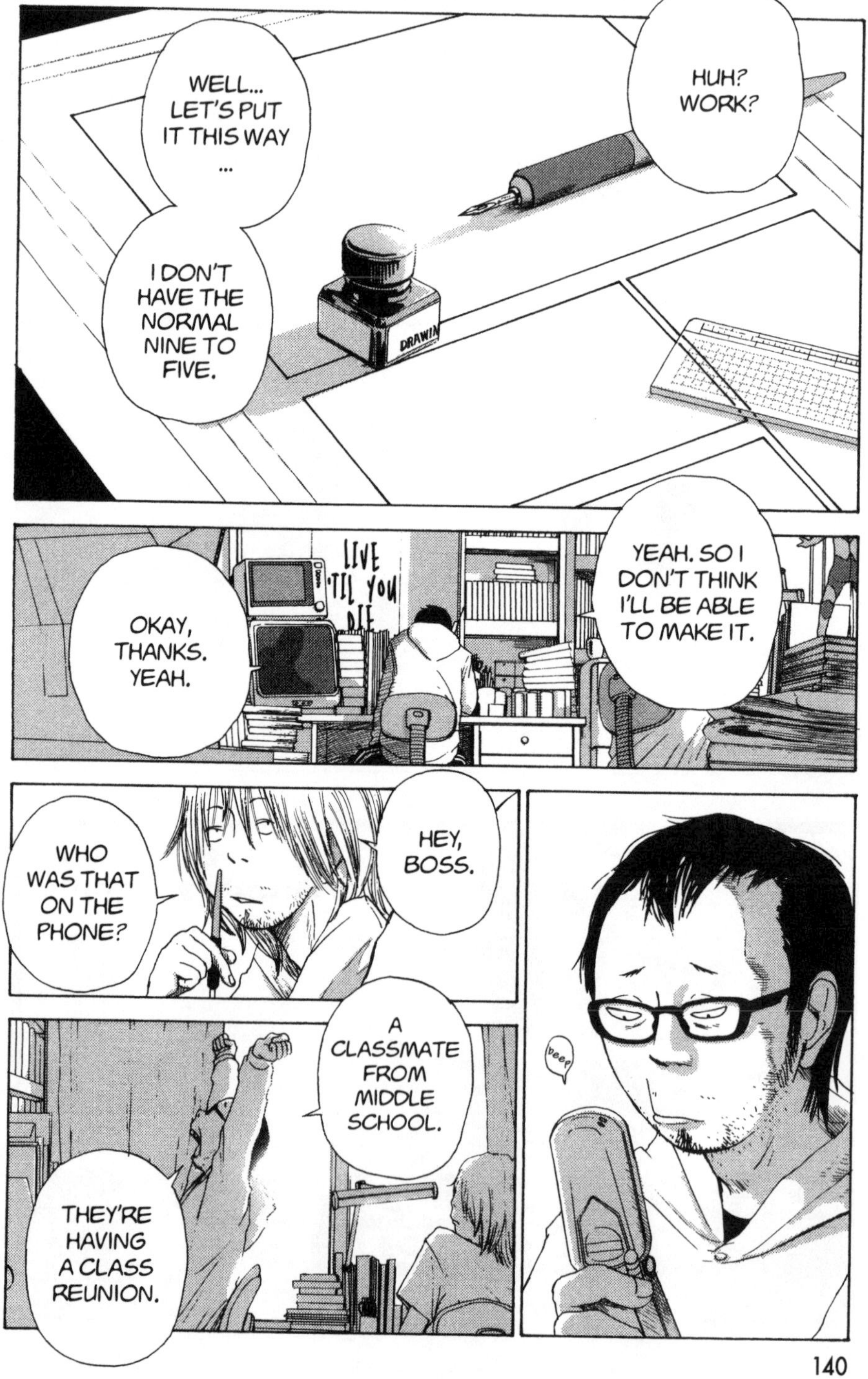
HUH? WORK?
WELL... LET'S PUT IT THIS WAY ...
I DON'T HAVE THE NORMAL NINE TO FIVE.
DRAWIN
YEAH. SO I DON'T THINK I'LL BE ABLE TO MAKE IT.
LIVE 'TIL YOU DIE
OKAY, THANKS. YEAH.
beep
HEY, BOSS.
WHO WAS THAT ON THE PHONE?
A CLASSMATE FROM MIDDLE SCHOOL.
THEY'RE HAVING A CLASS REUNION.

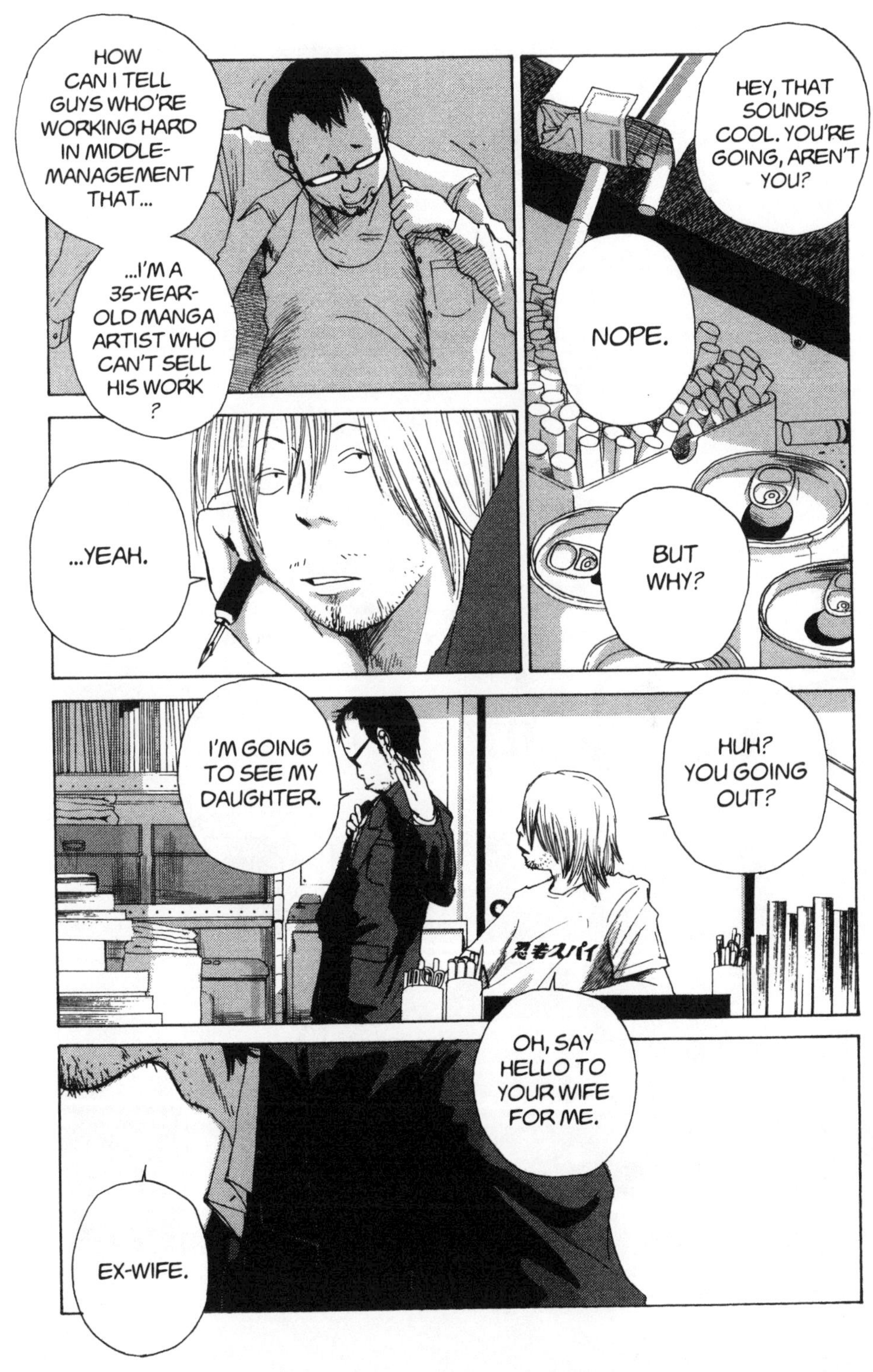
HEY, THAT SOUNDS COOL. YOU'RE GOING, AREN'T YOU?
NOPE.
BUT WHY?
HOW CAN I TELL GUYS WHO'RE WORKING HARD IN MIDDLE-MANAGEMENT THAT...
...I'M A 35-YEAR-OLD MANGA ARTIST WHO CAN'T SELL HIS WORK?
...YEAH.
HUH? YOU GOING OUT?
忍者スパイ
I'M GOING TO SEE MY DAUGHTER.
OH, SAY HELLO TO YOUR WIFE FOR ME.
EX-WIFE.

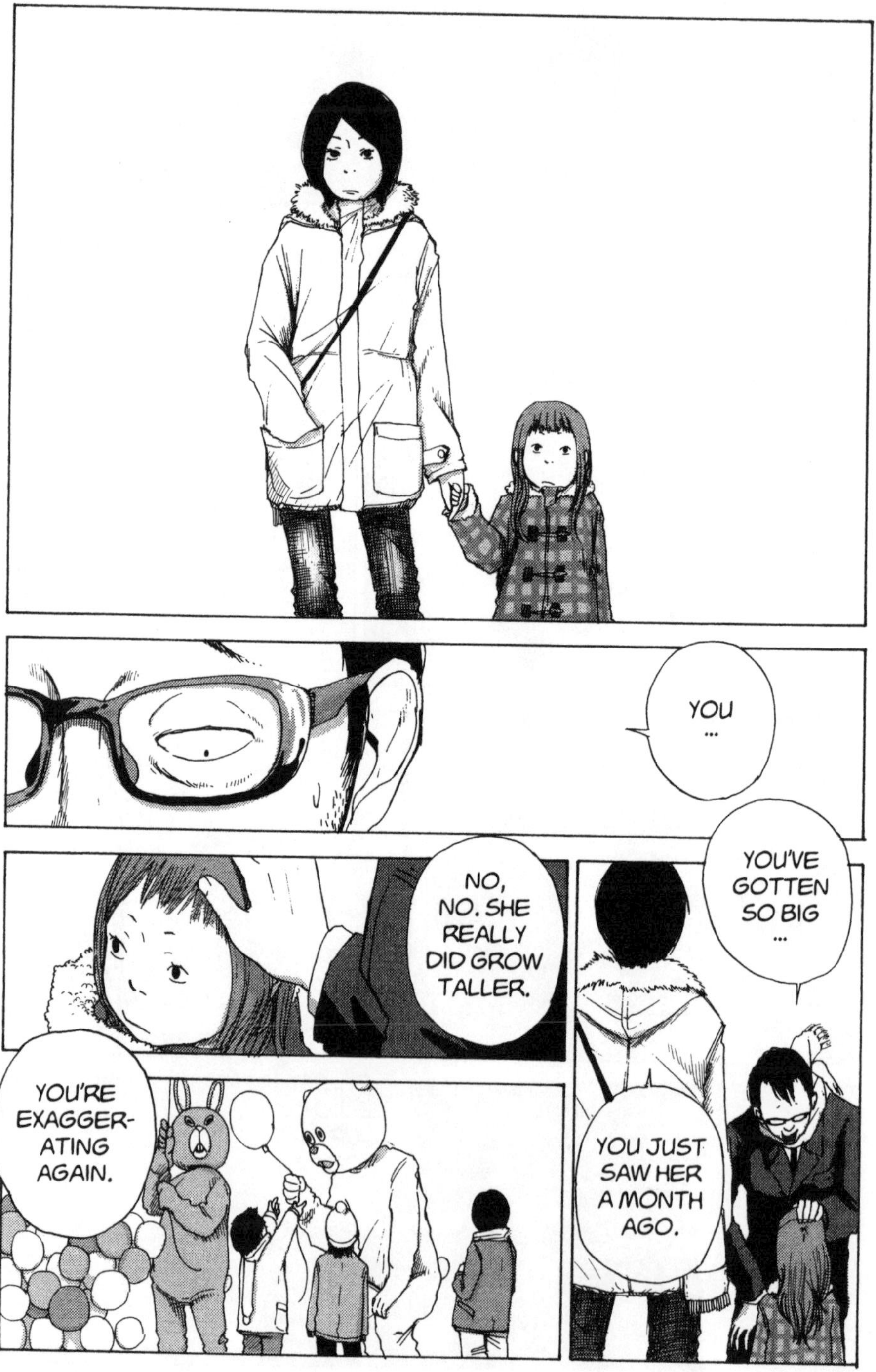
YOU ...
YOU'VE GOTTEN SO BIG ...
YOU JUST SAW HER A MONTH AGO.
NO, NO. SHE REALLY DID GROW TALLER.
YOU'RE EXAGGER-ATING AGAIN.

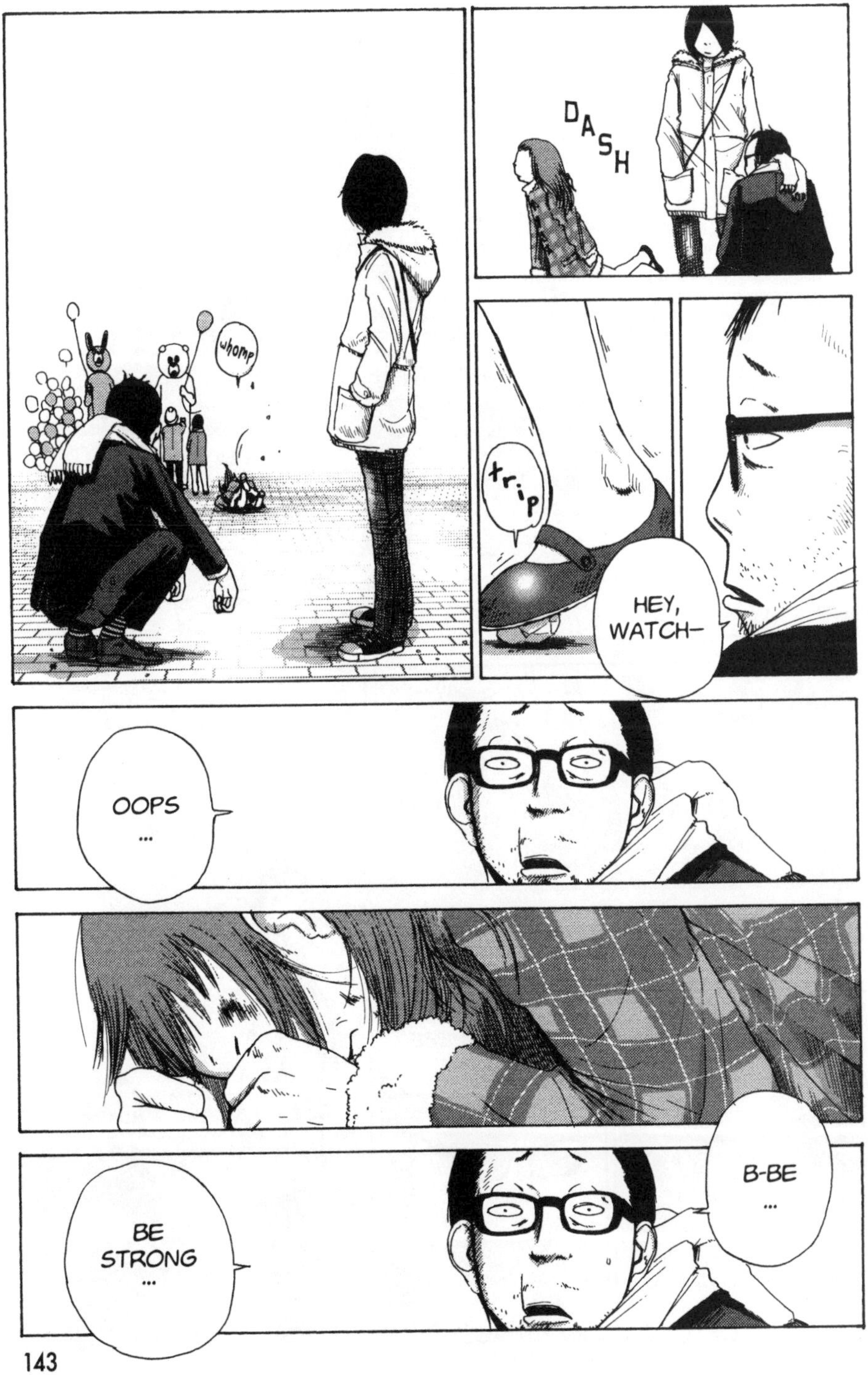
DASH
HEY, WATCH-
trip
whomp
OOPS ...
B-BE ...
BE STRONG ...

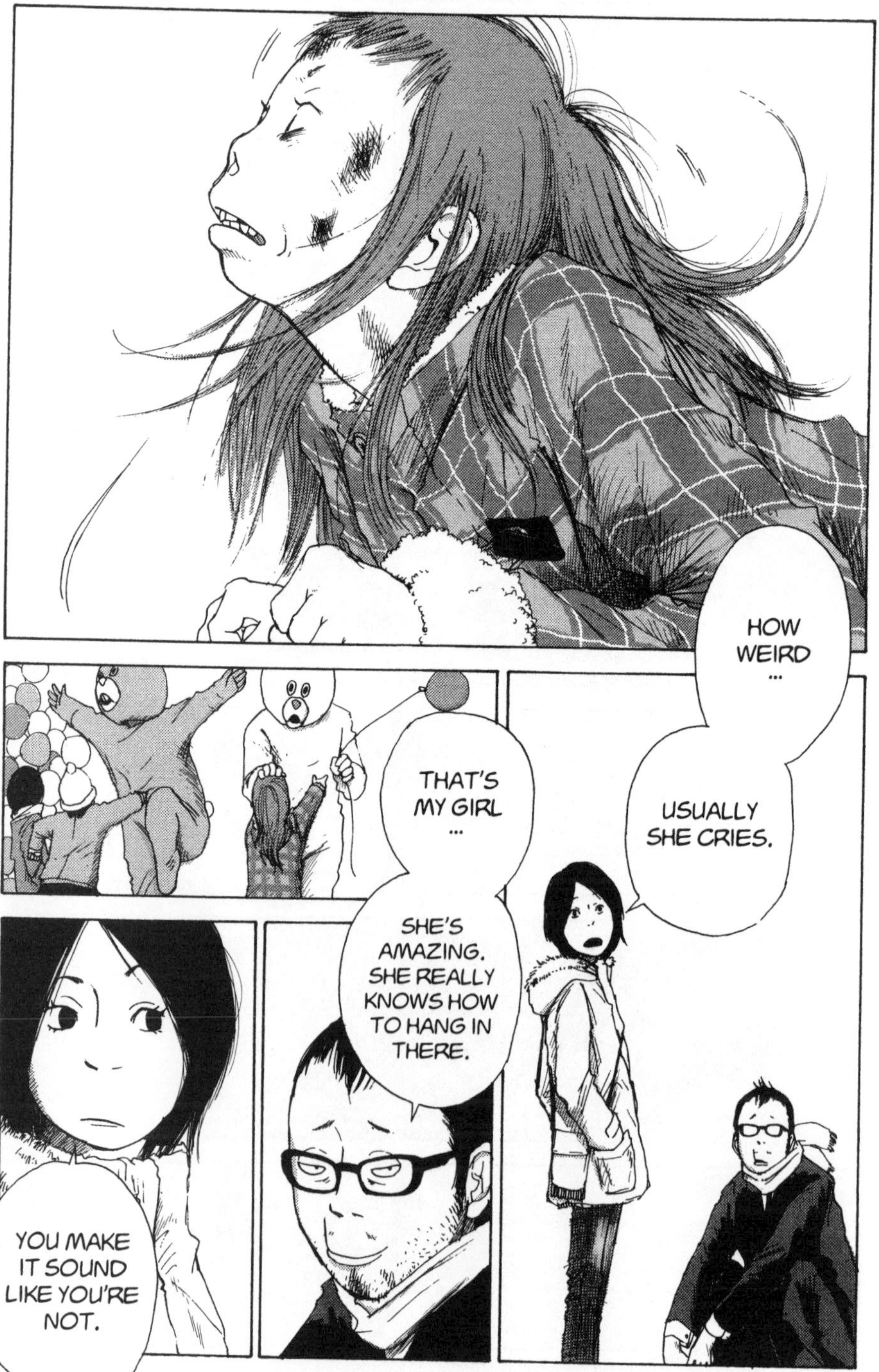
HOW WEIRD ...
USUALLY SHE CRIES.
THAT'S MY GIRL ...
SHE'S AMAZING. SHE REALLY KNOWS HOW TO HANG IN THERE.
YOU MAKE IT SOUND LIKE YOU'RE NOT.

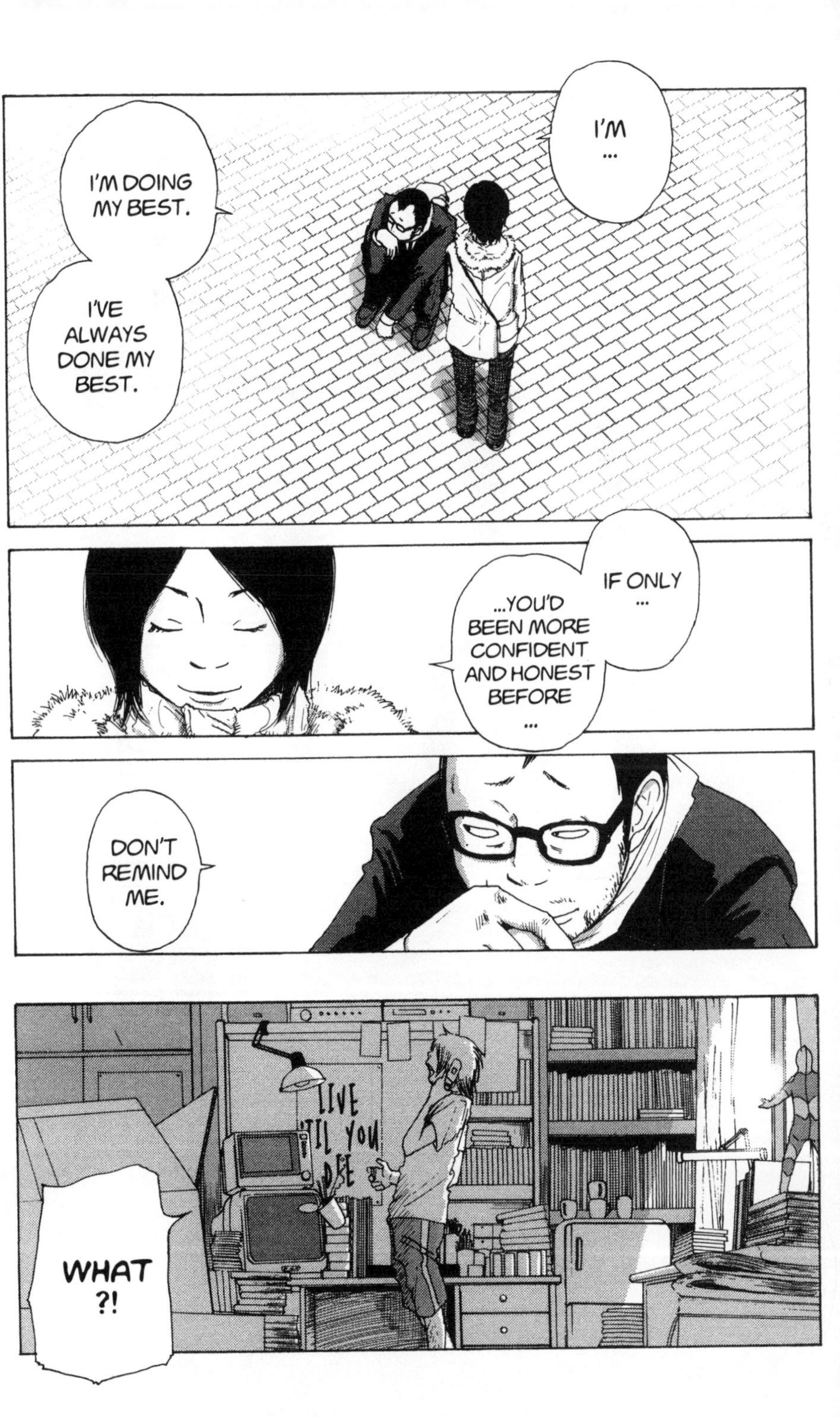
I'M ...
I'M DOING MY BEST.
I'VE ALWAYS DONE MY BEST.
IF ONLY ...
...YOU'D BEEN MORE CONFIDENT AND HONEST BEFORE ...
DON'T REMIND ME.
LIVE
TIL YOU
WHAT ?!

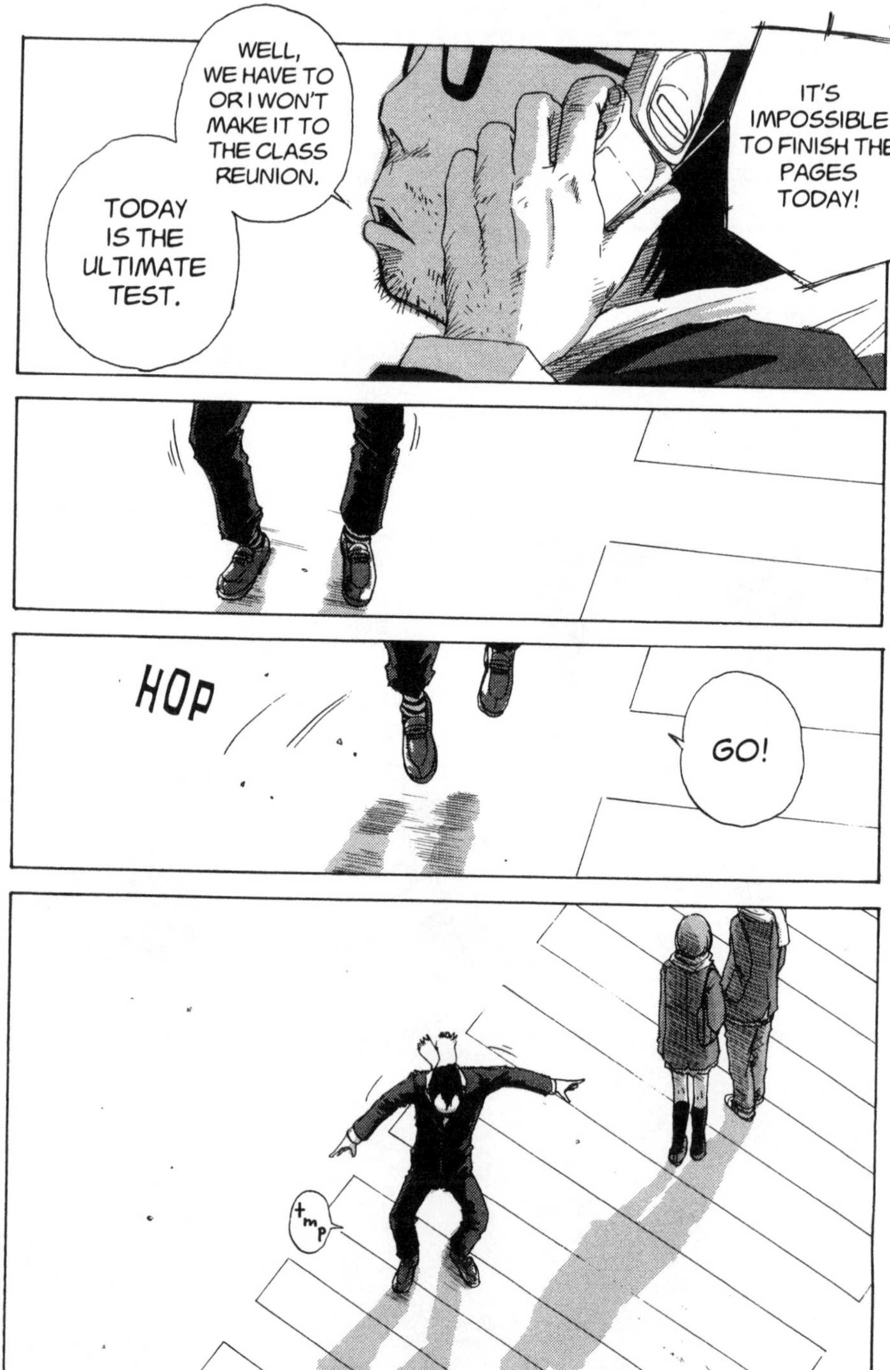
IT'S IMPOSSIBLE TO FINISH THE PAGES TODAY!
WELL, WE HAVE TO OR I WON'T MAKE IT TO THE CLASS REUNION.
TODAY IS THE ULTIMATE TEST.
GO!
HOP
tmp

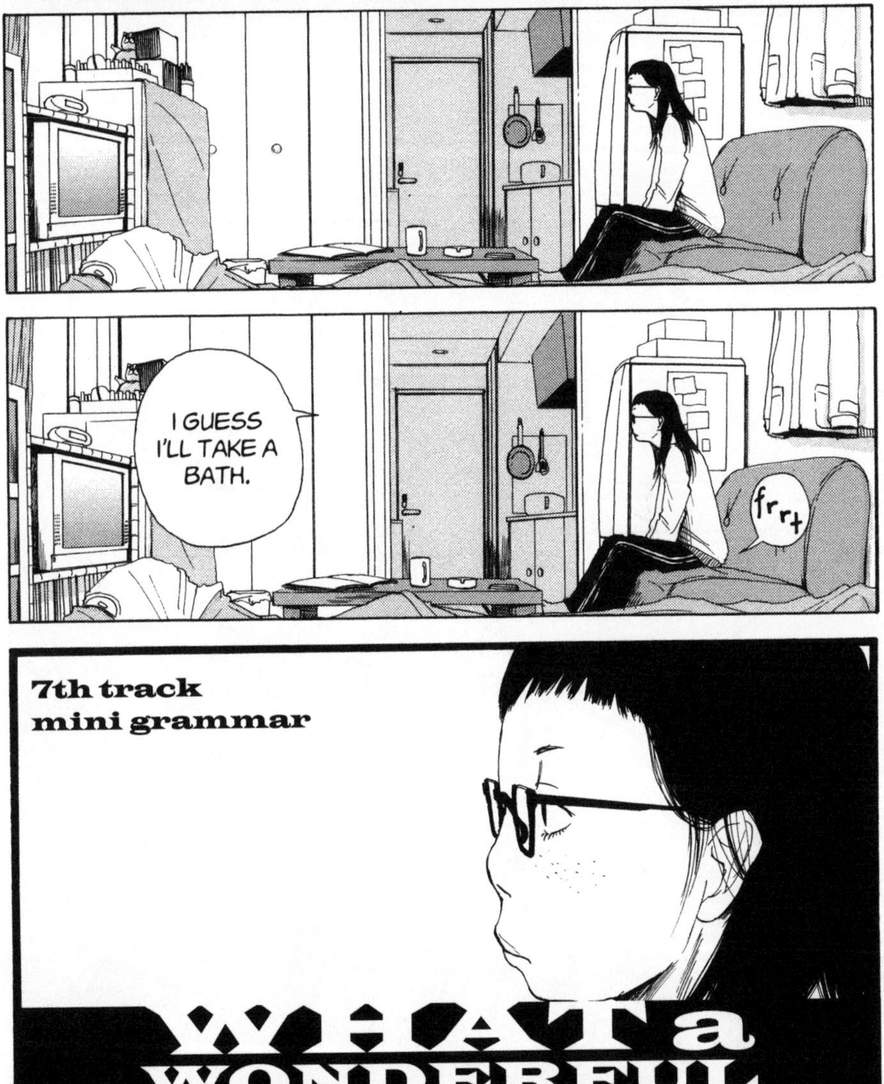
I GUESS I'LL TAKE A BATH.
frrt
7th track
mini grammar
WHAT a WONDERFUL WORLD!

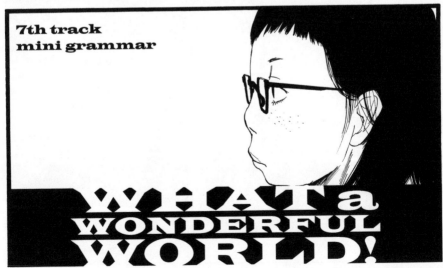

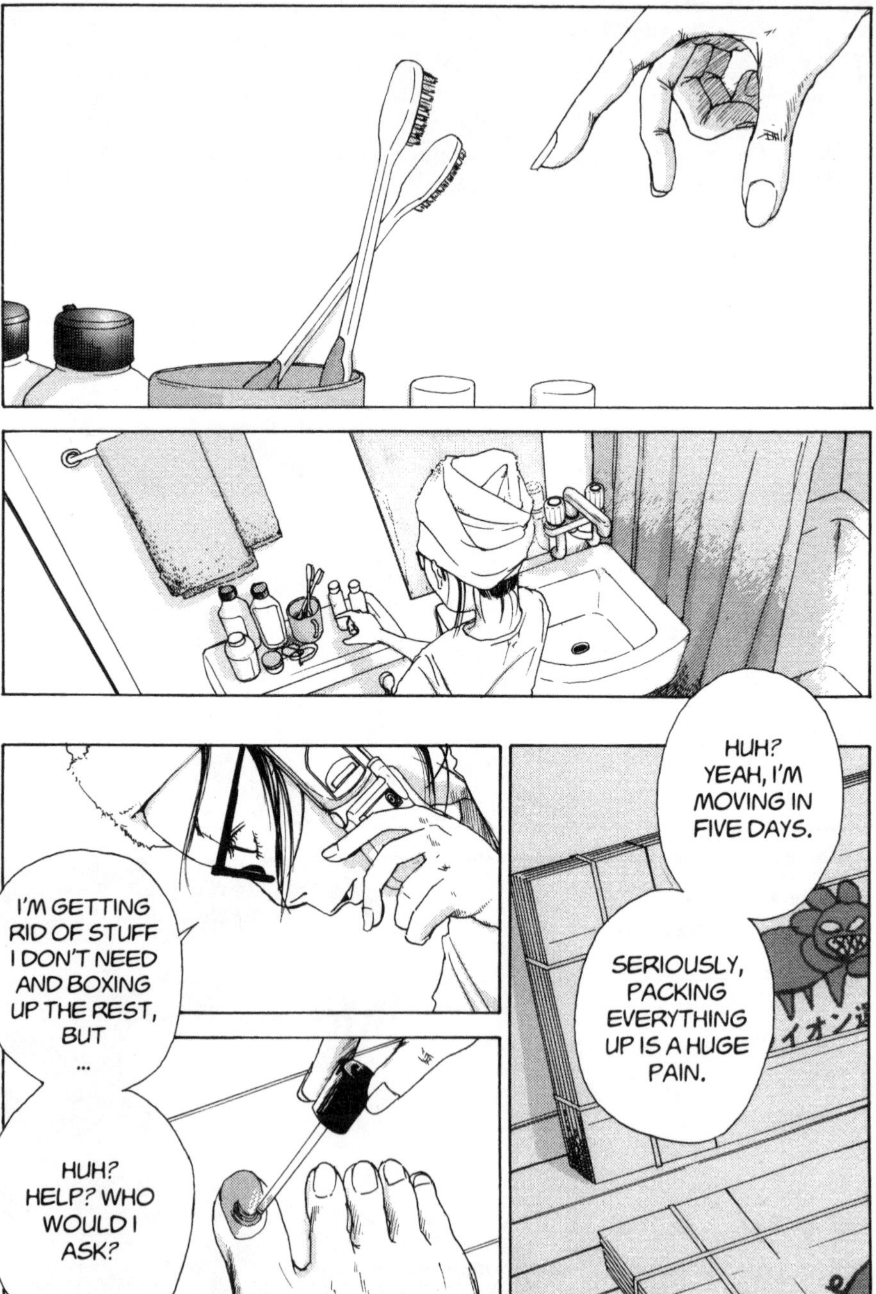
HUH? YEAH, I'M MOVING IN FIVE DAYS.
SERIOUSLY, PACKING EVERYTHING UP IS A HUGE PAIN.
I'M GETTING RID OF STUFF I DON'T NEED AND BOXING UP THE REST, BUT ...
HUH? HELP? WHO WOULD I ASK?

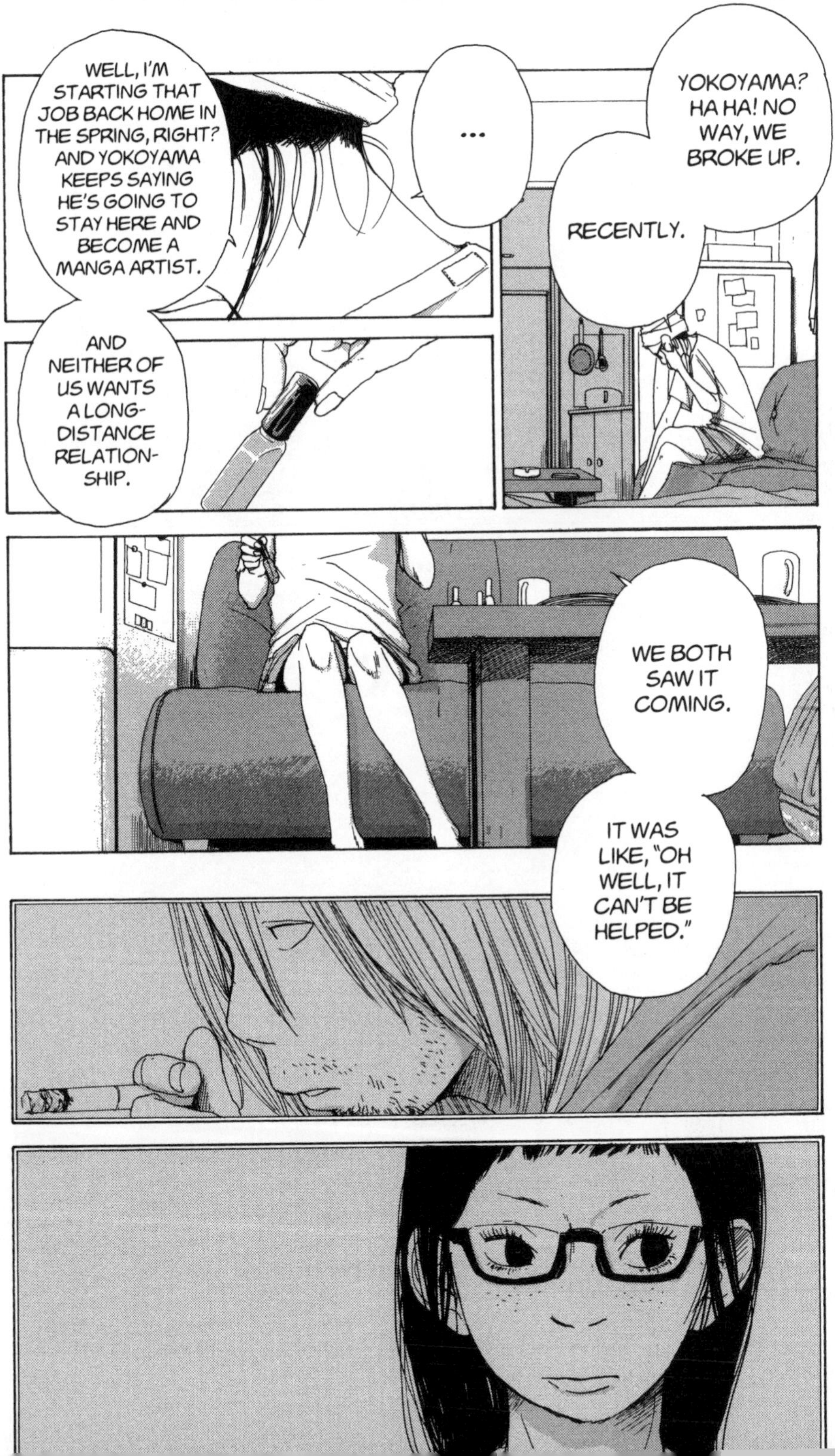
YOKOYAMA? HA HA! NO WAY, WE BROKE UP.
RECENTLY.
...
WELL, I'M STARTING THAT JOB BACK HOME IN THE SPRING, RIGHT? AND YOKOYAMA KEEPS SAYING HE'S GOING TO STAY HERE AND BECOME A MANGA ARTIST.
AND NEITHER OF US WANTS A LONG-DISTANCE RELATION-SHIP.
WE BOTH SAW IT COMING.
IT WAS LIKE, "OH WELL, IT CAN'T BE HELPED."

...YEAH.

I JUST
SPACED
OUT.

HA
HA HA.

SORRY.

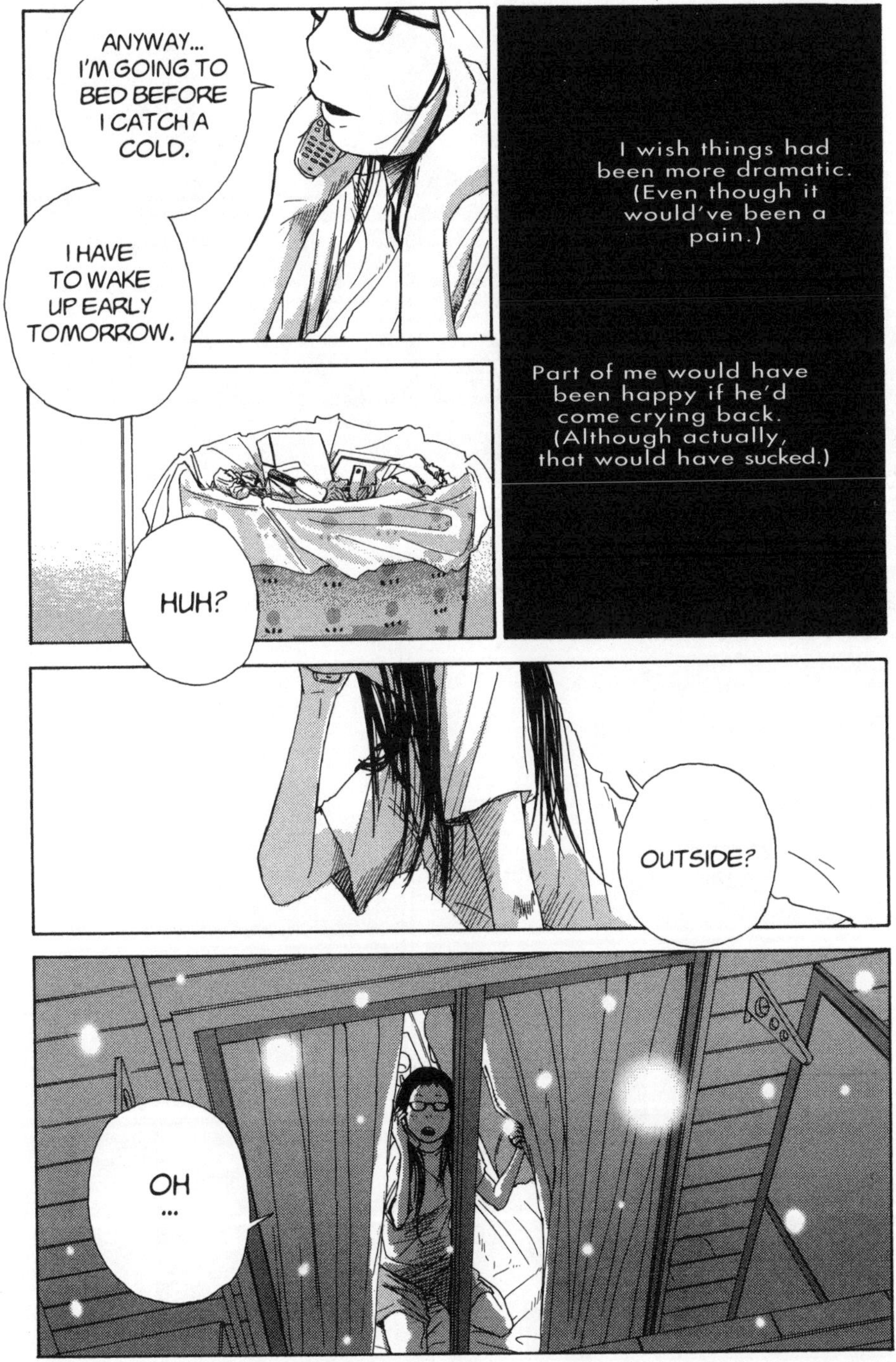
I wish things had been more dramatic. (Even though it would've been a pain.)
Part of me would have been happy if he'd come crying back. (Although actually, that would have sucked.)
ANYWAY... I'M GOING TO BED BEFORE I CATCH A COLD.
I HAVE TO WAKE UP EARLY TOMORROW.
HUH?
OUTSIDE?
OH...

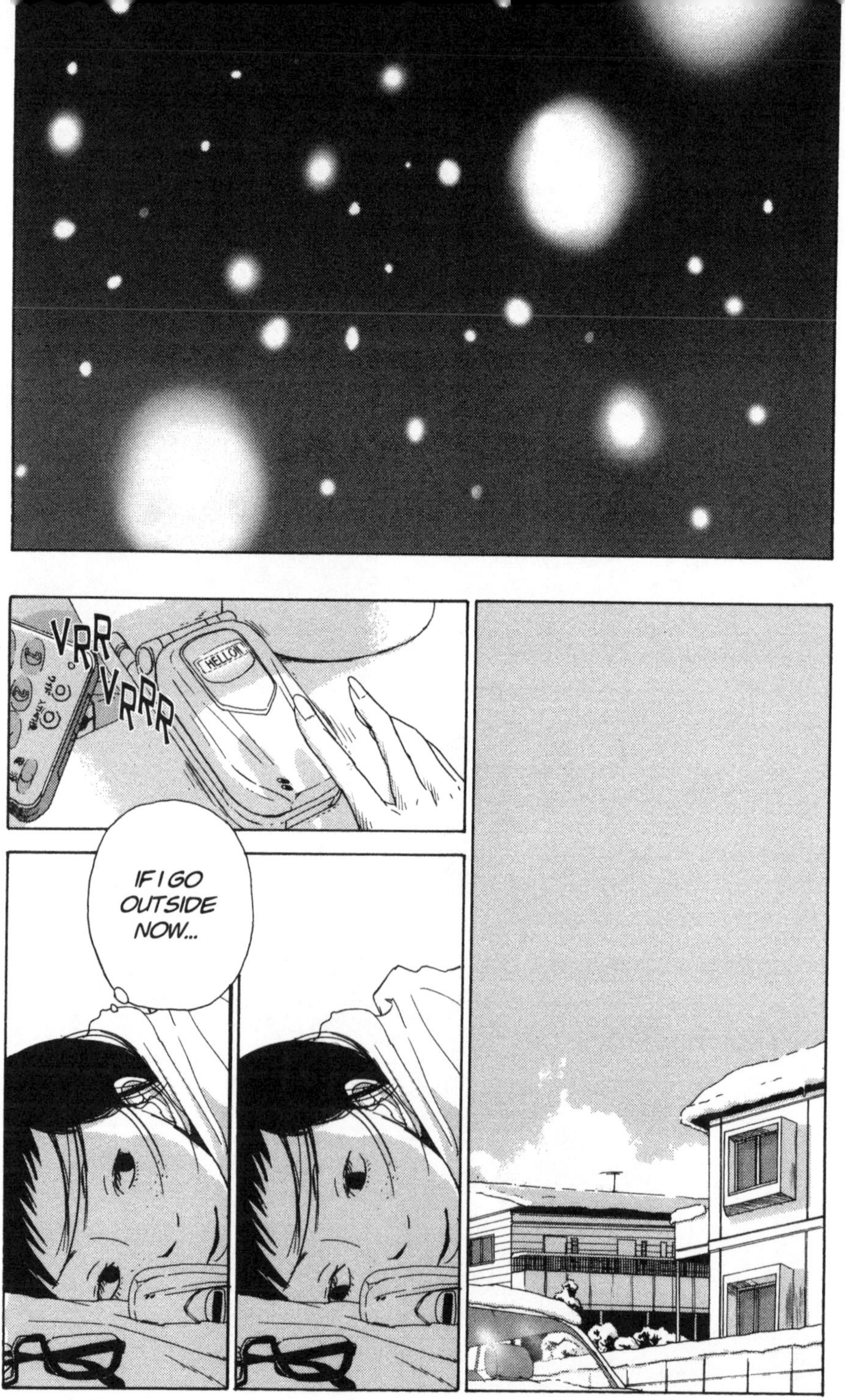
VRR
VRRR
HELLO
IF I GO OUTSIDE NOW...

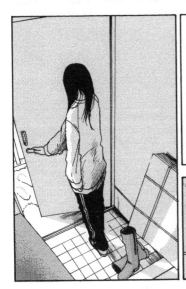

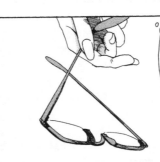

...I CAN HAVE THE SNOW ALL TO MYSELF BEFORE ANYONE ELSE TOUCHES IT.
He must've just left because his footprints were still there, along with a little snowman.
And as the snowman melted, it revealed a ring that fit my finger perfectly...

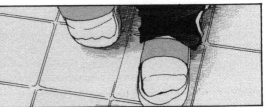

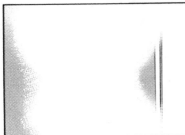

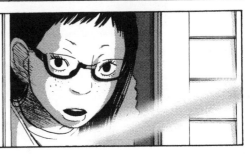

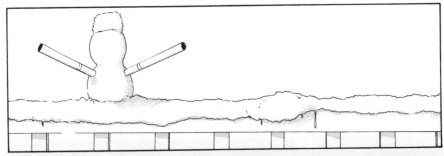

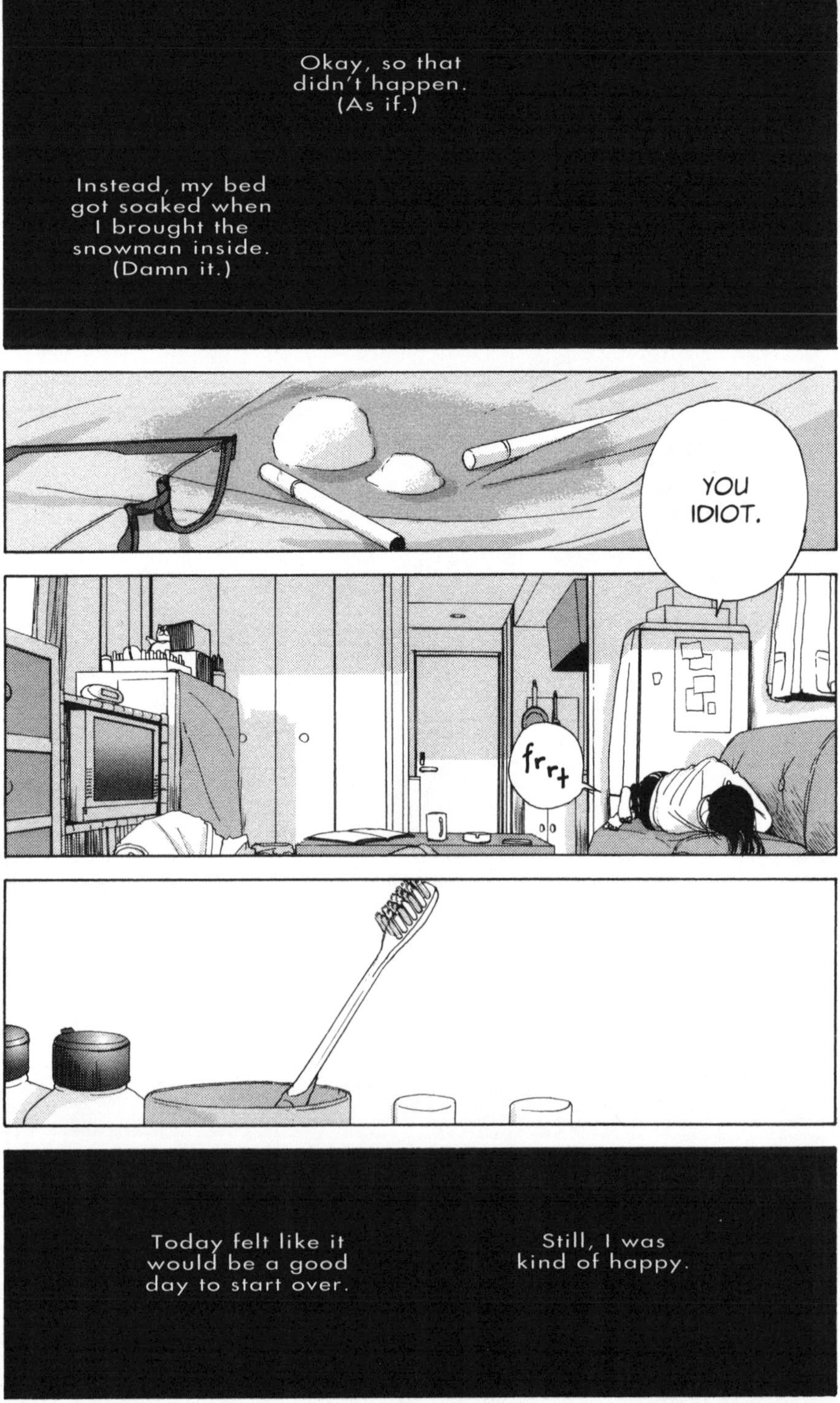
Okay, so that didn't happen. (As if.)
Instead, my bed got soaked when I brought the snowman inside. (Damn it.)
YOU IDIOT.
frrt
Still, I was kind of happy.
Today felt like it would be a good day to start over.

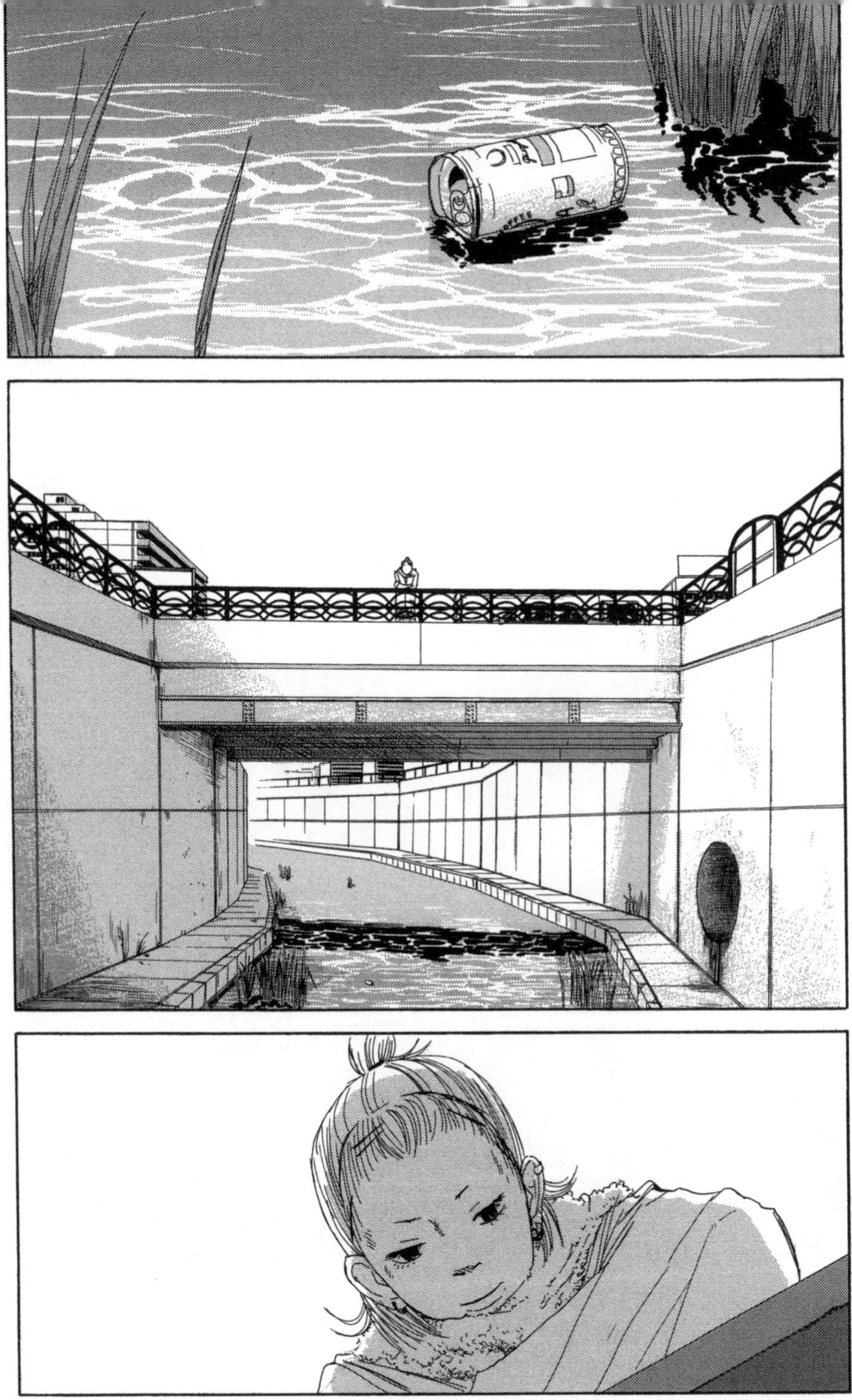

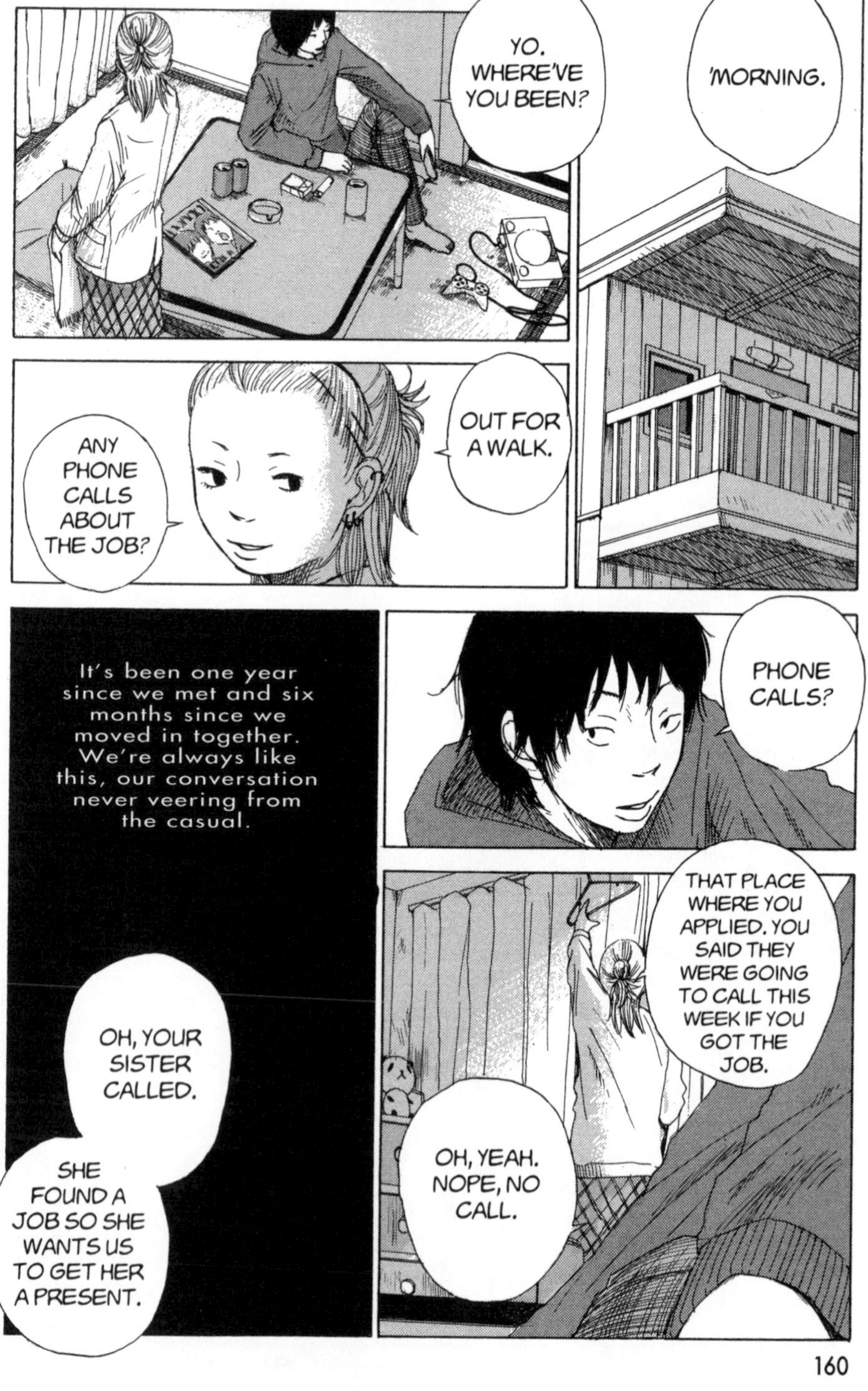
'MORNING.
YO. WHERE'VE YOU BEEN?
OUT FOR A WALK.
ANY PHONE CALLS ABOUT THE JOB?
PHONE CALLS?
THAT PLACE WHERE YOU APPLIED. YOU SAID THEY WERE GOING TO CALL THIS WEEK IF YOU GOT THE JOB.
OH, YEAH. NOPE, NO CALL.
It's been one year since we met and six months since we moved in together. We're always like this, our conversation never veering from the casual.
OH, YOUR SISTER CALLED.
SHE FOUND A JOB SO SHE WANTS US TO GET HER A PRESENT.

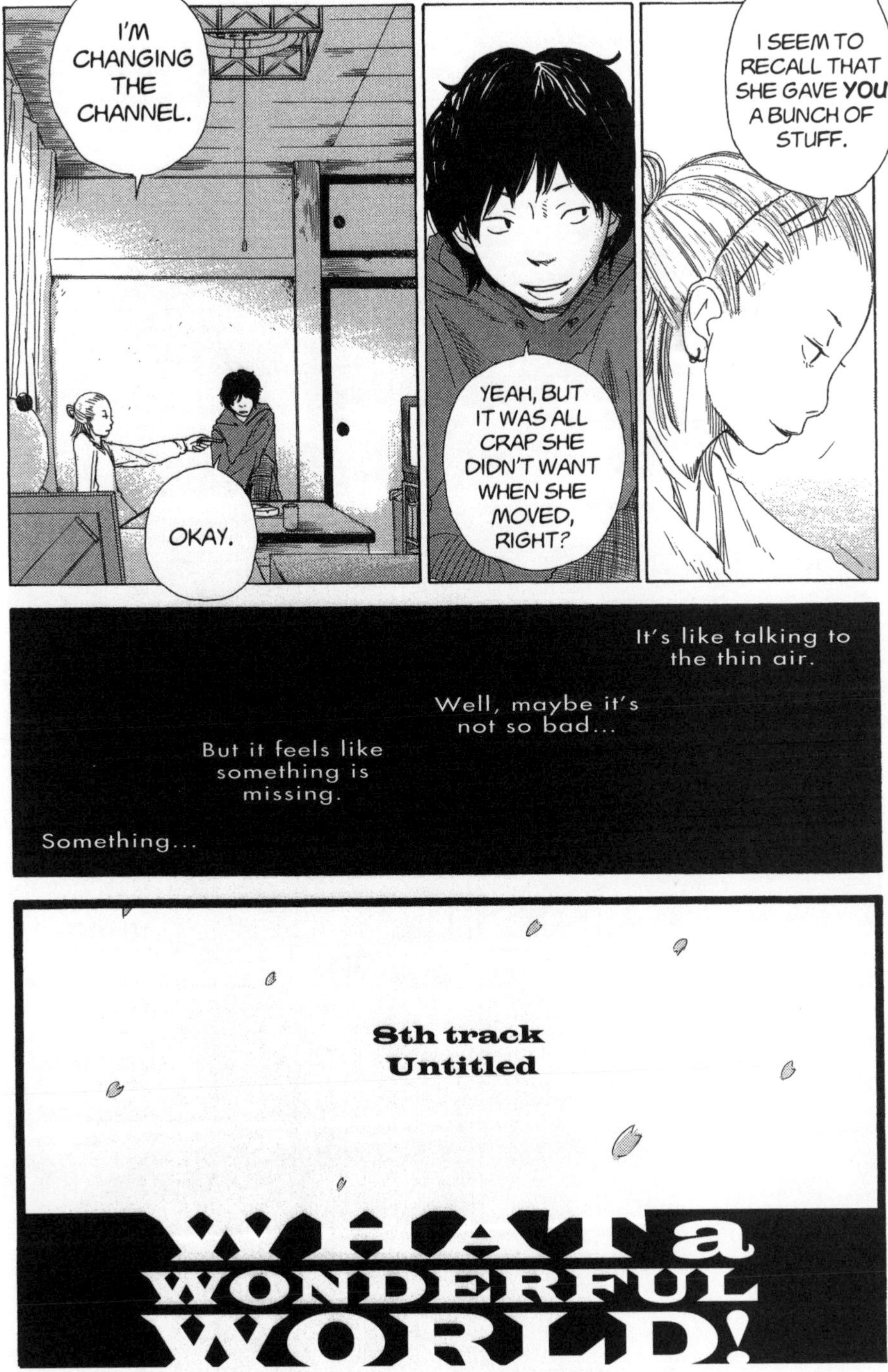
I SEEM TO RECALL THAT SHE GAVE **YOU** A BUNCH OF STUFF.
YEAH, BUT IT WAS ALL CRAP SHE DIDN'T WANT WHEN SHE MOVED, RIGHT?
I'M CHANGING THE CHANNEL.
OKAY.
It's like talking to the thin air.
Well, maybe it's not so bad...
But it feels like something is missing.
Something...
8th track
Untitled
WHAT a WONDERFUL WORLD!

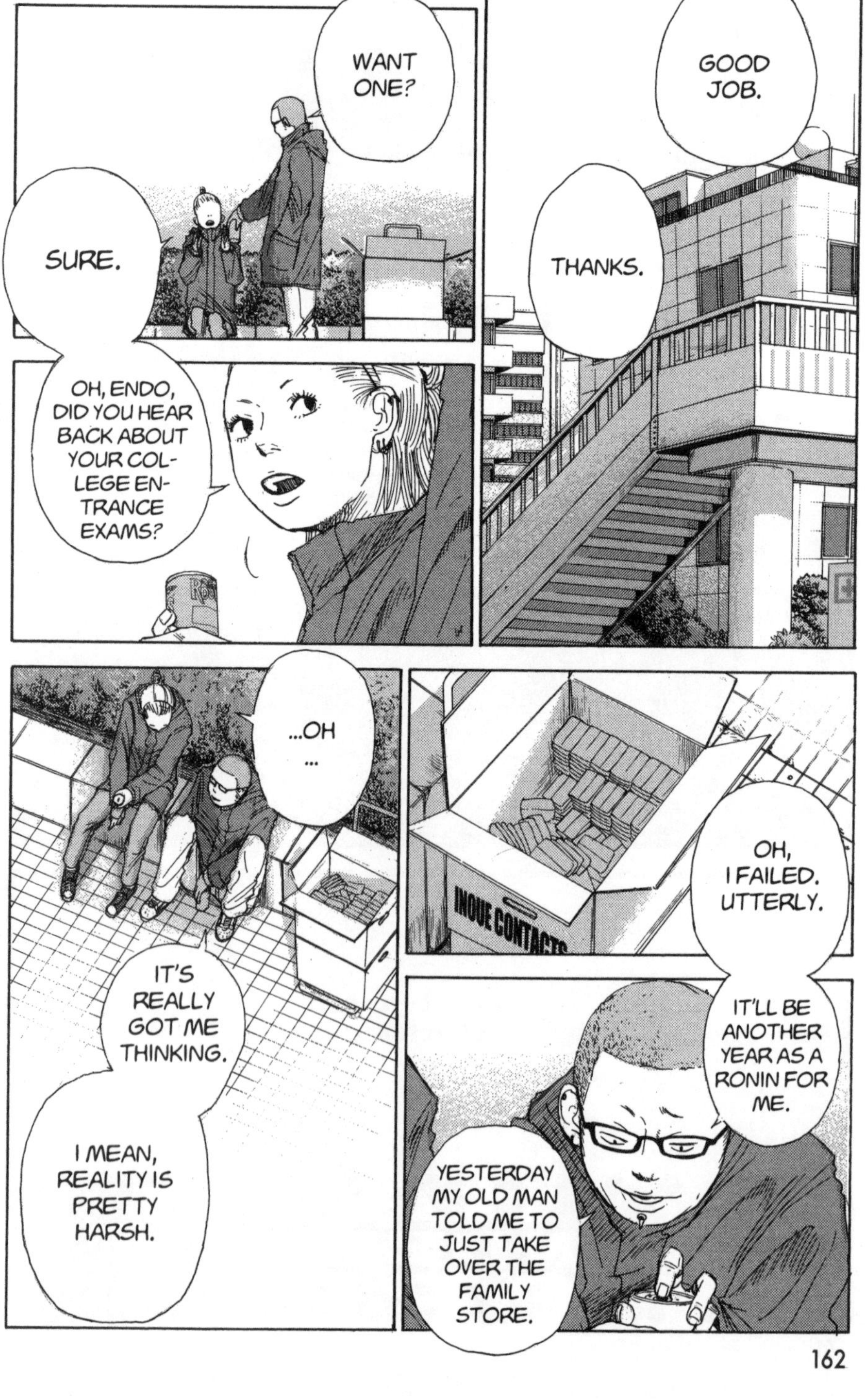
GOOD JOB.
THANKS.
WANT ONE?
SURE.
OH, ENDO, DID YOU HEAR BACK ABOUT YOUR COL- LEGE EN- TRANCE EXAMS?
INOUE CONTACTS
OH, I FAILED. UTTERLY.
IT'LL BE ANOTHER YEAR AS A RONIN FOR ME.
YESTERDAY MY OLD MAN TOLD ME TO JUST TAKE OVER THE FAMILY STORE.
...OH ...
IT'S REALLY GOT ME THINKING.
I MEAN, REALITY IS PRETTY HARSH.

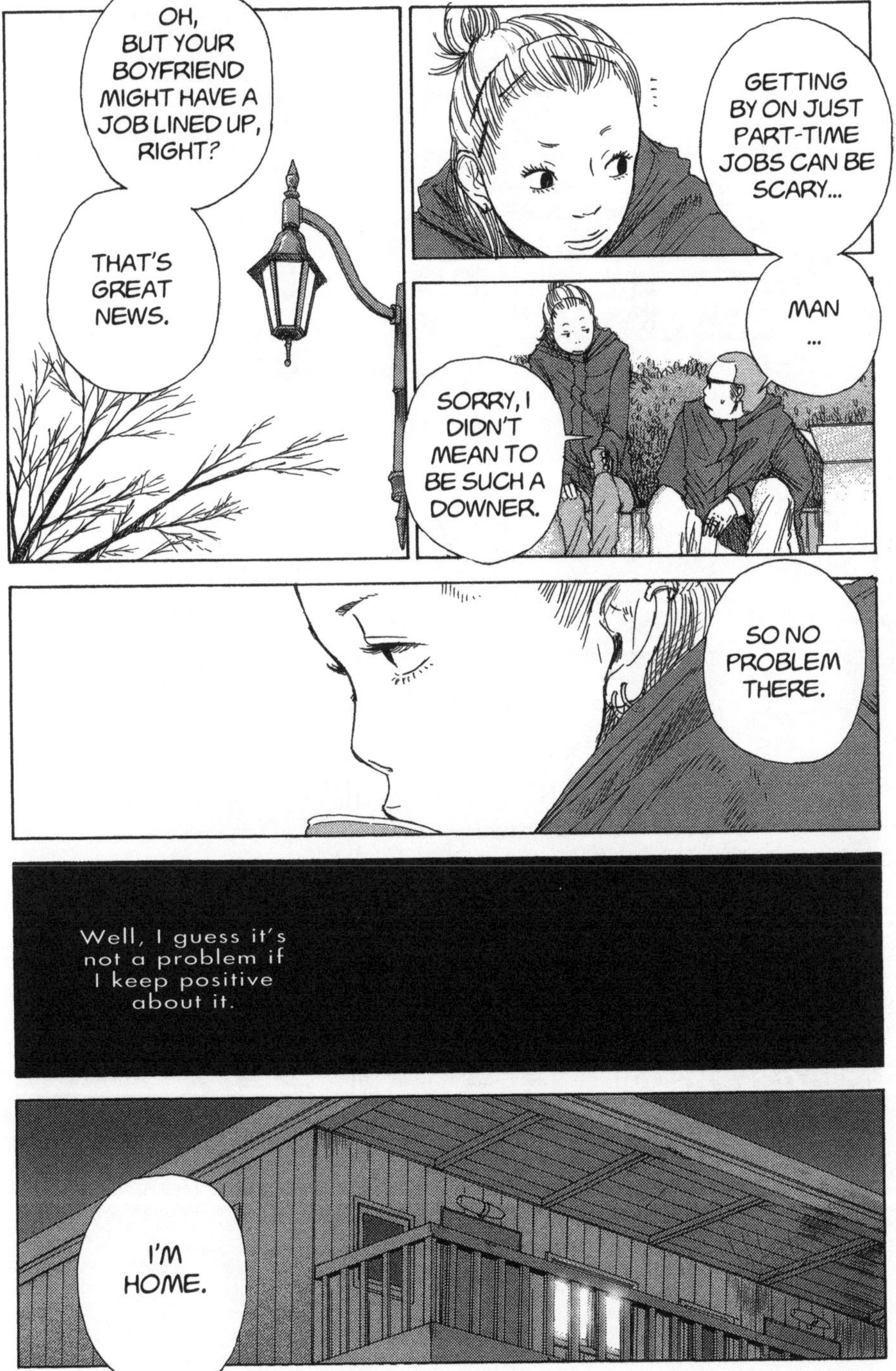
GETTING BY ON JUST PART-TIME JOBS CAN BE SCARY...
MAN ...
SORRY, I DIDN'T MEAN TO BE SUCH A DOWNER.
OH, BUT YOUR BOYFRIEND MIGHT HAVE A JOB LINED UP, RIGHT?
THAT'S GREAT NEWS.
SO NO PROBLEM THERE.
Well, I guess it's not a problem if I keep positive about it.
I'M HOME.

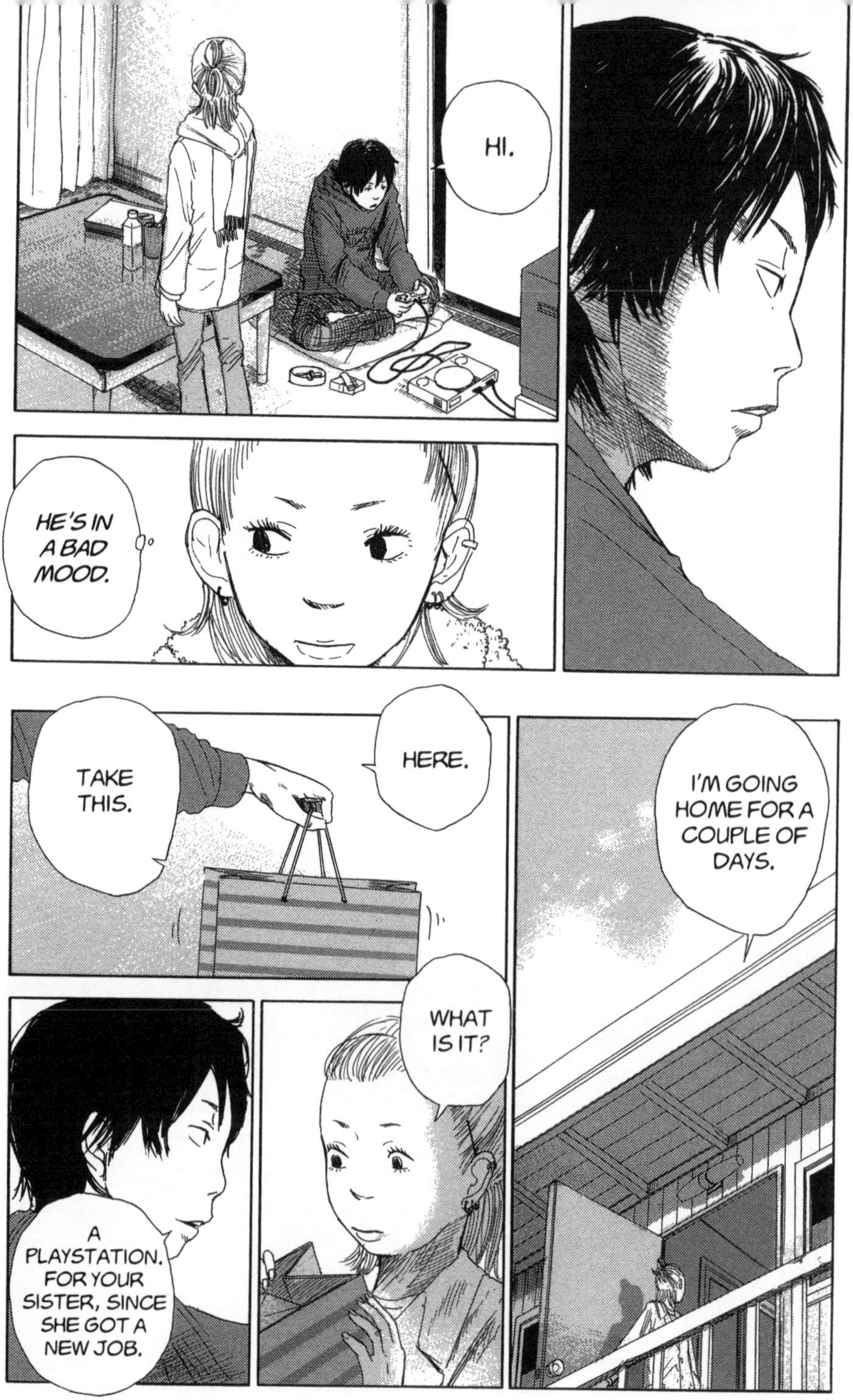
HI.
HE'S IN A BAD MOOD.
I'M GOING HOME FOR A COUPLE OF DAYS.
HERE.
TAKE THIS.
WHAT IS IT?
A PLAYSTATION. FOR YOUR SISTER, SINCE SHE GOT A NEW JOB.

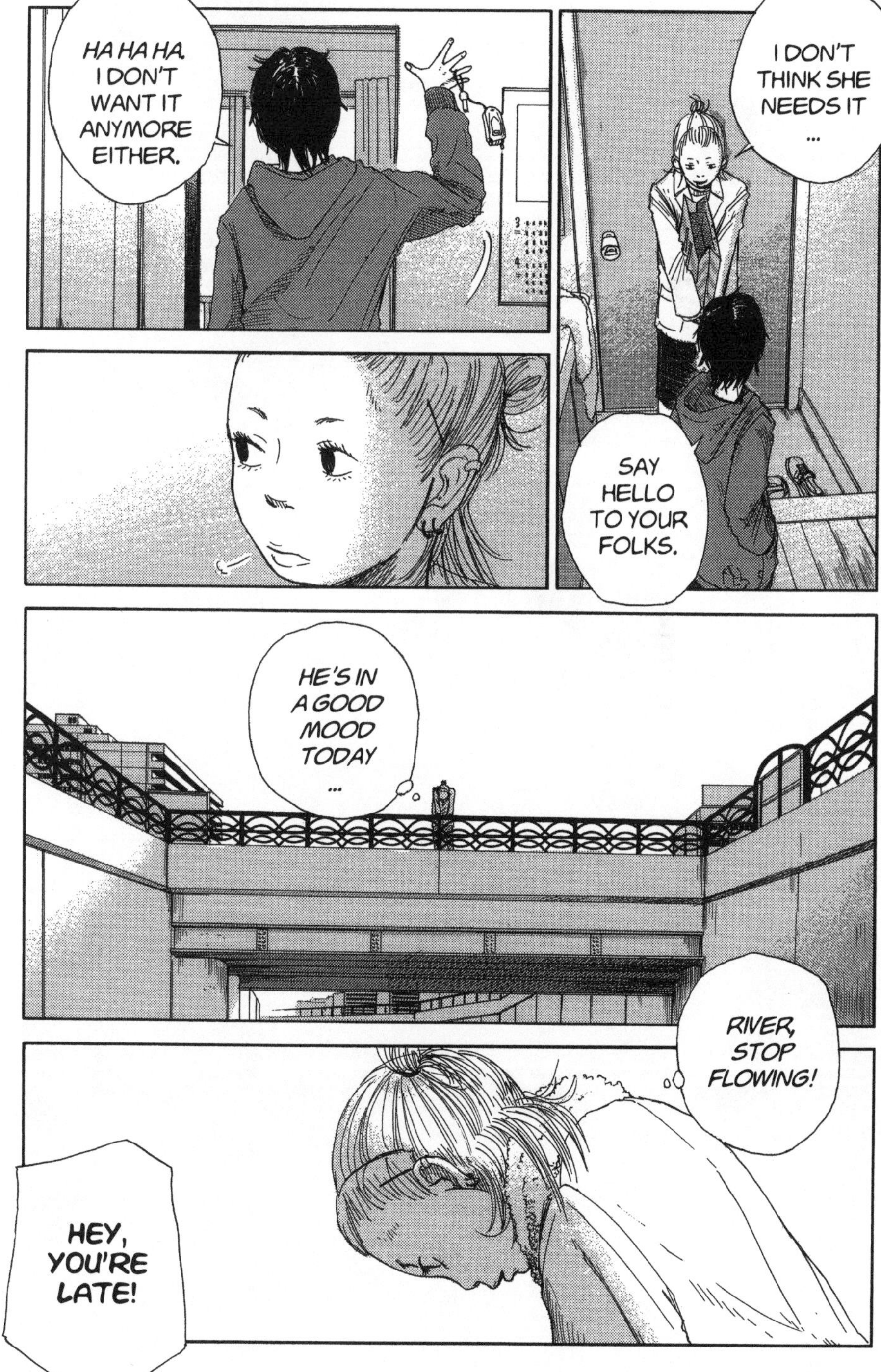
I DON'T THINK SHE NEEDS IT ...
SAY HELLO TO YOUR FOLKS.
HA HA HA. I DON'T WANT IT ANYMORE EITHER.
HE'S IN A GOOD MOOD TODAY ...
RIVER, STOP FLOWING!
HEY, YOU'RE LATE!

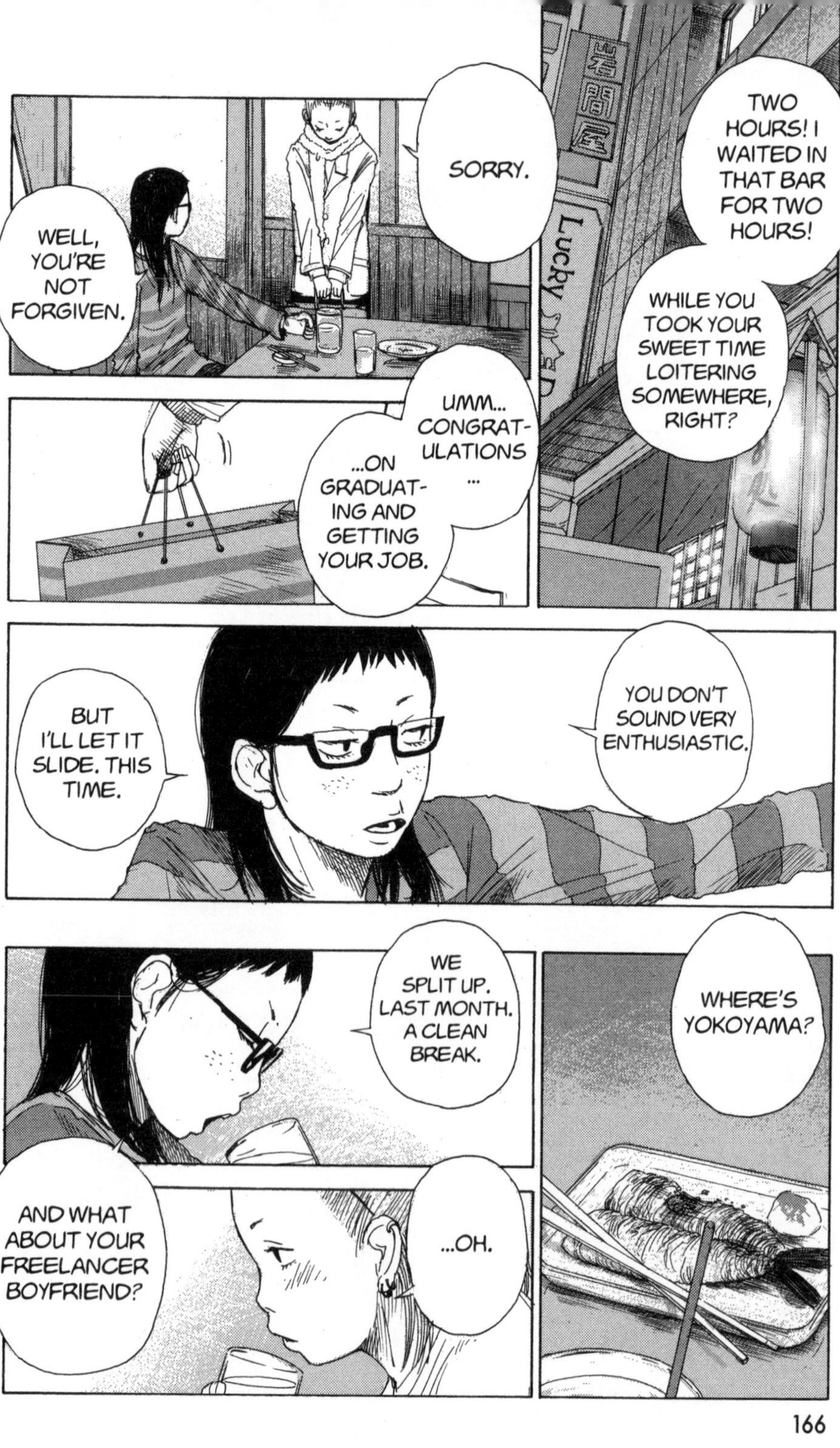
Lucky
TWO HOURS! I WAITED IN THAT BAR FOR TWO HOURS!
WHILE YOU TOOK YOUR SWEET TIME LOITERING SOMEWHERE, RIGHT?
SORRY.
WELL, YOU'RE NOT FORGIVEN.
UMM... CONGRATULATIONS ...
...ON GRADUATING AND GETTING YOUR JOB.
YOU DON'T SOUND VERY ENTHUSIASTIC.
BUT I'LL LET IT SLIDE. THIS TIME.
WHERE'S YOKOYAMA?
WE SPLIT UP. LAST MONTH. A CLEAN BREAK.
...OH.
AND WHAT ABOUT YOUR FREELANCER BOYFRIEND?

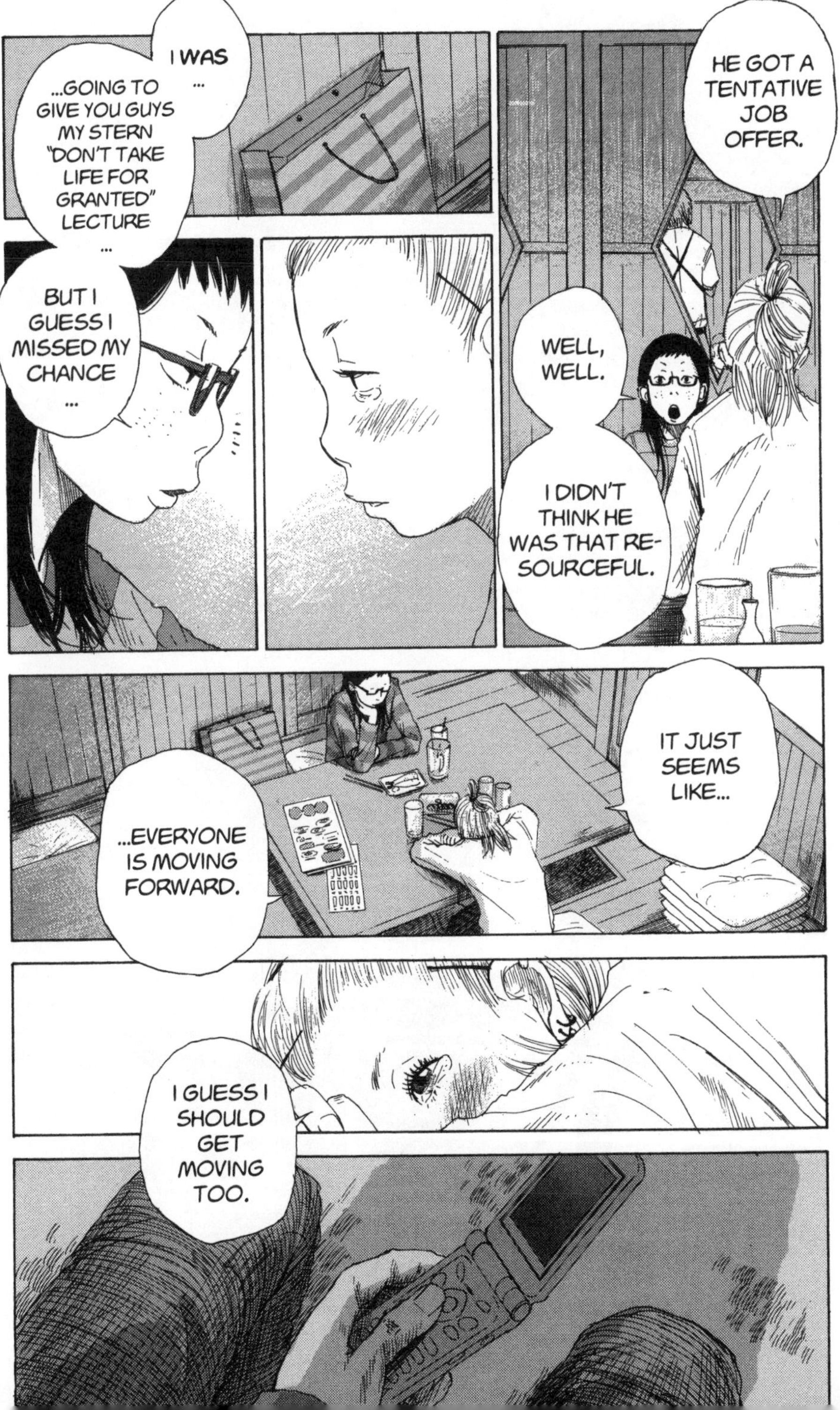
HE GOT A TENTATIVE JOB OFFER.
WELL, WELL.
I DIDN'T THINK HE WAS THAT RE-SOURCEFUL.
I WAS ...
...GOING TO GIVE YOU GUYS MY STERN "DON'T TAKE LIFE FOR GRANTED" LECTURE ...
BUT I GUESS I MISSED MY CHANCE ...
IT JUST SEEMS LIKE...
...EVERYONE IS MOVING FORWARD.
I GUESS I SHOULD GET MOVING TOO.

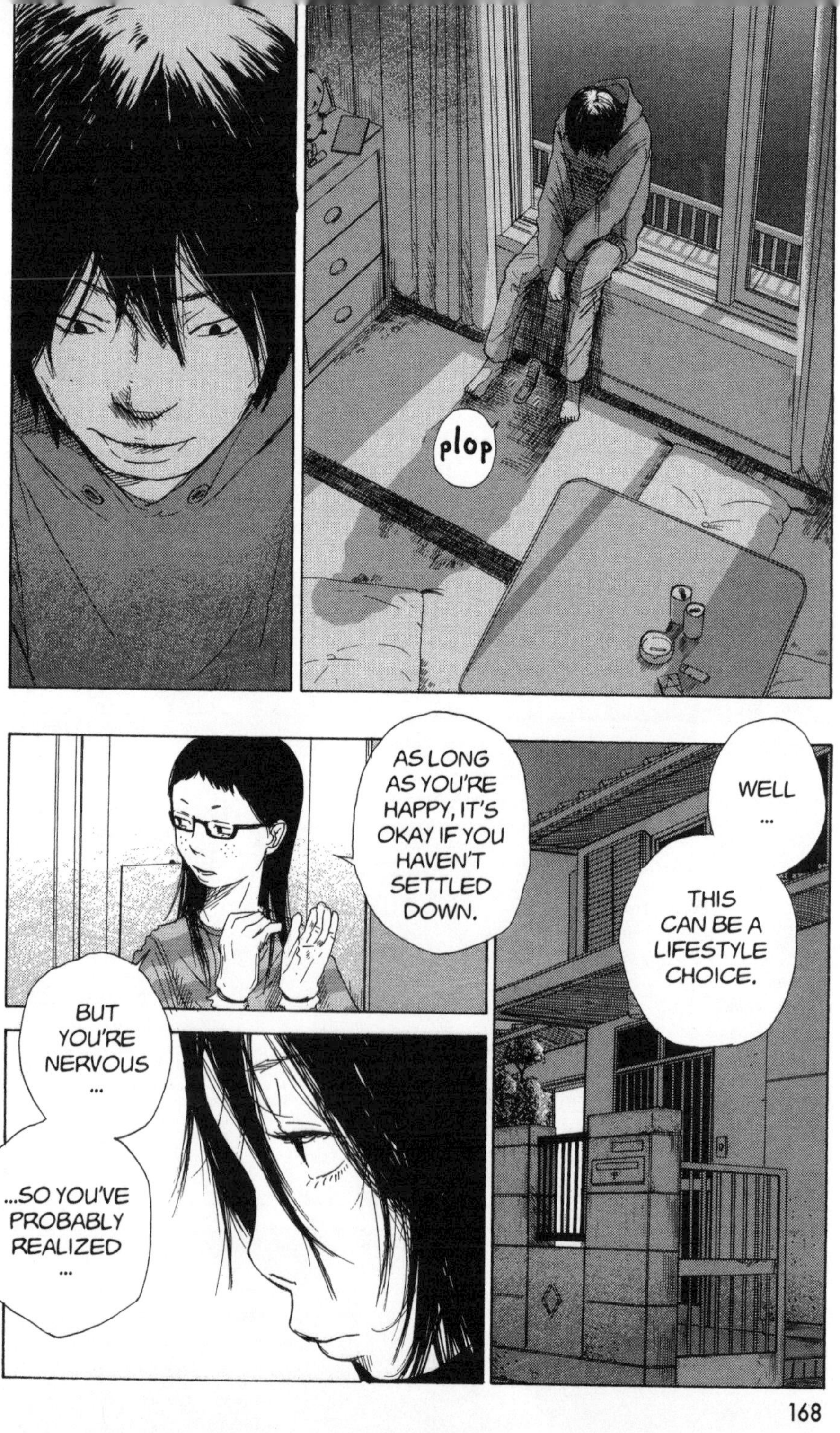
plop
WELL ...
THIS CAN BE A LIFESTYLE CHOICE.
AS LONG AS YOU'RE HAPPY, IT'S OKAY IF YOU HAVEN'T SETTLED DOWN.
BUT YOU'RE NERVOUS ...
...SO YOU'VE PROBABLY REALIZED ...

...THAT HAPPINESS NEVER LASTS.

snip

That's true.

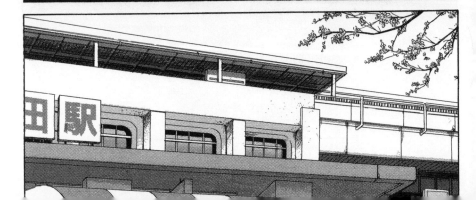

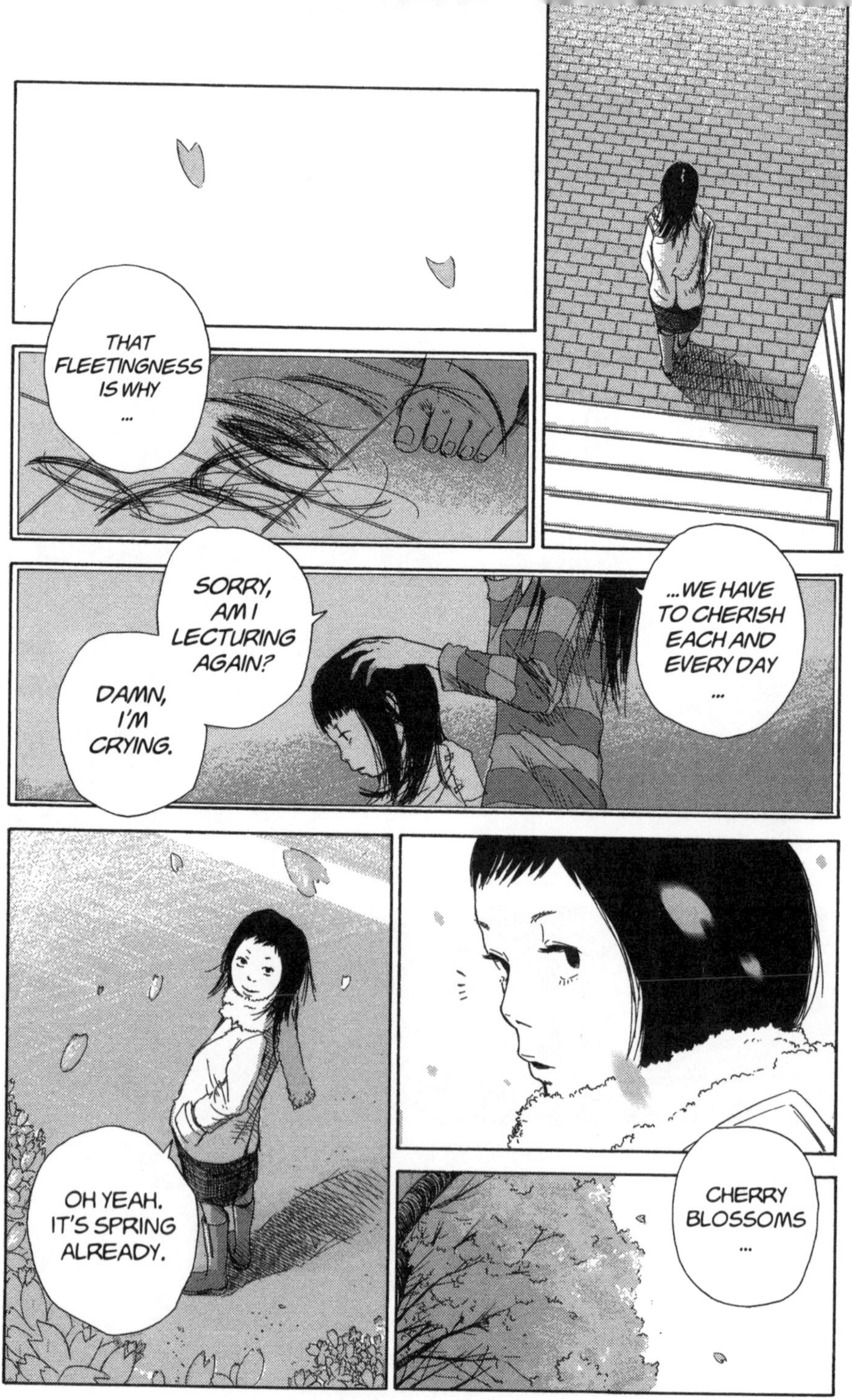
THAT FLEETINGNESS IS WHY ...
...WE HAVE TO CHERISH EACH AND EVERY DAY ...
SORRY, AM I LECTURING AGAIN?
DAMN, I'M CRYING.
CHERRY BLOSSOMS ...
OH YEAH. IT'S SPRING ALREADY.

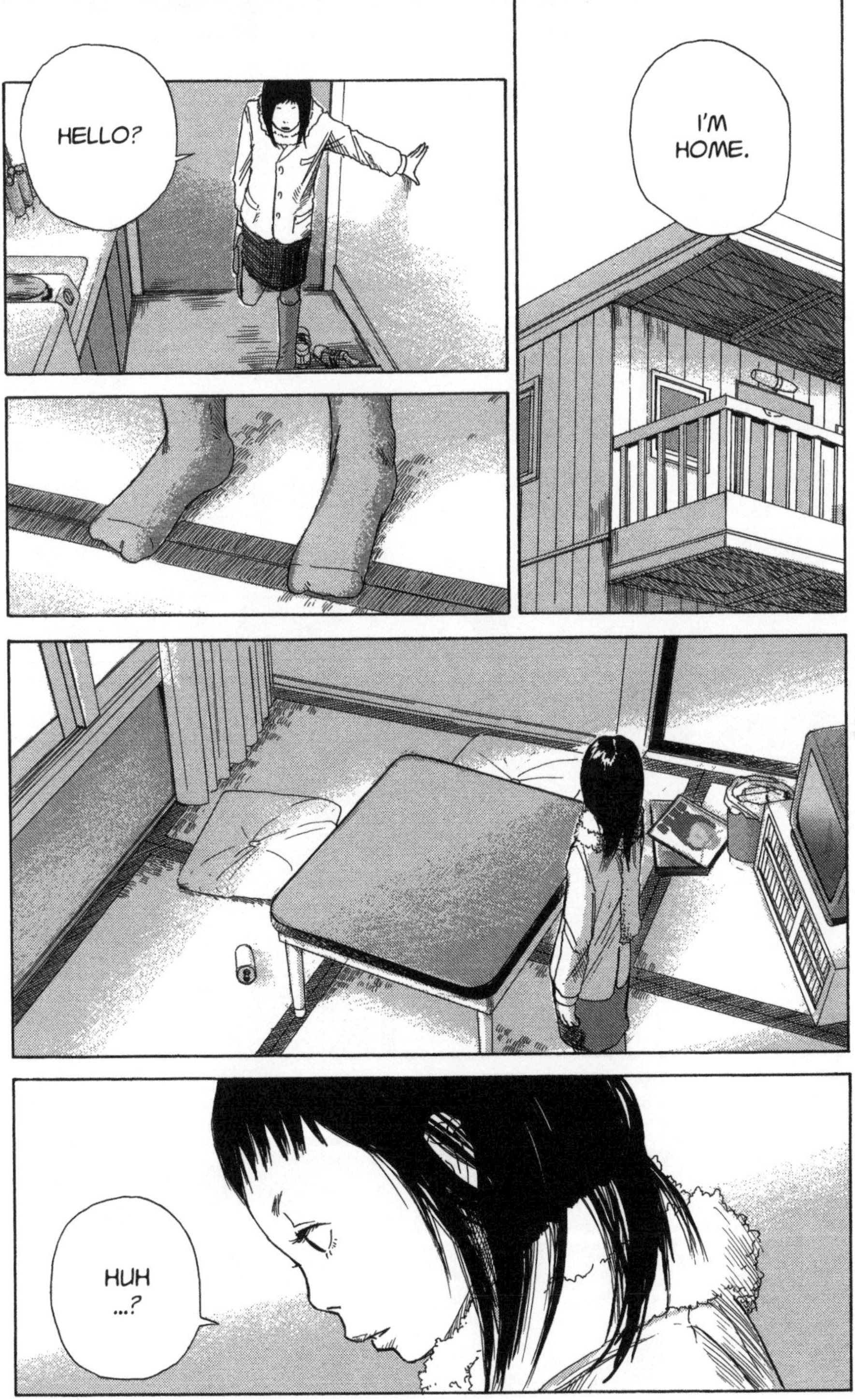
I'M HOME.
HELLO?
HUH ...?

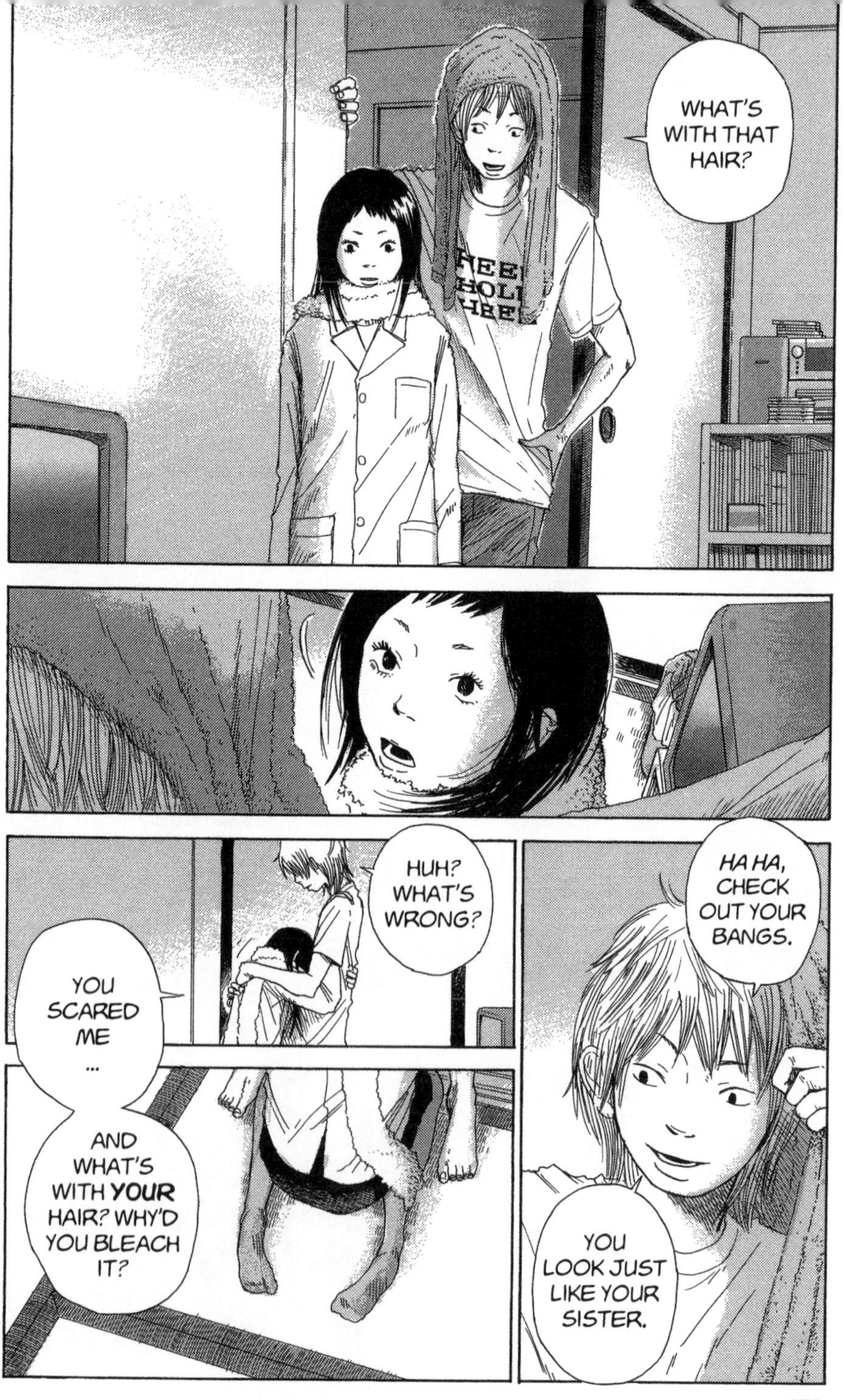
WHAT'S WITH THAT HAIR?
HA HA, CHECK OUT YOUR BANGS.
YOU LOOK JUST LIKE YOUR SISTER.
HUH? WHAT'S WRONG?
YOU SCARED ME ...
AND WHAT'S WITH **YOUR** HAIR? WHY'D YOU BLEACH IT?

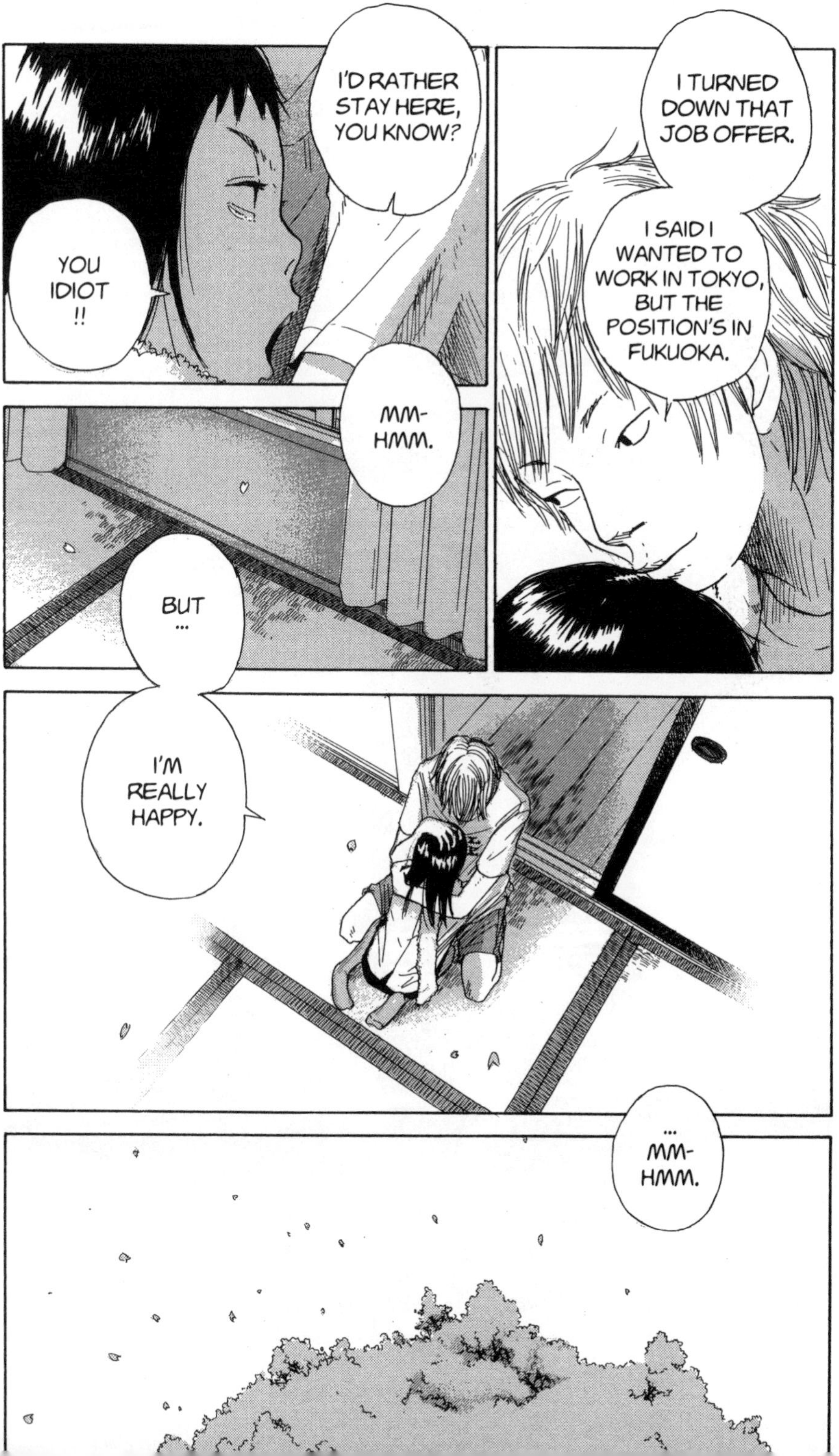
I TURNED DOWN THAT JOB OFFER.
I SAID I WANTED TO WORK IN TOKYO, BUT THE POSITION'S IN FUKUOKA.
I'D RATHER STAY HERE, YOU KNOW?
YOU IDIOT !!
MM-HMM.
BUT ...
I'M REALLY HAPPY.
... MM-HMM.

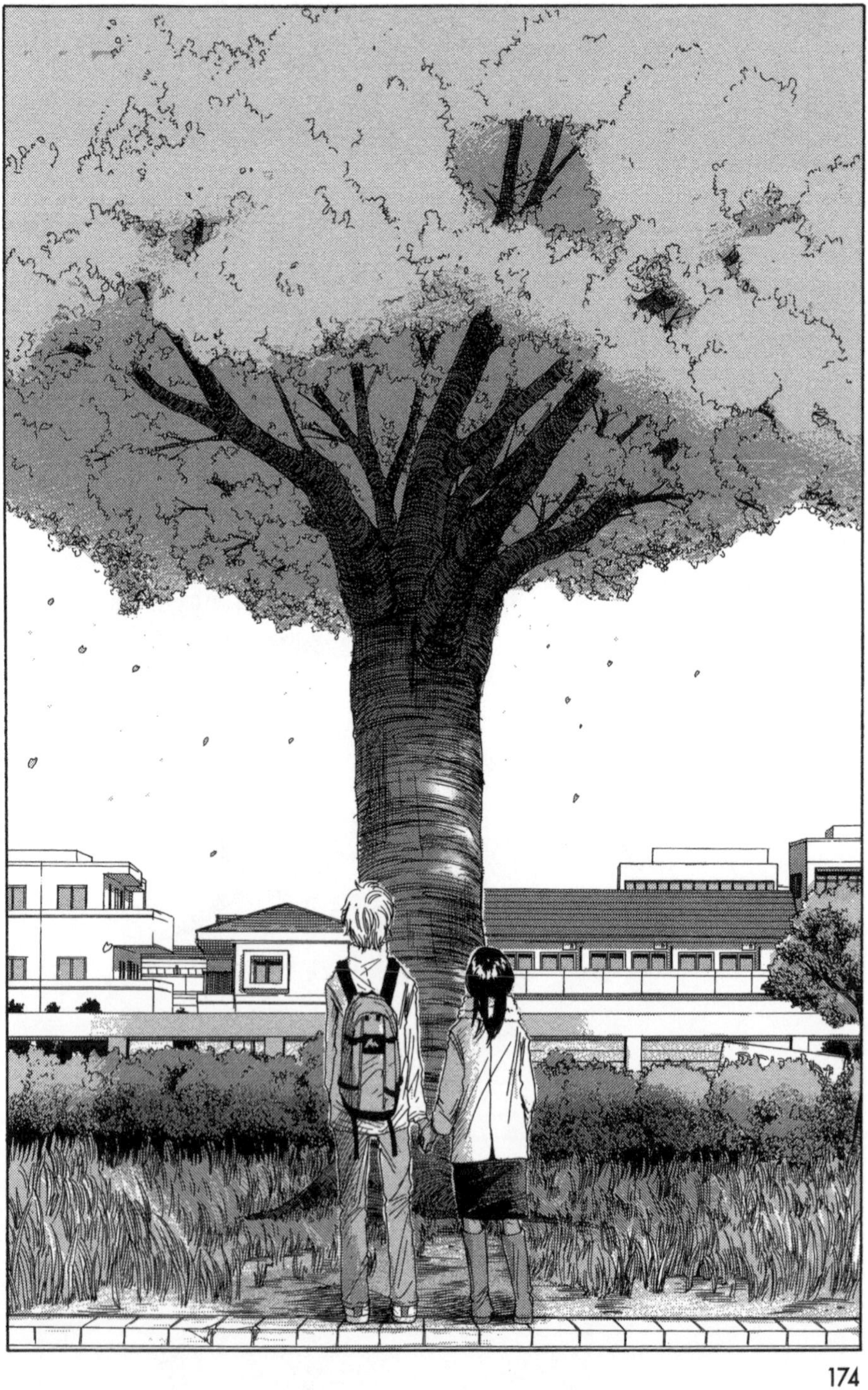

I DIDN'T KNOW ...
...THIS HUGE TREE WAS EVEN HERE.
IT'S SO PRETTY.
IT SURE IS.
Let's come to see it again next year.

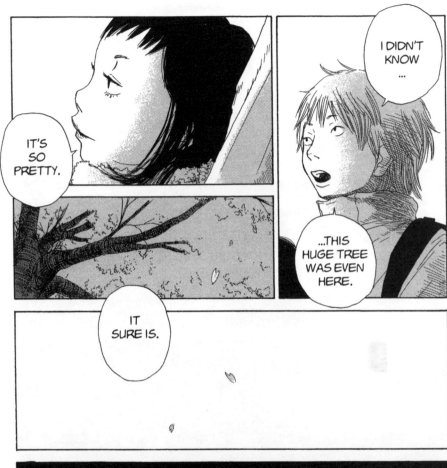

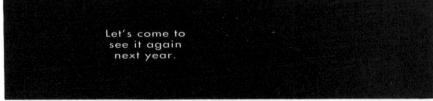

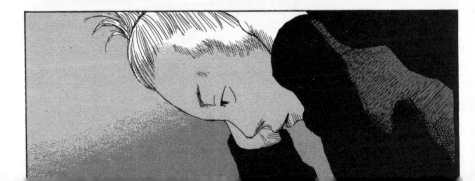

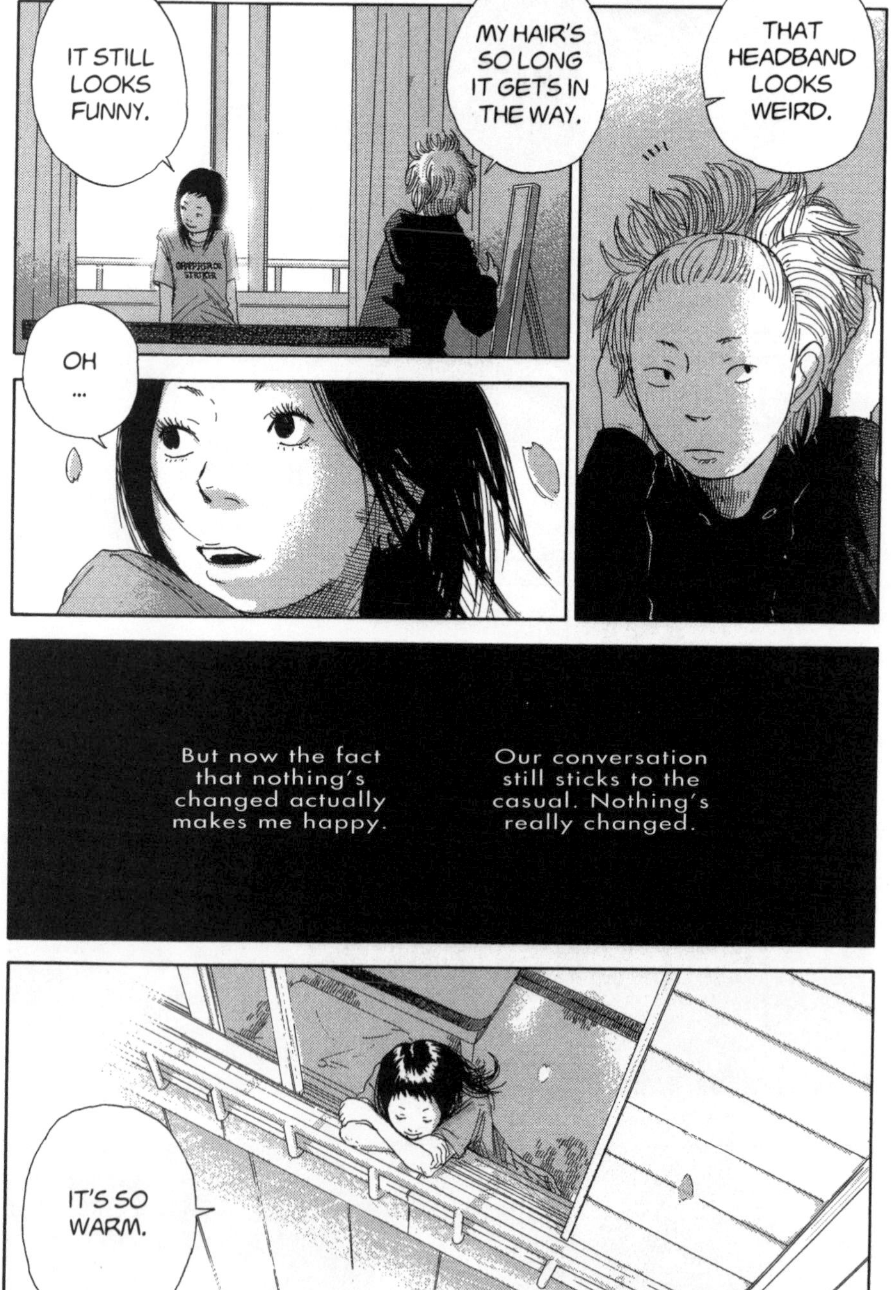
THAT HEADBAND LOOKS WEIRD.
MY HAIR'S SO LONG IT GETS IN THE WAY.
IT STILL LOOKS FUNNY.
OH ...
Our conversation still sticks to the casual. Nothing's really changed.
But now the fact that nothing's changed actually makes me happy.
IT'S SO WARM.

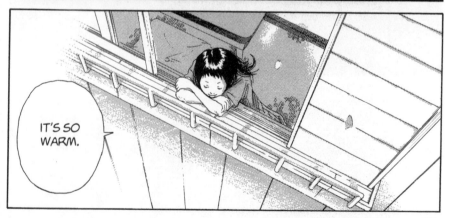

9th track Syrup

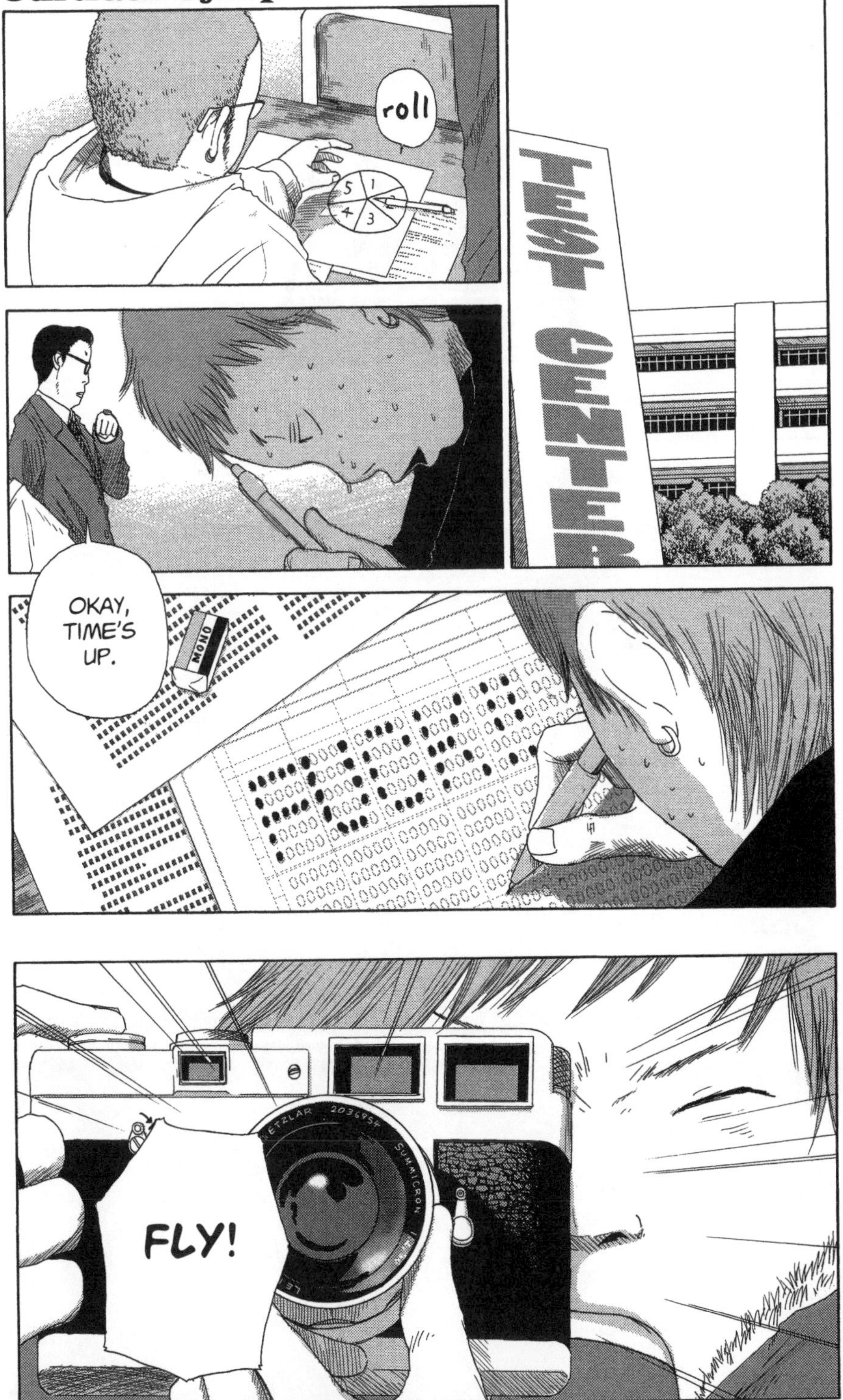
TEST CENTER
roll
OKAY, TIME'S UP.
MONO
SUMMICRON
FLY!

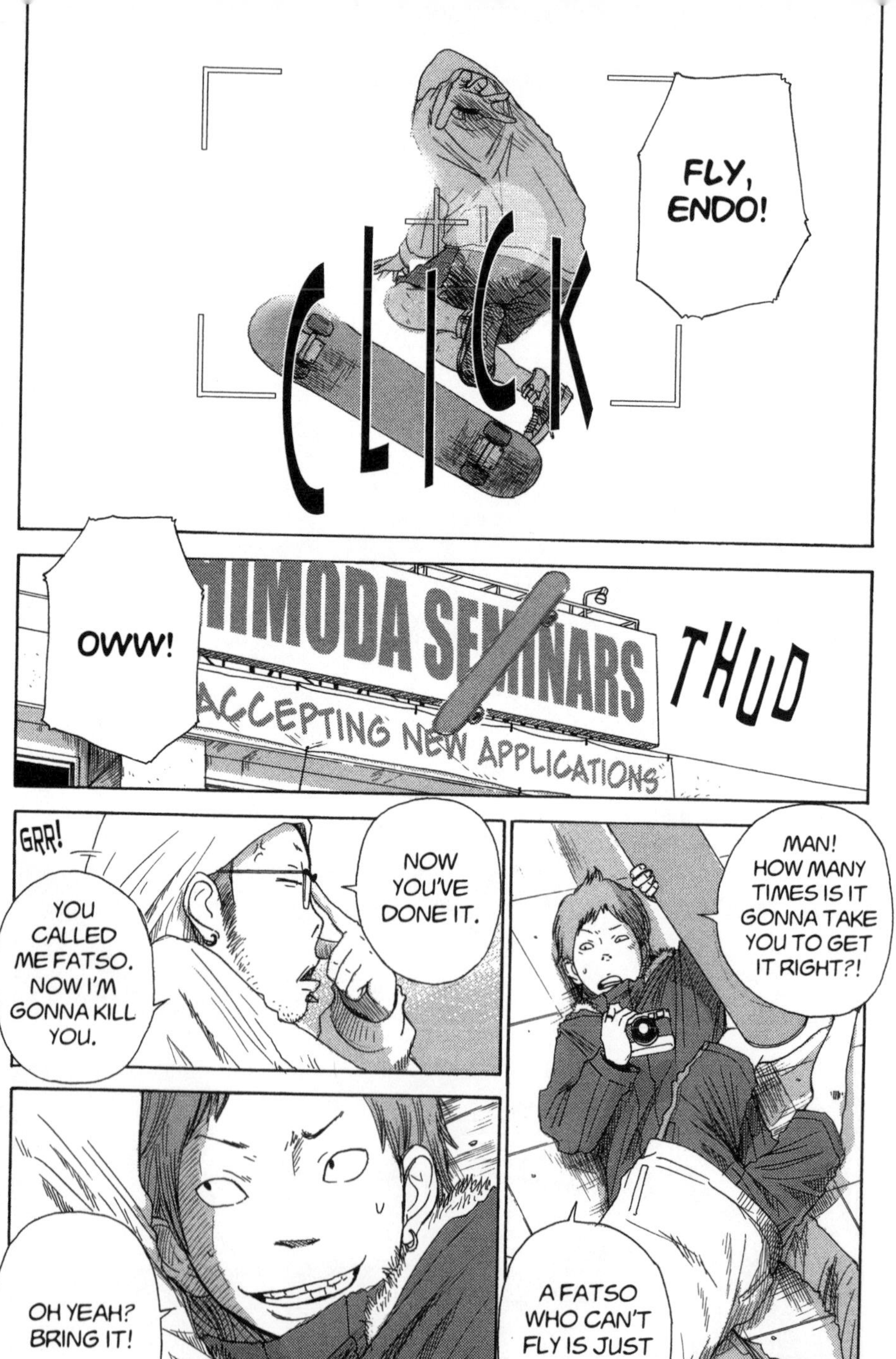
FLY, ENDO!
CLICK
THUD
OWW!
ACCEPTING NEW APPLICATIONS
MAN! HOW MANY TIMES IS IT GONNA TAKE YOU TO GET IT RIGHT?!
A FATSO WHO CAN'T FLY IS JUST A FATSO!
GRR!
NOW YOU'VE DONE IT.
YOU CALLED ME FATSO. NOW I'M GONNA KILL YOU.
OH YEAH? BRING IT!

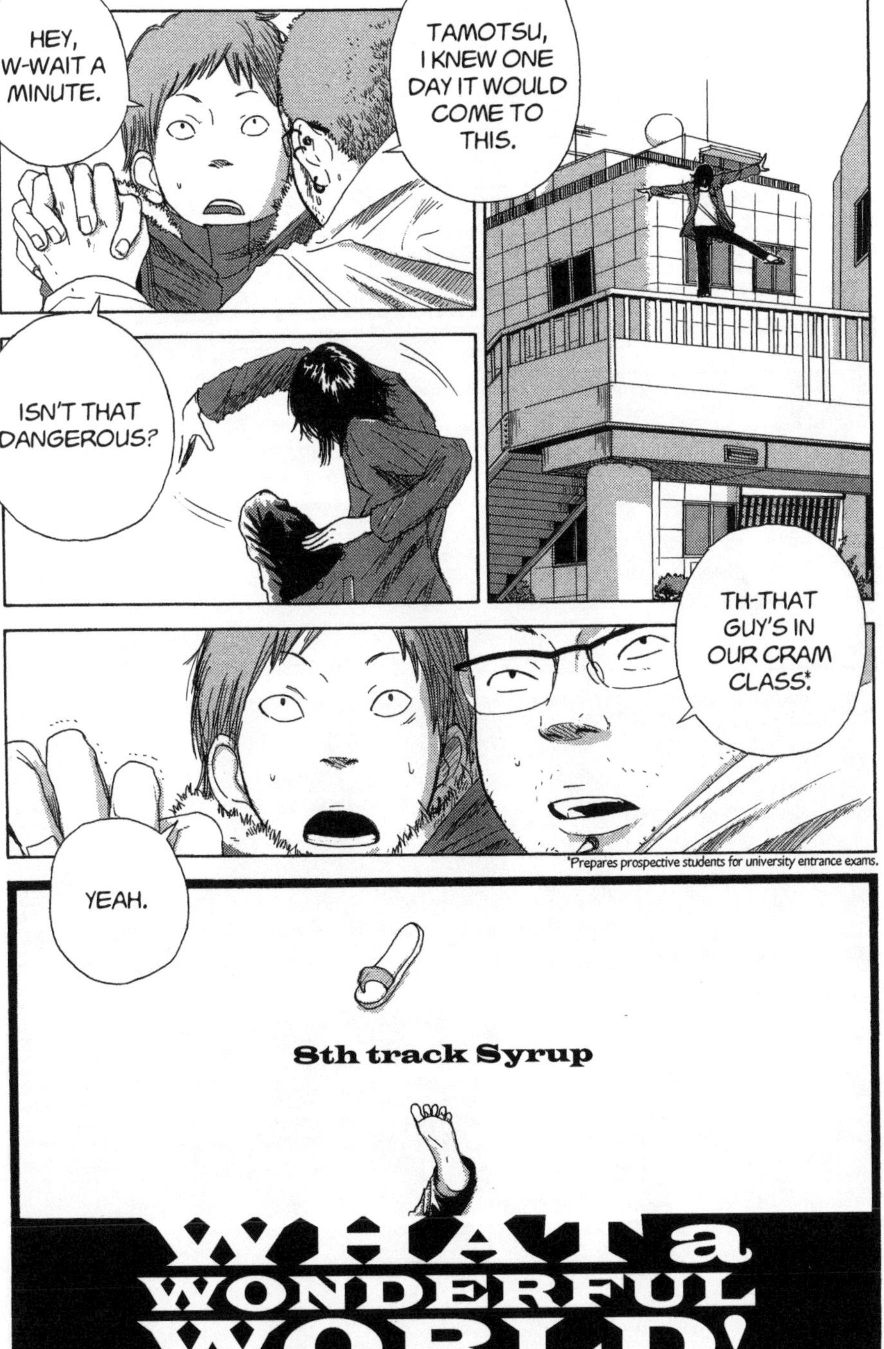
TAMOTSU, I KNEW ONE DAY IT WOULD COME TO THIS.
HEY, W-WAIT A MINUTE.
ISN'T THAT DANGEROUS?
TH-THAT GUY'S IN OUR CRAM CLASS.*
YEAH.
8th track Syrup
WHAT a WONDERFUL WORLD!
*Prepares prospective students for university entrance exams.

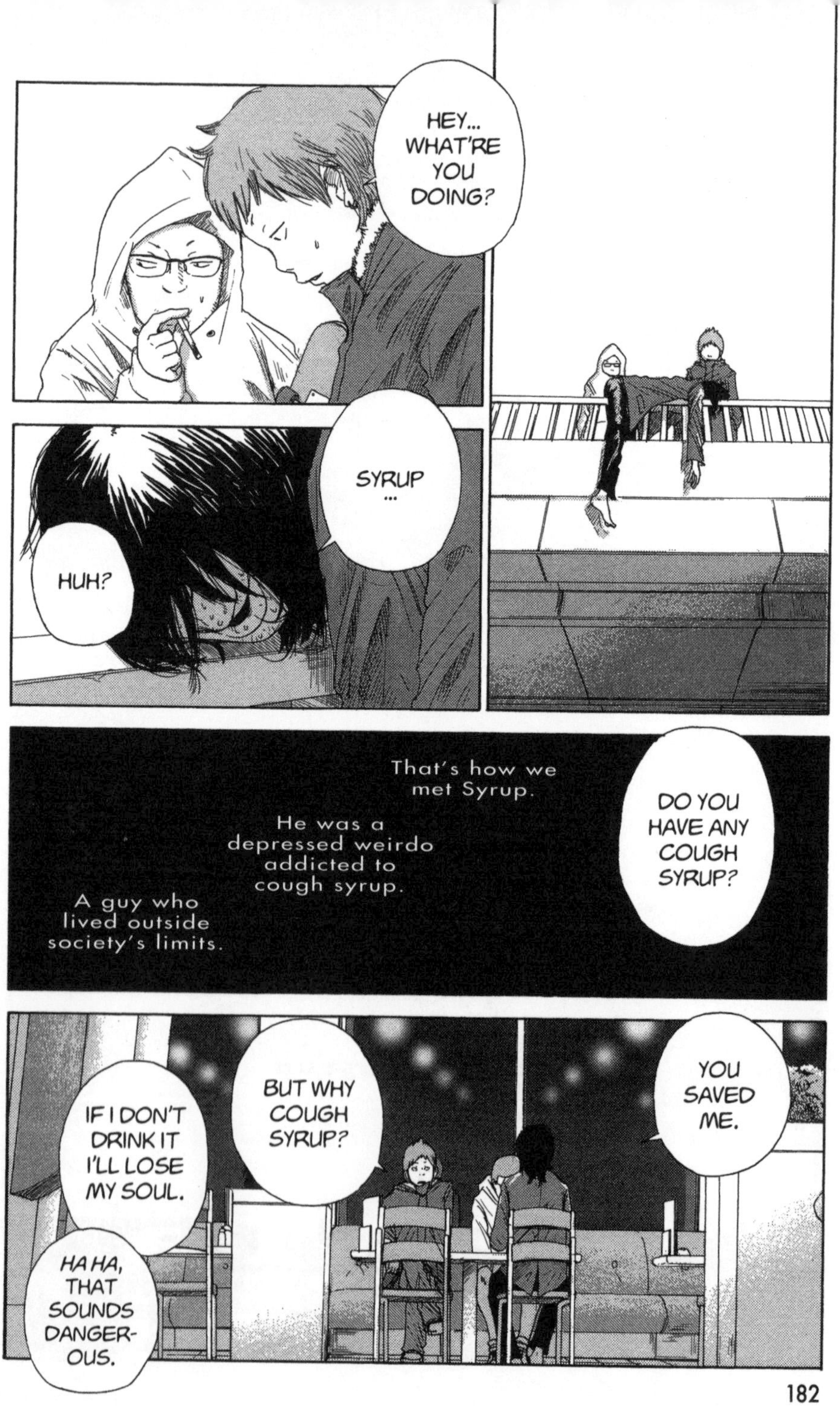
HEY... WHAT'RE YOU DOING?
SYRUP ...
HUH?
DO YOU HAVE ANY COUGH SYRUP?
That's how we met Syrup.
He was a depressed weirdo addicted to cough syrup.
A guy who lived outside society's limits.
YOU SAVED ME.
BUT WHY COUGH SYRUP?
IF I DON'T DRINK IT I'LL LOSE MY SOUL.
HA HA, THAT SOUNDS DANGER-OUS.

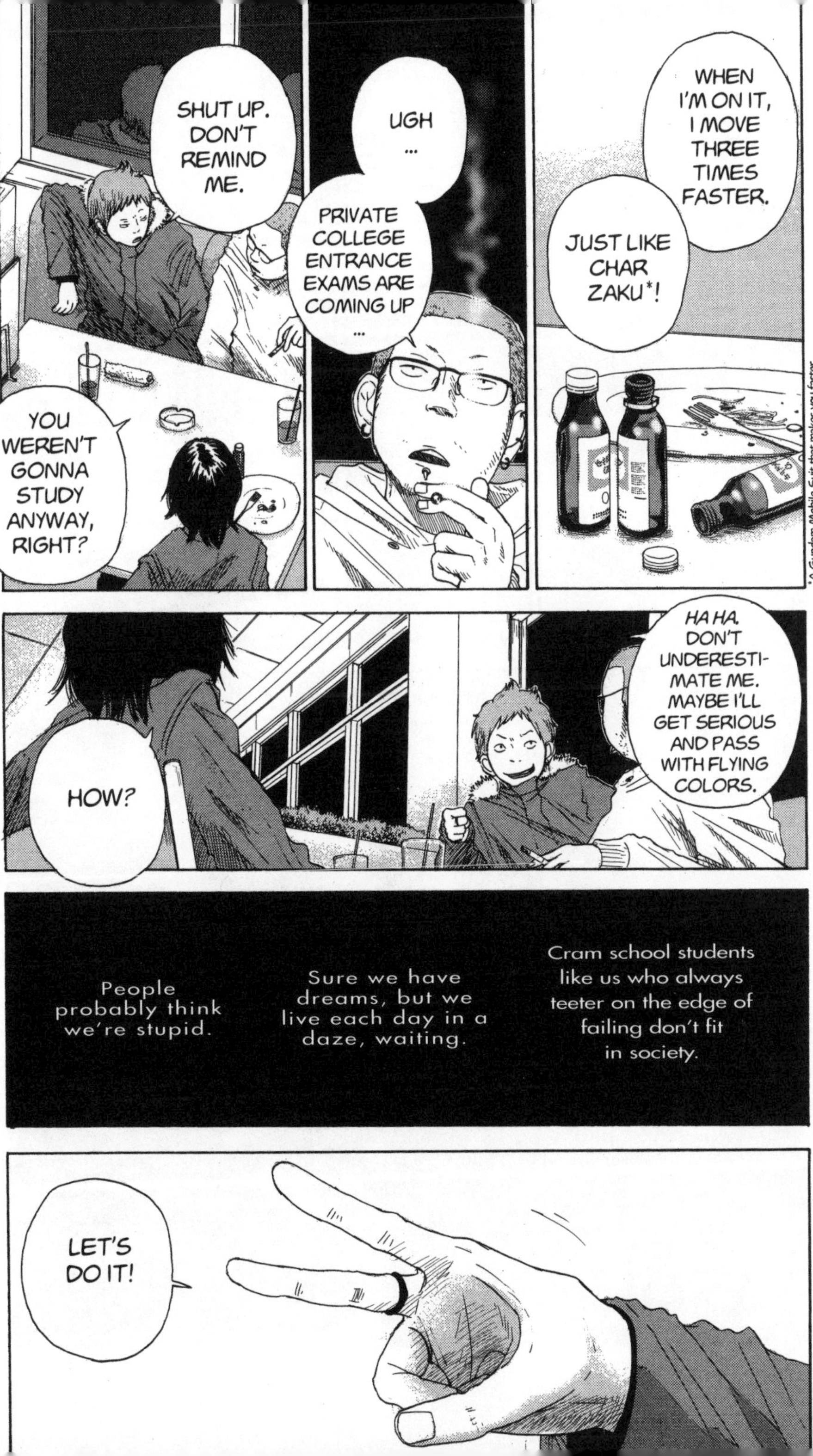
WHEN I'M ON IT, I MOVE THREE TIMES FASTER.
JUST LIKE CHAR ZAKU*!
UGH ...
PRIVATE COLLEGE ENTRANCE EXAMS ARE COMING UP ...
SHUT UP. DON'T REMIND ME.
YOU WEREN'T GONNA STUDY ANYWAY, RIGHT?
HA HA. DON'T UNDERESTI-MATE ME. MAYBE I'LL GET SERIOUS AND PASS WITH FLYING COLORS.
HOW?
Cram school students like us who always teeter on the edge of failing don't fit in society.
Sure we have dreams, but we live each day in a daze, waiting.
People probably think we're stupid.
LET'S DO IT!

*A Gundam Mobile Suit that makes you faster.

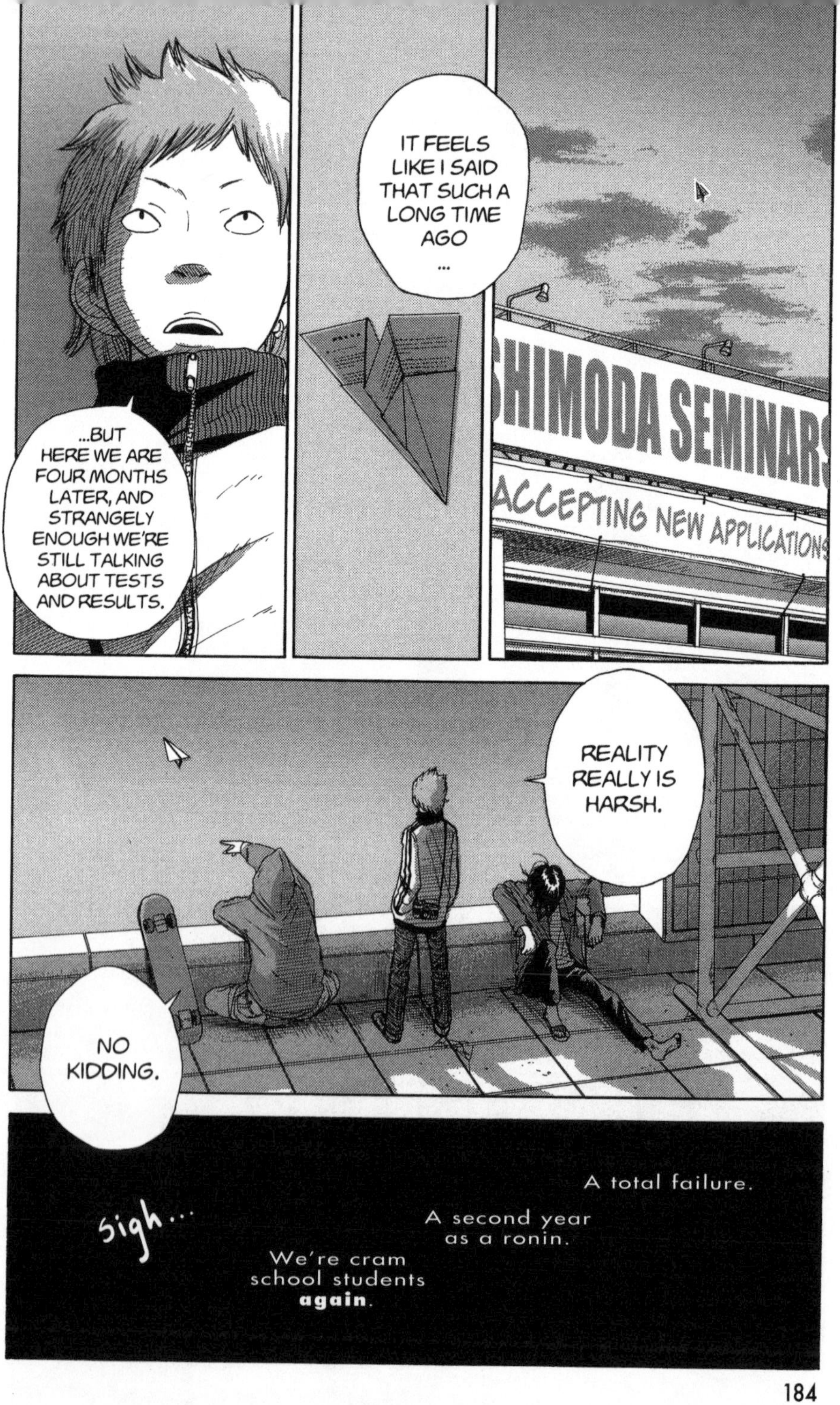
SHIMODA SEMINARS
ACCEPTING NEW APPLICATIONS
IT FEELS LIKE I SAID THAT SUCH A LONG TIME AGO ...
...BUT HERE WE ARE FOUR MONTHS LATER, AND STRANGELY ENOUGH WE'RE STILL TALKING ABOUT TESTS AND RESULTS.
REALITY REALLY IS HARSH.
NO KIDDING.
A total failure.
A second year as a ronin.
We're cram school students **again**.
Sigh...

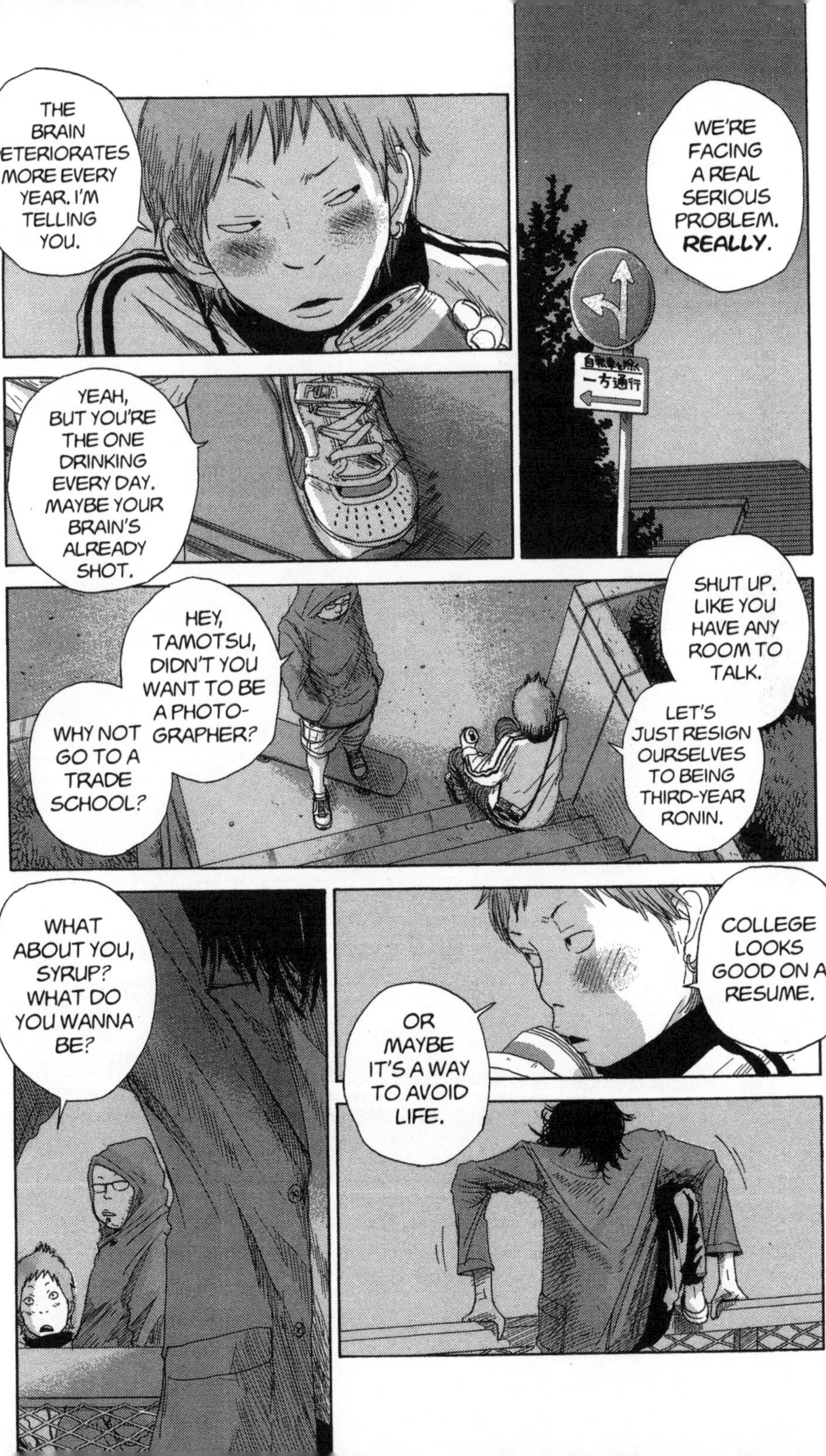
WE'RE FACING A REAL SERIOUS PROBLEM. **REALLY**.
自転車を除く
一方通行
THE BRAIN DETERIORATES MORE EVERY YEAR. I'M TELLING YOU.
YEAH, BUT YOU'RE THE ONE DRINKING EVERY DAY. MAYBE YOUR BRAIN'S ALREADY SHOT.
SHUT UP. LIKE YOU HAVE ANY ROOM TO TALK.
LET'S JUST RESIGN OURSELVES TO BEING THIRD-YEAR RONIN.
HEY, TAMOTSU, DIDN'T YOU WANT TO BE A PHOTO-GRAPHER?
WHY NOT GO TO A TRADE SCHOOL?
COLLEGE LOOKS GOOD ON A RESUME.
OR MAYBE IT'S A WAY TO AVOID LIFE.
WHAT ABOUT YOU, SYRUP? WHAT DO YOU WANNA BE?

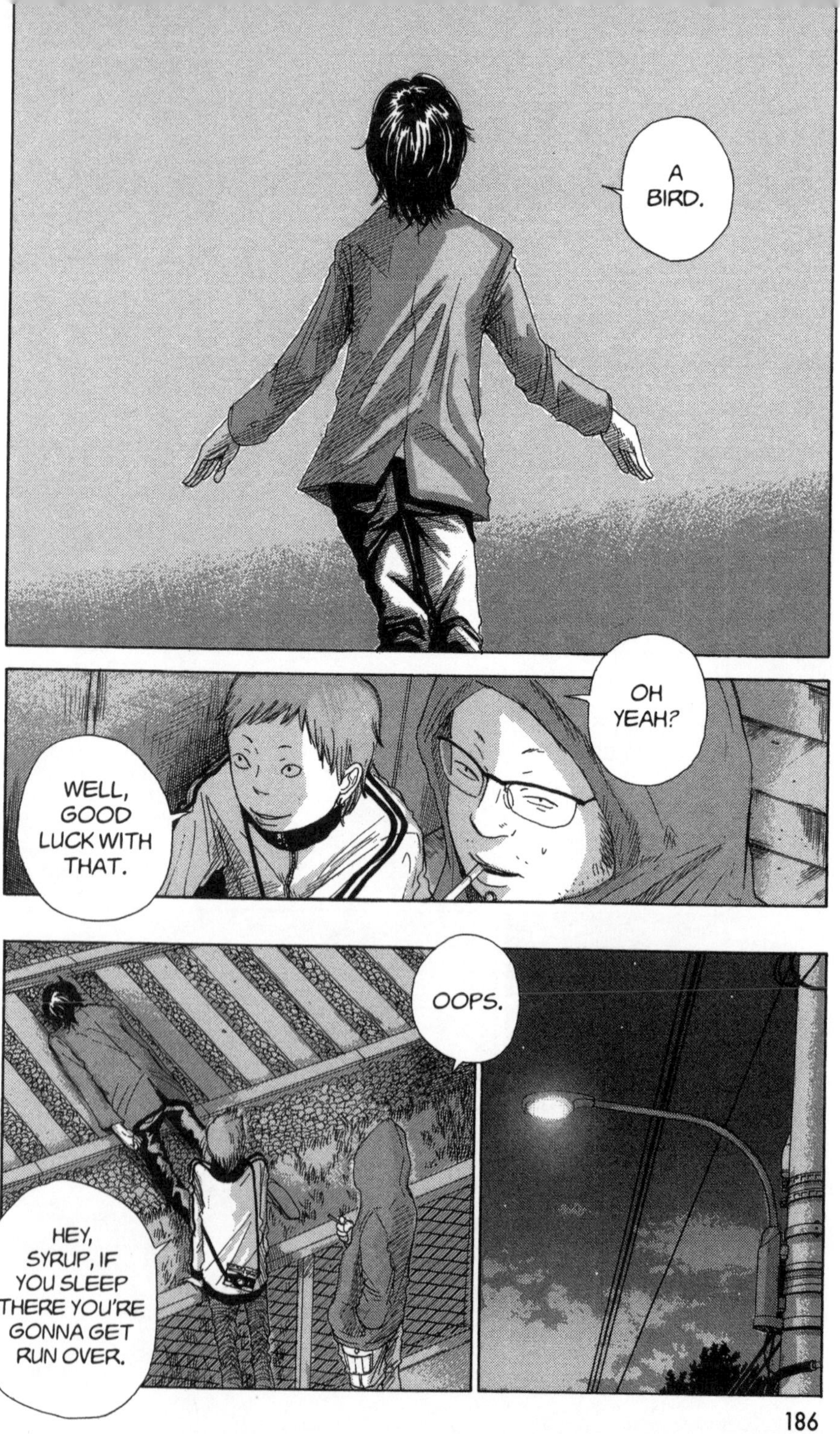
A BIRD.
OH YEAH?
WELL, GOOD LUCK WITH THAT.
OOPS.
HEY, SYRUP, IF YOU SLEEP THERE YOU'RE GONNA GET RUN OVER.

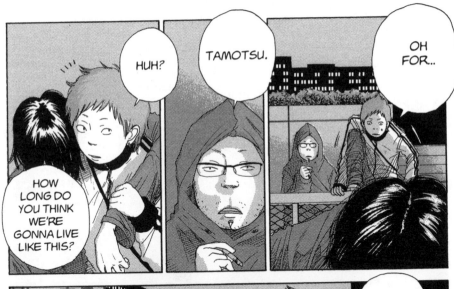

OH FOR...
TAMOTSU.
HUH?
HOW LONG DO YOU THINK WE'RE GONNA LIVE LIKE THIS?
WHAT BROUGHT THAT UP?
NOTHING'S WORSE THAN A CRAM SCHOOL STUDENT WHO DOESN'T STUDY, RIGHT?
WE'RE TOO COM-PLACENT.
WE'RE WAY TOO COMPLA-CENT.
QUIT MUMBLING AND HELP ME, WILL YA?
I'M GONNA TAKE OVER THE FAMILY STORE.
HUH ?!

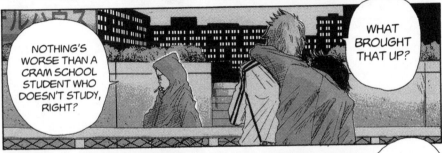

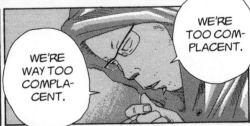

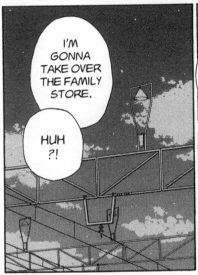

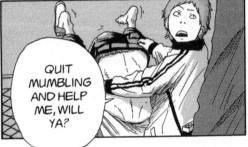

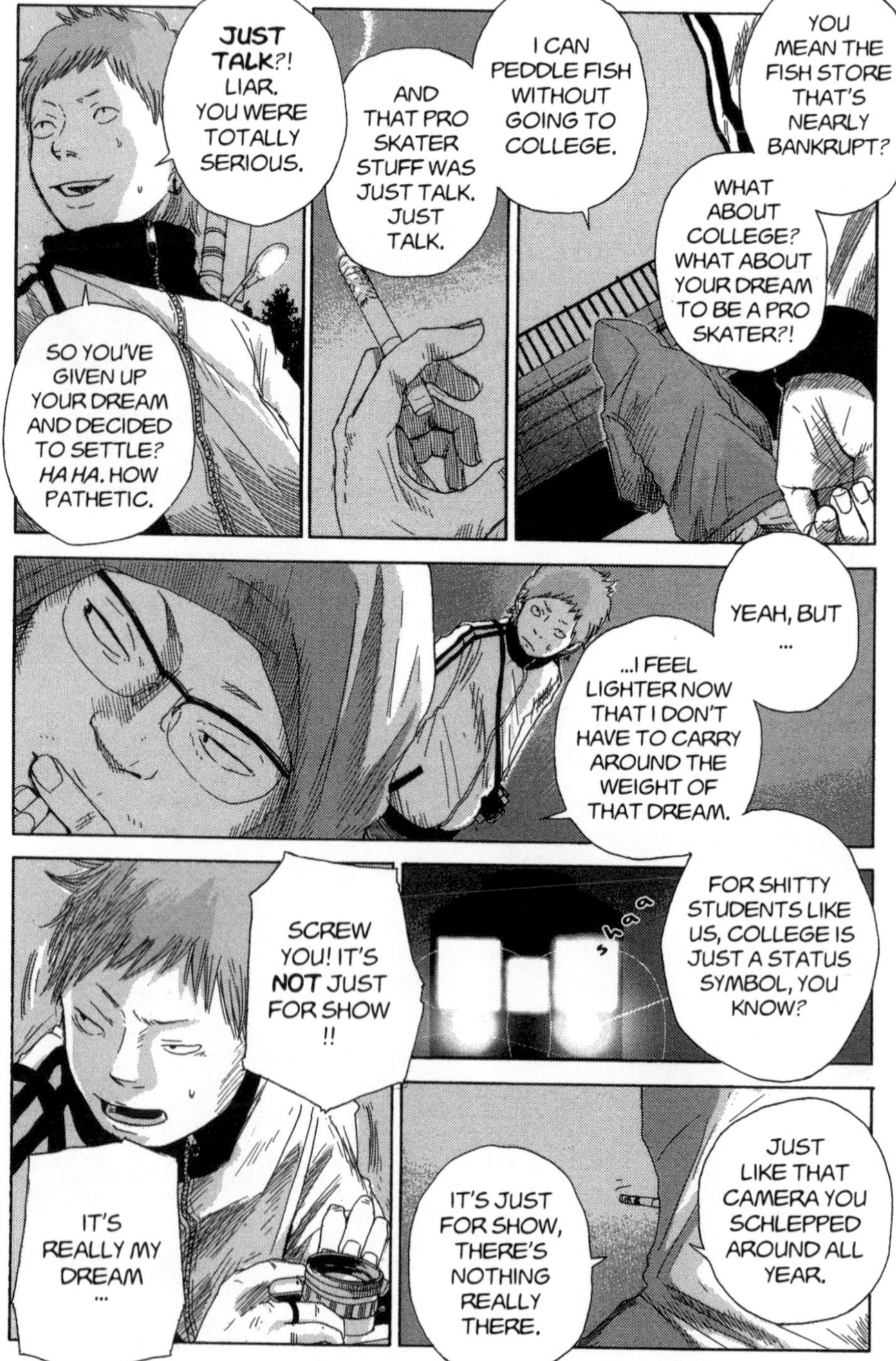
YOU MEAN THE FISH STORE THAT'S NEARLY BANKRUPT?
WHAT ABOUT COLLEGE? WHAT ABOUT YOUR DREAM TO BE A PRO SKATER?!
I CAN PEDDLE FISH WITHOUT GOING TO COLLEGE.
AND THAT PRO SKATER STUFF WAS JUST TALK. JUST TALK.
JUST TALK?! LIAR. YOU WERE TOTALLY SERIOUS.
SO YOU'VE GIVEN UP YOUR DREAM AND DECIDED TO SETTLE? *HA HA*. HOW PATHETIC.
YEAH, BUT ...
...I FEEL LIGHTER NOW THAT I DON'T HAVE TO CARRY AROUND THE WEIGHT OF THAT DREAM.
FOR SHITTY STUDENTS LIKE US, COLLEGE IS JUST A STATUS SYMBOL, YOU KNOW?
shaa
JUST LIKE THAT CAMERA YOU SCHLEPPED AROUND ALL YEAR.
IT'S JUST FOR SHOW, THERE'S NOTHING REALLY THERE.
SCREW YOU! IT'S **NOT** JUST FOR SHOW !!
IT'S REALLY MY DREAM ...

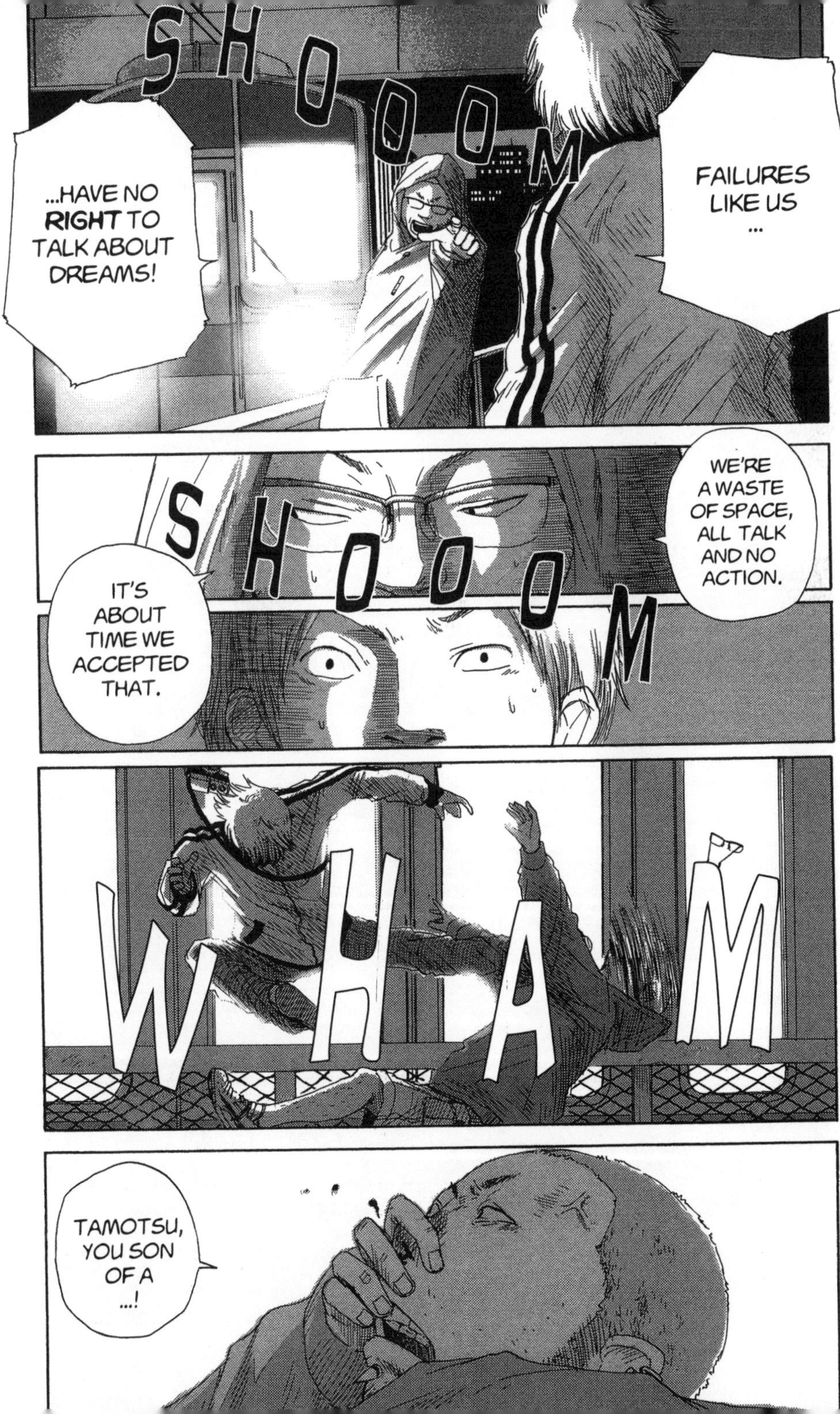
FAILURES LIKE US ...
SHOOOM
...HAVE NO **RIGHT** TO TALK ABOUT DREAMS!
WE'RE A WASTE OF SPACE, ALL TALK AND NO ACTION.
SHOOOOM
IT'S ABOUT TIME WE ACCEPTED THAT.
WHAM
TAMOTSU, YOU SON OF A ...!

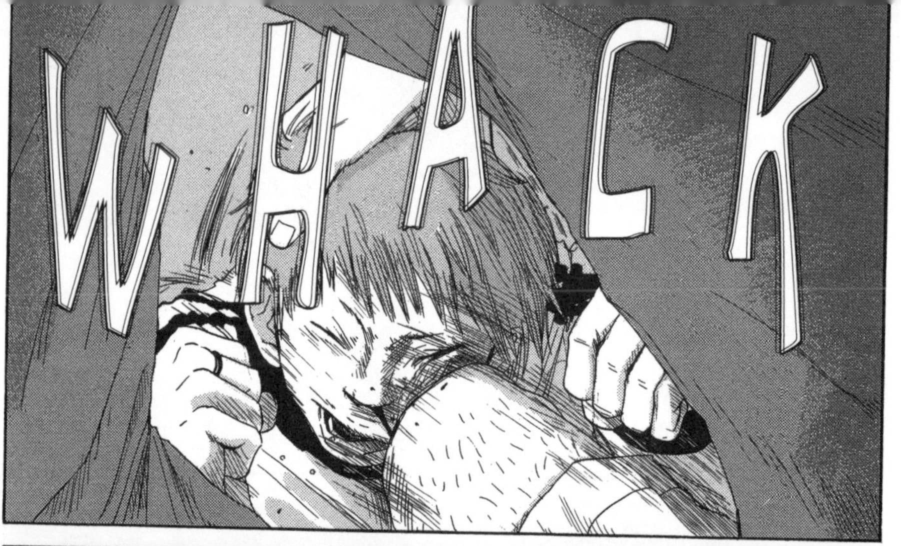
WHACK

I know that! Don't you think I know that?!

I've always known that about myself!

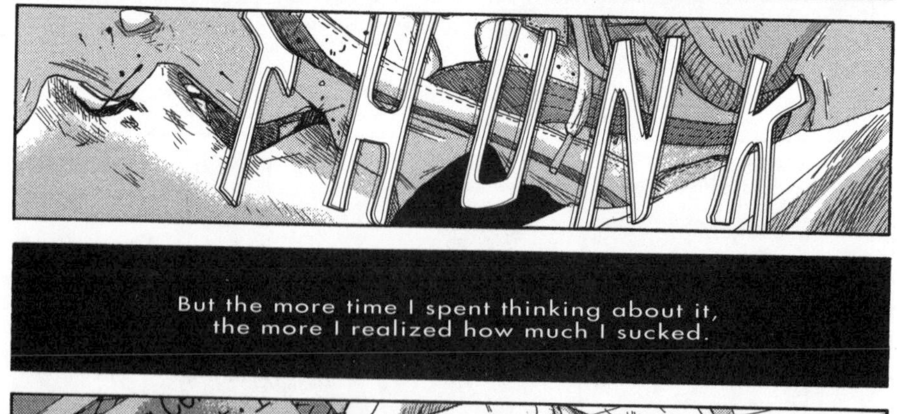
THUNK

But the more time I spent thinking about it,
the more I realized how much I sucked.

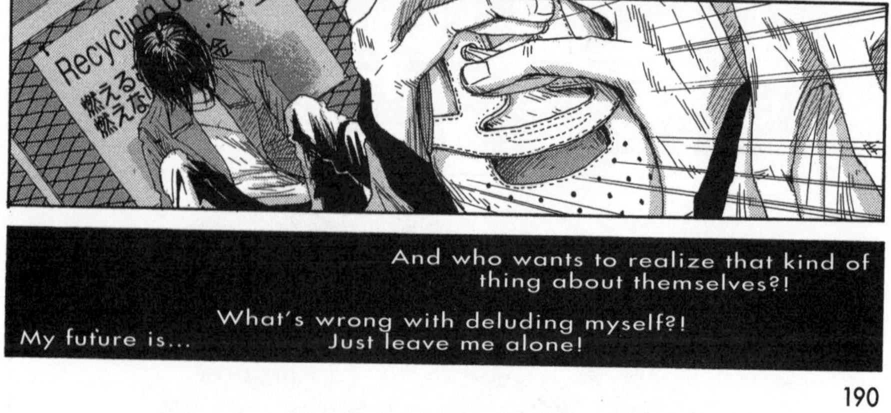
Recycling

And who wants to realize that kind of
thing about themselves?!

What's wrong with deluding myself?!
Just leave me alone!

My future is...

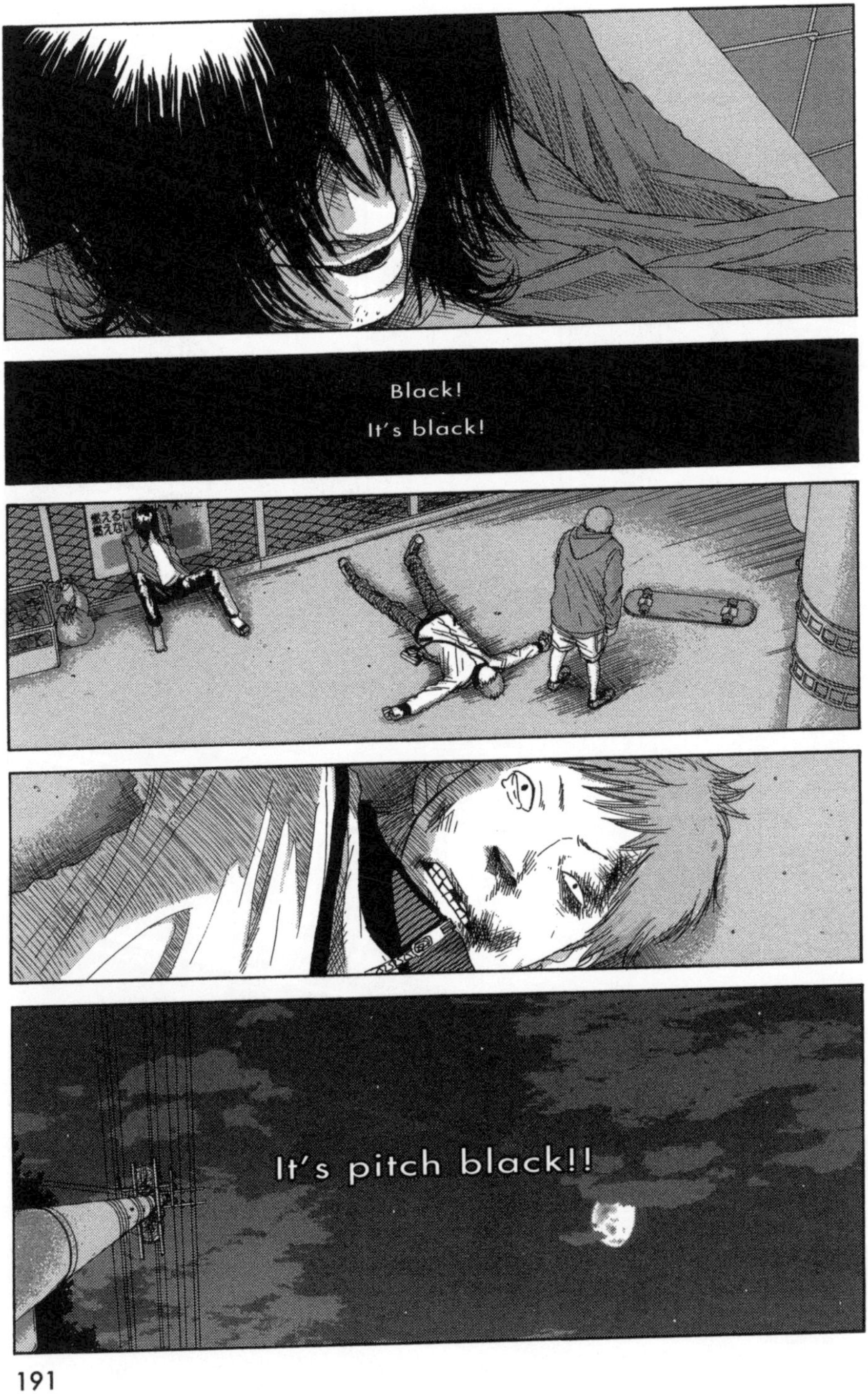
Black!
It's black!
It's pitch black!!

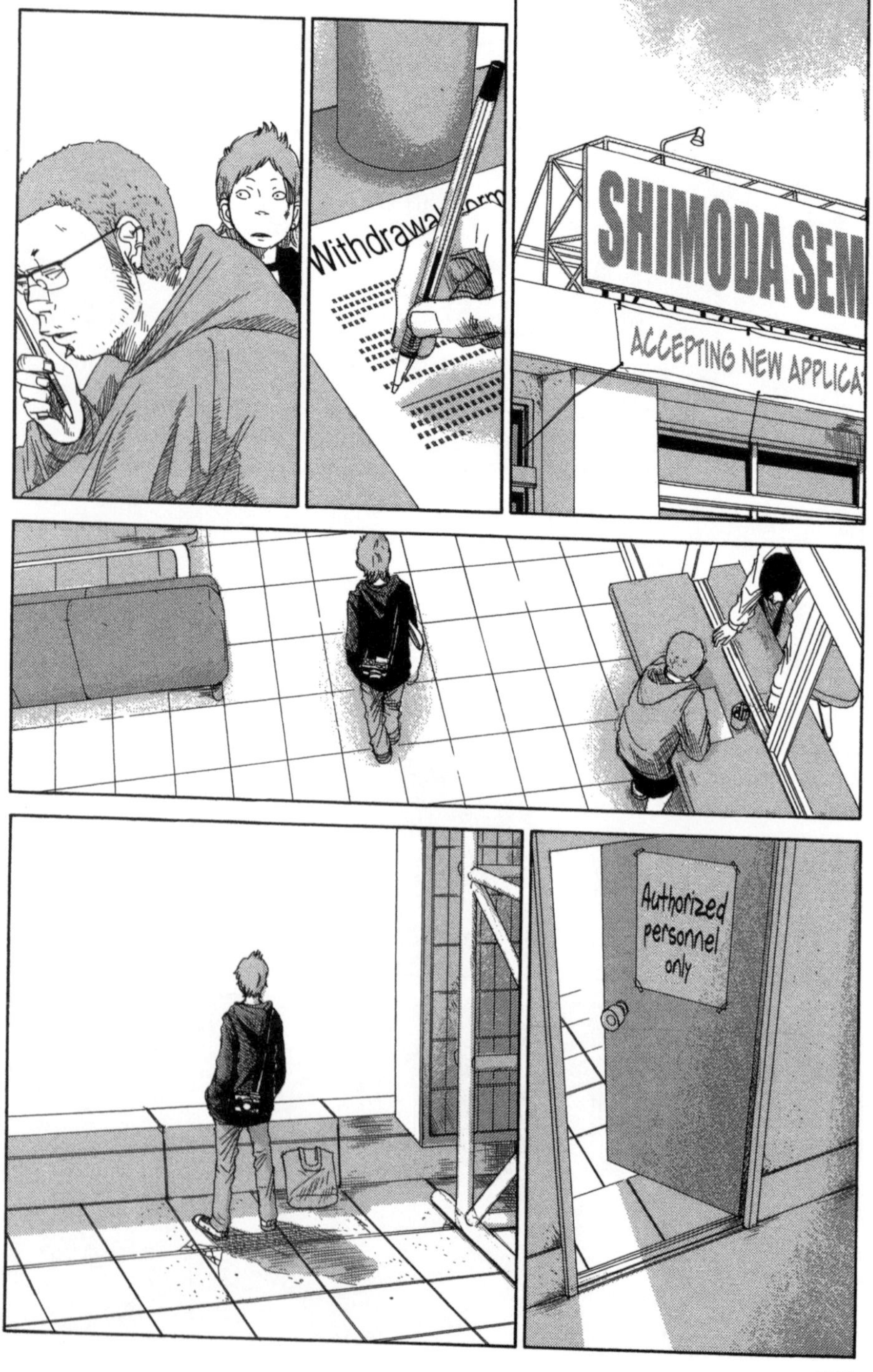
SHIMODA SEM
ACCEPTING NEW APPLICA
Withdrawal
Authorized personnel only

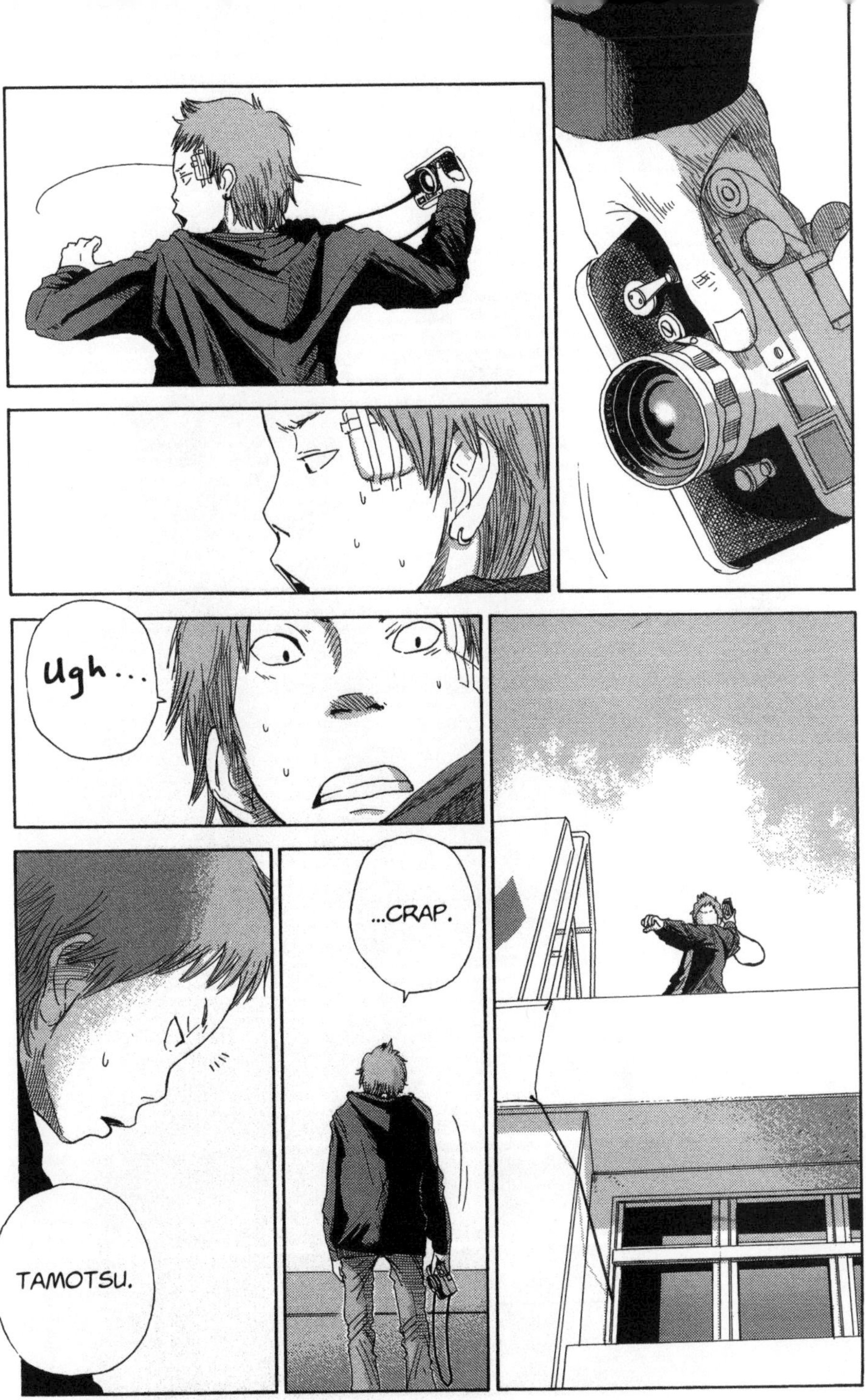
Ugh...
...CRAP.
TAMOTSU.

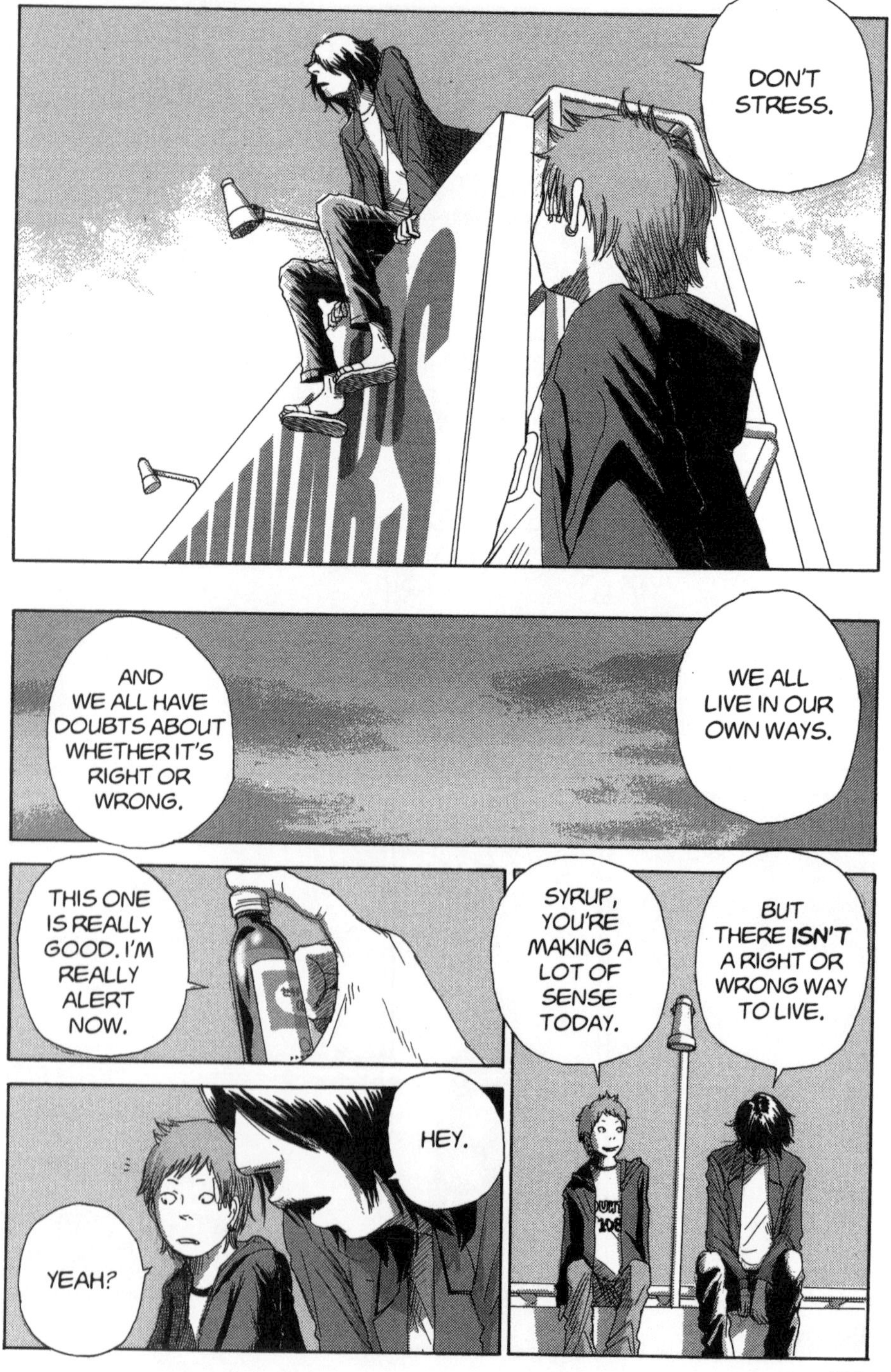
DON'T STRESS.
WE ALL LIVE IN OUR OWN WAYS.
AND WE ALL HAVE DOUBTS ABOUT WHETHER IT'S RIGHT OR WRONG.
BUT THERE **ISN'T** A RIGHT OR WRONG WAY TO LIVE.
SYRUP, YOU'RE MAKING A LOT OF SENSE TODAY.
THIS ONE IS REALLY GOOD. I'M REALLY ALERT NOW.
HEY.
YEAH?

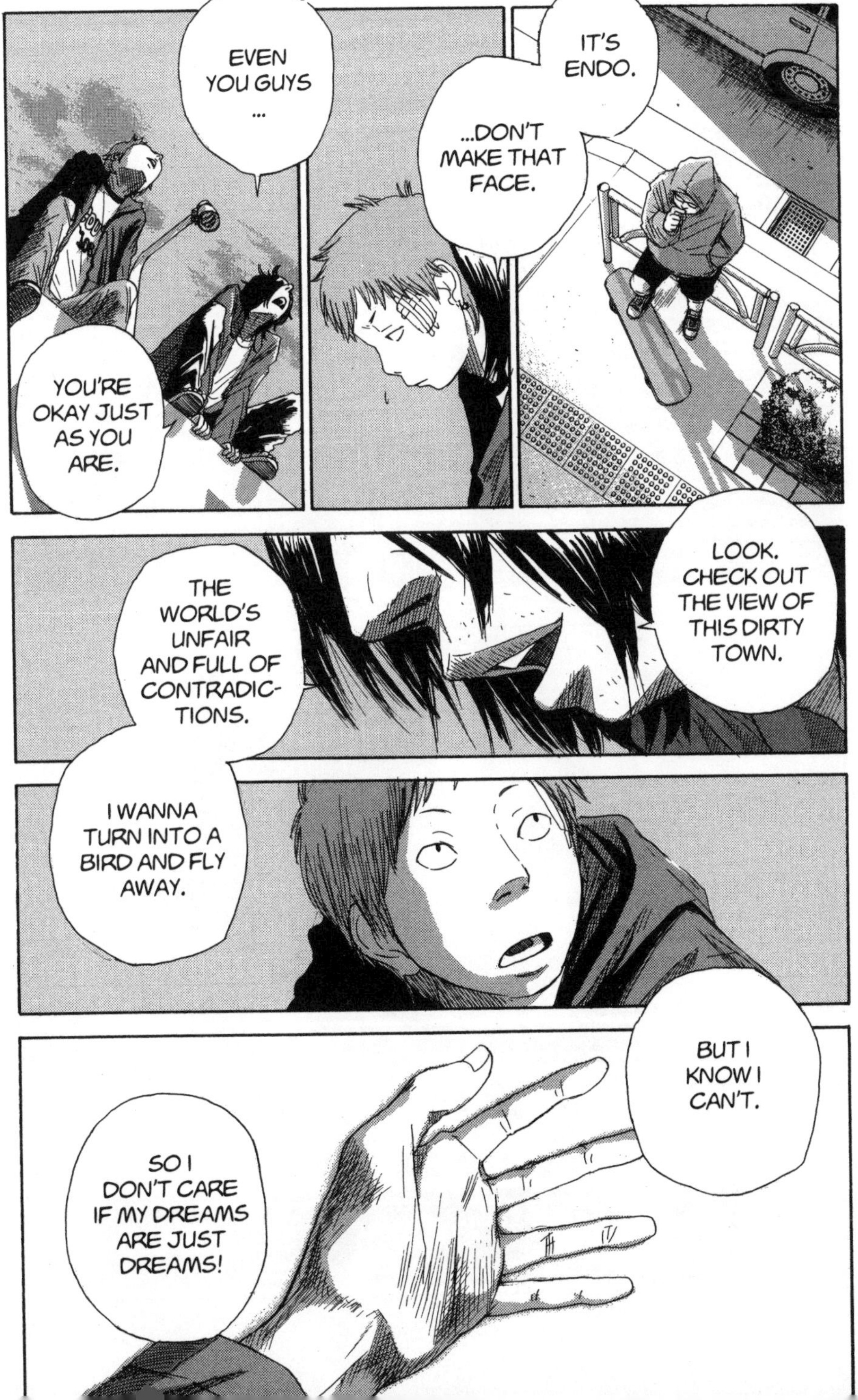

IT'S ENDO.
...DON'T MAKE THAT FACE.
EVEN YOU GUYS ...
YOU'RE OKAY JUST AS YOU ARE.
LOOK. CHECK OUT THE VIEW OF THIS DIRTY TOWN.
THE WORLD'S UNFAIR AND FULL OF CONTRADIC-TIONS.
I WANNA TURN INTO A BIRD AND FLY AWAY.
BUT I KNOW I CAN'T.
SO I DON'T CARE IF MY DREAMS ARE JUST DREAMS!

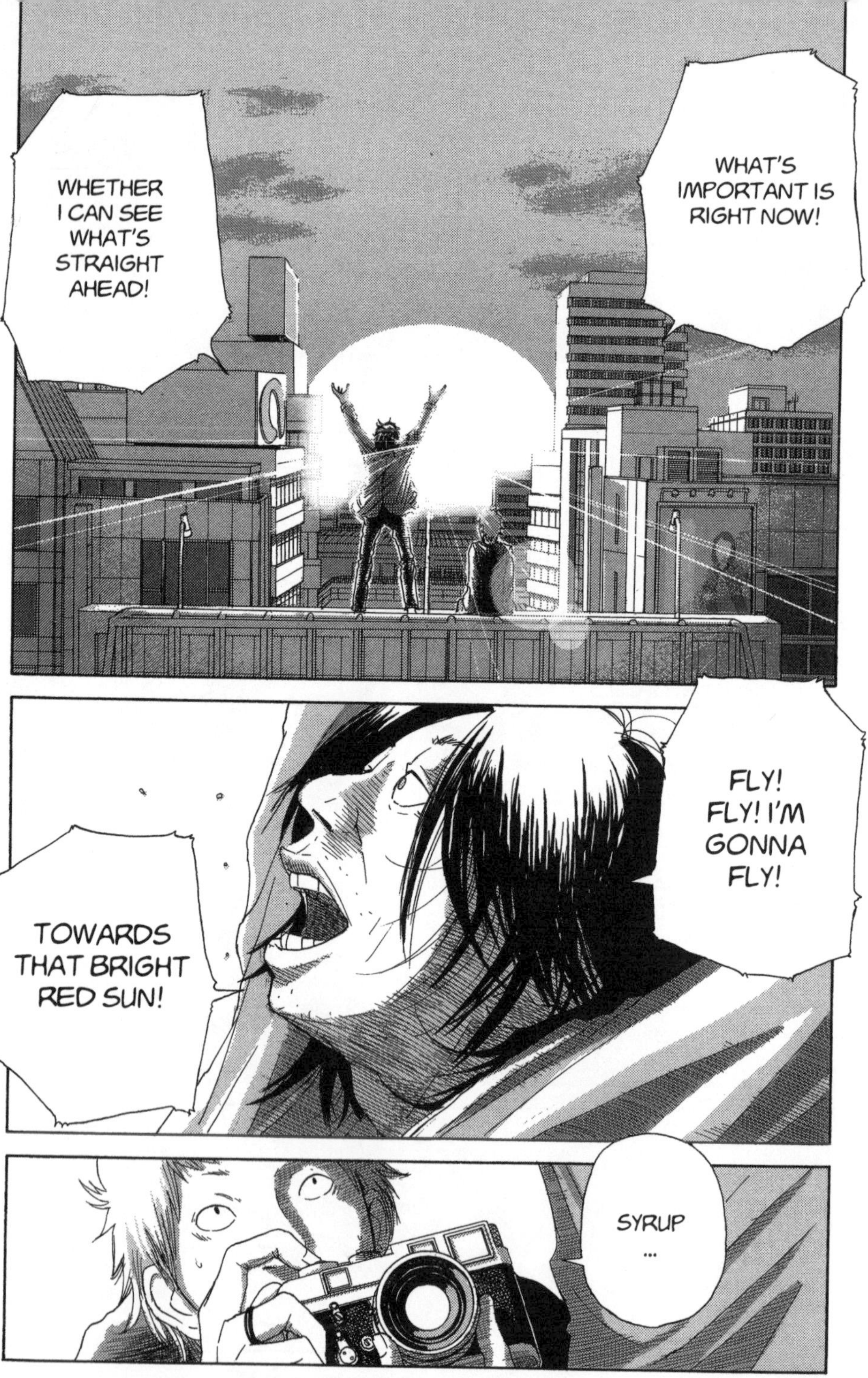
WHAT'S IMPORTANT IS RIGHT NOW!
WHETHER I CAN SEE WHAT'S STRAIGHT AHEAD!
FLY! FLY! I'M GONNA FLY!
TOWARDS THAT BRIGHT RED SUN!
SYRUP ...

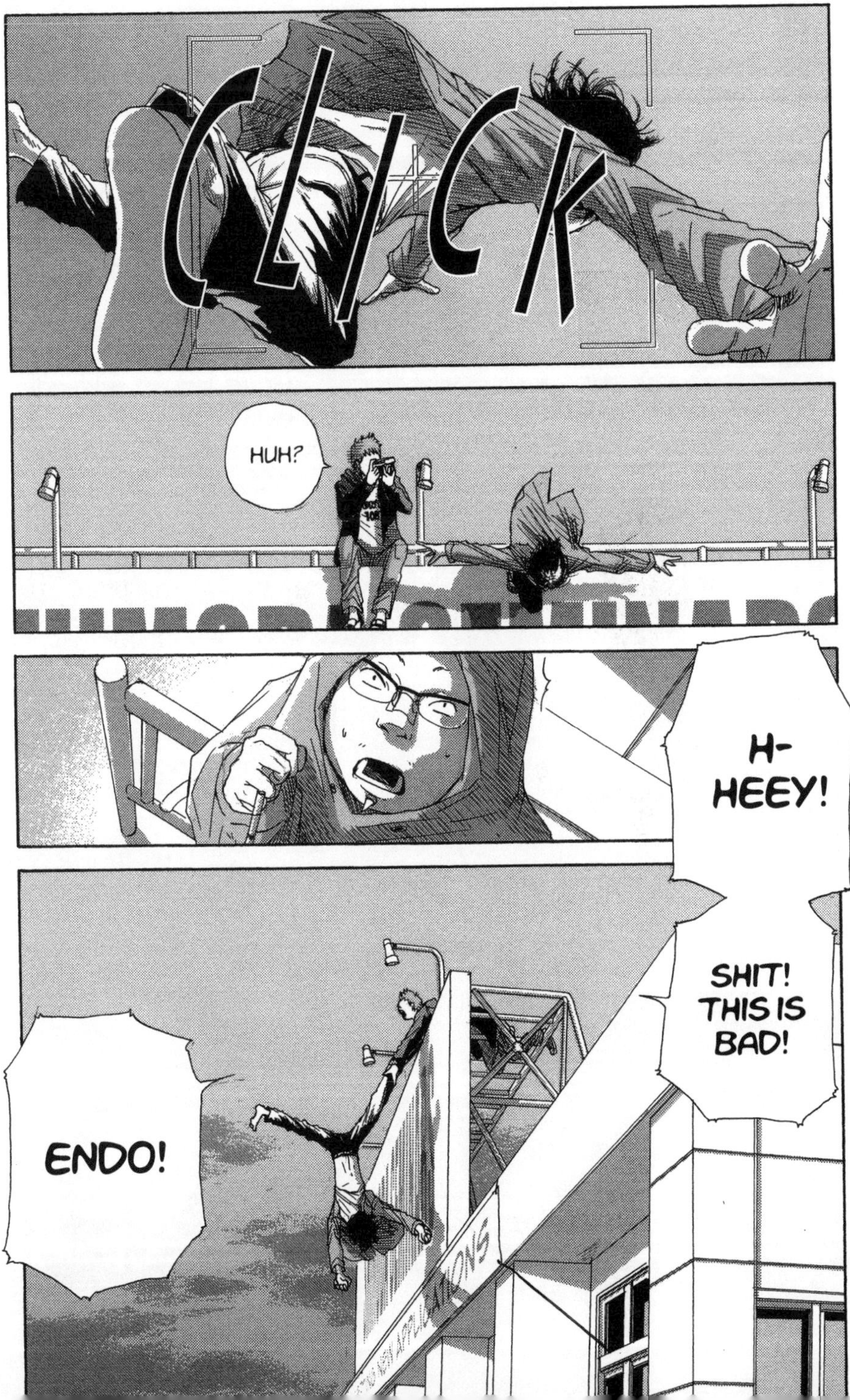
CLICK
HUH?
H-HEEY!
SHIT! THIS IS BAD!
ENDO!
APPLICATIONS

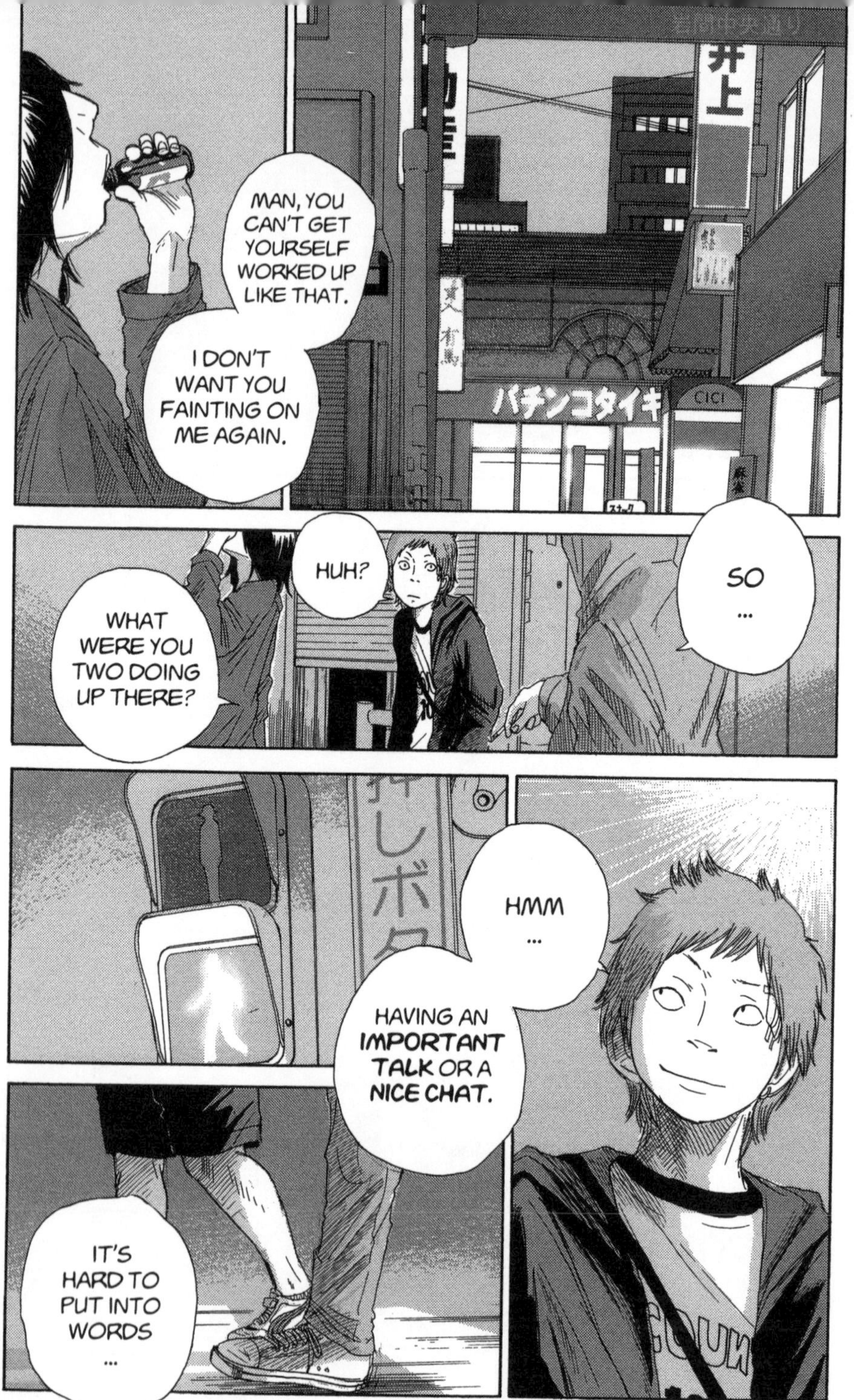
井上
パチンコタイキ
CICI
MAN, YOU CAN'T GET YOURSELF WORKED UP LIKE THAT.
I DON'T WANT YOU FAINTING ON ME AGAIN.
SO ...
HUH?
WHAT WERE YOU TWO DOING UP THERE?
HMM ...
HAVING AN **IMPORTANT TALK** OR A **NICE CHAT.**
IT'S HARD TO PUT INTO WORDS ...

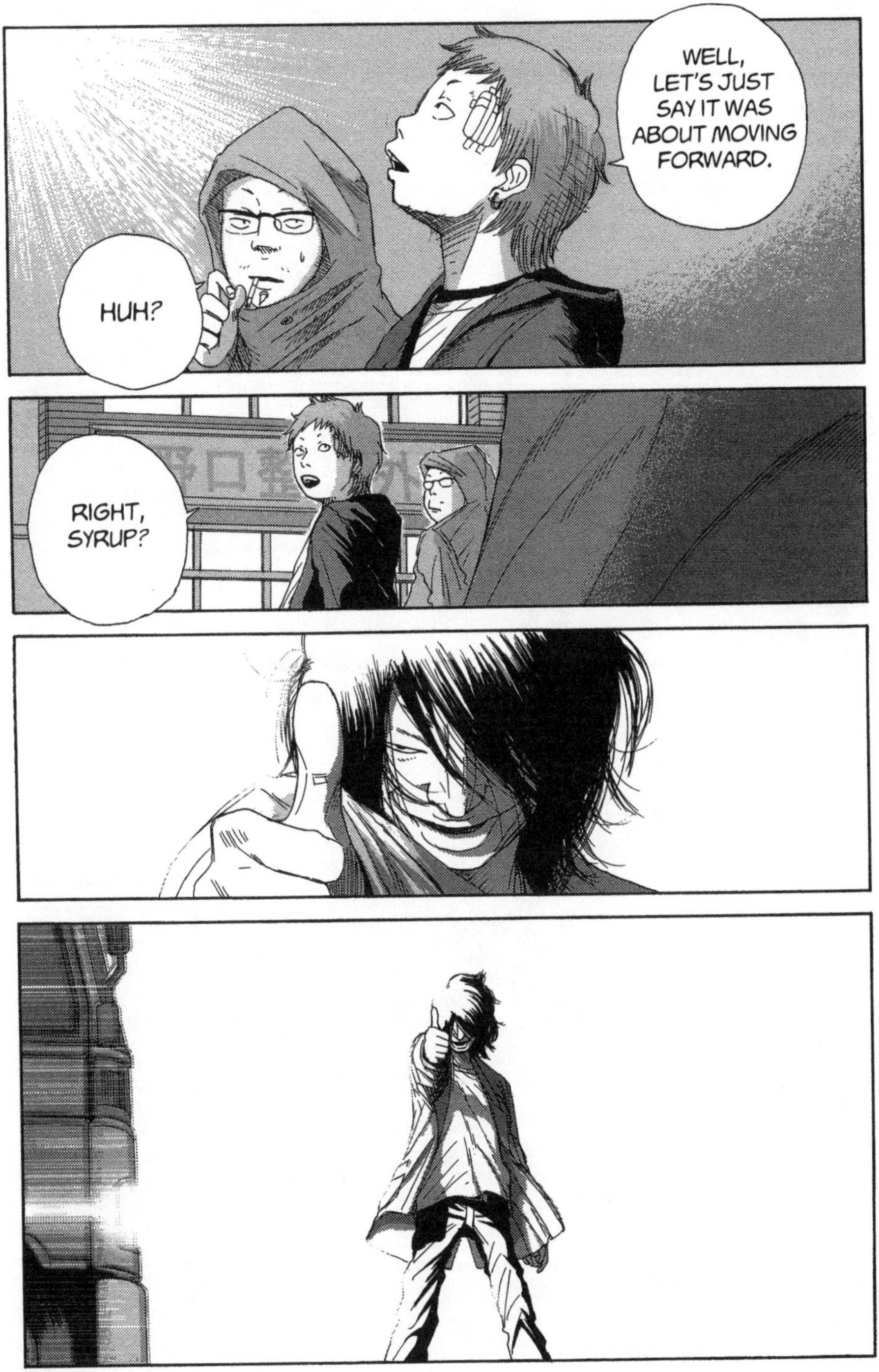
WELL, LET'S JUST SAY IT WAS ABOUT MOVING FORWARD.
HUH?
RIGHT, SYRUP?

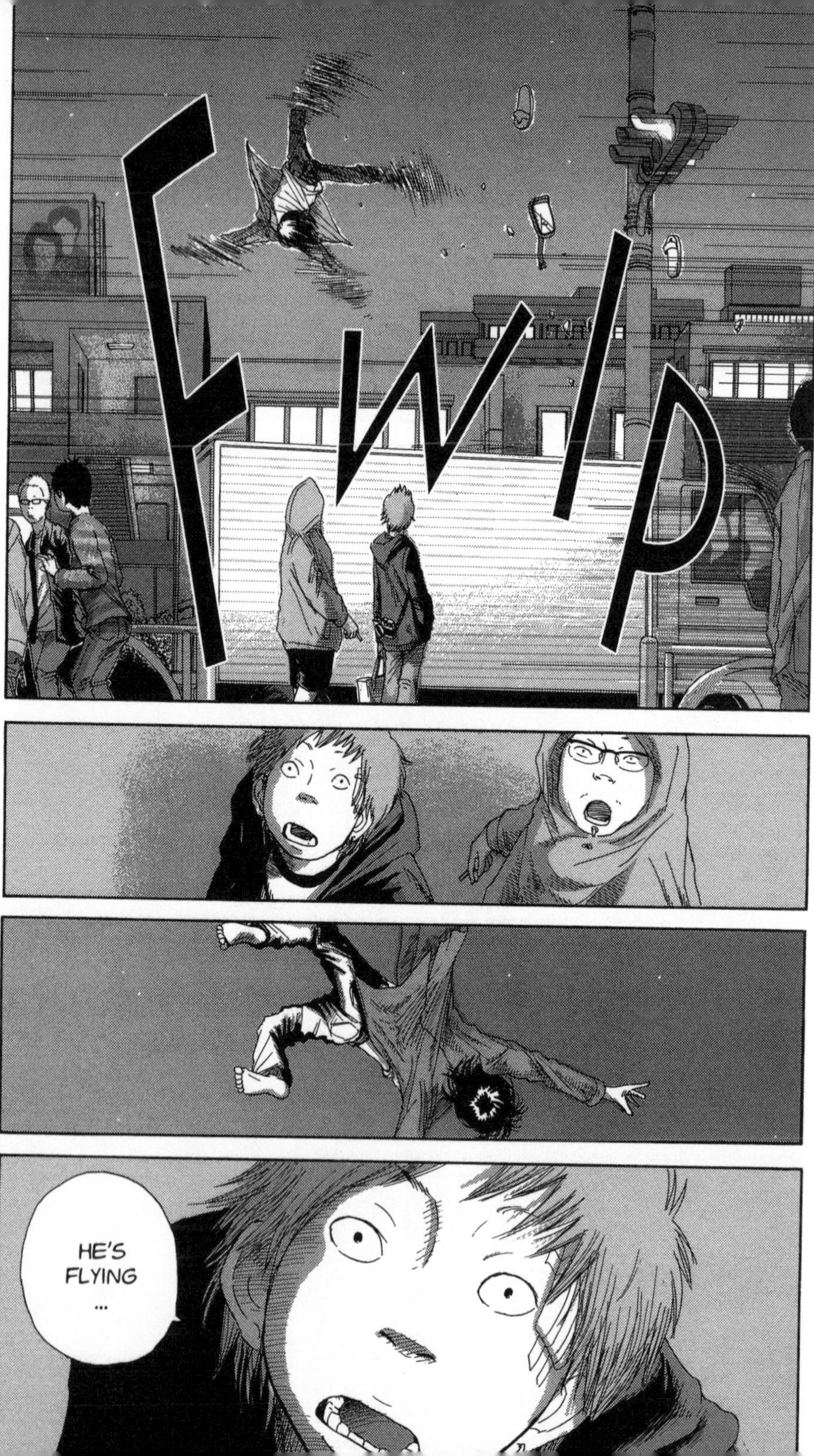
FWIP
HE'S FLYING ...

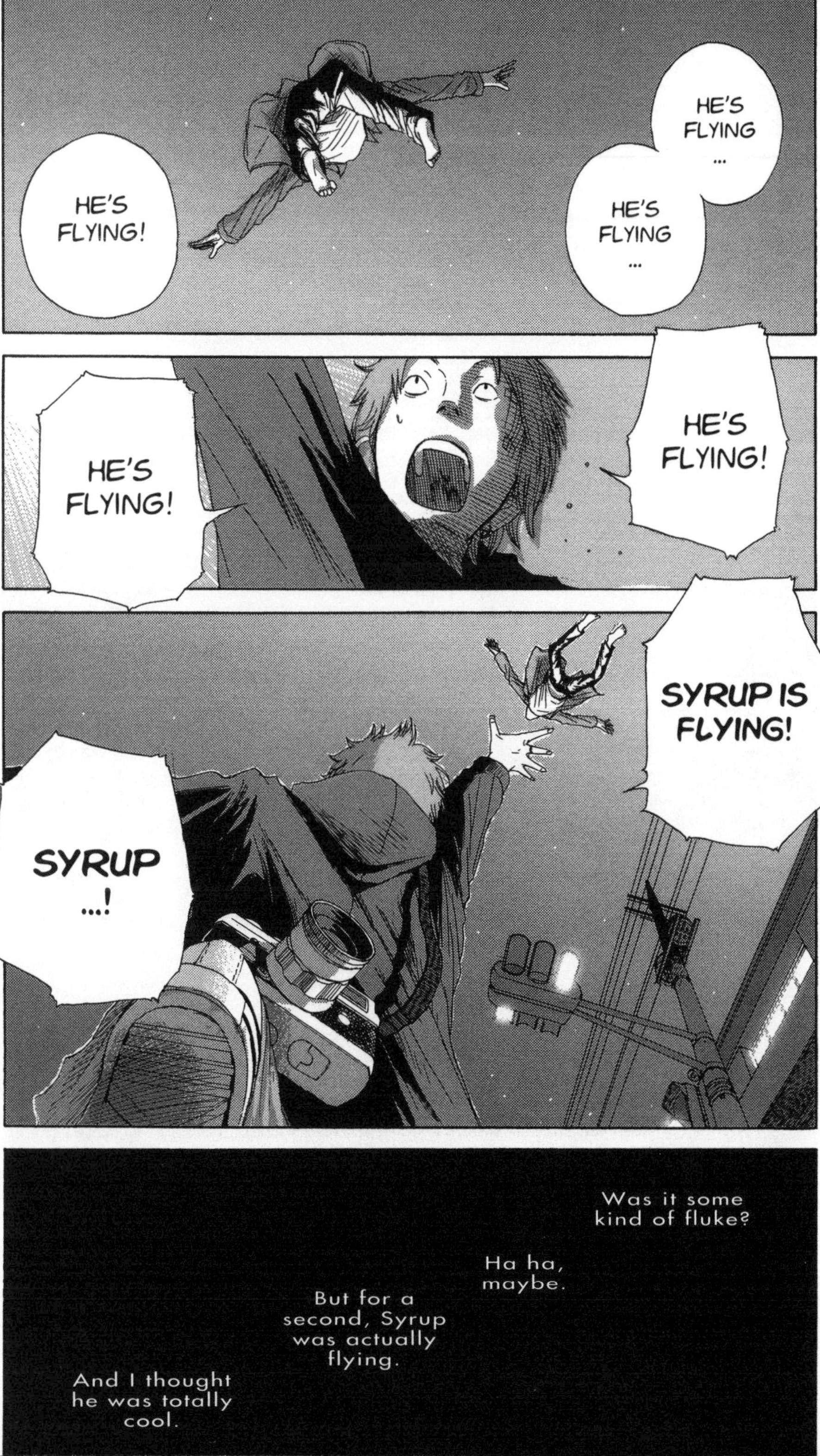
HE'S FLYING ...
HE'S FLYING ...
HE'S FLYING!
HE'S FLYING!
HE'S FLYING!
SYRUP IS FLYING!
SYRUP ...!
Was it some kind of fluke?
Ha ha, maybe.
But for a second, Syrup was actually flying.
And I thought he was totally cool.

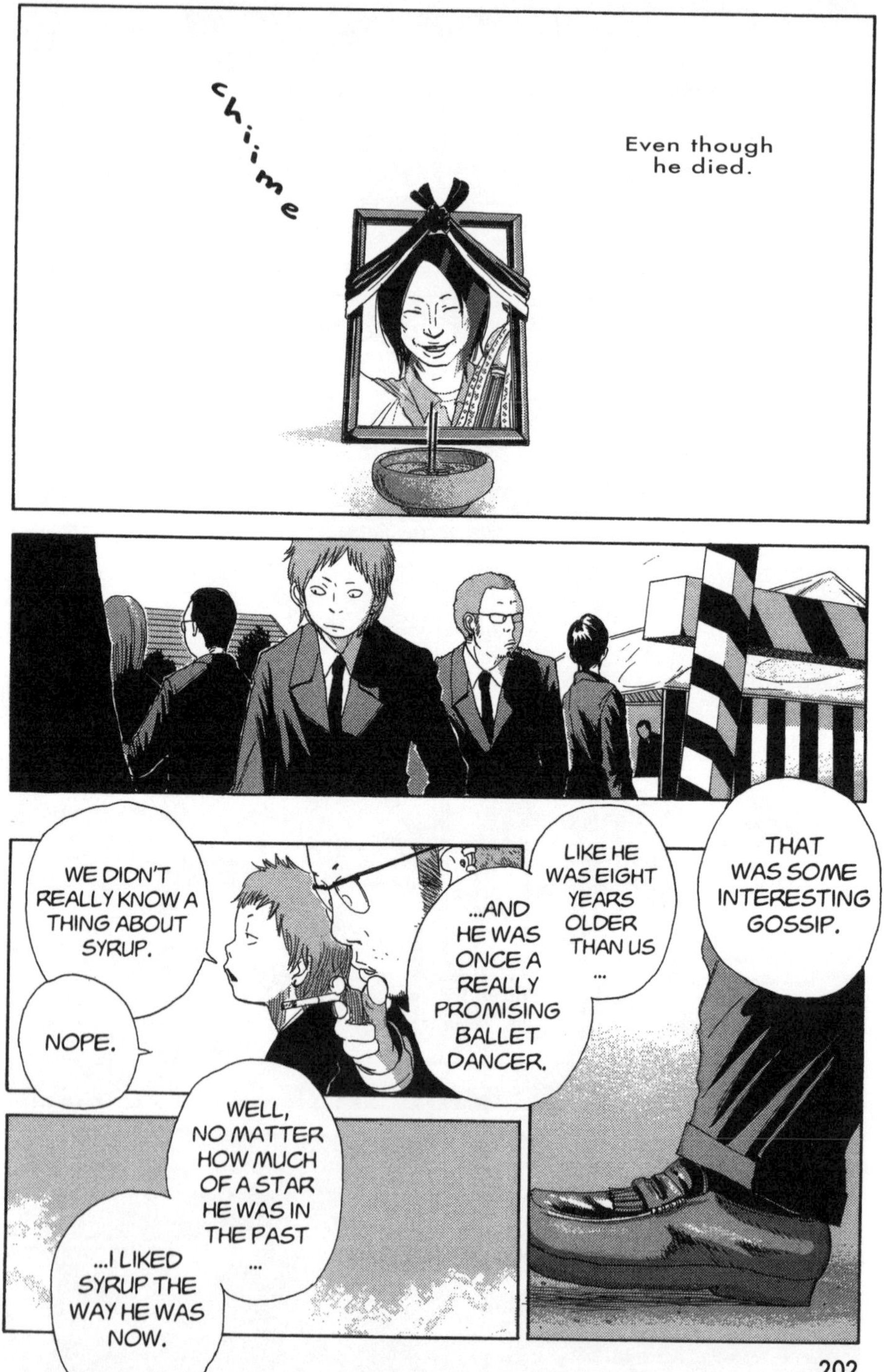
chime
Even though he died.
THAT WAS SOME INTERESTING GOSSIP.
LIKE HE WAS EIGHT YEARS OLDER THAN US ...
...AND HE WAS ONCE A REALLY PROMISING BALLET DANCER.
WE DIDN'T REALLY KNOW A THING ABOUT SYRUP.
NOPE.
WELL, NO MATTER HOW MUCH OF A STAR HE WAS IN THE PAST ...
...I LIKED SYRUP THE WAY HE WAS NOW.

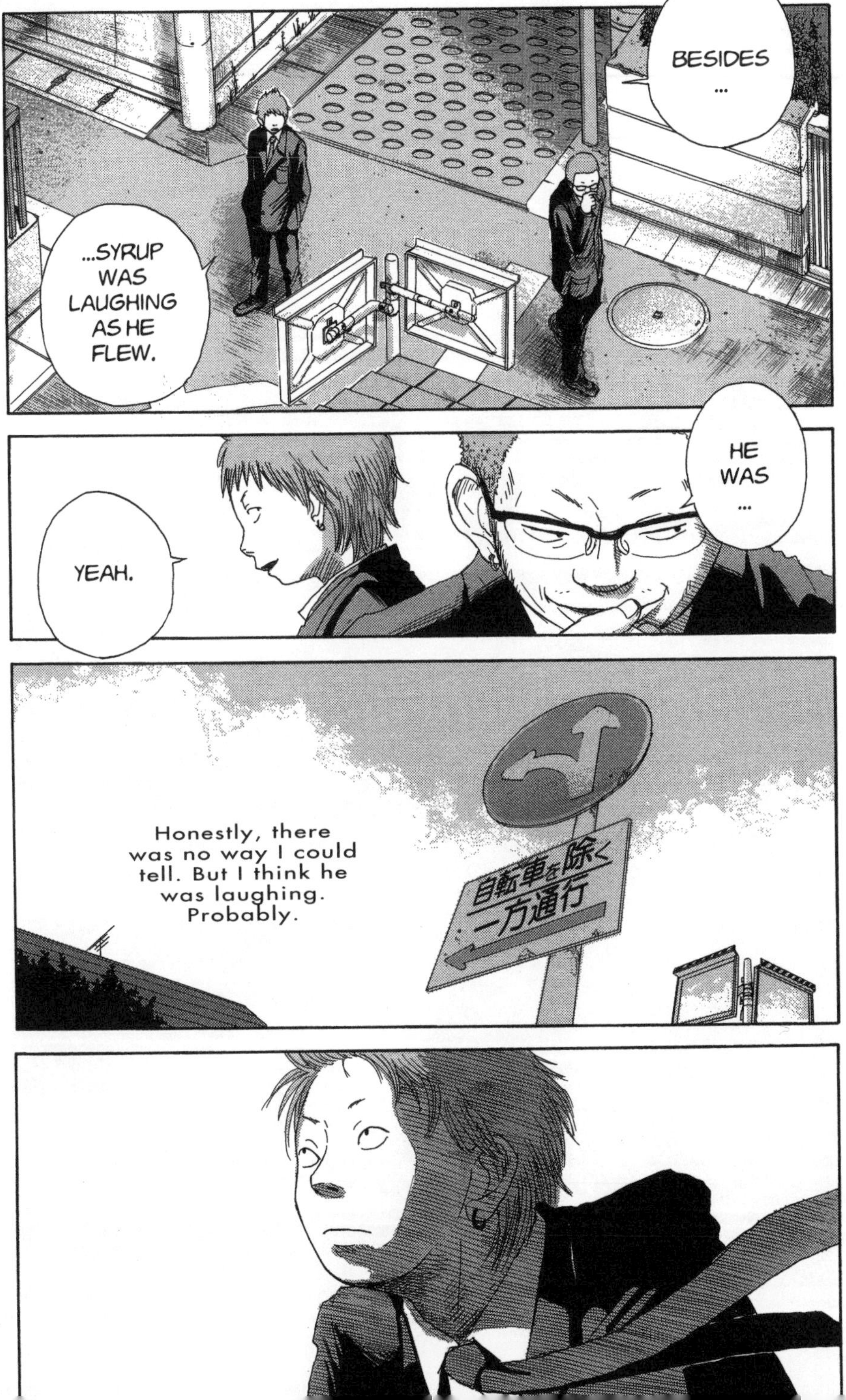
BESIDES ...
...SYRUP WAS LAUGHING AS HE FLEW.
HE WAS ...
YEAH.
自転車を除く
一方通行
Honestly, there was no way I could tell. But I think he was laughing. Probably.

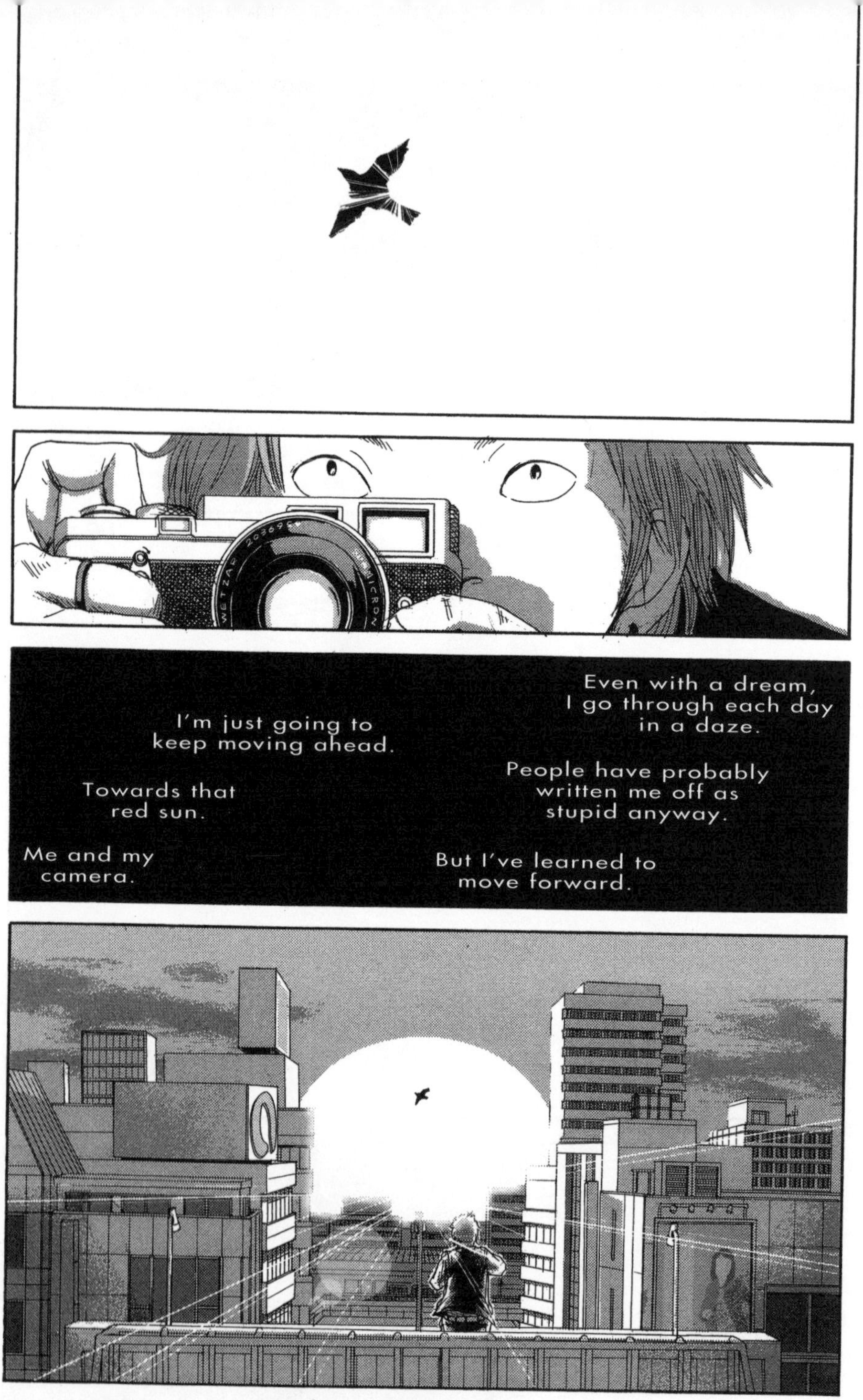
Even with a dream, I go through each day in a daze.
People have probably written me off as stupid anyway.
But I've learned to move forward.
I'm just going to keep moving ahead.
Towards that red sun.
Me and my camera.

What a Wonderful World Volume 1 - The End

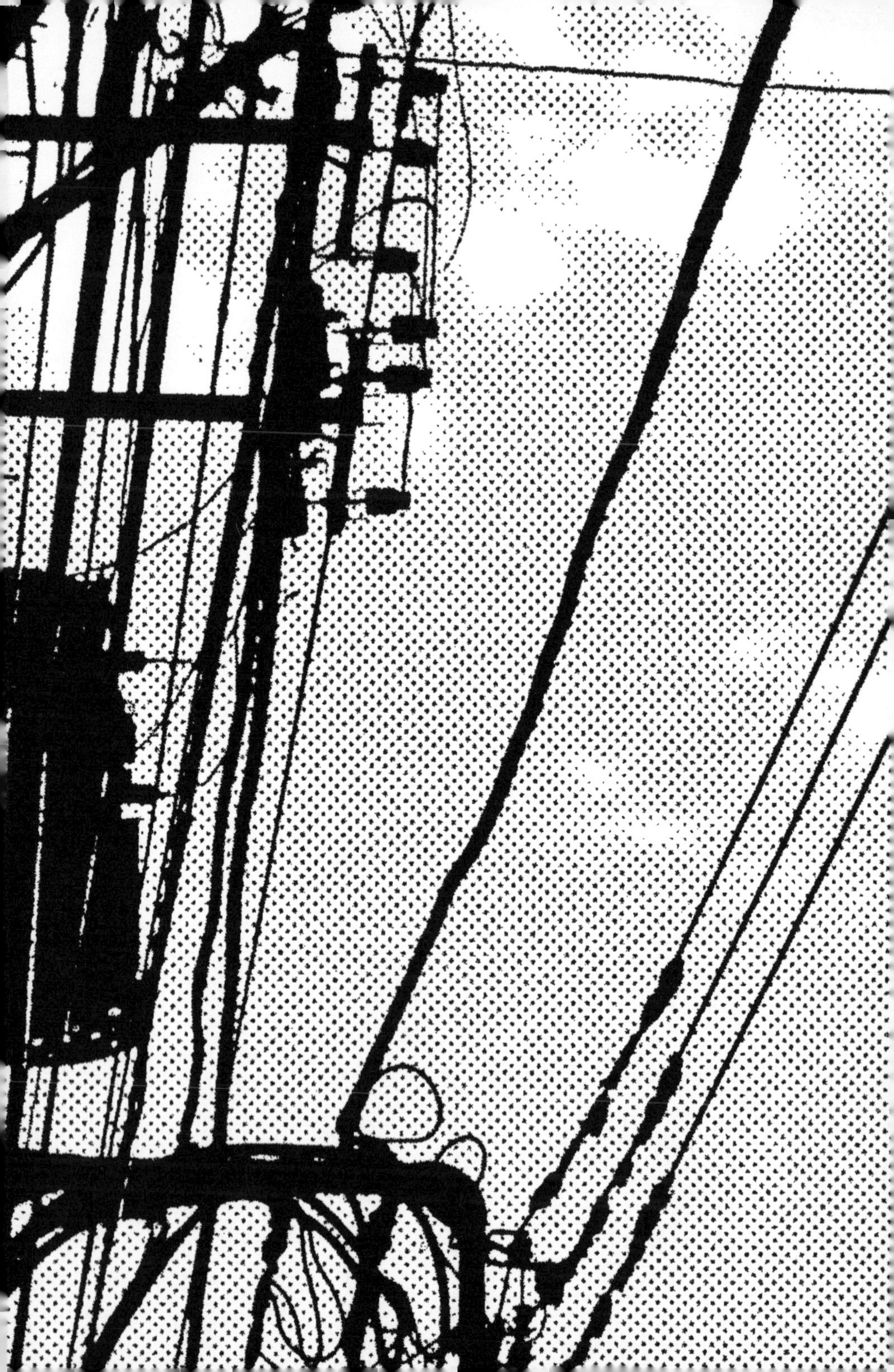

What a Wonderful World! 1

VIZ Signature Edition

Story and Art by Inio Asano

© 2003 Inio ASANO/Shogakukan
All rights reserved.
Original Japanese edition "SUBARASHII SEKAI"
published by SHOGAKUKAN Inc.

MORI NO KUMASAN
Used by permission of JASRAC
License No. 0907906-901

GIZA GIZA HEART NO KOMORIUTA
Words by Kan Chinfa
Music by Hiroyuki Serizawa
© 1983 by YAMAHA MUSIC PUBLISHING, INC.
All Rights Reserved. International Copyright Secured.

Translation/JN Productions
Touch-up Art & Lettering/Joanna Estep
Design/Frances O. Liddell
Editor/Pancha Diaz

Printed in the U.S.A.

Published by VIZ Media, LLC
P.O. Box 77010
San Francisco, CA 94107

10 9 8 7 6 5 4 3
First printing, October 2009
Third printing, May 2016

www.viz.com   www.vizsignature.com

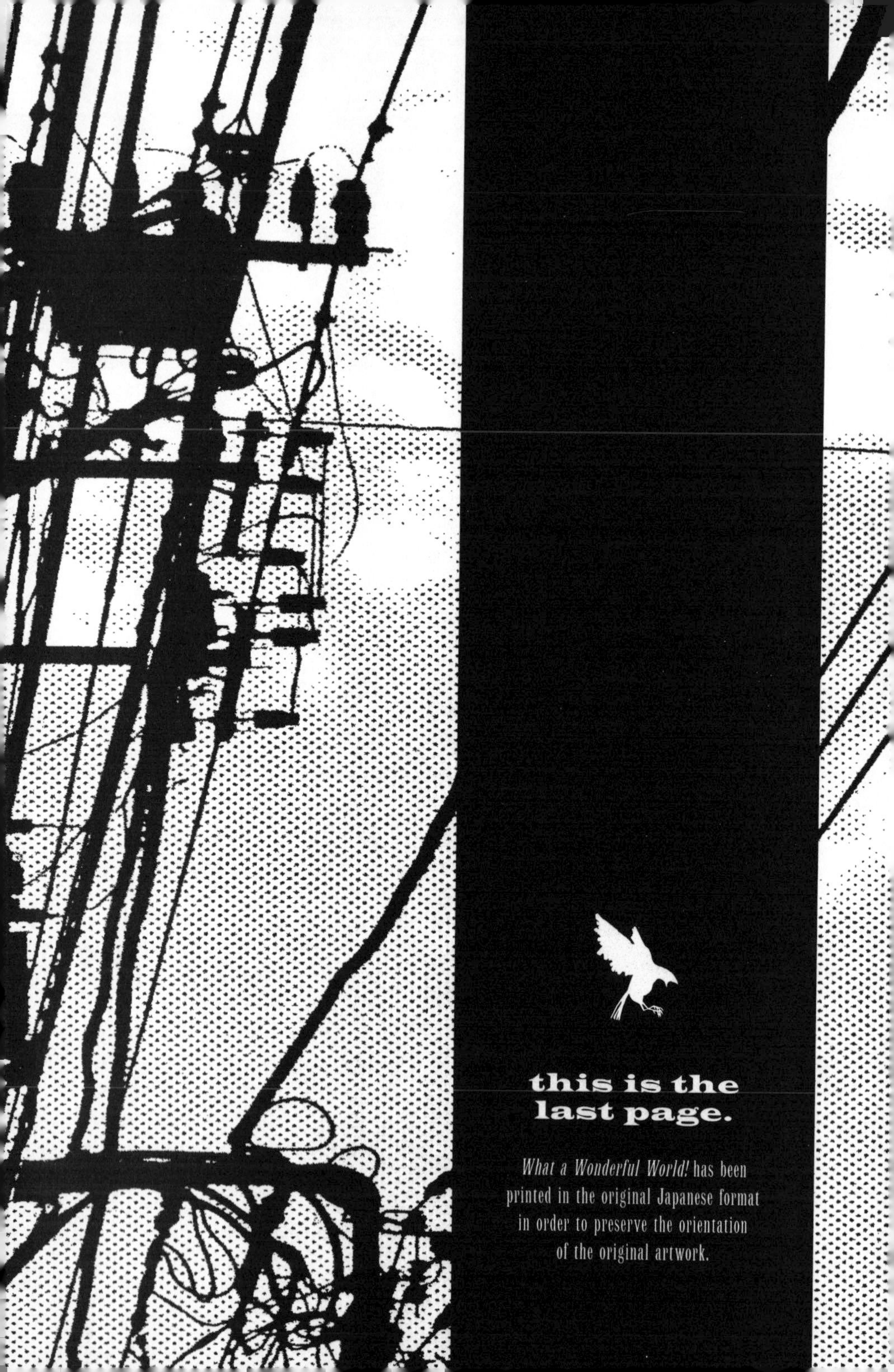

this is the last page.

What a Wonderful World! has been printed in the original Japanese format in order to preserve the orientation of the original artwork.